Moses

A PSYCHODYNAMIC STUDY

Moses

A PSYCHODYNAMIC STUDY

Dorothy F. Zeligs, Ed.D.

HUMAN SCIENCES PRESS, INC.
72 FIFTH AVENUE
NEW YORK, N.Y. 10011

Copyright © 1986 by Dorothy F. Zeligs
Published by Human Sciences Press, Inc.
72 Fifth Avenue, New York, New York 10011

All rights reserved. No part of this book may be reproduced by any means, nor transmitted, nor translated into a machine language without the written permission of the Author.

Library of Congress Cataloging in Publication Data

Zeligs, Dorothy F. (Dorothy Freda)
  Moses : a psychodynamic study.

  Bibliography: p. 428
  Includes index.
  1. Moses (Biblical leader) 2. Bible O.T.—Biography.
I. Title.
BS580.M6Z4 1986   222'.10924 [B]   84-19265
ISBN 0-89885-236-6

Dedicated to the memory of my father and mother, Joseph *and* Betty Mirkin Zeligs.
They valued most those aspects of life which enriched the spirit and enlightened the mind.

Contents

Acknowledgments 9

Permissions 13

Introduction 15

1. Birth and Rescue 25
2. Moses in Midian 47
3. On the Way Back to Egypt: *Moses Encounters the Daemonic Aspect of God* 79
4. Moses and Pharaoh: *Struggle and Liberation* 92
5. In the Wilderness: *On the Way to Mount Sinai* 118
6. The Covenant at Mount Sinai: *The Birth of a People* 134
7. The Golden Calf: *Regression, Guilt, and Reparation* 161
8. The Tabernacle: *A Sanctuary in the Wilderness* 195
9. Further Hardships in the Wilderness: *Maternal Aspects in the Personality of Moses* 211

10. Moses and His Siblings: *Rivalry and Love* 225

11. The Report of the Spies: *Conflict Between Faith and Fear* 239

12. Moses Faces the Revolt of Korah: *A Crisis in Leadership* 249

13. Why Did Moses Strike the Rock? *The Role of Unconscious Fantasy* 266

14. Final Years in the Wilderness: *Adversities and Triumphs* 286

15. The Story of Balaam: *The Paradoxical Prophet* 302

16. The Moses of Deuteronomy: *The Final Tasks of Leadership* 323

17. Moses on Mount Nebo: *The Last Theophany* 392

18. Additional Notes on Deuteronomy 405

19. A Psychoanalytic Note on the Function of the Bible 417

20. Some Brief Remarks on Biblical Exegesis 420

Suggested Bibliography 428

Notes 429

References 432

Glossary of Psychoanalytic Terms 438

Index to Biblical References 443

Index 451

Acknowledgments

I WANT TO express my appreciation to those who read all or parts of my manuscript and gave me both their helpful criticism and the warmth and encouragement of their responses. I am also grateful to the many who read some of the studies in this book as they appeared in journals and wrote to tell me of their interest.

My special thanks go to one of my former teachers, Dr. Philip H. Phenix, Arthur I. Gates Professor Emeritus of philosophy and education, Teachers College, Columbia University, who has continued to be a source of strengthening influence in the furtherance of this book. Dr. Phenix, who served on my doctoral committee and whose seminars I had the privilege of attending, was the first to suggest that I apply the methods utilized in my first volume in this field to the awesome task of the study of Moses. His responses to my studies were of special significance, coming as they did, from someone with a unique background in theology and science as well as philosophy and education. Dr. Phenix was awarded the Nicholas Murray Butler Medal in Silver from the above-named institution for the "flawlessness of his inspired teaching. "

To Rabbi Arthur J. Lelyveld, Fairmount Temple, Cleveland, Ohio, I want to express my thanks, not only for his scholarly evaluation of my material, but also for the warmth and encouragement that emanated from his communications. Although occupied with many responsibilities, both in his rabbinic role and his various positions of leadership in the area of American Reform Judaism and the social and moral issues of the day, Rabbi Lelyveld took the time to read lengthy portions of my manuscript with the care and perceptiveness that made his responses so meaningful. I am also indebted to him for the foreword to my first volume, *Psychoanalysis and the Bible: A Study in Depth of Seven Leaders.* Rabbi Lelyveld holds the degrees of *Master of Hebrew Literature* and (hon.) *Doctor of Divinity*, bestowed by his alma mater, the Hebrew Union College-Jewish Institute of Religion.

I want to thank Dr. Mark Kanzer, noted psychoanalyst and author, for his generous expenditure of time and thought in reading several chapters of my manuscript. The insightfulness of his comments and the spontaneity of his reactions to the material added to the value of his communications. Dr. Kanzer, emeritus clinical professor of psychiatry and emeritus director, division of psychoanalytic education, State University of New York (Downstate), is known for his many contributions to the field of psychoanalytic interpretations of literary and mythical figures—seminal studies which have enriched this area of applied psychoanalysis. He also serves as consultant on the editorial board of the journal, *American Imago*. Among Dr. Kanzer's publications is the volume, *The Unconscious Today* and the recent series of Downstate Anniversary Volumes.

I owe thanks to Dr. Harry Slochower, editor-in-chief of *American Imago*, for the encouragement that came from his acceptance of a number of my studies for publication in that journal. His wide background of scholarship in the field of literature and mythology made his editorial evaluation of my material especially meaningful. His well-known volume, *Mythopoesis*, has become a classic in itself.

To Dr. Murray H. Sherman, colleague and fellow member of the National Psychological Association for Psychoanalysis, I want to express my appreciation for his critical reading of several chapters of my manuscript and his thoughtful reactions to my interpretations. He served as editor of *The Psychoanalytic Review* during its formative years and has subsequently been active as consultant on its editorial board. His own contributions to the field of psychoanalytic writings have been extensive.

To Dr. Raphael Patai who, from the first, was supportive of

Acknowledgments 11

my efforts in this uncharted area of investigation, I wish to express my sincere thanks. Known for his many scholarly contributions, especially in the fields of the Bible and the ancient Near East, Dr. Patai's responses to my material were most helpful. I had the privilege of contributing one of my biblical studies to the volume, *Fields of Offerings: Studies in Honor of Raphael Patai*, issued by Dr. Patai's colleagues in honor of his seventieth birthday, under the editorship of Prof. Victor D. Sanua.

I want to thank Dr. Richard C. Robertiello, psychoanalyst and author, for reading and responding creatively to some of my material. In addition to his own numerous contributions to the literature, Dr. Robertiello has been associated with the editorial board of the *Journal of Contemporary Psychotherapy*.

I appreciate the time and thought given by Rabbi Ira Eisenstein, in reading part of my manuscript. In addition to his scholarly contributions, Rabbi Eisenstein is known for his leadership in the Jewish Reconstructionist Movement, especially since the retirement and death of its founder, Rabbi Mordecai M. Kaplan, and has been influential in making it a vital influence in the religious life of American Jewry.

I regret that two other scholars to whom I owe gratitude for reading and evaluating parts of my manuscript are no longer among us. Dr. Samuel Sandmel, whose books, *The Hebrew Scriptures* and *The Enjoyment of Scripture*, I found especially helpful, was on the faculty of the Hebrew Union College-Jewish Institute of Religion. Dr. Edward T. Sandrow, distinguished scholar and communal leader, was associated with the Jewish Theological Seminary.

It should be noted that the scholars mentioned here came from various schools of thought in regard to biblical exegesis. The interest they manifested in my work does not necessarily imply full agreement with the frame of reference in these studies.

I welcome this opportunity to thank the editorial staff of Human Sciences Press for their helpful and cooperative attitudes. I am especially grateful to Norma Fox, editor-in-chief, for her understanding and flexibility and for the creative spirit in which she initiated and guided the publication of this book from the beginning to its completion. I am also deeply appreciative of the help given by Donna Matthew, assistant editor, under whose able management the work was carried out. Her ready availability to me whenever questions arose or assistance was needed smoothed the path for me along the way. My thanks go, also, to Marilyn M. Houston for her excellent and painstaking work as copyeditor and in the preparation of the Indexes.

Permissions

I WISH TO thank the following publishers for permission to reprint a number of my studies, listed below, which originally appeared in their publications.

Wayne State University Press: *American Imago*: "The Family Romance of Moses," 23:2. (1966); "Moses in Midian: The Burning Bush," 26:4. (1969); "Moses Encounters the Daemonic Aspect of God," 27:4. (1970); "Moses and Pharaoh: A Psychoanalytic Study of their Encounter," 30:2. (1973).

Fairleigh Dickinson University Press and Herzl Press: In the volume "Fields of Offerings: Essays in Honor of Raphael Patai," Edited by Victor D. Sanua. "Why Did Moses Strike the Rock?, A Psychoanalytic Study." (1983).

I also wish to thank the following publishers for their kind permission to quote material from other sources referred to in this volume:

The Jewish Publication Society of America: "The Holy Scriptures, According to the Masoretic Text." (1917 version); also, "The Legends of the Jews," by Louis Ginzberg. (vols. 1-7). (1909-1938).

Introduction

THE ONLY SOURCE of information we have about the life and personality of Moses and his awe-inspiring accomplishments is the Bible itself. Therefore, our understanding of this great leader and lawgiver depends largely on how we interpret the biblical material. It might be noted, however, that regardless of how the biblical narratives are interpreted, few scholars today would question the basic historicity of the man Moses (*IB*, 1:842).

This story of his life, from the time of his birth in Egypt to his death on a mountaintop in Moab, deals with a psychodynamic analysis of the personality and character traits of this scriptural hero. It makes use of psychoanalytic concepts and techniques in an effort to get a greater in-depth image of this mysterious figure who dominates so much of the Pentateuchal literature. He emerges not only as the well-known phenomenal leader under whose aegis the Children of Israel as a people were brought into being but also as a genuine human being, whose modes of behavior and patterns of thought show a remarkable consistency throughout his life, leaving a convincing impression of his psychological validity as a whole person.

The content under consideration here is the so-called *received text*, the Bible as we have known it for more than two thousand years. It is this Bible of everyday usage, the text that has been read and treasured and puzzled over by the people, that is the source of the *psychic reality* from which the figure of Moses has emerged (Ginsberg 1904, 309). *This familiar text is therefore a legitimate object of psychological interest and investigation, in and of itself, apart from how it came to be.*

The approach utilized here seeks neither to affirm nor deny the various theories of Higher Biblical Criticism, a school of thought that has been the dominant one in biblical scholarship since the mid-eighteenth century.* Their scholars have contributed much to our understanding of the Bible, especially in terms of a more objective approach to the hitherto inviolate text. Their methods involved a separation of the text into a number of hypothetical sources or documents, which, it was theorized, were then put together by redactors and editors at different periods of history. The criteria for this division of the text was mainly on externals of language and style, together with elements of historical data indirectly referred to in the content. The interpretation of this data was understandably limited by the available knowledge of that period of history. This scholarly work was carried on mainly during the nineteenth and early twentieth centuries.

The main body of material subjected to the above process was, of course, the Pentateuch, which was fragmented and restructured in terms of the so-called documentary theory, leading to the formation of what might be called the Bible of the Scholars.

The concentration of interest on the technical analysis of the text and the reshaping of the Pentateuch had the effect of creating an impasse in the work of interpreting the inner meanings of the familiar Bible, the received text. As an authority who holds a prestigious position in Higher Biblical Criticism expressed this thought, "It may seem odd to claim that scientific historical criticism, the specific aim of which was to set the biblical text in full historical context, actually suppresses the text" (Funk 1976).

My own approach assumes an underlying unity in the biblical theme that goes beyond the theoretic diversity of the sources. Without such cohesiveness of purpose and meaning, the Bible could not have played the role it has in the history of Judeo-Christian culture (Goldman 1948, p.48; Roheim 1955, n.169). And indeed, the present study as well as my earlier ones, has

---

*See "Some Brief Remarks on Biblical Exegesis," Chapter 20.

strengthened convincingly the sense of psychological constancy that animates the scriptural narratives.

The French philosopher Paul Ricoeur (1970), known for his penetrating analysis of Freud's writings, maintains that the psychology of religious belief can be understood only by studying the texts in which man had indirectly expressed and formulated his beliefs. He points out that Freud used the *direct approach* in his *Moses and Monotheism* when he attempted to apply a general theory concerning the origins and growth of religion to a hypothetical reconstruction of Hebrew biblical history. Freud's weakness in this respect, Ricoeur explains, was in "thus circumventing an exegesis of the *texts* in and through which the religious man has 'formed' and 'educated' his belief." Further emphasizing this point, Ricoeur states, "there can be no question of grasping the meaning of the religious man apart from the meaning of the texts that are the documents of his belief." (p. 544).

However, it should be said in support of Freud that in the above-mentioned book he was basically concerned with the more general aspects of the evolution of monotheistic ideas in the light of his theories in this area. In spite of controversial aspects, the nature of which he himself openly presents, Freud laid the basis in this remarkable book for an understanding of the religious roots in the nature of man.

Although it has been assumed as obvious, perhaps it should be stated that these studies are not concerned with the problem of the nature of God in an objective or philosophic fashion. Such an approach lies outside the realm of psychoanalytic exploration, as Freud has stated on several occasions (Freud 1912, 1928).

Concepts and Methods of Applied Psychoanalysis

Psychoanalysis as a method of research is different in certain respects from its use as a therapy. In the latter situation, the chief goal is therapeutic, and the interpretation of observed facts is limited by rules of technique in which timing and the nature of the transference are of paramount importance. Also, in therapy the material dealt with is different since it constitutes not only the attempted free associations of the analysand but the totality of his or her behavior as a living presence.

When used as an instrument of research, psychoanalysis has a different goal. It can make full use of its psychological observations without regard for therapeutic consequences but is more limited in the areas and scope of the material that is under consideration.

In order to find new meanings in a given situation, it is often helpful to start with the mind as a tabula rasa, a clean slate as it were. This mental set involves the temporary abeyance of previous formulations so that the emergence of new impressions will be facilitated. It was in this frame of mind that I thought about the biblical narratives to be explored. Putting aside theories of how this material may have come into being, I asked myself questions regarding its present state. *From whose viewpoint in the narrative itself was the story being told?* Whose motivations, thoughts, feelings, and fantasies were reflected in the wording and style? Whose voice from the distant past was recounting these meaningful human experiences?

I was impressed with the fact that the teller of the story showed a remarkable degree of empathy with the hero. This finding reminded me of the work of Otto Rank (1909) and his studies on myths (p. 81). Both he and Freud determined that the hero of the myth, like the hero of the creative writer's inventions, really represented *the ego of the storyteller* (Freud 1908, 173–83). I wondered if a similar relationship might hold true in regard to biblical personalities, even though they were different in significant respects from Rank's mythic heroes. The question could then be worded as follows: *Would the psyche of the biblical hero reflect that of the storyteller?* The problem of who that storyteller might have been was put aside as unanswerable in our present state of knowledge and beyond the frame of reference for this study. It would be sufficiently challenging to determine whether the narratives under consideration were being told *as if* the hero himself were recounting the event, thus giving expression unconsciously to what was going on within himself psychically. I found this hypothesis worthy of being put to the test.

Thus, my basic assumption was formulated. I theorized that *the story was being told from the viewpoint of the hero.* The situation was now psychologically viable. Having established what my perspective would be, I could utilize an indispensable tool of my trade, empathy with the teller of the story, theoretically, the hero himself.

Empathy is a psychic process by which one puts oneself imaginatively into the situation of another person in order to experience how the latter thinks and feels. It is done unconsciously by all people, at times, in their efforts to relate meaningfully to others. The psychoanalyst learns to use this technique consciously when listening to a patient so that he can understand emotionally what the latter is trying to communicate.

The words of the biblical text became the voice of the personality under consideration. I tried to understand the relationship between these words and what was going on in the mind and heart of the biblical analysand. My task was to explore not only the surface meaning but also the stream of unconscious fantasy that motivated and colored the production of the biblical story.

With the use of other psychoanalytic concepts and techniques, surprising things began to happen. Not only did the thoughts and feelings of the scriptural hero come to light more clearly but his underlying conflicts and defenses were also revealed in a fashion that had convincing psychological validity. Previously obscure references in the text became meaningful, symbolic expressions lent themselves to interpretation, causal connections could be established between incidents that seemingly had been unrelated, and hidden motives could be disclosed.

As is well known, the biblical narratives are full of baffling features. They contain passages that do not seem to make sense on a rational basis, sentences that appear to be out of context, words and phrases that are omitted, repetitions of incidents that are often contradictory, and so forth. Many attempts have been made by scholars over the years to unravel these mysteries of the text and many theories propounded concerning them.

These numerous obscurities of the biblical text are attributed by scholars of Higher Biblical Criticism to causes external to the content of the material itself. They see these puzzling features as resulting from the work of redactors and editors of the final compilation of the Pentateuch, which, as indicated above, is considered to be a composite work, made up of a number of original documents from different times, places, and sources of authorship.

My own study explores the text from an entirely different viewpoint. It assumes that the material as it stands may have an inner unity of its own and tries to determine if the inconsistencies might have psychological significance as an inherent part of the setting in which they are found.

It was not the purpose of this study to attempt so ambitious an undertaking as a new approach to the problems of the biblical text. But when confronted with puzzling aspects of the material under scrutiny and finding no satisfactory answers on the basis of available exegesis, I was impelled by my training to seek psychological explanations. I approached these hindrances to the meaning of the text in the same way that resistances in the flow of free associations in a patient are dealt with in the treatment process. This kind of investigation was frequently successful, leading to that moment of surprise so well described by Theodor Reik (1948), when a hidden piece of knowledge suddenly comes to light and the fragments of a puzzle fall into place (pp. 270–71).

When one is in a state of unconscious conflict, troubled by opposing feelings, the resulting tension may reveal itself in small ways of which the person is unaware. In the biblical writings, as in the free associations of the analysand, seemingly insignificant details that did not fit into the context often proved to be an important source of insight. Such small disharmonies could signify an eruption of unconscious content into an otherwise rational presentation. Another way in which the unconscious manages both to reveal and to conceal its troubled secrets is through the device of ambiguity.

The fruitfulness of this pattern of working had already been established in my earlier experiences with the biblical material as depicted in my first volume in this field, which deals with a number of personalities from the time of Abraham through the period of Solomon (Zeligs 1974). It was the encouraging reception of these studies that prompted me to undertake what I thought at first would be only limited aspects of that greatest of all Hebrew biblical heroes, Moses himself. The work led me on and on because of the rewarding insights it brought and the consistency of the personality that was revealed. The great man's motivations, his areas of intrapsychic conflicts, the specific ways in which his ego defended itself against forbidden impulses and wishes, and the unconscious fantasies that colored his thinking and feeling became comprehensible as the ambiguities of the text gave way to psychoanalytic interpretations.

In my studies of the biblical personalities referred to above, certain basic intrapsychic problems stemming from relationships in the family were manifested. Similar conflictful situations, varying in degree and quality, also were revealed in the life of Moses. It was my finding throughout that *obscurities and inconsistencies in the text occurred most often at those points where the content dealt with forbidden aspects associated with the oedipal situation, such as sexuality in relation to incestuous objects and rivalry between fathers and sons.*

These familiar human areas of intrapsychic conflict are part of the developmental process in every man's growth and maturation. However, for Moses, the man with a mission, the man with a special relationship to his God, there were more than the usual superego pressures to contend with in such situations.

Many aspects of the inner life of Moses come to light in these studies. A meaningful picture emerges of his relationship to his parents, Amram and Jochebed; his other authority figures, Pharaoh and Jethro, both ambivalently perceived; his Midianite wife, Zipporah; his two largely ignored sons, Gershom and Eliezer; his siblings, Miriam and Aaron; and his long-time aide and successor-to-be, Joshua.

Most significant of all, there emerges a developmental view of his relationship with God. What becomes clear is the lifetime quest for greater intimacy with the Deity and the conflicting fear of such closeness, with its dangers of the loss of self-identity. There was a struggle between the wish for fusion, for being one with God, and the anxieties inherent in such a situation.

Perhaps it was these opposing needs that led Moses to evolve a special way of being-with-God. This psychic process manifested itself in those frequent theophanies that were, even for a biblical prophet, so large a part of his mystical experiences. In these states of altered consciousness, Moses was able to *regress in the service of the ego* (Kris 1952; 60, 289–302) and yet maintain a strong hold on reality, as his role of leadership demanded.

The attempts of Moses to get close to the Presence of God,

and the fear of doing so, stimulated a continuing struggle for a higher degree of spirituality. But the full attainment of such a goal was not realistically possible, for such a state would have denied the validity of the body and its physical nature.

Within the undercurrents of the biblical literature could be discerned the vestiges of certain tabooed aspects of instinctual life that biblical man tried to renounce in his forward movement toward a higher level of religion and morality. This long and difficult journey is marked many times by a *return of the repressed* in disguised or symbolic form.

Nor should we be too surprised by these findings. The Bible is primarily a religious literature. Its basic purpose was to set forth the vicissitudes of a people in relation to its God and His commandments. It thus depicts the struggles associated with the emergence of a *collective superego*, expressed most dramatically in the individual lives of its leaders.

As a product of religious feelings and beliefs, the biblical narratives contain those psychological elements that prompt the formation and development of religion. These forces are largely of an unconscious nature. They stem, in part, from man's unfulfilled childhood longings for an idealized father, a longing perpetuated by the adversities of adult life (Freud 1910, 103; 1928, chap. 4; 1939, 208ff). Together with this desire for a protective and loving father come the feelings of ambivalence and guilt and the wish for absolution that are characteristic of this relationship in its human form as well. Elements of conflict are therefore intimately involved, in both manifest and hidden ways.

The traditions of biblical religion exemplify in certain respects Freudian concepts about the psychological sources of religious feelings as these involve the figure of the father and have their roots in family life (Freud 1910, 103; 1939, 208ff). Beginning with Abraham, the leaders and heroes were father figures. The oedipus complex, having its basis in instinctual feelings, influences man's development as a human being. But the *source* of these feelings does not necessarily set the limits to man's power for spiritual growth (Ginzberg 1904, 309; Ricoeur 1970, pp. 531ff). The biblical heroes reveal some of these greater achievements of the human spirit. The man who came down from Mount Sinai with the light of Divinity shining on his face was able to relate to both his God and his fellowmen with extraordinary capacities in the roles of prophet, teacher, and leader.

The Leader and the Group

The Bible presents the narrative portions of its contents through the dramatic personal experiences of its individual leaders and heroes. But in a basic sense, the true hero of the biblical drama is the group itself, the Children of Israel. Its leaders, therefore, can be fully understood only in relation to the roles they play in the group and the functions they serve in regard to it. We shall find that in a curious, often mystifying way the psychic processes at work in the leaders reflect the same psychological forces dominant in the group at a given period of its developmental history. The true leader, it seems, is able to evoke only what is potential but dormant in his followers.

The words *leader* and *hero* are used synonymously here because both aspects are related to their roles. In contrast to the heroes of other ancient mythologies, whose aim usually was the gratification of their instinctual wishes, especially in the act of *overcoming* the father, the heroic deed of the biblical hero was to *identify* with the Father and His commandments. This process involved a constructive resolution of the oedipal conflict along the lines of sublimation and renunciation.

In terms of the functions pertaining to the leadership of the group, scholars have observed that if this literature had not presented us with such heroes as Abraham and Moses, it would have been necessary to assume their existence in order to explain the tasks accomplished in their names.

The biblical leader, experiencing himself as consecrated by God as His prophet, acted as the voice of the Deity to the people. Thus, he fulfilled the function of a superego. But since he was at the same time a human being, with his own inner growth a continuing process, he can better be understood as an example of the superego in *statu nascendi*, the *state of becoming*. Thus, the human weaknesses of the biblical personalities, their occasional falls from grace, were an understandable, even a necessary part of the biblical concept of man, with an awareness and acceptance of both his frailties and potentialities.

Concerning the relationship of the leader to the group, the words of Freud are especially applicable when the role of Moses is considered. Freud said: "It can be maintained that the community, too, develops a superego, under whose influence cultural evolution proceeds. . . . The superego of civilization originates in the same way as that of an individual. It is based on the impression left behind them by great personalities, men of outstanding force of mind, or men in whom some one human tendency has developed in unusual strength and purity (Freud 1930, 136–37). Moses, in his passion for morality in the name of monotheism, left such a lasting impression on civilization.

Birth and Rescue

 CHAPTER ONE

VERY LITTLE concerning the childhood of Moses is recorded in the Bible. The story of his birth takes place against the background of Pharaoh's expressions of enmity toward the Hebrew population in his land. A royal decree goes forth to destroy all newborn male infants. The mother of Moses succeeds in concealing her baby for three months, then fearful that he would be discovered, puts him in a watertight basket and places him on the brink of the Nile River, among the reeds. The daughter of Pharaoh comes to bathe in the river and finds the infant. Through the intervention of Miriam, the sister, who has concealed herself at a distance to watch over the child, he is given into the care of a Hebrew nurse, who is, in reality, his own mother. After the period of weaning, the young Moses is brought to the princess, who adopts him as her son. (2:1–10)* Nothing further is said about the early years of his life.

---

*All biblical references in this chapter, unless otherwise noted, are to the book of Exodus.

The Reality of Myth

In *Moses and Monotheism* Freud did not question the mythological character of the rescue story (p. 11). It fit into the pattern of the myths of the birth of a hero commonly found in the traditions of other ancient peoples. The original factor contributed by Freud was his interpretation of one element in the myth that he saw as significant for his hypothesis that Moses was an Egyptian nobleman by birth. Freud pointed out that in the typical myth the family that abandons the child is the noble one, whereas the second family, in which the child grows up, is the one of humble background. In the biblical narrative, the situation is reversed. Moses comes from a Hebrew family, a despised and outcast group in the hierarchy of Egypt, and is brought up as an Egyptian prince.

Freud then presents a new approach to the interpretation of the typical myth. He suggests that the second family, the one in which the child grows up, is the real one. Freud therefore assumes that the royal household in which Moses was brought up is his original background, and the Hebrew family represents the people whom he later adopted.

In regard to mythological personalities, Freud points out, the two families, both the real and the fictitious one, are actually the same. The purpose of such a myth is to provide a noble lineage for the hero of the story. Myths involving historical personalities such as Moses have to be understood on a reality level also, Freud says, adding that one of the families represents the real one into which the hero was born, whereas the other is fictitious. The motive of the biblical story, he suggests, stems from the desire of the people to provide a Hebrew origin for the Egyptian Moses.

The controversy that this interpretation aroused has been vehement and widespread. What critics seem to overlook is the very tentative fashion in which Freud presents his hypothesis. He clearly conveys the feeling that he would very much like to have proof of the Egyptian origin of Moses, for such a theory would provide a firmer foundation for other ideas of great significance that he wished to develop. However, he felt that his arguments required confirmation from other directions. Indeed, Freud himself stated that the element of reversal in the myth, on which he relied so heavily for his theory, might not in itself be convincing proof of what he wished to establish. And in fact, as A. Fodor (1951) reminds us, even in the Babylonian myth concerning the birth of Sargon I, after which it is believed the Moses myth was patterned, the infant was born to lowly parents and also brought up by one of humble estate, a gardener, before achieving his kingly role (p. 198). Thus, that myth too was not typical.

Freud relinquishes his interpretation of the myth of the birth of Moses as conclusive evidence for his theory, saying, "The objection is likely to be that the circumstances of the origin and transformation of legends are too obscure to allow of such a conclusion as the preceding one, and that all efforts to extract the kernel of historical truth must be doomed to failure in the face of the incoherence and contradictions clustering around the heroic person of Moses and the unmistakable signs of tendentious distortions and stratification accumulated through the centuries. I myself do not share this negative attitude, but I am not in a position to confute it." He ends this aspect of the subject rather sadly with the conclusion, "and therefore it will be better to suppress any inference that might follow our view that Moses was an Egyptian" (pp. 16–17).

The pressure of a great idea nevertheless forces Freud to continue his work at a later time, and in this last book he contributes some of his most brilliant and basic ideas about psychological factors underlying the development of religion. Significantly, he resumes his stimulating theme regarding the contribution of Moses and of monotheistic religion in general, under the heading *"If Moses was an Egyptian"* (italics added) (p. 21).

It seems to this writer that the wish to make Moses into a Hebrew, which was the motive Freud attributed to the myth, would belong to an *ego* level of functioning and relate to secondary processes of thinking rather than to the primary modes of the unconscious, which provide the basic ingredients of the myth. It would have been alien to the spirit of the biblical literature to conceal a fact of so much significance regarding the birth of its greatest leader. There is a quality of basic integrity in the Bible that would forestall such an attempt at falsification. Perhaps, however, there is indeed a kernel of truth in the myth, as there generally is, stemming not from historic sources but from the unconscious, a significant psychological truth relating to the personality of Moses himself. It is this aspect that we shall now explore.

In *Moses and Monotheism* Freud mentions but does not develop the theory that the inner source of the myth of the birth of the hero is the so-called *family romance* of the young boy, a typical fantasy (p. 11). The myth thus stands in a special relationship not only to the nocturnal dream but also to the daydream. Concerning this matter, Otto Rank and Hanns Sachs (1913), as coauthors, observe, "The ambitious and erotic phantasies of boyhood and puberty return in the myth structure. . . . Thus, for example, the myth of the exposure of the newborn hero in a little basket in water, his rescue and nursing by poor people and his ultimate victory over his persecutor (usually the father) is familiar to us as an ambitious phantasy of boyhood lined by erotic wishes which recurs in the *family romance*" (p. 43).

In the latter situation the youth, disappointed in his own parents, who have fallen short of his earlier idealization of them, seeks to console himself in the world of fantasy. He imagines that one or both of them are not his real parents but that he was adopted under some special circumstance that varies with the individual myth. The young hero of the daydream usually provides a more exalted lineage for himself than the real one, further to gratify his egocentric wishes (Freud 1909, 74ff). The oedipal conflict, which is usually involved in this period of disillusionment, leads to frustration regarding the unconscious wish for the mother as a love object and to increased hostility toward the rival father. The whole process helps to free the child from his attachment to the original family in the developmental task of growing up.

Géza Roheim (1955) also sees the myths of the birth of heroes, with their theme of adoption by foster parents, as representing a common fantasy or daydream of children. He feels that Freud's use of the biblical myth as a basis for assuming that Moses was an Egyptian was a mistake. Roheim goes on to say: "This universal fantasy proves only one thing. That is, that the Hebrews have retold an Egyptian myth and made one of their mythical or historical personages the hero of the myth" (p. 211). One wonders why the Hebrews had to borrow from the Egyptians if myths of this kind are universal as he himself states.

The view to be presented here is that the brief biblical story describing the exposure of the infant Moses and his subsequent rescue can be understood as a *condensation* of the myth of the birth of a hero and the later boyhood daydream, or family romance, of the young Moses himself, projected backward in time. The above interpretation does not exclude another possibility —that the story may be factually true. Dr. Reik (1959) suggests that such a happening was within the realm of the possible if not the probable (p. 16).

Coming back to our view of the birth and rescue story as a family romance, Moses is born a Hebrew, the child of an enslaved, despised people. In a fantasy suitably daring to the adventurous spirit and creative genius of the young daydreamer, Moses is adopted by the daughter of Pharaoh. Thus, he rids himself of his lowly estate and of his parents as well.

We must assume that the youth felt some discontent with his mother and father and had ambivalent feelings toward them, a situation typical of young people around the age of puberty. At any rate, in the fantasy under consideration Moses reveals a wish to be other than what he is, to occupy a more elevated position in life. That he does not wholly want to reject the mother of his earliest years is indicated by the role she retains as his nurse until the time of his weaning. Evidently the young daydreamer cannot relinquish even in fantasy this precious relationship of his infancy.

Otto Rank (1909) makes the striking observation that myths seem to be formed from the viewpoint of the hero himself (pp. 81–82). And Freud (1908) points out that in both the daydream and the fictitious characters of the creative writer the main role is occupied by *His Majesty, the Ego* (pp. 180ff). How much more then would this egocentric aspect be present in the child-centered family romance!

With this frame of reference let us view some of the actual wording of the biblical text dealing with the birth and rescue story. Exodus 2 opens with the statement, "And there went a man of the house of Levi, and took to wife a daughter of Levi." This is indeed an impersonal way for the Bible to introduce the parents of a great hero. Commentators on the book of Exodus invariably explain that the names of these nonspecific people are given four chapters later (6:20). Even then they are mentioned only as part of a genealogical list. But clearly, their omission at the beginning of the story was not due to a lack of knowledge of their identity. If the narrative is an expression of the discontented young daydreamer himself, it would seem that he is detaching himself emotionally from his parents. They are not the highly personalized Amram and Jochebed. They are only "a man of the house of Levi, who took to wife a daughter of Levi." These are the *insignificant* people the child was ready to discard for more exalted parents.

The text continues, "And the woman conceived, and bore a son." Biblical scholars have been puzzled, because this wording sounds as if Moses was the first-born child. Yet it is known that he had a sister, Miriam, considerably older than he, who is, in fact, mentioned several verses later. Moreover, he had a brother, Aaron, three years his senior. Why then this *as if* presentation? One is reminded of clinical examples where analysands tend to tell their life story as if they had no siblings, wishing to deny the existence of their rivals. May Moses also be engaging in this fantasy? Perhaps even stronger was the wish to be the first-born son, a position of greater prestige in the family.

The next phrase of the text is also meaningful from our viewpoint, although unclear to commentators. It says, "and when she saw that he was a goodly child, she hid him three months." What a clever condensation of hostility toward the mother and narcissistic gratification for the child! The only reason his mother bothered to save his life, the fantasy implies, is because he was such a beautiful baby. Otherwise, she might have discarded him immediately, at the command of the cruel father-king.

Nevertheless, the more genuine affectionate feelings for the mother emerge. "When she could not longer hide him," she took great pains to make sure the ark in which she would place him was waterproof. She "daubed it with slime and pitch." Moreover, "his sister Miriam stood afar, to know what would be done to him." They probably loved him after all. They exposed him only to save him.

There is an aspect in the rescue story that impresses one particularly as reflecting the egocentric attitude typical of such daydreams, together with the accompanying lack of empathy for the other members of the cast. The daughter of Pharaoh sees the infant in the basket, feels compassion for him, and decides to adopt him. Then, without allowing herself to enjoy the maternal satisfaction of closeness with the child, she follows Miriam's suggestion and turns him over to a *Hebrew nurse* for a period of years. Certainly there could have been no reality reason why the princess, who probably lived in a separate apartment of the palace, as was the custom, could not have taken both the baby and the Hebrew nurse home with her. Only in the fantasy of a young boy could such a lack of identification with the feelings of a motherly woman be likely. The princess performed her role strictly in terms of what the young daydreamer desired for himself.

That the youthful Moses also regarded his sister Miriam as a maternal figure is indicated by her part in the rescue story. She watches over him as he lies in the basket at the river's edge, even as she must have guarded him at home, bringing him then also to be nursed by his mother.

It is of interest that Amram, the father of Moses, plays no role in the rescue story. Only women participate in saving the life of the infant. This omission of the father figure, on both the side of the original and of the foster family, is indicative of the hostility toward the father that is one of the characteristics of the family romance. Indeed, it is Pharaoh, most cruel of all fathers, whose decree endangers the life of the infant Moses in the first place.

The hypothesis presented in this study—that the exposure of the infant Moses and his rescue plays the dual role of a myth of the birth of a hero and the family romance of the hero himself—would reveal new aspects regarding the period of growth and development in the personality of Moses. That even in a fantasy typical of the prepuberty period he could exchange his identity for that of an Egyptian prince must have significance. Was the young Moses unhappy not only with the stresses of adolescence but also with his feelings of self-identity as a member of the Hebrew group?

As noted, apart from the birth and rescue story the Bible tells us little about the childhood and youth of Moses. We do know that he came from a Levite family. Tradition has it that the Levites received special consideration from Pharaoh and were not subjected to slavery as were the rest of their brethren. (Ginzberg

1909–1938, 5:391) If this was so, it would provide a reality background for the portrayal of Moses as one who had been spared the degrading experiences of life as a slave.

As the son of a Levite, Moses would have been brought up in an atmosphere conducive to the fostering of the traditions of his people. The authenticity of the Patriarchal Era has been definitively established in recent decades by the findings of archeology and from the studies of comparative history and religion of the ancient Near East. The theory of some scholars that Moses probably belonged to a family that was familiar with Egyptian culture and ways of life seems logical. Certainly there must have been a group of well-to-do, educated Hebrews who escaped the fate of their less fortunate brethren. Both Martin Buber (1936, 35) and Theodor Reik (1959, p.16) concur in their opinion that Moses had a background of Egyptian culture. Reik even speculates that the youth may have been an important personage at the Egyptian court, whether or not he was actually adopted by the daughter of Pharaoh.

Thus, it would be understandable that Moses, caught in a conflict of cultures, might have suffered from feelings of insecurity in his sense of self-identity. The problem that troubled him during his adolescent years may have been *not who he was, from a biological aspect, but who he wanted to be*, psychologically and culturally. If the story of his Hebrew birth and the adoption by an Egyptian princess was actually true, then the reasons for such a conflict would be even greater, for the Bible clearly indicates that Moses knew his real family origin.

Freud may have experienced a similar problem in his own adolescence regarding his self-acceptance as a Jew, although consciously he reacted strongly, with anger and some bitterness, to the signs of anti-Semitism in his own environment. In the biblical situation under discussion, may Freud have been projecting his feelings onto Moses and trying to solve his own problem by making the latter into an Egyptian who later became a Hebrew and a hero among his adopted people?

Another aspect of ambiguity surrounding the historical identity of Moses is the derivation and meaning of his name (Buber 1936, 35–36). A widely accepted view is that it is of Egyptian origin, meaning *child*, or *born*. Others point out that in this sense the word is generic and would not be given as a name. Usually it is combined with another part, such as Thotmose, *child of Thot*, an Egyptian god (Benno 1942). Hertz thinks that it may be a Hebraized reproduction of an Egyptian word that probably means *child of the Nile* (Hertz 1936, 211).

Others claim a Hebrew derivation, tracing the name to the Hebrew root, *Masha, to draw out of the water*. Literally, in Hebrew *Moses* means *a drawer-out of the water* or *one who draws out*.

Martin Buber (1936) thinks that the Hebrew form can only mean *he who draws forth*, adding, "and it seems to me, it was the covert purpose of the etymology to indicate this: that the intention was to characterize Moses as the one who drew Israel forth from the flood" (pp. 35–36) (while crossing the sea during the exodus).

And indeed, it is characteristic of birth stories in the Bible that the circumstances under which a child is born has some relationship to his mission in life or reveals some aspect of his personality. Thus, Jacob struggles with his twin brother, Esau, within the mother's womb, symbolic of the later conflict between them. Isaac is born under a special dispensation from God in spite of Sarah's earlier barrenness and the advanced age of both parents. He is in a sense the *gift* of God to Abraham, a gift that the latter feels *called upon* to return, with its subsequent dramatic outcome.

Joseph too is born after years of frustrating barrenness on the part of Rachel. He was especially treasured and became a treasure also to his people, as well as to the Egyptians. The birth of Samuel is of particular dramatic quality. His mother, Hannah, promises the child to God as a lifelong priest and servant if only she may be redeemed from the unfruitfulness of her womb. This prenatal commitment on the part of his mother vitally affects Samuel's relationship to God and to Israel.

It is of interest also to note that the only reference in the Bible to the early life of Abraham, first Patriarch of Israel, is the statement of his birth (Gen. 11:26). Abraham begins his biblical mission at the advanced age of seventy-five. The biblical story moves immediately from his birth to his marriage. This treatment seems appropriate to the particular function he serves. Abraham, the *father of a multitude of nations*, is a father figure par excellence. His earlier life is therefore seemingly irrelevant.

The life of Moses begins as an infant. Symbolic of the people, Israel, he is the spiritual son who succeeds the fathers, Abraham, Isaac, and Jacob.

Psychoanalytically, the process of being drawn out of the water is a familiar symbol of birth. In the youthful fantasy of Moses, he is *born again*, this time to a new mother, the Egyptian princess. The biblical explanation is explicit. "And the child grew, and she [the Hebrew mother] brought him unto Pharaoh's daughter, and he became her son. And she called his name Moses, and said: 'Because I drew him out of the water'" (2:10); that is, she gave birth to him. By accepting him as her son, she declared herself to be his mother, as the young daydreamer wished. That the new mother in all probability did not know Hebrew, and was therefore unaware of the Hebrew derivation of the name Masha was no obstacle to the fantasy, a world where all things are possible.

From the viewpoint of its function in the saga of a people, this story of the birth of Moses, his rescue and adoption, makes clear that these happenings involve no supernatural intervention. The human origin of Moses is thus indirectly established. At the same time, the episode highlights the hand of destiny from the start. These two influences, Moses as the human being and Moses as the special child of God, find repeated if subtle reverberations throughout his life story.

There is a curious gap in the biblical text regarding the early life of Moses. In a few highly concentrated sentences we are told about his birth and rescue. In the very next verse, Moses is already a grown man. Certainly there was much to challenge the imagination in the dramatic event of a Hebrew child, progeny of a despised caste, being reared within the palace walls of the great Egyptian ruler. Legends from extrabiblical sources have utilized this situation with lively fantasies about the experiences of the young Moses in this setting (Ginzberg 1909–1938, 1:89ff). Why then was this period omitted in the Bible itself?

If, as suggested, the family romance of the youthful Moses gave indications of intrapsychic conflict regarding his feelings of self-acceptance as a Hebrew, Moses would have *preferred to forget* about the period of his life that intervened between the time of his adoption and his emergence into manhood. The gap in the text referred to above can then be understood as representing a repression. It would coincide largely with the period of latency, a developmental stage during which infantile amnesia normally takes place. Under conditions of conflict this period could involve a longer span of time than usual. Moses was clearly a person of intense feelings and vivid imagination. The common psychological experiences of maturation would tend to affect him more profoundly than most. Deep emotions must have been involved in his efforts to detach himself from his original family and his group. Equally strong would have been the spiritual awakening, the return of his first loyalties. Moses may thus have gone through a long and stormy adolescence. Freud says that family romance fantasies usually start in childhood but may persist until long after the puberty period.

If the unconscious fantasy of Moses was occupied with themes of freeing himself from ties of family and of group, there would be associated feelings of guilt. As a reaction, the youth's quest for personal emancipation may have been converted into a greater cause, a process not uncommon in the development of adolescence. Not only would the young dreamer free himself, he would liberate his entire people who were so shamefully enslaved. Thus, the family romance of the growing boy may have provided the impetus for the later achievements of the man. This kind of psychic development is interestingly described in Greenacre's (1963) concept of the *collective alternatives* utilized by creative people. (pp. 14–15).

It is certainly not without significance that the first recorded act in the adult life of Moses is an unequivocal assertion of identification with his own people. He goes out among them and strikes down an Egyptian who is beating a Hebrew slave. The text says, "And it came to pass in those days, when Moses was grown up, that he went out unto his brethren, and looked on their burdens; and he saw an Egyptian smiting a Hebrew, one of his brethren. And he looked this way and that way, and when he saw that there was no man, he smote the Egyptian and hid him in the sand" (2:11–12).

The intensity of feeling expressed in this initial gesture conveys a quality of overcompensation, as if emotions long withheld were now breaking forth. He not only had compassion for the suffering Hebrew slaves but he identified with them. *They were his brethren.*

At the same time there is an impliction in the biblical verses quoted above that Moses went out among his brethren and observed their hardships, not only on this momentous occasion but as a customary practice. For the text refers to "those days when Moses was grown up," a continuing period. The act, therefore, although giving the impression of a strong impulse breaking from control, may unconsciously have been moving toward this outcome for a long time.

Despite the brevity and restraint so characteristic of the biblical style, we are informed *twice* that Moses knew he was a Hebrew (2:11). One wonders *how* he acquired this knowledge of his biological origin, since ostensibly he had been brought up by the princess as her son. The Bible does not enlighten us regarding this matter.

Up to this point, we have emphasized that aspect of the family romance that stems from the unconscious motivation of the prepuberty youth to achieve emotional independence from his original family. This kind of fantasy also has an erotic base, the very wishes that tie the boy to his first love object, the mother. This emotional state is accompanied by unconscious hostility to the father.

On the theory presented here that the birth and rescue story contains also the family romance of Moses, the question arises, Are there further indications in the text of a disguised oedipal fantasy that would give added confirmation to the hypothesis presented here? Let us explore in further detail the behavior of Moses both in the act already mentioned and in another episode the next day that led him to flee from Egypt in fear for his very life.

Before striking the Egyptian, Moses reveals an element of caution. He "looked this way and that way." There is a certain incongruity in this detail. If Moses was truly an Egyptian nobleman, would he have to be so fearful of doing injury to a menial taskmaster? Ironically, it was a Hebrew who saw him and who became the source of Moses' fear of discovery and punishment. The text relates the brief narrative in this fashion: "And he went out the second day, and behold, two men of the Hebrews strove together; and he said to him that did the wrong, 'Wherefore smitest thou thy fellow?' And he said, 'Who made thee a ruler and a judge over us? thinkest thou to kill me, as thou didst kill the Egyptian?' And Moses feared, and said: 'Surely the thing is known.' Now when Pharaoh heard this thing, he sought to slay Moses. But Moses fled from the face of Pharaoh, and dwelt in the land of Midian" (2:13–15).

It seems that Moses was justified in his fear. Pharaoh was prepared to mete out the most dire punishment. But the narrative contains some puzzling features. Why should Pharaoh be so punitive to a foster grandson who had been brought up from early childhood within the palace gates? In the totalitarian regime of ancient Egypt, human life, particularly that of an ordinary overseer, was cheap. Realistically, it would be of little significance if such a person were struck down by a nobleman. Moreover, how did Pharaoh find out what Moses had done? Surely, the quarrelsome Hebrew, threatening and blustering though he was, had no access to the royal ear. He had in fact voiced no actual threats. Nor had he suffered any injury from Moses that would have justified such retaliation. How, therefore, did Pharaoh "hear of this thing"? A further puzzle: Did the Hebrew know the true identity of Moses? The text implies it. The Hebrew recognizes Moses as the one who slew the Egyptian the day before; there is no clear indication that he really knew who Moses was. Why then would he be so hostile toward one who was clearly on the side of his own people? It seems evident that the Hebrew was not afraid of Moses even after witnessing the latter's act of violence. Perhaps he had also noted the gesture betraying caution. The quarrelsome Hebrew was clearly playing on Moses' sense of fear and guilt.

It is also possible that Moses' identity was known, since he was accustomed to walking among his brethren while they toiled. In that event we can assume that the hostility of the Hebrew was aroused by envy and hatred toward one of his own race who had been elevated to such a lofty position. Under any circumstances, however, it seems unrealistic that a menial Hebrew slave would speak so boldly and threateningly to an Egyptian prince.

When analyzed thus, in the light of objective reality, the facts of the biblical story do not seem to stand up. Perhaps the main question is why the text is so cryptic, so meager in the information it gives. Why does it conceal so much? The episode may have evoked emotions relating to repressed fantasies of a conflictful nature, thus adding to the anxiety and terror Moses experienced. Intuitively, the sages of old, responding with their own unconscious to the inner disguised content of the biblical text, help to solve the puzzle.

A story from the Midrash gives us a clue. According to this legend, the Egyptian killed by Moses was a man who abused a certain Hebrew, Dathan by name. The latter was one of the petty officers appointed to a position of responsibility over a certain number of Hebrew slaves. Dathan, the story relates, had a beautiful wife of whom the Egyptian taskmaster was enamored. He once made Dathan leave his home early for work, then forcibly took the woman and dishonored her. Dathan returned home and discovered him. The Egyptian was so angered that he oppressed Dathan unmercifully at his work. Moses observed his cruelty and killed the Egyptian. According to the story, Moses did not have to use violence to accomplish this act of retribution. He pronounced the name of God and the deed was done.

Curiously, in the aftermath of this incident, the legend goes on, Moses found two Hebrews quarreling and sought to stop them. One of them, also named Dathan, threatened to reveal his knowledge of what Moses had done. The latter then had to flee for his life (Ginzberg 1909–1938, 2:279–80).

The biblical narrative describing the two acts of Moses before he flees to Midian, namely, the slaying of the Egyptian and the effort to intervene in the fighting of the two Hebrews, can be understood psychoanalytically as a continuation of the fantasy of the family romance. The anger of Moses toward the Egyptian taskmaster is aroused, not only by the latter's cruelty to the Hebrew slave but even more by the omitted part of the fantasy, the act of sexual violence on a Hebrew woman. This kind of fantasy is typical of a young boy at puberty who resents the father's sexual relationship with the mother, picturing it as a sexual attack on the helpless woman.

The Egyptian taskmaster and the Hebrew officer, Dathan, who plays the role of the wronged husband, are indeed one and the same in this story, since both are *sexual attackers*. They also may represent a projected image of Moses himself in the unconscious oedipal fantasy. Moses is here striking down not only the rival father but also his own childhood incestuous wishes, as he strives to return to the group and join them as his brethren.

But the angered Hebrew whom Moses reproves threatens retaliation on the young man for acting in a superior role as judge and ruler. In the legend the two men who quarrel are brothers. We have here a further indication of sibling rivalry between Moses and Aaron. Dathan is not only the father, he is the angry and envious brother as well. Significantly, two brothers, Dathan and Abiram, play a role in the biblical story later on as bitter enemies of Moses.

Such an incident as described in the Bible actually may have occurred. It is a commonplace event for an onlooker at a brawl to attempt the role of peacemaker. But what might such an experience have evoked in Moses at that particular time? To his unconscious, the two Hebrews may have represented Aaron and himself during one of their boyhood quarrels. On the basis of a sibling rivalry fantasy the resentment of the Hebrew toward Moses takes on further meaning. But now Moses desires to make peace with his brother as well as with his people. At the same time the unconscious childhood fears of retaliation for his own hostility toward the rival sibling would be stirred up by the reality factor.

On the level of the underlying stream of unconscious fantasy, the man who was reproved would know who Moses was. The implied threat may have been, "I'll tell father on you. I saw *you* fighting yesterday. Why then do you act so superior!"

Other puzzling elements in the biblical text now become understandable. The characters in the story possess knowledge the source of which does not need explaining, for it is the secret knowledge of the unconscious expressed through projection. Thus, Moses *knows* that he is a Hebrew in spite of any conflict he may have had regarding his sense of identity. In fact, the emphasis on his identification with the Hebrew slaves is the main motif of the story. Under the guise of the liberator, the youthful hero can also allow himself a reactivation of his oedipal feelings.

Pharoah *knows* of the act of violence committed by Moses. It is clear now why the latter fears such extreme punishment by the father-king. The fantasied retribution for patricide is death. The Egyptian taskmaster, Dathan, and Pharaoh are all father figures.

We can see the biblical incident, then, on two levels. On a reality basis the first two acts recorded of the adult Moses may indeed have taken place as described. But the wording of the narrative, its omissions and ambiguity, provide clues that can be utilized to uncover that other level of significance, the unconscious psychic forces that ever relentlessly prove that the child is father to the man.

There is indeed a rather impressive cohesiveness of meaning in this underlying stream of content in the material we have thus far analyzed. A developmental pattern is discernible. First, there is the myth of the birth of a hero, which is subtly combined with the family romance of the young boy, extending far into adolescence. The subsequent gap in the narrative can be understood as a period of amnesia, or repression, characteristic of the latency period.

Freud has emphasized the importance of a latency phase in the development of religious feelings, both in the individual and the group. (Jones 1957, 3:366) It is in the return of the intense but repressed feelings of childhood that the later emotions of equal intensity have their source. In his book *Mystery on the Mountain* Theodor Reik makes the following assertion regarding the psychic development of Moses: "Whatever were the vicissitudes of Moses during his early years, he was alienated from his people and came back to them on a detour that led him to Midian. It was there that he had the vision of the Burning Bush. His religious conversion was, as in most cases of this kind, preceded by a rejection of the traditional religion. Only a great inner experience, in which he deeply felt the misery of his people was powerful enough to make him aware of their destiny and to make him decide to share it with them" (p. 16).

The sudden eruption into activity on the part of Moses marked his emergence into manhood. This final break for psychological as well as physical freedom occurs with the initiative expressed in actions that could symbolize the attempt to overcome the hostile father and make peace with the brother figures. However, the latter effort fails, for the hostility of the brother becomes merged with the reactivated dread of the powerful oedipal father. The youth flees from the land that belongs to Pharaoh, leaving behind him the mother of his childhood, the woman who also belongs to Pharaoh. But in his very first encounter in the land of refuge he overcomes successfully another hostile group of *fathers and brothers,* makes a conquest of the woman who is to become his wife, and makes peace with the good father, Jethro.

It seems that we have here, in the second chapter of Exodus, a remarkable condensation of what may be both historical truth and psychological biography. The two are so merged that they become indivisible. It is this interweaving of the unconscious of the individual hero with the saga of the group that lends to the biblical literature some of its aura of mystique.

The Hero and the Group

The first two chapters of Exodus present an interesting parallel. The opening chapter deals with the group situation, the scene on a national scale, which provides the background for ushering in the hero in chapter 2. There are strong indications that the first chapter does more than present the stage for the exploits of the hero. This introductory chapter does, in fact, contain a little drama of its own, neatly concealed in a veil of ambiguous wording and other defensive maneuvers. Its hidden content is closely related to the underlying meanings in chapter 2, with which we have just dealt.

The style and manner of presentation in the biblical text is often significantly related to its content. Martin Buber (1936) expresses a similar thought when he remarks, "In the course of dealing with this text over a period of many years, I have been ever more strongly reaching the conclusion that the form frequently, as one might say, rounds off the content, i.e., that we are often shown something important by means of it" (p. 9).

We are told in the opening chapter of Exodus that a new Pharaoh arose who "knew not Joseph." He experiences the presence of the Hebrews as a threat, although the reasons for this attitude are not entirely clear. He says: "Behold, the people of the children of Israel are too many and too mighty for us. Come, let us deal wisely with them, lest they multiply, and it come to pass, that when there falleth out any war, they also join themselves unto our enemies, and fight against us, and get them up out of the land" (1:9–10).

The only crime of which the people, Israel, stands accused is that of existence. They dare to exist, to multiply, and to flourish. The threat to Pharaoh seems to be of a twofold nature. The Hebrews may turn hostile and join forces with the enemies of Egypt. Or in such a time of disturbance they may leave the country. With a curious ambivalence Pharaoh can neither live with the Hebrews nor without them, an attitude he maintained throughout his dramatic conflict with Moses.

The plot now unfolds. Pharaoh enslaves this freedom-loving people, accustomed to a seminomadic existence in the land of Goshen, the eastern delta of the Nile. No doubt many Hebrews were by this time living in other parts of Egypt as well, in towns and villages. The text says: "and the land was filled with them" (1:7).

But even the most oppressive labor to which they were subjected did not satisfy Pharaoh. He therefore gives an order to have all newborn male infants destroyed. The illogic of this step has impressed biblical commentators. If the Hebrews were a threat in times of war, a more immediate remedy would have been to get rid of the adult males. Moreover, if Pharaoh didn't want the Hebrews to increase in number, wouldn't it have been more practical to annihilate the female children instead of the male? (Benno 1942).

Psychoanalytically, we can perceive here a familiar configuration: like the father of the primal horde, Pharaoh was anxious about the growing strength of his sons, particularly since he saw them as potentially hostile stepsons. His aggression is directed primarily toward the male progeny. The women are seen as belonging to the father in a special sense, to be preserved for his exploitation and enjoyment.

How does Pharaoh go about the task of having the newborn males eliminated? He entrusts this bloody undertaking to the two midwives, Shiprah and Puah. This latter detail is indeed a curious one. In the midst of a narrative characterized by a tone of generalization and vagueness, where no mention is made concerning the number of Hebrews involved except the fear that they may multiply, a highly specific factor is suddenly introduced, that of the midwives who are *two* in number. The ruling Pharaoh himself is not given a name; the midwives are. This change in the style of presentation creates a certain element of incongruity in the text. It is similar to the eruption of an inappropriate detail in the *free associations* of an analysand. As in the latter situation, a breakthrough of unconscious content may be indicated here.

The text says, "And the king of Egypt spoke to the Hebrew midwives, of which the name of one was Shiprah, and the name of the other, Puah; and he said, 'When ye do the office of a midwife to the Hebrew women, ye shall look upon the birth-stool: if it be a son, then ye shall kill him; but if it be a daughter, then she shall live'" (1:15–17). Interestingly, the terms *son* and *daughter* are used rather than the more impersonal *male* and *female* designations.

It also seems strange that the matter of communicating the order is handled in this intimate way. The king himself speaks to the midwives, telling them what to do. One would have expected an official of the court to perform this task, not the exalted potentate of Egypt in person.

This significant detail, the familiarity of Pharaoh with the two midwives, reveals the mythlike quality of the story, with its unconscious content. In this oedipal fantasy, the hero must again be identified as the youthful Moses. Safeguarded by the defensive structure, he momentarily takes the place of Pharaoh himself.

The two midwives, we are told, feared God and did not carry out the king's commands. Instead, they delivered the male infants safely. The text then makes a rather cryptic statement: "And it came to pass, because the midwives feared God, that He made them houses" (1:21). Here again scholars are puzzled. A Talmudic interpretation is that He gave them *families* or increased their prosperity. Another explanation is that the pronoun *them* in the biblical verse refers to the people of Israel as a whole (Hertz, 1936, 209). Such a thought, however, would be unrelated to the context. Why should God give all Israel houses because the midwives feared Him? Clearly, the act of God was intended as a reward for the midwives themselves.

What is the unconscious content that may be concealed in

this obscurity? God, the potent Father, will reward the kind, merciful mothers by making them fruitful, giving them families. They who had allowed others to keep their children would receive a like reward. The unmentioned hero of the fantasy here identifies himself with God. The image of the father thus fluctuates between Pharaoh and God.

A Hebrew expression for husband is *baal habayit*, lord or master of the house. The *house* and the *woman* are one and the same. The concealed wish in the sentence under discussion is a forbidden oedipal one and thus can be expressed only ambiguously. "He gave them houses" may be interpreted to mean "he took them as houses" and gave them families.

The rabbinic interpretation mentioned above therefore contains the kernel of truth but omits a necessary connection. This kind of intuitive understanding is often found in the legendary and interpretative material and can be used as one of the confirmations of a psychoanalytic analysis of the text.

Who were the two women, Shiprah and Puah? Although they are referred to as the Hebrew midwives, Hertz (1936) says the expression means *midwives to the Hebrews* and thinks the two women were Egyptians, since the king could hardly expect that Hebrew women would kill their own infants (p. 208). The *Cambridge Bible* commentary interprets the phrase literally and considers them Hebrews (Driver 1911, 6). There is therefore a further element of ambiguity here. Were Shiprah and Puah Hebrew or Egyptian? This question arose in ancient times and was a matter of controversy in the Talmud.

Rabbinic legend makes an interesting identification of the two midwives. It says that Shiprah and Puah represent Jochebed and Miriam, the mother and sister of Moses (Ginzberg 1909–1938, 2:279–80). The psychological source of such an association seems clear. It confirms that an oedipal drama is being enacted here. The dominant feature of this fantasy is its collective aspect. The father-king is the group lord and master. His aggression is directed against the people, Israel, whose male infants collectively are to be destroyed.

Chapter 1 of Exodus portrays the group drama within which the individual oedipal drama is defensively concealed. The two midwives are not only protective and maternal figures but also incestuous objects. As in the family romance described earlier, the act of repression falters and weakens where the mother image is concerned. The attachment to the mother must indeed have been a strong one. It is only she who is allowed to rescue Moses in both the collective and the individual fantasy. But the gap in the defense must be mended. It is the *other women* who perform the actual deed of saving him.

The derivation of the two names, Shiprah and Puah, are also significant. *Shiprah* closely resembles the Hebrew word for *bird* and *Puah* for *red*. These words readily symbolize maternal and sexual concepts, particularly on the basis of infantile, aggressive fantasies regarding coitus. There is a further association. The woman whom Moses weds in Midian is named Zipporah, which means *bird*.

We have in this chapter an example of the peculiar relationship between the group and the hero that is characteristic for Israel and is especially significant in the life of Moses, a phenomenon that will manifest itself with increasing significance in the further studies of this volume.

We know that every fantasy has its origin in an individual mind. Then empathically it can be adopted by the group, whose latent thoughts and wishes it expresses. If Moses identified himself so strongly with his people that at times he unconsciously represented them, then the kind of narrative we have in Exodus 1 would be entirely understandable. Moses uses the group as concealment for his unconscious individual oedipal fantasy. The one is lost among the many, and the many become the one. These mechanisms of defense would explain the ambiguity of the text.

Freud (1930) has contributed the concept that the cultural development of a group repeats the history of individual social maturation (p. 133). Perhaps one of the aspects of uniqueness in regard to the biblical Hebrews is the extent to which an empathic relationship existed between the leaders and the group. The patriarchal setting and the monotheistic God provided the stimulating background for such a development. The hero in a special sense becomes the *collective ego* of the group. Moses performs this role with peculiar intensity and clarity. His distinctiveness, however, lies in a broader scope. His life story is synonymous with the development of the collective superego of the group.

An underlying danger that Moses and his people had to face was keeping the hero clearly a human figure. It is this stubborn need to maintain God as the One and Only that keeps Moses from becoming a Son of God in the sense that Jesus did later. Instead of becoming merged with the Deity, Moses becomes at times psychologically one with his people. Thus, the myth of the birth of a hero, expressive of the group, and the family romance, the *personal myth*, become united in the fantasy of the leader and the saga of the group.

Moses in Midian

 CHAPTER TWO

THE PERIOD OF time that Moses spent in Midian as a member of the household of Jethro is one of preparation, of inner unfolding and growth. It was in the quietness of this family life, in the tranquil pursuits of a Bedouin shepherd, that the transformation must have taken place that propelled him back to Egypt for the great task awaiting him there.

This epoch in the life of Moses can be understood as a developmental stage, when he leaves his adolescence behind him and emerges fully into manhood. The exact age at which Moses left Egypt is not mentioned, but the biblical text refers to the time of his appearance among the enslaved Hebrews as "those days when Moses was grown up" (2:11),* (literally, *when he became great*), that is, reached his physical maturity, probably at age eighteen or twenty, according to Talmudic opinion (Ginzberg 1909–1938, 5:406).

---

*All biblical references in this chapter, unless otherwise noted, are to the book of Exodus.

It will be recalled that the impetus for his flight from Egypt came after Moses struck down an Egyptian taskmaster who was beating a Hebrew slave. The text says, "Now when Pharaoh heard this thing, he sought to slay Moses. *But Moses fled from the face of Pharaoh, and dwelt in the land of Midian; and he sat down by a well*" (2:14–15) (italics added).

There are several noteworthy aspects about this last verse. First, there is a compression of time. Moses is brought from Egypt to Midian without the mention of any intervening events. But if Midian here actually refers to the homeland territory of this nomadic people, Moses would have trekked across the entire width of the Sinai Peninsula to the northeastern shore of the Gulf of Aqaba. Certainly much time and many periods of rest would have been required for him to make this perilous journey alone through the wilderness. This passage of time is treated as though it had not occurred.

It seems that only what is directly relevant to the forward movement of the main theme of the narrative, the coming together of Moses and his task, is considered important enough to be recorded in the sacred literature. Moses alone in the desert, struggling toward an unknown destination, is just a man concerned with the problems of survival, as far as we know. Yet this journey must have taught him a great deal about how life could be sustained in the wilderness and helped to prepare him for the leadership of his people in that same unfriendly but awe-inspiring terrain.

Folklore relating to biblical events, however, seems to abhor a vacuum. What the Bible itself leaves out, popular fantasy generously fills in. In the Haggada, the story portion of the Talmud, and in the wider body of such literature known as the Midrash, this gap of biographical detail in the life of Moses abounds with vivid fantasies of the experiences Moses went through between the time he leaves Egypt and arrives in Midian. He becomes involved in wars between Ethiopia and lands to the East, performing heroic feats on behalf of the former. There are also wars between Ethiopia and Egypt itself. In some of these legends he fights on one side; in some, on the other, but always his exploits are remarkable beyond the wildest dreams. He defeats great armies, conquers hitherto unconquerable cities, is made a king of Ethiopia, marries a princess of that land but, interestingly, does not consummate that marriage and is finally dethroned by that understandably frustrated queen. (Ginzberg 1909–1938, 2:283–89). All this happens before Moses reaches Midian, where his real task awaits him.

Is there any relationship, one is led to conjecture, between these exaggerated tales of remarkable exploits and the reality situation of Moses at this time? Were the storytellers identifying with their hero in his lonely wanderings across that desolate land and the thoughts and feelings he must have been experiencing? For, indeed, it seems plausible that Moses might have had daydreams of that very nature. It would have been comforting to think of himself as performing those astounding military deeds instead of dwelling on his real situation, fleeing from his homeland, afraid for his very life. It would have been psychologically helpful to visualize himself as being crowned king by a grateful people, perhaps his own brethren, whom he had rescued from the enemy. Since the queen would, unconsciously, be a mother figure, he could not, of course, fulfill the marital role. In defeating and displacing powerful rulers, Moses would be fighting and conquering Pharaoh himself, here the dreaded oedipal father.

It is not surprising, however, that the biblical narrative itself omits this phase in the life of Moses and brings him, as if by magic, from the time when "he fled from the face of Pharaoh" to the moment when "he sat down by a well in Midian." Personal hardships and adolescent dreams of an unrealistic nature did not belong in this history of a people and the psychobiography of its leader. However, Moses must have fled from Egypt in a mood of turbulent feelings. In one act he had uncompromisingly asserted his sense of self-identity through compassion for his suffering brethren. At the same time he had found himself capable of aggression in its most violent form, the taking of a human life. By this deed he severed the bonds with his native land and was faced with the imperative of finding new paths and purposes for himself. Moving from a familiar and protected environment into homelessness is an action prompted by both desperation and courage. To have taken a human life and to be threatened by a powerful father-king must indeed have been anxiety-provoking, and we are told that "Moses feared."

On the positive side, it can be assumed that the youth experienced a new found strength in his sense of identity and self-assertion. His flight was not only to escape from the wrath of Pharaoh but also to reach a locality where he could gather his inner resources for an undertaking that on a certain level of self-awareness he may already have accepted for himself. Indeed, the postbiblical legends described above seem to point in that direction.

That Moses was unconsciously acting out a part of the oedipal fantasy when he struck down the Egyptian is suggested in the preceding chapter. Associated with a growing independence from the father figure is the second part of the fantasy, the conquest of the woman. There is an underlying logic, therefore, in bringing Moses directly from the events in Egypt to those that are about to take place at the well in Midian, even to the extent of including these two localities within the compass of a single sentence. In the biblical literature, *sequence* frequently suggests *connection*. And indeed, a well is a place traditionally favored in the Bible for meeting one's future wife.

In the Household of Jethro

The description of what occurs is made with characteristic brevity: "Now the priest of Midian had seven daughters; and they came and drew water, and filled the troughs to water their father's flock. And the shepherds came and drove them away; but Moses stood up and helped them, and watered their flock" (2:16–17).

Here another omission may be noted. No reference is made to the methods used by Moses to drive away the unruly shepherds. It is hardly likely that his mere presence was enough to intimidate them in their efforts to use the already filled troughs for their own flocks. Certainly Moses must have engaged in some form of aggressive behavior toward them, even if only in terms

Moses in Midian 51

of a verbal protest. But all we are told is that he stood up and helped the girls.

Might there be some underlying connection between the need to deny the aggressive behavior here and the act of violence that Moses committed in Egypt? Was he now experiencing a kind of reaction to the earlier deed, so that even aggression on a milder scale and in the realistic service of the women could only be expressed in the narrative by implication? In terms of what was conscious and what was repressed, the situation at the well in Midian represents the opposite of what took place in Egypt. The rescue of the woman is related, whereas the hostility toward the man is ignored.

That the two events have a connection in the unconscious is also suggested by a Talmudic legend relating that when the girls expressed their gratitude to Moses for helping them, he replied, "Your thanks are due to the Egyptian I killed, on account of whom I had to flee from Egypt. Had it not been for him, I should not be here now" (Ginzberg 1909–1938, 2:291–95). That is, only when the cruel father is disposed of can the woman be rescued.

It might be noted that the same Hebrew word, *yeshev*, is used to express both *he sat down* and *he dwelt*. A well is a place of communal meeting. The statement that he sat down in this place may also have been a way of saying that Moses was ready to join the community in this new environment. Immediately thereafter he does indeed come in contact with those who are to play important roles in his life.

The action moves forward when the young women relate the experience to their father. He replies, "And where is he? Why is it that ye have left the man? Call him, that he may eat bread" (2:20).

Why indeed, one may wonder, did the girls, daughters of a priest, fail to perform this gesture of hospitality so valued in the desert? The father here emerges as a more real person than the girls. And perhaps that is the explanation. The women may have had to retain their quality of unreality for Moses, a point to which we shall return shortly.

The narrative continues with the same brevity. "And Moses was content to dwell with the man: and he gave Moses Zipporah his daughter. And she bore a son and he called his name Gershom: for he said: 'I have been a stranger in a strange land'" (2:21–22).

There are recurrent themes in the stories of the biblical heroes, yet the experience of each is distinctively and significantly different. Jacob also meets his future wife at a well. But there the similarity ends. The colorful romance of Jacob and his beloved Rachel stands in bright contrast to the brief factual statement regarding the marriage of Moses and Zipporah. It seems that not only aggression but also sexuality are presented in muted tones concerning Moses in Midian. Their presence is implied as facts of life, but the brevity and omission of affect with which they are treated point to repressive tendencies.

Let us look more closely at the elements involved in the meeting and marriage of Moses and Zipporah. As Moses sits at the well, the newcomers to the story are introduced with the statement: "Now the priest of Midian had seven daughters." The number seven has a fairy tale quality. It makes Zipporah one of many, thus denying her any real individuality. One of the functions of fantasy is as a defense against reality. There is not a single personal attribute describing Zipporah at this point that makes her stand out among her sisters. Nor does the text contain any expression on the part of Moses that indicates the slightest interest or feelings of warmth for the woman he makes his wife. In fact, even the word *wife* or *marriage* is not mentioned in the text. All we are told is that "he gave Moses Zipporah his daughter."

Hebrew values stress the importance of marriage and children. It would have been incongruous for the great future lawgiver of Israel to have remained a celibate. Moses does fulfill the minimal requirements in the roles of husband and father. But there is clearly a reluctance in the biblical narrative to make much of these customary events of the ordinary man in the life of Moses, especially where sexuality was concerned.

The psychological development of Moses in Midian centers largely around his relationship to the father figure. It is important, therefore, to understand the role that Jethro plays in the life of Moses at this time.

An aura of mystery obscures the figure of the father-in-law

of Moses. He is referred to by several different names in the course of the biblical story, thus raising the question of whether one or two personalities were actually involved. On some occasions he is known as Reuel, but most commonly as Jethro. In other parts of the Bible he is referred to or associated with the name of Hobab (Num. 10:29; Judg. 4:11).

Names were of particular significance in antiquity and special meanings were attached to them. A name often expressed an attribute of the person. Therefore, there may be some reason underlying the several names relating to the father-in-law of Moses and the confusion of identity regarding these.

The hypothesis presented here is that the obscurity surrounding this personality served an unconscious purpose for Moses, the hero of the story. It made possible the splitting of the father image to serve various functions. This process is similar to the mechanism found in dreams and myths, when different figures represent certain aspects of a relationship to the dreamer or hero.

First, when introduced as the father of the seven girls whom Moses meets at the well, he is the impersonal "priest of Midian." This designation serves the useful function of describing his status and role. Moreover, it creates a protective emotional distance from a still unknown but potential father figure.

The next mention of him is as Reuel, on the occasion when his daughters return and tell him of the kind stranger who came to their aid. Their father's response, as noted earlier, bids them summon the man to partake of their hospitality, a virtue highly valued in the desert. The name Reuel, Assyrian in origin, means *the friend or companion of God,* thus bringing to mind the personality of Abraham, who was known in a special way as the *friend of God* and whose origins did indeed stem from the lands to the northeast. Practicing hospitality in regard to strangers is vividly associated with this first Patriarch.

Extrabiblical legendary sources explain that the priest of Midian gave up idolatrous worship and became a believer in the One God. This story too follows the pattern of the Abraham legends in which the founding father turns away from idols and comes to the realization of the true God. As for Moses himself, the flight from idol-worshipping Egypt to the purity of the wilderness can be compared with Abraham's departure from Ur and Haran, also to escape the polluted atmosphere of those centers of idolatry.

It would be psychologically understandable if leaving Egypt also represented for Moses a dimly felt, hardly conscious wish to return to the life and traditions of his own people of an earlier age, the Patriarchal Era. The figure of Jethro may therefore have been endowed with composite meanings, as in a dream. In the quest for a renewed sense of identification with his people and with his past, Moses may have perceived in the idyllic figure of the priest of Midian the prototype of Abraham himself. The name Reuel may thus represent the Abraham-like aspects of Jethro, with which he could identify.

When Moses has become a part of the family and is pursuing his daily routine, his father-in-law is called Jethro, probably his given name. Some describe it as expressive of his attributes, in its meaning of *overflowing with excellent qualities* (Ginzberg 1909–1938, 2:290).

Rabbinic tradition inclines toward the view that Reuel was another person altogether and is the father of Jethro. The text itself, however, clearly points to the designation of Reuel and Jethro as being the same person. The Talmudic rabbis may have been responding with their usual sensitivity to unconscious connotations in the text. If Reuel does indeed symbolically represent Abraham, then he would have to be a father figure, an ancestor. As such, he would stand above Jethro, the more earthly and real human being, who lived in the present.

The name Hobab is first mentioned after the exodus from Egypt, when Moses is leading his people through the unknown wilderness and is not sure of the path he should follow. The text says, "And Moses said unto Hobab, the son of Reuel the Midianite, Moses' father-in-law . . . 'Leave us not, I pray thee; for as much as thou knowest how we are to encamp in the wilderness and thou shalt be to us instead of eyes'" (Num. 10:29,31).

Hobab is here described as the son of Reuel, but the identity of the latter in this context is unclear. If it is Reuel who is the father-in-law of Moses, Hobab would be a brother-in-law. The function Hobab serves here, as the *eyes* of Moses, is reminiscent of Aaron's role, when he becomes the *mouth* of Moses, making up for his brother's lack of verbal fluency when the two confront Pharaoh. Hobab can therefore be understood as a mythlike duplicate of Aaron.

The need for a splitting of the father-brother images may be indicative of ambivalence in Moses. At the same time, the specific content points to a longing for the good father and the good brother, who will respond to his need for help.

The hero of mythology is one who rises in revolt against the father and overcomes him. But the hero in the world of reality is one who makes peace with the father, who identifies with him in constructive ways and tries to emulate his strength and virtues. In the complex process of maturation, the problems of ambivalence, the splitting of the father figure into good and bad images, the feelings of guilt and efforts at atonement are part of the growth experience.

The role of Jethro as a significant father figure must have been of considerable importance in the life of Moses during this period of development and change. It is through this relationship that Moses enters into those two areas basic to maturity—love and work.

Jethro can be seen as a kind of transitional father figure in a relationship preparatory to the encounter with the Father-God Himself. It is only after making peace with an earthly father that Moses is ready for the greater confrontation. Of his two previous fathers, Amram, the biological parent, must have been experienced as one who abandoned him. The foster grandparent, Pharaoh himself, according to the biblical story, was the one whose threats to slay him forced Moses to flee from Egypt. Pharaoh was the tyrannical father who eventually would have to be faced and conquered in the fashion of the mythical hero.

But even with the idealized figure of Jethro an undercurrent of ambivalence in this relationship finds expression in the rabbinic traditions and legends concerning him. These contain two different views on the subject of Jethro's attitude toward the marriage of Moses and Zipporah. One favored the biblical approach that Jethro welcomed Moses as a son-in-law. The other view presented the Midianite priest as opposed to this union, an attitude finding expression in legends that Jethro subjected Moses to severe ordeals in an effort to disqualify the latter from winning the hand of Zipporah. One of these relates that Jethro tried to take Moses' life by throwing him into a pit, where he lived for seven years, secretly fed by Zipporah (Ginzberg 1909–1938, 2:291–95). These tales represent the folk fantasy of how Jethro must have felt about Moses as a son-in-law, an aspect not treated in the Bible itself. The trial by ordeal is also, of course, a regular feature of the fairy-tale course of events through which the aspiring suitor, the hero, is expected to go. It expresses the familiar ambivalence of the father toward the man who deprives him of his daughter.

In his book *Moses and Monotheism* Freud assigns to the priest of Midian a role that is of interest here. He is indeed a father-in-law of Moses, but of a *native Midianite Moses*, a different person entirely from the Egyptian Moses, the two being separated in time by several generations or more (pp. 49–51). In his reconstruction of the development of the Hebrew religion during this crucial epoch, Freud theorized that the Moses of biblical tradition was a composite figure, a merging originally of two powerful leaders among the Hebrews. One was the earlier Egyptian Moses, follower of the so-called monotheist king, Iknaton. This was a Moses of noble Egyptian lineage, who *adopted* the Hebrew slaves as his people, brought them through the exodus, and taught them his religion of ethical monotheism. Freud postulated that this Moses met a violent death at the hands of some of his rebellious followers. However, the religious concepts he taught them lived on in these *Moses people*. After a number of years this group joined related tribes who had not gone through the experience of slavery in Egypt but had maintained their nomadic existence. They occupied the area between the eastern border of the Sinai Peninsula and the western edge of Arabia, around the springs of Kadesh. Freud's theory is that this group worshipped a volcano-god called *Yahveh*, who was a much more primitive deity than the highly spiritual god of the Egyptian Moses. The joining of these two groups resulted in a compromise religion that retained some of the features from both sets of traditions. In the process of time the two figures of Moses became merged into one personality in the minds of the people.

This hypothesis of Freud's, presented by him in highly tentative fashion, can be understood from another viewpoint. There were indeed two figures of Moses. One was the Egyptian-clad youth, identified with the upper-class culture of his native land, who was described by the daughters of Jethro as *the Egyptian* who helped them. The other was the Moses who returned to the nomadic simplicity of his ancestors and took on a new aspect, in identification with the Abraham-like aspects of Jethro and as an assertion of his true sense of identity. Thus, Moses may indeed have represented a merging of two personalities but in quite a different fashion from that conjectured by Freud. It was the *personal exodus* of Moses from Egypt and his psychological transformation while in Midian that brought about this synthesis. The Egyptian Moses merged with the Midianite Moses in this psychological sense, to become the integrated personality of the great leader and emancipator, the Moses of Jewish tradition (2).

The Burning Bush

The theophany of the burning bush belongs to an era more than three millenia removed from our own. To what degree can one really hope to understand the nature and quality of such an experience from a psychological viewpoint? Perhaps we do not know under what conditions of a different social order and religious climate capacities for experiences can be evoked that lie dormant and unused in our lives today.

To present the biblical theophanies as hallucinatory (Arlow 1951) is to describe rather than to explain. Yet perhaps that is the best we can do. A profound religious experience such as a theophany involves a quality of psychic functioning that is particularly mysterious to us.

It is in his humble and peaceful role as a shepherd, guarding the flocks of his father-in-law, Jethro, that Moses has his first mystic experience, the theophany of the burning bush. The groundwork for this moment had been laid. When Moses arrived in Midian, he was dressed as an Egyptian, referred to as such by the daughters of Jethro. In the desert he casts aside this garb and returns to the life of his nomadic ancestors. He accepts the basic responsibilities of adulthood—marriage, paternity, and work. And now the man and the task are to be brought together.

This *call from God* was indeed a psychological inevitability for Moses. It was the coming to fruition of his intrapsychic struggle in Egypt, his flight from that land, and the period of preparation in Midian.

Let us first consider what psychic factors might have played a role in precipitating the theophany. News about the death of the king of Egypt and the rise to power of a new Pharaoh probably had reached Midian. Moses must have felt that the hour for decision was close at hand. In the aloneness of his shepherd's task, his mind must have been in a state of preoccupation with dimly formed ideas regarding his brethren in Egypt and what his role might be regarding them. But only a confrontation with God could give form and purpose to that which was stirring restlessly and conflictfully within him. The setting in which he moved was one to inspire contemplation and awe, an influence to which the people of biblical days were peculiarly sensitive. The vast expanse of wilderness, the towering mountain peaks with their copperish glow characteristic of that region, all would lend themselves to the awaited experience. It must have been with barely repressed feelings of both dread and expectancy that Moses spent his days preceding the momentous event. He was now in an environment reminiscent of the traditional home of his forefathers, worshippers of the God he was actively seeking.

The text says, "Now Moses was keeping the flock of Jethro his father-in-law, the priest of Midian; and he led the flock to the farthest end of the wilderness, and came to the mountain of God, unto Horeb. And the angel of the Lord appeared unto him in a flame of fire out of the midst of a bush; and he looked, and behold, the bush burned with fire, and the bush was not consumed. And Moses said: 'I will turn aside now, and see this great sight, why the bush is not burnt.' And when the Lord saw that he turned aside to see, God called unto him out of the midst of the bush, and said: 'Moses, Moses.' And he said: 'Here am I.' And He said: 'Draw not nigh hither; put off thy shoes from off thy feet, for the place whereon thou standest is holy ground.' Moreover He said: 'I am the God of thy father, the God of Abraham, the God of Isaac, and the God of Jacob.' And Moses hid his face; for he was afraid to look upon God. And the Lord said: 'I have surely seen the affliction of my people that are in Egypt, and

Moses in Midian 59

have heard their cry by reason of their taskmasters; for I know their pains and I am come down to deliver them out of the hand of the Egyptians, and to bring them up out of that land unto a good land and a large, unto a land flowing with milk and honey; . . Come now therefore, and I will send thee unto Pharaoh, that thou mayest bring forth My people the children of Israel out of Egypt.' And Moses said unto God: 'Who am I, that I should go unto Pharaoh, and that I should bring forth the children of Israel out of Egypt'" (3:1–11). Thus runs the first part of the dialogue.

The episode of the burning bush contains the basic elements found in the theophanies of other biblical prophets (Arlow 1951). These include the summons to prophecy in a dramatic revelation of the Divine Presence and the induction of the prophet into his task. The use of fire as a manifestation of divinity is a common one and has appeared in the visionary experiences of other biblical prophets. Each theophany, however, is also highly individual in character and, it is suggested here, *is related to the personality of the prophet.*

The question then arises of why God appears to Moses in the particular guise of the burning bush. Explanations of scholars regarding the significance of this phenomenon vary from mythological interpretations characteristic of the school of Higher Biblical Criticism (Buber 1936, 40; Reik 1959, 113) (3) to suggestions that natural causes may have illumined the bush giving it the appearance of being on fire. (4) An external stimulus of some kind may indeed have played a role in the experience. But it could only have been utilized by Moses in the way described because it met his psychic need of the moment.

We shall assume that the entire configuration of the burning bush, with fire issuing from its midst and the voice of an angel speaking from the flame, was a symbolic representation occurring in a dreamlike or hallucinatory state. The bush is a female symbol. Fire expresses sexual potency and related libidinal and aggressive impulses (Arlow 1955). Moses is filled with awe and hides his face. This affect is associated developmentally with the small child who witnesses the powerful phallus of the father (Greenacre 1956, 9–30).

In the text, however, attention is not called directly to the fire itself but to the angel of the Lord who appeared to him in a flame of fire. An angel represents a nonsexual, spiritualized being. Thus, we have here a dramatic representation of the psychic process of sublimation, the conversion of sexual energy into superego function.

The ground on which Moses has so unexpectedly intruded is holy and sacrosanct. Moses is warned, "Draw not nigh hither; put off thy shoes from off thy feet for the place whereon thou standest is holy ground." Old rabbinic sources state that the command to Moses bidding him remove his shoes conveyed the desire of God that Moses should give up conjugal life. "For," the Midrashic legend expounds, "God says, 'Moses has begot children, he has done his duty toward the world. I desire him now to unite himself with the *Shekinah*, that she may descend upon earth for his sake'" (Ginzberg 1909–1938, 2:316).

The *Shekinah* is a mystical presence, feminine yet wholly spiritual in nature. It is appropriate, therefore, that at this moment, when a profound change is taking place in the psychic life of Moses, libidinal desires should be transformed into a spiritualized, sublimated form. And indeed, tradition maintains that Moses lived apart from his wife after his selection by God.

Why the removal of his shoes signified the giving up of conjugal life is not explained, of course, by the scholars of old, but the symbolic meaning was unconsciously comprehended. The displacement of genital significance to the foot and shoe is a common form of symbolism, the removal of the shoes expressing separation from the woman.

We still face the difficult question concerning a more specific origin for the choice of symbols represented in the burning bush. I will try to show that the form and structure of this configuration suggests a latent content reminiscent of a reactivated childhood memory dealing with the primal scene. It is known psychoanalytically that the repressed affects of the child can provide a springboard for the most profound experiences of the human spirit.

Let us consider the verbal exchange between God and Moses that now takes place. Moses says, "I will turn aside now, and see this great sight, why the bush is not burnt." The emphasis here is on the scopophilic aspect. The impulse to see and to understand the mystery of what one sees is here expressed with childlike simplicity. What seems to be repressed is the anxiety that would normally accompany such an experience.

In the attempt to master the anxiety associated with the childhood trauma, Moses may have altered some of those very aspects that would have been most disturbing to him in the forgotten episode. The matter-of-fact attitude in which he investigates the unusual phenomenon of the burning bush is understandable as a defense. The childhood act of guilty observation is here converted into a rational, almost scientific manner. The scopophilic impulse is sublimated into intellectual curiosity, a familiar developmental process.

The next verse has an odd quality. "And when the Lord saw that he turned aside to see, God called to him out of the midst of the burning bush, and said: 'Moses, Moses.' And he said: 'Here am I.'"

What can be the meaning of this rather strange behavior on the part of God? The text clearly states that God spoke to Moses only after observing that the latter turned aside to see. Certainly it was within God's power to *cause* Moses to turn aside to see. And certainly God knew that Moses would do so. Why then does the narrative present God as being in a state of uncertainty about the rather simple matter of attracting the attention of his prophet to be?

A possible interpretation is that God's waiting *to see* if Moses would turn aside *to see* may be a reversal of the original situation in which Moses himself, as a small child, waited to see if *he* was being observed by his father. The child guiltily and stealthily goes out of his way in the hope of observing a primal scene and may wonder uneasily if he himself is being observed. Another instance of *looking* comes to mind here. Moses "looked this way and that way" before striking down the Egyptian taskmaster who was beating a Hebrew slave (2:12). *Looking* is evidently associated with an aggressive act or fantasy and thus with anxiety. In following the line of our argument, it might be considered that the uncertainty on the part of God, waiting to see if Moses would turn aside to see, may have had its origin in the uncertainty of Moses himself, as a small boy, when he conflictfully wondered if *he* should turn aside, perhaps in order *not* to see. In the biblical text Moses does, in fact, actually see the burning bush *before* he turns aside to see "this great sight, why the bush is not burnt." It seems more reasonable to assume that Moses would have turned *toward* the burning bush rather than *aside* in order to see it. One turns aside as an avoidance rather than a going forth to view something. So we have here another incongruity that rises from the latent content.

Moses responds to the sound of his name by saying, "Here am I." How different again from the childhood situation! The fear that father would see him and call out reprovingly, bidding him leave the forbidden area, is turned into its opposite. Now God actively summons him. And Moses, instead of retreating in fearful confusion, answers bravely and boldly, "Here am I."

It is true that this response on the part of a prophet who is being called is not an unusual one. But there may indeed be a common factor, for the prophet who is thus summoned for initiation into his new role is expected to surrender a portion of his sexuality in the psychic transformation that follows. He who answers "Here am I" thus announces his readiness for such renunciation.

And then follows this puzzling statement: "Moreover, I am the God of thy *father*, the God of Abraham, the God of Isaac, and the God of Jacob" (italics added). The expected wording would be "I am the God of *thy fathers*," a form of expression commonly used throughout the Bible. Why then the use of this word in its singular form?

One attempt to deal with this difficulty was made in a first-century translation of the Pentateuch by simply interpreting the word in its collective sense, as referring to the descriptive phrases that follow (Hertz 1936, 214). More widely held rabbinic tradition, however, accepts the literal meaning and clearly refers the appellation to Amram, the father of Moses. The Midrash explains that God spoke to Moses in his father's voice in order not to alarm him by the sudden and unexpected sound (Ginzberg 1909–1938, 2:316). This interpretation could be understood as a defensive reversal of the original situation, for a child would certainly be alarmed at hearing his father's voice under the conditions described above.

God did indeed speak to Moses in the voice of the father of his early childhood. For the voice of the father becomes the voice of the superego, rising from the oedipal conflict of the child, a process so graphically depicted in the elements of this theophany. Moreover, we have here another indication of the fact that Moses had been influenced in his early years by his biological parent, the Hebrew Amram, as well as by his Egyptian milieu.

God now moves directly to the purpose of His summons. He makes known that He has heard the cry of the Children of Israel in Egypt and says to Moses: "Come now therefore, and I will send thee unto Pharaoh, that thou mayest bring forth my people the children of Israel out of Egypt." "And Moses said unto God: 'Who am I, that I should go unto Pharaoh, and that I should bring forth the children of Israel out of Egypt'" (3:10–11).

In this exchange God is clearly choosing Moses for this mission. And yet the words "Come now, and I will send thee" indicate that God wishes Moses to accept willingly. The latter, however, immediately questions God's choice. His reluctance is based on the phrase "Who am I?"

A comparison with the reaction of another prophet in the same situation may be helpful here. God said to Jeremiah, who lived in the sixth and seventh centuries B.C. "Before I formed thee in the belly I knew thee, and before thou camest forth out of the womb I sanctified thee; I have appointed thee a prophet unto the nations" (Jer. 1:5).

Here there is no allowance for questioning or retreat. God clearly declares His purpose. Jeremiah's reluctance to accept the call stemmed from the feeling of unreadiness. He responds, "Ah, Lord God! behold, I cannot speak: for I am a child."

Jeremiah had no doubt about his identity as a person and what his life mission was to be. However, he was frightened at the task, for it was indeed a fearful one. It was to be his destiny to predict the destruction of the Jewish state and the dispersal of the people, a message that would make him vastly unpopular in the eyes of the whole nation.

The response of Moses, however, can be understood as coming from a different source psychologically. His words may indicate a sense of doubt about his self-identity. Who indeed was he? It was an old question, and at this crucial moment Moses had to face it anew. He had to know who he himself was before he could accept the responsibility confronting him.

God's reply to Moses is practical and to the point. The problem of self-identity, if that issue was indeed involved, is not answered directly. God says, "Certainly I will be with thee; and this shall be the token unto thee that I have sent thee: When thou has brought forth the people out of Egypt, ye shall serve God upon this mountain" (3:12).

The implication is that it doesn't matter who Moses is. The fact that God will be with him in this undertaking is the only identity that is relevant. *Moses is the man chosen by God*; that is his identity. Moreover, the token or sign that he is indeed the appointed one is the statement that the Children of Israel shall serve God on that very spot where he now stood. Moses is here associated and identified with his people as a whole. When they escape from Egypt, as he himself escaped, they too will come to this same place and also witness the revelation of God. At this moment Moses experiences within himself the two great forces that hereafter dominate his entire life—an identification with God and at the same time with his people, Israel.

The next part of this astonishing dialogue between God and Moses is of particular interest in terms of the problem of identity. "And Moses said unto God: 'Behold, when I come unto the children of Israel, and shall say unto them: The God of your fathers hath sent me unto you; and they shall say to me: What is His name? What shall I say unto them?' And God said unto Moses: I AM THAT I AM; and He said: 'Thus shalt thou say unto the children of Israel; I AM hath sent me unto you'" (3:13–14).

God had clearly defined earlier who He was, in terms of His relationship to the fathers of Israel. What then could the question of Moses mean and the cryptic answer? Biblical scholars have understandably been puzzled, and much has been written about the significance of God's reply. One opinion is that the query referred, not to *Who* God was, but *how great* was His name. "What are the mighty deeds which thou canst recount of Him, what is His power, that we (the people) should listen to thy message from Him" as Hertz puts it (1936, 215).

But for Moses, in this first profound experience with Deity, standing without shoes on holy ground and hiding his face from the Awful Presence, it would indeed be incredible, at such a time, to ask God for credentials regarding His power.

In its Hebrew form, *Ehyeh asher Ehyeh* is grammatically in the imperfect tense, signifying a process of being or becoming as well as continuity. Some scholars prefer to translate it "I will be what I will be," as expressive of a more active manifestation of God's existence. Martin Buber (1936) strongly emphasized this sense of the active presence of God that he finds inherent in the phrase (p. 40).

But perhaps of even greater psychological interest is the question itself. What might have prompted Moses to ask God by what name He should be called? There is a significant sequence in the first two questions Moses asks. The first one is *Who am I?* (that I should go unto Pharaoh). The second is *Who are You?* (in whose Name am I being sent?).

Both questions may be concerned with the same theme of self-identity. Moses, as we assume, was biologically a Hebrew but culturally, to a large extent, Egyptian, and spiritually, in conflict between those two (Reik 1959, 16). Here in Midian he was seeking to discover his true sense of self. Indeed, his own name, of doubtful origin, lacked a specific meaning, whether considered as derived from the Egyptian word meaning *child* or *born*, or the Hebrew, vaguely involving his *being drawn from the waters*. Thus, the question, *Who was this God*, which is the essence of the query, may have been, in part, a projection of the uncertainty Moses felt about himself.

In the theophany Moses enters into a new relationship with God. It is a form of initiation, a solemn covenant. On such occasions a new name is commonly part of the ceremony. But here an unusual feature is introduced. It is God who appears under a new name rather than the novitiate. If, as suggested, Moses was to find his own sense of identity through his relationship with God, then the identity of God was indeed all-important.

Moses may here be momentarily doubting the validity of his own theophany. How could he be sure that the voice and the vision of the burning bush did indeed belong to the God of his fathers? He had been brought up in a land of many gods. The answer God gives him is reassuring. *I AM* is the God of continued existence, the God who *was* and *is*. The new name expressed the new relationship, the rediscovery of Moses and of Israel, with the God of their fathers. Three times, within the next few verses of the text, God again makes clear His true identity as the Deity who had revealed Himself to the Patriarchs.

Knowing God's name was also a way of drawing closer to Him. This aspect is brought out on a later occasion when Moses more openly voices the wish to know God better. He argues that God should grant him this privilege because "Thou hast said, I know thee by name and thou hast also found favor in My sight" (33:12).

God now proceeds to tell Moses explicitly what message he is to bring the Children of Israel.* He depicts in vivid terms what Moses is to say and do when he arrives in Egypt.

And then, in the midst of the inspiring words that instruct Moses to tell the people of their coming escape from Egypt, a jarring note, out of tune with the rest of the content, is suddenly introduced by God Himself. It is a mundane, materialistic note. God says, "And I will give this people favour in the sight of the Egyptians. And it shall come to pass, that, when ye go, ye shall not go empty; but every woman shall ask of her neighbor, and of her that sojourneth in her house, jewels of silver, and jewels of gold, and raiment; and ye shall put them upon your sons, and upon your daughters, and ye shall spoil the Egyptians" (3:21–22).

Theologians throughout the centuries have been embarrassed by these words and have tried to find rationalizations for the rather unadmirable aspect of the Deity reflected in them. I shall attempt to explore their meaning here as another eruption of the unconscious, projected by Moses onto God.

When habitual psychological patterns of response are shaken by some momentous event and a new integration of psychic forces is in process, derivatives of repressed infantile wishes and fears also may be reactivated. We can expect that as God describes what would take place in Egypt, a whole complex of related thoughts and feelings are stirred up in Moses. He experiences in fantasy the role he is to play before Pharaoh, a powerful father figure who is to be overcome and forced to accede to the request of Moses that the Children of Israel be permitted to leave Egypt. Unconsciously associated with the conquest of the father

---

*Differences in capitalization between the biblical quotations and the author's text will be found throughout. The purpose was to maintain the integrity of the biblical text on the one hand, and allow the author present-day usage on the other.

is the sexual submission of the woman, the mother. But this forbidden aspect of the oedipal pattern must indeed be greatly disguised in order to find expression. Not lending itself to sublimation, the wish emerges in distorted form and as a discordant note. The underlying impulse, unconscious to Moses himself, and the responsibility for which is projected onto the Deity, is the conquest of the woman. The symbolic significance of a woman's *treasure chest*, her jewels of gold and silver, is psychoanalytically familiar. Her clothes, or raiment, also represent her person.

The Hebrews are to be instructed to *spoil*, or *strip* the Egyptians, the connotation of which can be *to despoil sexually*. But the retort can immediately be made that the text clearly states that the *Hebrew women* are to perform this act. This would seem to rule out definitely any interpretation of a sexual meaning to this content.

One must ask, however, why the text so specifically states that the Hebrew *women* are to ask for these treasures from the Egyptian *women*? Why this limitation in terms of sex if the object is only a materialistic one, that of recovering from the Egyptians a monetary recompense for the years of enforced and unpaid labor endured by the Hebrew slaves? For this latter explanation is the one that seemed most understandable to many scholars. Another theory says that the Hebrew women would desire to have appropriate garments in which to celebrate the religious festival for which they were ostensibly leaving Egypt. But surely, at a time as momentous as the escape from Egypt, finery for the performance of religious worship could hardly become so important. It is interesting to reflect that much of these material goods, which were actually obtained by the Hebrews, according to the text, was later donated by the women for use in furnishing and decorating the tabernacle that was built in the wilderness. We have here a nice symbolic expression of sublimation, the renunciation of sexual for superego values.

There is further evidence pointing to the sexual meaning of the phrase "and ye shall spoil the Egyptians." Hertz (1936) has suggested that the traditional translation of the text is incorrect and should be rendered "and ye shall *save* the Egyptians," a direct reversal of the apparent content. The reason given for this change is that the Hebrew verb *nitzal* has other meanings, among them, "to rescue." Grammatically, it refers to the *person* rather than to *that which is taken from the person*. His interpretation is that the Hebrews would actually be *saving the Egyptians* from a lasting sense of guilt by obtaining this deserved recompense from their former oppressors (p. 217). This rather desperate rabbinic need to rationalize an unacceptable situation confirms the psychoanalytic view here presented—that the underlying impulse, as stemming from the unconscious of Moses, was directed at the *person* of the Egyptian woman herself, of which her jewels and raiment were but a displacement.

The ambiguity of the Hebrew word *nitzal* may indeed contain two contradictory connotations in the fashion of the antithetical meaning of words (Freud 1910, 4:184). The desire to conquer the mother, *to despoil* her, may also involve the opposite idea, *to rescue or save* her from the sexual attack of the rival, in this case the Egyptian man and ultimately Pharaoh himself. Both factors are contained in the oedipal fantasy of the little boy. He is at once the attacker and the knight-errant, eager to rescue the beloved mother.

The instruction that the Hebrew women are to do the asking from the Egyptian women can be understood as a displacement, a form of disguise often occurring in dreams. It is to hide the underlying wish that the *men* are to do this. And the men collectively represent the man Moses himself.

It is also significant that the text clearly says that these possessions of the Egyptian women are to be attained by the friendly process of *asking* for them. The use of force is thus definitely denied. This element too may be a defensive one against the unconscious impulse of the man to make a forbidden, forceful conquest of the woman.

When viewed as stemming from the unconscious, the phrase "every woman shall ask of her neighbor, and of her that sojourneth in her house" may express the relationship of *closeness* to the woman from whom the asking is to be done. It is either the woman in one's own home or the familiar figure of a neighbor, both representative of the most familiar woman of all—the mother.

The Hebrew word *sha-al* (to ask), frequently used in the Bible, is interpreted variously as meaning *to demand, to request, to obtain by entreaty*. Some versions of the Bible translate the word in the context under discussion as meaning *to borrow*, thus adding an element of deceit to the behavior of the departing Hebrews, much to the indignation of some Jewish scholars. Only once, as Hertz (1936) points out, is the word used in that sense, and in this instance its grammatical construction is different (p. 217).

Another phrase in these verses has a further element of incongruity. God, with a puzzling degree of interest in this matter, instructs Moses how the jewels and raiment thus obtained are to be used: "and ye shall put them upon your sons and upon your daughters." Why not on husbands and wives?

This detail can be better understood as a further disguise of the hidden wish already referred to. The displacement to sons and daughters, a more distant relationship, removes the deed farther from the source, thus helping to conceal the original wish. At the same time, since it is a *son* who is having the wish, it also brings it closer to its origin, in a characteristic compromise between impulse and defense.

The carrying out of this action must have been quite important to Moses, for it is mentioned on two other occasions. During the period of the confrontations with Pharaoh, just before the final disaster of the tenth plague, God again instructs Moses as follows: "'Speak now in the ears of the people, and let them ask *every man of his neighbor*, and *every woman of her neighbor*, jewels of silver, and jewels of gold.' And the Lord gave the people favour in the sight of the Egyptians. Moreover, the man Moses was very great in the land of Egypt, in the sight of Pharaoh's servants, and in the sight of the people" (11:2–3) (italics added).

Here the situation changes. The *men* evidently are to make this request of the Egyptian *men* and the women from those of their own sex. This change brings the men into the scene also, thus carrying the underlying impulse closer to the surface.

In the third reference to the plan, at the time when it is actually fulfilled, there is a further change in who is to do the asking and from whom. Now an even wider generalization takes place. The text says, "And the children of Israel did according to the word of Moses; and *they asked of the Egyptians* jewels of silver, and jewels of gold, and raiment. And the Lord gave the people favour in the sight of the Egyptians, so that they let them have what they asked. And they despoiled the Egyptians" (12:35–36) (italics added).

In the mood and atmosphere of that fateful time, when the

Egyptians had already suffered the horrors of nine plagues and were facing further dangers, the need to placate the Hebrews may have been strong. Perhaps only asking was required to make the guilt-ridden Egyptians willing to pay this conscience money to their mistreated slaves, in the hope, perhaps, of avoiding further catastrophe.

The unconscious significance for Moses of this action, carried out at his behest, retains the original impulse that prompted it —the conquest of the Egyptian woman, the foster mother, a fantasy symbolically acted out through the process of projection and displacement. Moreover, in the actual excitement of the impending departure, the sexual aggression toward the woman, the bad mother who had not protected Moses from the wrath of Pharaoh in earlier years, making it necessary for him to flee from the land, is now extended to the Egyptians as a whole. This mood of angry retaliation could have found a ready response among the Hebrews, so long maltreated and themselves despoiled, not only of material goods but of human dignity as well.

The need to conceal the true character of this action points both to its unconscious incestuous source and forbidden aggressive impulses. Let us consider further some of the defenses with which this behavior was surrounded, indications that such action was carried out against inner scruples.

The plan is introduced with the statement that God will give the Hebrew people favor in the eyes of the Egyptians. This expression is repeated each of the three times the action is referred to. In other words, the Egyptians would first be seduced into giving away their treasures, a process certainly having sexual connotations. It also gives emphasis to the fact that force was contraindicated. Finally, the statement "Moreover the man Moses was very great in the land of Egypt, in the sight of Pharaoh's servants, and in the sight of the people," points to a return of the original narcissistic source of the action.

"And ye shall not go empty." When Moses fled from Egypt, in danger of his life, he probably did go empty, leaving behind him not only all the material wealth he may have possessed but also any attachments he may have had to women in that land. The need to undo this wrong may have lingered and become identified with the hurts suffered by his people as a whole.

The same phrase occurs later in biblical law relating to a slave who must be freed in the seventh year of his servitude. The master of the house is charged as follows: "Thou shalt not let him go empty; thou shalt furnish him liberally out of thy flock, and out of thy threshing-floor, and out of thy winepress; as the Lord thy God hath blessed thee thou shalt give unto him. And thou shalt remember that thou wast a bondman in the land of Egypt, and the Lord thy God redeemed thee; therefore I command thee this thing today" (Deut. 15:13–15). One might conjecture with some basis, that out of the above incident in Egypt came the commandment regarding the compensation of freed slaves.

There are other discrepancies in this portion of the text, the understanding of which helps to confirm the meanings presented here. In the course of His pronouncements, God says, "And I know that the king of Egypt will not give you leave to go, except by a mighty hand" (3:19). The last phrase in the above verse is unclear. *Whose* mighty hand is here being alluded to? In the statement immediately following, God talks about *His* mighty hand. "And I will put forth My hand, and smite Egypt with all My wonders which I will do in the midst thereof. And after that he will let you go" (3:20).

The ambiguous reference to "a mighty hand" that will force Pharaoh to submit can be understood as unconsciously revealing a wish on the part of Moses that it should be *his* hand which would bring the ruler of Egypt to terms. Is Moses here competing with God as well as with Pharaoh? Such a motive of personal power, which makes Moses so understandably human, would create conflict with the more idealistic goals that animated him at this time.

A further textual problem now manifests itself, strengthening the interpretation of conflictful feelings within Moses at this time. First, God describes what is to take place—the victorious escape of the Hebrews and the added triumph they would enjoy as recipients of jewels and clothing from the Egyptians. Chapter 3 closes on this note. Then there is a striking nonsequitur. Chapter 4 begins by completely ignoring the above material (verses 19–22): "And Moses answered and said: 'But, behold, they will not believe me, nor hearken unto my voice: for they will say; The Lord hath not appeared unto thee'" (4:1).

This response, expressing anxiety and distrust, shows concern not about the frightening task of appearing before Pharaoh and making a daring demand but that his own people, the Hebrews, would not accept him. This feeling is not even expressed in the form of a doubt but as a certainty. It is a direct reply to verses 16–18 of Chapter 3, bidding him call the elders together and tell them of his mission. He seems also to forget completely God's concluding words of assurance with which those verses end: "And they shall hearken unto thy voice."

Higher Biblical Criticism attempts to explain this hiatus in the sequence by attributing the intervening verses to a different source. Why they should have been placed by later editors in a location where they separate a statement made by God and the direct reply to this declaration, made by Moses, is not clarified.

However, from a psychological viewpoint, ignoring these verses could express an unconscious avoidance brought about by conflict. The sensitive material they deal with, namely, the defiance and defeat of the father and the seduction of his women, represent the two aspects of the oedipal fantasy, which Moses is being told to carry out. This prospect, stemming from a reactivation of his own unconscious, stimulated by the prospect of facing the hated and feared ruler of Egypt, would be a frightening one for the novitiate prophet, trembling before his first encounter with the Deity.

In this mood, how could he expect the elders of Israel to accept him as leader and prophet! For we shall assume that there is an unspoken or omitted part to the response that Moses makes to God. This repressed portion would be: "If part of my motive in returning to Egypt is a questionable one, that of gratifying my own desire for revenge against the father and my wish to take possession of the mother, *Behold, they will not believe me* (that I have been sent by God to save them)."

God responds to the feelings of inadequacy in Moses by invoking three signs, all of magical significance, a dramatic display of supernatural powers. "And the Lord said unto him: 'What is that in thy hand?' And he said: 'A rod.' And He said: 'Cast it on the ground.' And he cast it on the ground, and it became a serpent; and Moses fled from before it. And the Lord said unto Moses: 'Put forth thy hand, and take it by the tail—and he put forth his hand, and laid hold of it, and it became a rod in his hand—that they may believe that the Lord, the God of their fathers, the God of Abraham, the God of Isaac, and the God of Jacob, hath appeared unto thee'" (4:2–5).

The first sign is that of phallic potency, using as a source that, symbolically representing the phallus, belongs to Moses himself, his shepherd's staff. God says, "What is that in thy hand?" Certainly both He and Moses know what the latter is holding in his hand. The implied import of the question therefore may be, "You have power but you don't know it because you are afraid of it." And indeed, when the rod becomes a serpent, Moses flees from it in fear.

The rod of God, as it becomes known, plays an important role in the dramatic contest of wills between Moses and Pharaoh. However, as the story progresses, the possessor of the rod is sometimes Moses, sometimes Aaron, and sometimes there is no clear indication which of the two is performing the magical act. On other occasions God himself intervenes and becomes the direct source of the supernatural performance. It seems as if Moses dares not arrogate this power to himself consistently. Designated originally to demonstrate before the Hebrews, the rod of God is used even more dramatically in the struggle with the Egyptian fathers.

The second magical sign is a more subtle one. "And the Lord said furthermore unto him: 'Put now thy hand into thy bosom.' And he put his hand into his bosom; and when he took it out, behold, his hand was leprous, as white as snow. And He said: 'Put thy hand back into thy bosom.' And he put his hand back into his bosom; and when he took it out of his bosom, behold it was turned again as his other flesh" (4:6–7).

Does this second manifestation of magic have any relation to the first one? It is a clinically familiar situation that a movement toward self-assertion in a person fearful of such a step is often followed by a return to passivity as a result of attendant anxiety. The first sign deals with phallic potency. The second one expresses a regressive state, a return to the mother's breast, the fantasied *mighty hand* now momentarily useless (Hirsch 1960, 41–42) (5). But in the process of undoing, Moses gains new strength and a sense of mastery, not only over himself but of others. It is clear, however, that only at God's command, as Moses now experienced it, could that arm and hand be outstretched in power or lie inactive on the bosom.

The third sign of miraculous ability that God bestows on Moses is described as follows: "And it shall come to pass, if they will not believe even these two signs, neither hearken unto thy voice, that thou shalt take of the water of the river, and pour it upon the dry land, and the water which thou takest out of the river shall become blood upon the dry land" (4:9).

Here the demonstration moves from the person of Moses to the land itself. The waters of the Nile can be turned to blood at the command of Moses. This catastrophe later occurs as the first of the ten plagues visited on the Egyptians. For use as a sign to the Hebrews themselves, however, it is to be carried out only on a small scale. The water is first to be poured out on the dry land and then it is turned to blood. Viewed as an unconscious fantasy, this third magical gesture represents an attack on the land itself, symbolically, the mother.

What is the possible relationship between the second sign and the third? If, as suggested, the second manifestation represents a return to the mother, a retreat to passivity and the consequent punishment, then a motive for retribution against the mother would be activated. The child blames the mother for its dependency on her. As the waters of the Nile provide life, so does the milk from the mother. Because the breast is so tempting as a retreat from life, it must be punished too, for encouraging passivity. Also, the angry infant will, on occasion, bite the mother's breast if it does not respond magically to the child's wishes. Thus, the blood spurts forth on the *dry land.*

These signs may express Moses' own response to the frightening task presented to him. The wish to undertake this mission, the basic purpose that brought him to this moment, is accompanied by feelings of powerlessness brought on by his daring to think of himself in the role of leader and emancipator. The increased phallic potency represented by the rod of God is needed to counteract these feelings. But to accept the paternal phallus as his own, with its implication of competitiveness, stirs up even greater anxiety and leads to a momentary regression of complete passivity. Such retreat is unbearable, equivalent to death itself in terms of the adult ego. The reaction is a renewed awareness of dependency on the Father and anger toward the mother who tempts one to this infantile state, with a consequent symbolic attack on her.

The whole tone of this latter part of the theophany, as well as its content, is on a different plane from the preceding portion. The nature of God Himself seems to change. He becomes a teacher of magic, with Moses as His pupil. Some consider this material as a later supplement. Psychoanalytically, the need for support in terms of magic represents a regression on the part of Moses. He retreats to the stage of magical thinking and sharing in God's omnipotence for the reasons discussed above. The Egyptian influence in the field of magic and some of its favorite manifestations are apparent here.

And now Moses reacts in a most unheroic fashion. Once more he pleads his inadequacy, saying, "Oh Lord, I am not eloquent, neither heretofore, nor since Thou hast spoken unto Thy servant: for I am slow of speech and of a slow tongue" (4:10). It seems as if his need for reassurance is insatiable. But if Moses was more frightened by the signs of miraculous power he had just witnessed than convinced of his own strength to use them, the reaction is understandable.

The feelings of impotence are now displaced from below upward, from the phallus to the mouth. However, the words also contain an implied reproach, for Moses points out that his lack of eloquence has not changed since God revealed Himself to him. Is Moses now making a further demand as a condition for accepting the task placed before him?

But God does not accede to this implied request. He answers, "'Who hath made man's mouth? or maketh a man dumb, or deaf, or seeing, or blind? is it not I the Lord? Now therefore go, and I will be thy mouth, and teach thee what thou shalt speak.' And he said: 'Oh, Lord, send, I pray Thee, by the hand of him whom Thou wilt send'" (4:11–13).

This reply of Moses conveys a purposeful ambiguity. He does not accept the mission wholeheartedly but places the responsibility for making the choice on God. The text says, "And the anger of the Lord was kindled against Moses."

Instead of complying with the implied wish to make him

powerful vocally, as He had given him symbolic phallic power, God responds in a different fashion. He says, "Is there not Aaron, thy brother the Levite? I know that he can speak well. And also, behold, he cometh forth to meet thee; and when he seeth thee, he will be glad in his heart. And thou shalt speak unto him, and put the words in his mouth; and I will be with thy mouth, and with his mouth, and will teach you what ye shall do. And he shall be thy spokesman unto the people; and it shall come to pass, that he shall be to thee a mouth, and thou shalt be to him as God. And thou shalt take in thy hand this rod, wherewith thou shalt do the signs'" (4:14–17).

This elaborate speech of instruction and reassurance indicates that God is understanding of how Moses feels but is also firm in His purpose. Moses is reminded, as it were, of Aaron's existence. One wonders why the descriptive phrase "the Levite" is employed here. Since the two were brothers, both would be Levites. A possible explanation is as follows: *"Thy brother the Levite"* describes two states of social distance: one (the brother) is a close relationship; the other (a Levite) marks him as one of many. The intimate tie of brotherhood is here diluted by the much more distant tribal relationship. *"Thy brother the Levite"* may be indicative of Moses' own feelings toward Aaron, from whom he has been separated for so long, not only by time and distance but also by ambivalent feelings.

"I know that he can speak well." Moses here acknowledges Aaron's superiority in this respect. It is a skill that must have impressed Moses in his early childhood. When he was just learning to talk, Aaron, three years older, could already "speak well." Perhaps Moses' own disability in this area was an inhibition growing out of feelings of inferiority in relation to his older brother. A projection of these attitudes may have made him uneasy about how Aaron would greet him. God, the Good Father, reassures him on this point. Very likely, Moses himself "will be glad in his heart" to see Aaron but will not be able to put this emotion into words. And indeed, when the two brothers do meet, it is Aaron who takes the initiative and kisses him.

Moses needs and wants the supportive presence of a good father-brother figure in this gigantic undertaking, but it is a desire that is colored by competitive feelings. The ambivalence comes out much more directly in the highly specific fashion in which God describes their respective roles. God will communicate directly with Moses, and the latter will do the same with Aaron. The feelings of sibling rivalry in Moses are expressed in a burst of grandiosity, an unacceptable attitude, disguised by its projection onto God. "he shall be to thee a mouth, and thou shalt be to him as God." There follows also the reassurance that the magic rod would be in the hands of Moses himself, and he would perform the signs.

As is evident throughout this first theophany, Moses does not present the view of a man who immediately and submissively places himself at the disposal of God, fully ready to carry out the Divine command. Rather, we see a person full of uncertainty and self-doubt. In his impetuous flight from Egypt, Moses was acting out feelings of fear and anger toward the father, together with a sense of abandonment by the mother, as interpreted here. But life has taken on new meaning in his identification with his suffering brethren. However, it would take time for the personal hurts and conflicts to diminish. Such a time is provided in the peaceful atmosphere of Midian. But the very prospect of returning to Egypt must inevitably have evoked the old fears and conflicts once more and the attempts at mastery resumed. It was a struggle that was to go on throughout his life as he moved forward both in his great task and in his personal growth.

This first theophany of Moses emerges as a vivid and moving expression of the struggle within a great man for strength to undertake an awesome task. Coming at the beginning of his career as leader and prophet, the theophany can be understood as the climax of a developmental phase, when the psyche must make its major push toward maturity.

Moses here exemplifies the true culture hero of Hebraic biblical tradition. For the theophany of the burning bush depicts in dramatic imagery the growth of the superego along the lines of ethical monotheism. The taming of the instincts, the process of sublimation, the redirection of psychic energy to moral and religious purposes, are symbolically portrayed as Moses endeavors, in truly heroic yet significantly human fashion, to identify with the God of Israel and the superego He represents.

The mechanisms of defense employed in the narrative, familiar to us since the days of Freud, make him as understandably human in a psychological sense as he has been through the ages on a more intuitive level. As with all the biblical heroes, Moses did not have greatness thrust upon him—he achieved it. The imperfections common to man are clearly attributed to him. Thus, the human tendency to deify *the great father* is guarded against.

The period of Moses in Midian as a preparatory stage to his consecration can be compared to the time spent in the wilderness by the Children of Israel after their escape from Egypt. For the group also that was a period of trial and purification before the acceptance of God's Law. Legend says that during this interim, physical defects among the people, such as disease, blindness, or lameness, were magically eradicated by God so that the people might receive His Word in a state of wholeness, or purity.

The individual experience of Moses and the burning bush can be seen as a prelude leading to the even more significant event of the revelation at Mount Sinai, when the Children of Israel as a group become consecrated to God as a "kingdom of priests and a holy nation."

On the Way Back to Egypt

Moses Encounters the Daemonic Aspect of God

 CHAPTER THREE

IT IS ON his way back to Egypt to carry out the mission undertaken at the burning bush that Moses undergoes the bizarre and frightening experience of his second encounter with God. This time it was of a totally different nature from the first encounter. In Exodus 4:24–26 we are told: "And it came to pass on the way at the lodging place, that the Lord met him, and sought to kill him. Then Zipporah took a flint, and cut off the foreskin of her son, and cast it at his feet; and she said: 'Surely a bridegroom of blood art thou to me.' So He let him alone. Then she said: 'A bridegroom of blood in regard of the circumcision.'"*

This puzzling and obscure passage has challenged scholarly investigation over the years. Roheim (1955) sees this episode as a myth of the origin of circumcision. Theodor Reik (1959) views the biblical incident as a displaced reference to the puberty rite

---

*All biblical references in this chapter, unless otherwise noted, are to the book of Exodus.

(p. 115). Andrew Peto (1960) sees Zipporah in this situation as a reemergence of the ruthless, daemonic mother-goddess, originating in the early traditions of the desert Bedouins (pp. 326ff). Martin Buber (1936) interprets Zipporah's role along quite different lines. He views the circumcised son as representing symbolically the entire clan of Israel, which is thus consecrated to God by Zipporah, here the symbolic mother of the clan (pp. 56–58) (6).

My viewpoint is that this strange episode can be understood in terms of the personal psychodynamics of Moses himself, relating to the immediate circumstances. It can be viewed as a sequel to the theophany of the burning bush, stemming from that earlier event. The psychic processes that were then set in motion within Moses lead in a comprehensible fashion from the first experience to the second. Let us attempt to trace this developmental sequence.

Following the theophany at the burning bush, the text says, "And Moses went and returned to Jethro his father-in-law, and said unto him: 'Let me go, I pray thee, and return unto my brethren that are in Egypt, and see whether they be yet alive.' And Jethro said to Moses: 'Go in peace'" (4:18). "And the Lord said unto Moses in Midian: 'Go, return unto Egypt; for all the men are dead which sought thy life.' And Moses took his wife and his sons, and set them upon an ass, and he returned to the land of Egypt; and Moses took the rod of God in his hand" (4:19–20).

Moses does not reveal to Jethro the true reason for his wish to return to Egypt. We can only conjecture why. Does he perhaps fear that his story would sound implausible and grandiose? Does he wish to save himself from Jethro's possible disbelief and opposition? If so, one detects here a lack of trust in a father figure. The reason he presents to Jethro is a rational and acceptable one. And yet there is a peculiar quality in the sequence of the two verses quoted above. One scholar observes in this connection, "That Moses should now be commanded by God to do what he has already both determined to do, and obtained Jethro's permission to do, is remarkable; and . . . can only be explained by the fact that the verse is by a different narrator from Verse 18" (Driver 1911, 30).

Can we find another explanation along psychological lines?

As in the process of free association, *sequence* in the biblical narrative may denote an inner relationship even though on the surface *the impression is one of a nonsequitur*. The first thought, voiced by Moses himself, is that he wishes to return to Egypt to see whether his brethren are yet alive. The next verse, spoken by the Deity, can be considered as a response to that thought. God tells him to return to Egypt because "all the men who sought his life" are dead. These words seem to be more in the form of a reassurance than a command. What possible connection, however, can there be between the wish of Moses to see if his brethren are yet alive and the comforting reply that *all the men who sought his life* are dead? Why the cryptic wording? If the reference here was to Pharaoh and his aides, there was no reason why that fact could not have been openly stated. Was a subtle association being made here between the two groups, *his own brethren* and *all the men who sought his life*? This idea sounds rather fantastic, but perhaps that is where it belongs—in the realm of unconscious fantasy, the latent stream of thoughts and feelings that may have been activated in Moses at this time. The implication is that Moses was afraid to return to Egypt because of potential enemies in that land and that these hostile people were his own brethren, more specifically, his kinsmen.

In an earlier chapter it was indicated that his flight from Egypt had been motivated largely by his own unconscious oedipal fantasies and fears in which the figures of Pharaoh and his own father and brother were used interchangeably. Legendary sources declare that the men who had been seeking his life were indeed Hebrews, the brothers Dathan and Abiram, identified in the previous chapter with family figures in the fantasies referred to above. These two, the legend says, were now not actually dead but had been reduced to such an insignificant and poor estate that their existence was equivalent to death (Ginzberg 1909–1938, 4:327). Actually such a situation could have described the enslaved Hebrew people as a whole.

One wonders whether there might have been some confusion within Moses about who his real enemies were—the Hebrews or the Egyptians or both. His first doubts at the theophany of the burning bush concerned the Hebrews, his own people, and how they would receive him. It was before them that he was to display his magical powers first. Then suddenly it was the Egyptians at the royal court whom he would have to convince that he was God's messenger.

Moses had left his native land in a state of fear and guilt, feelings directed against Pharaoh, who wished to slay him, and the Hebrew slave who threatened to expose him for killing the Egyptian taskmaster. Thus, he anticipated enemies on both sides.

Moses had actually committed an act of violence against an Egyptian. He was the object of envy and hatred among some of his own brethren. Moreover, he had abandoned his people in their state of misery for the sake of his own safety. Now the future leader must return to face an angry Egyptian father-king and distrustful Hebrew brethren.

The realistic aspects of these feelings must have been considerably augmented by the more unconscious factors. God's assurance that all the men who sought his life were dead may contain a hostile wish against father and brother figures within Moses himself, stemming from early childhood. Unacceptable to the conscious mind, such a wish might have found an outlet through projection. It is *they* who are seeking *his* life.

Viewed in this light, the sequence of the two verses under consideration becomes understandable. Moses wishes to go to Egypt to see if his brethren are yet alive, a seemingly laudable request, which Jethro readily grants. But the Deity's response, that all the men who sought his life were dead, suggests that his wish to see if his brethren were yet alive was motivated largely by anxiety. These feelings, it seems, were not entirely put to rest by God's reassuring words. The verses, with their unspoken connection, contain an almost imperceptible nuance of the incipient anxiety growing out of the hostile wishes both against the Egyptian father-king and his own brethren. These underlying fears develop into a full-blown experience of stark terror during the night at the lodging place.

We are also presented with a contradiction in time sequence. The statement is made that Moses returned to Egypt, with the clear implication that he had already arrived (4:20). But in the verse immediately following, he is still on the way. "And the Lord said unto Moses: 'When thou goest back into Egypt, see that thou do before Pharaoh all the wonders which I have put in thy hand;

but I will harden his heart, and he will not let the people go. And thou shalt say unto Pharaoh Thus saith the Lord: Israel is My son, My first-born. And I have said unto thee: Let My son go, that he may serve Me; and thou hast refused to let him go. Behold, I will slay thy son, thy first-born.' And it came to pass on the way at the lodging place, that the Lord met him, and sought to kill him. Then Zipporah took a flint, and cut off the foreskin of her son, and cast it at his feet; and she said: 'Surely a bridegroom of blood art thou to me.' So He let him alone" (4:21–26).

We shall assume that the earlier statement of his return to Egypt as a completed act was only an anticipation in fantasy of this event. It may have been a reactivation of an earlier daydream at this moment when the reality loomed so close. Moses, the youth who had to flee from Egypt in fear for his life, would return, not only as a man with wife and children but as a conquering hero, ready to defy Pharaoh himself. Indeed, it is after this statement of his return that he had the rod of God in his hand. But although he is ostensibly ready and eager to perform his wonders before Pharaoh, the act suddenly becomes an anticipatory one, prefaced by the words spoken by God, "When thou goest back into Egypt." His original fears that his own people would not believe him seem to be forgotten at this point. In his fantasy Moses is preparing to face Pharaoh himself.

As indicated in verse 19, Moses is instructed by God just what to say in this prospective encounter with the mighty ruler when he gets back to Egypt. And now for the first time occurs a curious and oft-repeated feature of the struggle between the two, expressed here in the words spoken by the Deity, "but I will harden his heart and he will not let the people go" (4:21).

We get here another aspect of the Divine Being, which is puzzling and embarrassing to theologians. Does God deliberately make Pharaoh resist in order to provide greater opportunity to manifest His own powers? This seems inplausible, yet throughout the narrative the text states nine times that God hardened the heart of Pharaoh so that he would not let the people go. Also, ten more times we are told that Pharaoh himself hardened his heart, making a total of nineteen instances when this attitude on the part of Pharaoh is expressed (Hertz 1936, 42–43). Such a degree of repetition must have special significance. One would naturally expect that Pharaoh would not readily allow his valuable slaves to depart, even for the three-day festival to serve God in the desert, which was the form of the original request. But that this expected situation is aggravated by a deliberate act of God, often repeated, is puzzling.

Viewed as a projection of Moses himself, what can be the meaning of the emphasis given to this idea? It seems that Moses not only anticipates a tremendous contest of wills between Pharaoh and himself, but also *greatly desires* such a struggle. Here we see again that underlying the reality situation there is an unconscious fantasy that must have stemmed from an earlier time. Moses does not wish an easy victory. The struggle must be prolonged and difficult, with the hero finally and gloriously triumphant. Even more important, Pharaoh's stubbornness would be a justification for defeating him.

The anticipated conflict can be understood not only as a preparation in fantasy for mastering a feared situation in reality but also as a displacement of the oedipal struggle with the father. The royal family must indeed have played an important role in the imaginative life of the young Moses. In a land where society is divided sharply between the few who are mighty and the many who are powerless, the universal parental symbols of king and queen may become even more compelling in their effect on the unconscious mind of the child. The desire of Moses for a prolonged struggle with a father figure must have become libidinized, a process that is clinically familiar. A further aspect of a defensive nature is generally present as well. As long as the struggle goes on, the desired but feared victory can be postponed.

Let us return to the biblical text that ushers in the strange episode referred to earlier: "And thou shalt say unto Pharaoh, Thus saith the Lord: 'Israel is My son, my first-born: and I have said unto thee: Let My son go, that he may serve Me; and thou hast refused to let him go: behold, I will slay thy son, thy first-born."

We find here a significant sequence which, to my mind, contains the clue to the strange occurrence that follows. God threatens to slay the first-born son of Pharaoh because that stubborn monarch refused to let Israel, the *first-born son* of God, leave Egypt to serve Him. This dire event does take place later, as the tenth plague, during which the first-born sons of all Egyptians meet this fate. Why then, one wonders, is the threat presented now, in anticipatory fashion? Might it be because of some special meaning that such a happening would have for Moses? It should be noted that for the first time Israel is here called the first-born son of God. We can assume that Moses was now identifying himself with the whole of his people; *he* is the first-born son of God, chosen and preferred above all others at the theophany of the burning bush. Unconsciously, therefore, he himself must be the object of Pharaoh's enmity. The retaliatory threat expressed against the son of Pharaoh, although uttered in the words of God, may have been unconsciously an aggressive wish of Moses himself, growing out of unacceptable personal motives. The omitted connective in the biblical content under consideration would have completed the following thought in the unconscious fantasy of Moses: "*Because* I wish to kill the oldest son of Pharaoh, God the Father (Pharaoh, the father) will kill me in retaliation."

Interestingly, the verb in "thou hast refused" (to let Israel go) is in the past tense, as though Pharaoh had already committed the act, not only in Moses' fantasy but in reality. And indeed there is a relationship with the past. Pharaoh had at one time threatened the life of Moses if he remained in Egypt. At least, the latter had believed so. Now, on his way back, that unhappy memory must have returned forcefully to Moses, stirring up both fear and a wish for reprisal. Moreover, along another line of association, the crown prince may have represented Moses' own brother, Aaron, who also had the enviable good fortune of being the first-born. From his new advantageous position of power, Moses may now have wished to right the humiliation of being a younger son.

It is immediately following the disguised and projected aggressive wish of Moses that God approaches the latter with the intent to slay him. This event is here regarded as a psychic phenomenon, a projection of Moses himself, experienced as a nightmare or hallucinatory-like state. The form it took, the external aspects, may have utilized prevailing beliefs of a primitive kind, but its meaning for Moses must have been in terms of his own concepts of God. Certainly it is significant that, even in this early period of religious development in Israel, the daemonic God who thus attacked him was the same Deity whom Moses had earlier encountered as the God of mercy and deliverance. The monotheistic aspect is apparent here, God being the source of both goodness and retribution. If Moses actually went through a kind of hysterical attack during which death seemed imminent, then Zipporah's action may have been carried out in reality, with the purpose of appeasing God.

A quality of ambiguity pervades the biblical verses dealing with this event. First, there is an indefiniteness about *who* actually was attacked and threatened with death. The antecedent of *him* (verse 24) could refer to either Moses or his son. Second, it is unclear whom Zipporah touched with the foreskin, her husband or her child.

This ambiguity, so characteristic of dreams, may indicate a condensation of meanings. Moses may have played several roles here. He now saw himself as the son of God and therefore in a son role. He was also the father and, as such, identified with God in this relationship. The circumcision of the son was therefore a displacement from Moses to a son figure, thus alleviating the anxiety of being the direct object of the symbolic castration and allowing Moses himself to retain a reassuring aspect of the father-God status. In addition, the son can be understood psychoanalytically as an extension of the father, thus being identified with his own phallus.

Although we are told that Moses took both his sons with him, the text does not indicate which one was circumcised. In terms of the immediate situation, it should have been Gershom, for it was Pharoah's first-born that had been threatened. But in reality Moses was the second son, and on this basis could have been associated with Eliezer, his younger child, in masochistic identification with the victim. Other aspects of an unconscious nature could also have been involved in the dreamlike condensation of meanings. There may have been the hostility associated with the oedipal father-son jealousy, especially directed toward the eldest. Gershom may also have represented Moses' older brother, Aaron, and thus have stimulated sibling rivalry.

We now come to the dramatic and unusual role that Zipporah herself plays. It is the woman who performs the circumcision and thus by her quick action saves her husband's life. I see no evidence here of the primitive, castrating mother-goddess. Zipporah's act was a *symbolic* castration, not an actual one. Its motivation was to rescue, not to destroy.

Again, it is a woman who saves the life of Moses. As an infant, his life was endangered by the decree of Pharaoh and he was rescued by a mother figure. Thus, we have here a repetition of the same theme. The father threatens, the mother saves.

At whose feet does Zipporah cast the foreskin? Some scholars think the reference is to Moses; others think it was to the son. In terms of the interpretation given here, it must have been Moses, for he was the person undergoing this experience which, like all such psychic phenomona, is egocentric in nature.

That the symbolic partial castration was the price of saving the life of Moses can be understood in terms of the principle of *lex taliones*, in the light of the background of those times. That it was Zipporah who performed the ceremony could have been a kind of wish fulfillment on the part of Moses. The beloved woman saves and hurts at the same time, even as his mother did when she put him in a basket and abandoned him for the purpose of saving him.

The words with which Zipporah concludes the ceremony have a haunting quality: "Surely a bridegroom of blood art thou to me." They contain a note of sadness and resignation. And indeed, it is after this experience that Zipporah vanishes from the scene, not to reappear until much later in the narrative. Moses does become a bridegroom of blood, a sacrifice to God. For the time being, he is dedicated to the Deity.

Zipporah's cryptic words contain yet another puzzle. Why the repeated but slightly changed expression of the second phrase, "A bridegroom of blood in regard of the circumcision(s)" (4:26)? The word *circumcision* is plural in the Hebrew. It may convey the latent meaning that the son's sacrifice symbolically includes the father's, and also, in line with Buber's thought, the whole of Israel.

A number of precipitating factors could have been involved in this dramatic aftermath to the theophany of the burning bush. During the latter experience, Moses maintains a degree of control and *self-possession* unusual in a biblical prophet under the spell of the Divine Presence. He even pits his will against the will of God, demanding and receiving signs of God's support and of his own potency. It was only later, when Moses was actually on the road to Egypt, that the emotions related to the totality of the experience might have come upon him in full force. This would occur most naturally while he was relaxed or asleep at the lodging house where the party stopped for the night.

The abject terror that the presence of the Deity should have aroused in him at an earlier time may have taken place now. The situation is similar to the delayed reaction frequently experienced by people after facing a great danger during which they responded realistically and intuitively. The tension is relaxed at a safer time, and the full emotional impact of the earlier situation is then felt. In this second experience, Moses is indeed the passive recipient of an attack by an Awful Presence. Unconsciously, he may have felt that his life was in peril because he had encountered God.

Other psychic processes of a more specific nature also may have been involved, as indicated earlier. The underlying narcissistic aspects of his personality would have been stimulated by the theophany, with the feeling of being *the chosen one*. Fantasies of greatness and power, especially when colored by competitiveness and hostility, can readily be accompanied by guilt and fear. Moses had to achieve a greater degree of sublimation, a lessening of both aggressive and libidinal desires, a mortification of the flesh, as it were, in order to strengthen the superego qualities necessary for leadership. But together with the healthy aspects of such a process, one could expect elements of the more primitive, sadistic superego rising from childhood repressions to become activated. It could have been the projection of this part of his personality that provoked the encounter with the daemonic God, a reflection of the daemonic in Moses himself. The circumcision of his son, an act of submission to the Deity, could have brought to Moses the necessary relief from guilt and fear.

Immediately following this episode, another discrepancy in sequence occurs in the text. In verse 26 Moses and his family are at the inn, on their way to Egypt. In the following verse, a new locale and another person are introduced. "And the Lord said to Aaron: 'Go into the wilderness to meet Moses.' And he went, and met him in the mountain of God, and kissed him" (4:27). So here

Moses is back again at a geographic point that we assume he had left behind him. Moreover, there is no indication that Aaron also met the family of Moses.

We shall assume that the meeting between Aaron and Moses at Horeb has a symbolic meaning. In terms of psychological sequence, Moses has just undergone a terrifying experience involving, as we have interpreted, his competitive feelings with a father figure and death wishes against the rival first-born son of Pharaoh. Following this event, Moses meets Aaron in the mountain of God. The two, long separated, are now united, and Aaron affectionately kisses his younger brother.

This episode can be understood as a denial of Moses' hostile feelings and a reaction formation to them. In the presence of the Father, who loves them both, Moses allows his warm feelings for Aaron and his longing for a loving relationship with a brother to find expression. The mountain of God may here be a *recollection*, a return in fantasy to a time and place when God had said to him, "Is there not Aaron, thy brother?" The actual meeting may have occurred within Egypt itself or on its borders, for immediately afterward Moses and Aaron "went and gathered together all the elders of the children of Israel," thus setting in motion the wheels of their great undertaking.

The fact that the family of Moses is not referred to here also may be for psychological reasons. Moses eliminated them from his mind for the present. They are not mentioned again until much later, after the exodus, when Jethro, the good, permissive father, comes to visit Moses in the wilderness and restores his wife and children to him. Only at that time are we told that Moses had sent Zipporah and his sons back to Midian, presumably after his experience at the inn (18:2–5).

This silence is in itself significant. His wife and children disappear, as it were, and Aaron, a brother-father figure, suddenly comes on the scene. Moses thus replaces the woman and children with the man, returning to Egypt as he had left it, a younger brother.

This situation may involve not only a regression but also a form of sublimation. Moses, the man with a special destiny, is required to make a special sacrifice of his adult sexuality. For him, the act of submission as expressed in the ritual of circumcision is not enough. More is required of the leader and prophet. He must indeed give up the conjugal life altogether for a period of time and devote his energies solely to the task of leadership. The terrifying experience at the inn may therefore have the further meaning of a punishment for Moses because he had not been willing to make this renunciation earlier and had brought his family with him, close to the very borders of Egypt.

There may be another point of significance in the meeting of the two brothers at the mountain of God. Aaron, the Levite, is here performing the role he is to assume officially at a later time, that of a priest. He leads Moses back to God. It is Aaron who kisses Moses, thus participating in an active way, and the other receives the salutation as one might receive a priestly blessing.

This return geographically to an earlier position from which the journey had begun may represent a psychological regression. Perhaps Moses had to return there to make a fresh start, this time giving up to a greater degree his narcissistic wishes. The displacement of a psychological situation to a geographic locale is a phenomenon characteristic of dreams. We could therefore regard this meeting with Aaron as a continuation of the dreamlike episode contained in the preceding verses. The terror of the nightmare or hallucinatory state is concluded with a peaceful solution. Moses not only endures circumcision symbolically through his son but gives up family life completely for the time and returns to God, a necessary state of readiness for his coming task.

The period of Moses in Midian is particularly meaningful when viewed in the light of ego psychology. Moses overcomes the repressive and distorting effects of his conflicts in self-identity under which, we assumed, he labored during his early life in Egypt. He returns to his people and to the heritage of his ancestors. He fulfills the duties of manhood, taking on the responsibilities of marriage, parenthood, and work, all indications of a maturation of the ego. Then comes the turning point in his development as a leader, the theophany of the burning bush, at which Moses undergoes a significant change in his superego development characteristic in important respects of the transformations occurring in other biblical prophets during similar conditions. On his shoulders is now laid the heavy task that he himself had reluctantly but definitively chosen, which comes to full, conscious awareness at this awesome moment. Moses came to Midian as a youth in the throes of a crisis in self-identity. He returned to Egypt as a leader of phenomenal strength and resolution.

Complex psychological processes must have taken place within Moses during his stay in Midian. These must have included the overcoming to a greater extent aspects of the oedipal struggle, yet in a fashion differing from that of the ordinary man. Through the paths of renunciation and sublimation Moses surrenders more fully not only his incestuous wishes but also a part of his mature sexual desires. In their place comes a new and closer identification with God and a consequent special development of the superego (Arlow 1951).

Moses and Pharaoh

Struggle and Liberation

 CHAPTER FOUR

THE FIRST encounter of Moses with his brethren in Egypt turned out well. His anxiety that they would not believe him was quickly set at rest through the good offices of Aaron, whom Moses had immediately taken into his confidence. The biblical narrative says, "And Moses told Aaron all the words of the Lord wherewith He had sent him, and all the signs wherewith He had charged him. And Moses and Aaron went and gathered together all the elders of the children of Israel, and Aaron spoke all the words which the Lord had spoken unto Moses, and [he] did the signs in the sight of the people. And the people believed; and when they heard that the Lord had remembered the children of Israel, and that He had seen their affliction, then they bowed their heads and worshipped" (4:28–31).*

The implication is that Aaron himself performed the signs but some commentators think that the pronoun *he*, although generally omitted in the translations, refers to Moses himself (Driver 1911, 34). But why is the text ambiguous on this point? In identification with Moses himself an explanation is possible. The newly arrived prophet,

---

*All biblical references in this chapter, unless otherwise noted, are to the book of Exodus.

in that initial appearance before the elders, was wholly dependent on Aaron or at least felt himself to be, a situation that was never repeated later in the same way. Therefore, even if *Moses* performed the signs, as God had assured him he would (4:17), the leader was still in a position of being sponsored by Aaron, a state of affairs that could not have been entirely to the liking of the younger brother. In this role Moses withdraws psychologically and allows his identity to be obscured. The whole episode, which is so important to the success of the entire undertaking and one that Moses had initially feared, is presented with brevity and indefiniteness of detail, as if Moses wished to be finished with it as soon as possible.

We do not know what conditions made it possible for the two Hebrews, one of them a shepherd from Midian, to appear before the Pharaoh. In the ancient Orient it was customary for the common people to have an opportunity of petitioning their rulers at stated times to express a grievance or make some special request (James 1950, 16). This situation also may have existed in Egypt. The Bible does not mention any difficulty along those lines, saying only, "And afterward Moses and Aaron came, and said unto Pharaoh: 'Thus saith the Lord, the God of Israel: Let my people go, that they may hold a feast unto Me in the wilderness.' And Pharaoh said: 'Who is the Lord, that I should hearken unto His voice to let Israel go? I know not the Lord, and moreover I will not let Israel go'" (5:1–2). The two repeat their plea and again are sternly repudiated.

Pharaoh reproaches the two leaders and accuses them of turning the minds of the people away from their work and encouraging idleness. The taskmasters are forthwith commanded to make the burdens of the slaves heavier by withholding the straw necessary to mix with the clay in the process of making bricks. The Hebrews were now required to search the fields for their own straw and yet produce the same quota of bricks as before. This task was evidently an impossible one, and the Hebrew officers who supervised the work were treated harshly. They complained bitterly to Moses and Aaron, declaring that the two had put a sword into the hands of Pharaoh with which to slay them.

This first confrontation of Moses with Pharaoh and its resulting disappointment was clearly very upsetting to the novice prophet and leader. Moses turns to God and complains in his turn, asking, "Why is it that Thou has sent me? For since I came to Pharaoh to speak in

Thy name, he hath dealt ill with this people; neither hast Thou delivered Thy people at all" (5:22–23). These words of reproach to God are bitter ones, spoken in much the same tone and with the same complaint that the Hebrew officers had spoken to Moses himself. God answers reassuringly, saying, "Now shalt thou see what I will do to Pharaoh; for by a strong hand shall he let them go, and by a strong hand shall he drive them out of his land" (6:1).

This response, especially the opening words, do not have the sound of Divinity speaking. They resemble more the expression of an angry man, Moses himself. The second part of the statement has an ambiguous quality. By *whose strong hand* will he let them go? God generally does not hesitate to refer to His own might. Why then the indefinite article in the phrase "by *a* strong hand"? Disappointed and perturbed, does Moses wish to punish the ruler of Egypt *with his own strong hand*? If so, such a wish must be concealed by ambiguity. Spurned by Pharaoh and repudiated by his own people, Moses must have suffered a loss of self-esteem and sought thus to restore his injured narcissism.

The symbolism of the strong hand, an expression used frequently in the Bible to denote the power of God both to punish and to save, could have had a particular appeal for Moses, who evidently had impulses of a similar nature. The same metaphor is employed at the earlier theophany of the burning bush, and there too it results in an ambiguity of the text. God says in the course of His pronouncements, "And I know that the king of Egypt will not give you leave to go, no, not by a mighty hand" (3:19). Here also the possessor of the mighty hand is unclear. My view is that, in this instance, it belonged to Pharaoh, thus establishing him as a foe worthy of the powerful hand of God, Who in the following verse declares, "And I will put forth My hand and smite Egypt." Thus Moses, in identification with God, matches his power against that of Pharaoh, an attitude of personal competitiveness that must be repressed.

This wish *to be like God*, to punish Pharaoh with his own strong hand, comes briefly to the surface again in the immediate situation under discussion. And suddenly there is a complete break in the context. The following verse begins on an entirely different note: "And God spoke unto Moses, and said unto him: 'I am the Lord; and I appeared unto Abraham, unto Isaac, and unto Jacob, as God Almighty

[El Shaddai], but by My name *Yahweh* I made Me not known to them'" (6:2–3). God now repeats His promise to deliver the Children of Israel from bondage in Egypt and instructs Moses to convey this message to them.

God thus introduces Himself anew, as though no previous communication had taken place. Even traditional biblical commentary can find no satisfactory explanation for this nonsequitur and sees the content only in relation to the promise of redemption made at the burning bush (Hertz 1936, 232). The school of Higher Biblical Criticism also makes this association to the earlier theophany but explains these verses as a parallel account, coming from a different literary source and placed here by an editor at a later date (Driver 1911, 41). But neither commentary explains why this material was introduced *at this particular point*, where it disrupts the continuity of the text.

This distinction in the name by which God was known to the forefathers of Israel has played an important role in the history of biblical exegesis. It became a significant factor in Higher Biblical Criticism for determining the various literary and historical sources into which the Pentateuch was divided by scholars in this school of thought (Speiser 1964, xxiii). Their reasoning was that if God was not known to the Patriarchs as *Yahweh*, and the name is commonly found in the narratives of that period, then the Genesis account must have been put together from different sources, some of which would have been written after Exodus 6:3, where this revelation is made to Moses.

From a psychological viewpoint, the situation can be interpreted differently. It is assumed that communication with God, when viewed as an intrapsychic experience, takes place in an altered state of consciousness (Arlow 1951; Kris 1952, 292). A characteristic sequence of dynamics in terms of Moses seems to take the form of a transitory merging with God, a rise in anxiety, and a reactive withdrawal. If, momentarily, Moses confuses God's strong hand with his own—if, briefly, he merges his own identity with God, especially in a punitive role—both anxiety about this loss of self (Sandler 1960, 155) and the fear of retaliation for competitiveness with God must follow. Comparable to a break in the associations of an analysand when there is an increase in anxiety, the discontinuity of the text may represent a defensive measure. It is conjectured that Moses separates himself from God, withdrawing some of his libido from the Divine Imago (ego ideal) into his own ego in this intersystemic struggle (Kohut 1971, 153).

The next words in the text are: "And God spoke unto Moses and said unto him: 'I am the Lord'" (6:2), thus clearly defining and delineating their separate identities.

It is during such a period of withdrawal that Moses, in terms of this analysis, experiences a sense of relief at his separateness but also reactivates feelings of aloneness and inadequacy. He can tolerate neither too much closeness with the Deity nor too much distance. At this point it seems that reassurance is needed. It is not enough now to hear the familiar pronouncement that the God of his patriarchal fathers was addressing him. Moses had to know God in a *special* way, a need that must have been invested with strong emotions of a highly narcissistic nature. So the Deity now reveals Himself to His prophet by a *new* name which, *according to the fantasy of Moses*, had not been known to the revered forefathers, thus giving him a distinction, a sense of being special, that even they had lacked.

The sequence of events does indeed bear a striking similarity to the theophany of the burning bush. Both involve the mission of liberating his people and the reluctant attitude of Moses, suffering from a lack of confidence in himself, to undertake the task. On both occasions the matter of God's name is brought up. At the burning bush, it is Moses who asks God by what name the Deity should be called when he is asked by the Hebrews who had sent him. God then replies, "I AM THAT I AM; and He said: 'Thus shalt thou say unto the children of Israel: 'I AM hath sent me unto you'" (3:13–14).

Evidently the name by which God was known had great meaning for Moses. On both occasions the subject is introduced at a point when Moses retreats from an experience of identification with God and is left with feelings of inadequacy, unsure of his own identity. If God and Moses were separate entities, then the old problem of "Who am I?" would reassert itself. This question is again projected onto God, Who first describes Himself in familiar terms and then introduces Himself by a new name.

Names had special meaning in antiquity. Frequently, they expressed the *essence* of the bearer (Pedersen 1926, 1–2:245ff). Knowing God by a special name may also have implied a greater degree of familiarity and closeness for Moses (See chapter 2).

Some significance also must be attributed to the specific names of the Deity. *El Shaddai (God is Mighty)* is clearly mentioned as having been known to the Patriarchs. Interestingly, it is this attribute of God, His omnipotence, from which Moses had been retreating in guilt and anxiety. So now Moses meets God as *Yahweh*, the Ineffable Name, the most sacred by which the Deity was known. Rabbinic tradition associates this designation of God with the aspect that denotes His more personal relationship to man, especially in the role of one who forgives and shows mercy (Cohen 1947, 331).

Thus, in terms of the present situation, Moses turns from the God of Might to the God of Mercy, Who will forgive the prophet's transgression in the wish for omnipotence, which had a competitive quality with the Deity Himself. At the same time, in a fashion that is clinically familiar, the narcissism that is withdrawn from sharing in God's omnipotence finds expression in a substitute form, knowing God by a special name.

It may be that this name was repressed in the memory of Moses and indeed in the memory of his people, and that it now rises from repression and is experienced as new. Indeed, this entire theophany, with its repetitive quality, could be understood as a déjà vu experience, *I have been there before* (Freud 1913, 336–37).

A further association can be made. The name of Moses' mother is Jochebed *(God is my glory)* (Fodor 1951, 189–200). Buber (1936) states that it is the only recorded instance of a personal name formed from *Yahweh* before the time of Moses. He wonders if some early family tradition concerning this name might be involved (p. 50). The name of *Yahweh* is thus definitely associated with the mother image in regard to Moses. Psychoanalytically, this relationship is particularly understandable in the circumstance under discussion. In his hour of distress and alienation, Moses experiences the Deity not only as the God of his fathers but also as embodying an aspect of the comforting mother. Such an association would normally have remained under repression in this Father religion, with its particularly forbidden connotations of the oedipal fantasy and even earlier period of infantile symbiosis. The latter may here have been reactivated by the longing to merge with the Deity.

The concept of a *return of the repressed* in relation to the name *Yahweh* is also mentioned by Reik (1959), although he too, like Buber, considers the name as possibly referring to a forgotten family tradition rather than one formerly familiar to the group as a whole (p. 153). Stemming originally from a Hebrew family, brought up under the influence of Egyptian culture, and then living for many years among the desert Midianites, one of whose daughters he took as wife, it is not surprising that Moses should have moments of confusion both about his own identity and that of God's. Add to these reality factors the underlying tendency we are assuming for a shifting identification from his own ego to God, and the foundation is laid for psychological phenomena of this kind. There is indeed a similarity in this second call of Moses to what occurred at the burning bush, but the likeness is understandable as a repetition of psychological forces within Moses himself.

Encouraged by a renewed feeling of relationship with God, Moses speaks again to the people of Israel. But they also have been disillusioned and disheartened because of his first failure and they do not listen to him. Again, the effect of this rejection is traumatic. And at this point God adds to the tension by bidding Moses return to Pharaoh and repeat the demand to let the Hebrews go. This prospect is evidently too threatening for Moses. He replies, "Behold, the children of Israel have not hearkened unto me; how then shall Pharaoh hear me, who am of uncircumcised lips?" (6:12).

This is indeed a curious expression, *of uncircumcised lips*. Circumcision, the ritual of the covenant with God, bestows the right of adult sexuality through a symbolic partial castration, as an act of submission to God (Reik 1931, 105). Having "uncircumcised lips" must be a further reference to the lack of facility in speech that Moses had dwelt on at the burning bush. This difficulty could have been experienced unconsciously as a punishment for the wish to be omnipotent. It was thus a failure in sublimation related to an oedipal conflict, now reactivated by the need to defeat the father-king of Egypt. Such a sense of guilt, would indeed inhibit the power of speech when ostensibly Moses is pleading in behalf of others, a situation aggravated by the rejection of the people. Moreover, the competitive feelings may refer not only to Pharaoh but to God Himself.

Martin Buber (1936), when referring to the expression *uncircumcised lips*, comes close to a psychoanalytic interpretation, describing it as "not a mere defect in the instrument of speech, but a fundamental inhibition of expression" (p. 59). He attributes this situation to the fact that Moses acts as a *mouth* for God. And indeed, at the theophany of the burning bush, God says to him twice within the space of four verses, "I will be with thy mouth" (4:12–16). To be *a part of Divinity*, even in this symbolic sense, could have been very disturbing to one who indeed wished so strongly for this kind of relationship, a wish that we assume found utterance in these very words projected onto the Deity.

God's response to Moses' cry about his "uncircumcised lips" is made indirectly, almost unobtrusively. He repeats His instructions but now addresses Himself to *both Moses and Aaron*, although Aaron's presence had not been mentioned up to this point. Thus again, as at the burning bush, Aaron is suddenly brought into the picture. He is the brother of whom God had said on that earlier occasion, "Is there not Aaron thy brother the Levite. I know that he can speak well . . . he shall be to thee a mouth, and thou shalt be to him in God's stead" (4:14–16). Evidently the image of Aaron is to serve here again as a supportive figure, the good brother-father.

But in terms of our textual analysis this easing of the situation is not enough. Again there is a sudden shift in the continuity. Without any connecting thought, the narrative moves into a lengthy genealogical table, beginning, "These are the heads of their fathers' houses," and concluding with the words, "These are that Aaron and Moses to whom the Lord said: 'Bring out the children of Israel from the land of Egypt according to their hosts . . .' these are that Moses and Aaron" (6:14–27).

As in the instance mentioned earlier (6:2–3), the interruption occurs as a sequence to God's instructions regarding the liberation of the Hebrews. Both are situations that involve Pharaoh, a dreaded father figure. In the first, Moses is to witness what God will do to Pharaoh (6:1), a punitive attitude stimulated by Moses himself and with which he identifies. On the second occasion, Moses is charged again to appear before the monarch and demand the release of his people (6:13). Both situations must have been very anxiety-producing for Moses, emotions that lead to a discontinuity of the text, as if the thought itself was too difficult to pursue. In the earlier instance God reinforces His presence by appearing to Moses under a new name. The second time, Moses himself is given a special place among his people. Both of these responses were of a reassuring nature.

Evidently Moses could feel strengthened in two ways, both involving feelings of identity. One was through his relationship to God.

Moses was the man chosen by God; that was his identity. Thus he tries repetitively, through inquiries about the name of God, to determine who *He* was, both in the past and in the present. The other way was to see himself clearly in the relationship of the family tree of which he was a living part.

One commentator intuitively senses that the abrupt introduction of that table does have psychological significance (Hirsch 1960, 72). He sees its purpose as a reminder that Moses is human, that he comes from human origins, and the temptation on the part of his descendants to deify the great leader must be resisted. My own interpretation is that *Moses* was fighting the unconscious impulse toward deification, and in a reactive withdrawal from this temptation he had to *remind himself* of reality.

As a further, more realistic function, the genealogy may also satisfy the sense of historic mission that imbues this entire narrative. The escape from bondage in Egypt was an event of phenomenal importance in the history of a people. Every detail of this happening had to be commemorated. How much more then should the leaders who appeared before Pharaoh and initiated this delivery be plainly identified! This purpose, with its underlying narcissistic gratification, may also have helped to strengthen the courage of Moses at this crucial point. The two brothers are mentioned twice, first as Aaron and Moses, then shortly thereafter as Moses and Aaron, in a kind of even-handed justice concerning the matter of priority. This detail too may reflect the struggle of Moses against his narcissism.

Following the genealogy, God resumes the interrupted theme, again instructing Moses to speak to Pharaoh. He prefaces His command with the words, "I am the Lord; speak thou unto Pharaoh king of Egypt all that I speak unto thee." But again the distraught leader pleads his disability. "And Moses said before the Lord: 'Behold, I am of uncircumcised lips, and how shall Pharaoh hearken unto me?'" (6:30).

God is still patient at this point. He seems to understand the problem, saying reassuringly, almost seductively, "See, I have made thee a god to Pharaoh; and Aaron thy brother shall be thy prophet. Thou shalt speak all that I command thee; and Aaron thy brother shall speak unto Pharaoh, that he let the children of Israel go out of his land" (7:1–2).

God here smooths the path for Moses. He satisfies the sense

of omnipotence Moses seems so greatly to desire—"See, I have made thee a god to Pharaoh" —and at the same time diminishes his anxiety, for it is God Himself Who makes him a god to Pharaoh, thus giving permission to be greater than the oedipal father-king. God also comfortingly allows him to be a child: "Thou shalt speak all that I command thee." Here Moses remains under the protective authority of God, thus denying his own responsibility for guilty competitive wishes. Moreover, it is Aaron who is appointed to do the actual talking to Pharaoh, further relieving Moses of his sense of verbal inadequacy.

Here, as at the burning bush, God performs the function of the loving, protective father, an aspect that manifests itself with particular clarity in how God relates to Moses during his periods of despondency and low self-esteem. We shall return to this point later in the study.

The Ten Plagues

The conflict between Moses and Pharaoh finds dramatic expression in the biblical narrative of the ten plagues. These catastrophes were visited on the Egyptians in ever-increasing severity as a means of forcing the stubborn monarch to allow the Hebrews a three-day excursion into the desert, ostensibly for a religious festival. Both parties to the struggle understood that in reality the enslaved people would use this opportunity for an escape to freedom, and in the course of events this final outcome is tacitly accepted by both sides.

Modern scholarship is largely in agreement that the story of the exodus has a historical basis and that a series of calamitous events must indeed have taken place in Egypt at that time (Albright 1957, 255). All of the so-called plagues were intensifications of the natural disasters to which Egypt was prone. It is psychologically significant that the miraculous was thus rooted in the natural, the abnormal being an exaggeration of the normal. This factor indicates a closer relationship between reality and fantasy in the mythology of the Hebrews than was generally true of other ancient peoples.

The biblical narrative is a literary tour de force, giving full expression to the struggle not only between Moses and Pharaoh but, even more meaningful for our purpose, to the inner conflict within the heart and mind of the great Hebrew leader himself. The portrayal of Pharaoh for the most part lacks the quality of a real flesh and blood personality. He serves chiefly as a foil, an image of the powerful, bad father against whom Moses must pit his strength, not only in a reality struggle of gigantic proportions but one that is also psychologically fraught with an unconscious personal conflict here seeking externalization.

The repeated demand that Pharaoh comply with the request of Moses or suffer the punishment decreed by the God of the Hebrews is a direct challenge to the Egyptian ruler as the hitherto supreme authority figure, the semidivine king of the land. He is repeatedly put into the humiliating position of submitting to a mysterious, unknown figure, appearing suddenly out of the desert and speaking in the name of a strange God. Pharaoh's so-called obstinacy is understandable. No absolute ruler of those times, or other times, would readily allow himself to be divested of valuable slaves under such conditions. There were no foreign armies on the borders of his land demanding surrender. There was no revolution within the palace threatening to dethrone him. There were only Moses and Aaron, two strange men, probably clad in the simplest of garments and armed only with a shepherd's staff. It is also understandable, even more so, that under such circumstances Moses tended to be overcome at his own daring.

Yet the underlying uncertainty in the narrative seems to be not that Pharaoh will ultimately give in but that he may yield too easily. In that event the glory of the victory won by Moses would be diminished. Repeatedly we are told by God Himself that He would harden Pharaoh's heart so that the strength and glory of the Hebrew Deity would be abundantly displayed. We assume that the need for exhibiting such power was an expression of Moses himself, projected onto God.

A more specific analysis of the text gives evidence of this conflict between Moses' wish for omnipotence and the feelings of guilt and inadequacy. One element of the struggle can be seen in relation to the so called "rod of God" and the unpredictable way in which it is used, at times by Moses and on other occasions by

Aaron. Another aspect of this problem is the role of Aaron himself, whose appearances and disappearances are curiously erratic. The inconsistencies regarding the use of the rod and the participation by Aaron are explained by certain scholars of the school of Higher Biblical Criticism as a consequence of the interweaving of various sources (Driver 1911, 55ff).

Psychoanalytically, another view presents itself. The rod of God is first introduced and its magical powers demonstrated at the theophany of the burning bush, when Moses expressed the fear that his own people would not believe that he was God's appointed messenger to them. This obviously phallic symbol is thus used as a form of reassurance for Moses. It is mentioned again on the same occasion when God reminds him of Aaron's existence and the latter's role as helper, for Moses had complained about being of "slow tongue." But this image of Aaron must have been experienced not only as a supportive figure but also as a possible rival. So God says reassuringly that "he shall be to thee a mouth, and thou shall be to him in God's stead. And thou shalt take in thy hand this rod, wherewith thou shalt do the signs" (4:16–17).

Thus Moses is assured that *he* is the one who will hold the rod and perform the signs. This original plan is later disregarded, as will be noted.

The next mention of the rod occurs when Moses departs from Jethro after securing the latter's blessing. Here he leaves the supportive presence of the kindly father figure and the familiar home surroundings. "And Moses took his wife and his sons, and set them upon an ass, and he returned to the land of Egypt; and Moses took the rod of God in his hand" (4:20). The loss of the good father and the fear of facing Pharaoh in Egypt is compensated for by the possession of the rod.

It is in connection with the ten plagues that the staff is most frequently mentioned. It is utilized in a fashion that on the surface seems somewhat erratic, as though it were a matter of indifference whether Moses or Aaron handled this magical instrument. Yet when it is first introduced in the confrontation with Pharaoh, the wording of the text seems to express an unusual carefulness. God presents the subject as if He were trying to preserve a balance satisfactory to Moses regarding the degree of power that was being bestowed on each of the two brothers. "And the Lord spoke unto Moses and unto Aaron, saying: 'When Pharaoh shall speak unto you, saying: Show a wonder for you; then thou shalt say unto Aaron: Take thy rod, and cast it down before Pharaoh, that it become a serpent.' And Moses and Aaron went unto Pharaoh and they did so, as the Lord had commanded, and Aaron cast down *his* rod before Pharaoh and before his servants, and it became a serpent" (7:8–10) (italics added). Here Aaron not only uses the rod but it is referred to as *his*.

Why, one must wonder, is the text so explicit in its details about the respective roles of Moses and Aaron? We can assume here not only the problem of sharing in the omnipotence of the Father but also a struggle in sibling rivalry with Aaron. Guilt would be alleviated on both levels by allowing Aaron to participate in the display of power, a situation that might also unconsciously imply a sharing of the guilt.

Having granted Aaron so large a part in this first episode, Moses arrogates to himself a fuller degree of participation in the second meeting with Pharaoh. God now speaks to *Moses alone*, and Aaron temporarily vanishes from the scene.

The next confrontation with Pharaoh is to take place the next morning on the bank of the Nile. During the lengthy instructions to Moses God tells him to say to Pharaoh, "Thus saith the Lord: 'In this thou shalt know that *I* am the Lord: behold, *I* will smite with the rod that is in *my hand* upon the waters which are in the river, and they shall be turned to blood. And the fish that are in the river shall die, and the river shall become foul; and the Egyptians shall loathe to drink water from the river'" (7:17–18) (italics added).

As one biblical scholar remarked, "The transition from the *Divine I* just before to the *I of Moses* is very abrupt" (Driver 1911, 60). Psychologically, however, the juxtaposition of these two *I*s makes sense. Moses is here so closely identified with God that in his mind the two temporarily merge.

Then, as is to be expected, follows the retreat. For although Moses alone is addressed here by God and given a dramatic and powerful role to perform in the very presence of Pharaoh, the action is not actually carried out as here described. It can be assumed that the daring of Moses, which found an outlet in the spirited words uttered by God, with Whom Moses was now strongly identified, could not be carried through in action by Moses himself. The narrative now reverses itself: "And the Lord said unto Moses: 'Say unto Aaron: Take thy rod, and stretch out thy hand over the waters of Egypt . . . that they may become blood; . . . And Moses and Aaron did so, as the Lord commanded; and he lifted up the rod and smote the waters that were in the river, in the sight of Pharaoh, and in the sight of his servants; and all the water turned to blood" (7:19–20).

First, Moses alone is to perform the miracle. Suddenly Aaron is again brought into the picture and is allowed a greater share of the honors. The ambivalence, however, comes through in the ambiguity of the pronoun in the words, "and *he* lifted up the rod," thus reflecting the struggle within Moses. Was it he or Aaron who performed this gesture?

In the description of the second plague there is a similarity to the pattern followed in the first. God speaks to Moses only, bidding him go to Pharaoh with the command that he allow the Hebrews to leave. If he refuses to do so, God will bring a deluge of frogs on the land. God now unexpectedly brings Aaron into the situation. "And the Lord said unto Moses: 'Say unto Aaron: Stretch forth thy hand with the rod over the rivers, over the canals, and over the pools, and cause frogs to come up upon the land of Egypt.' And Aaron stretched out his hand over the waters of Egypt; and the frogs came up, and covered the land of Egypt" (8:1–2).

As with the first plague, it is again Aaron who performs the magical gesture, although the episode is introduced by the command of God to Moses that *he* is to go in and speak to Pharaoh. Another contradictory detail is that God instructs Moses to direct Aaron to stretch forth *his hand with the rod*, but in the following sentence, when the action is carried out, the text says, "And Aaron stretched out *his hand*," omitting the mention of the rod.

The description of how this second plague would bring distress to the Egyptians and particularly to the household of Pharaoh is so explicit and so vivid in its detail that one can only wonder what divine purpose such eloquence could serve. Indeed, there is an element of humor for the observant reader in these minutiae. The text says, "And the river shall swarm with frogs, which shall go up and come into thy house, and into thy bedchamber, and upon thy bed, and into the house of thy servants, and upon thy people, and into thine ovens, and into thy kneading troughs" (7:28).

The investment of emotion reflected in these graphic details can be attributed only to Moses himself. Involved is a projective identification with the Deity that becomes an important source of narcissistic gratification to Moses. This guilt-laden competitiveness once more brings with it the pattern of retreat. Aaron is then quickly brought into the picture to lessen the anxiety, but at the last minute the latter is deprived of the magical rod, using only his hand to accomplish the miracle.

It cannot be without significance that the most dramatic passages in the text dealing with the confrontations of Moses and Pharaoh are in the words spoken by *God to Moses*, who is to repeat them to the monarch, rather than in the direct addresses by Moses himself to Pharaoh. We may have here further evidence of why Moses suffered from a certain inhibition of speech. If words are libidinized and become a source of narcissistic pleasure, especially for aggressive purposes in triumphing over a rival, then such defensive measures as being of "slow tongue" and "uncircumcised lips" are psychologically understandable. Only during his transitory participation in the omnipotence of God can Moses allow himself eloquence.

Although disguised by projection onto God, this kind of verbal self assertion may also lead to an inhibition in the actual carrying out of the aggressive act. At such times, Aaron, serving as a kind of alter ego, fulfills this function for him.

In the course of the second plague, however, a comparatively lengthy verbal exchange does take place between Moses and Pharaoh. In this situation, it is Pharaoh who calls for Moses and Aaron, saying "Entreat the Lord, that he take away the frogs from me, and from my people; and I will let the people go, that they may sacrifice unto the Lord." Moses here utilizes his position of strength in an unusual way. He says to Pharaoh, "Have thou this glory over me, against what time shall I entreat for thee . . . that the frogs be destroyed . . . ?" (8:8–9).

Moses here takes it upon himself to let Pharaoh decide when the frogs should be removed, thus identifying himself clearly with the power of God. That this assumption of authority caused him uneasiness is manifested when we are told that "Moses *cried* unto the Lord concerning the frogs which He had brought upon Pharaoh" (italics added). Then the text states, "And the Lord did according to the word of Moses" (8:12–13). Thus, this act of rather daring initiative meets with success.

As the account of the contest between Moses and Pharaoh continues, the role of Aaron, a silent and shadowy figure at best, trails off into nothingness. Even the words, "And the Lord said unto Moses, 'Say unto Aaron,'" no longer appear after the third plague. The fourth catastrophe is introduced by God speaking to Moses only. Aaron appears briefly in the formula, "And Pharaoh called for Moses and for Aaron" in order to plead with them to remove the pestilence.

Moses plays an increasingly active role, and in the course of the last four plagues his confrontations with Pharaoh take on a somewhat different form. These addresses, although delivered with firmness, are always respectful in tone. They carry only a small part of the fervor and ringing determination that characterize God's own words as addressed to Moses, who is to repeat them to Pharaoh. We see here the difference between the dramatic eloquence of how one behaves in fantasy preparatory to action and the more subdued tones of behavior in reality.

As the plagues continue and the contest nears its end, the tension between the two opponents increases. In a gesture that Pharaoh must have deemed most generous, he announces to Moses, "Go ye, serve the Lord; only let your flocks and your herds be stayed; let your little ones also go with you" (10:24). But Moses is firm in his demands. All the flocks and herds must be allowed to leave with the people "there shall not a hoof be left behind" (10:26). Moses explains that they would need all their cattle because it was uncertain how many of them would be required for the sacrifices. Pharaoh is enraged. He responds, "'Get thee from me, take heed to thyself, see my face no more; for in the day thou seest my face thou shalt die' And Moses said: 'Thou has spoken well; I will see thy face again no more'" (10:28–29).

A seeming difficulty in the chronology of the narrative now presents itself. The impression is given that Moses left the presence of Pharaoh at this point although the text does not actually say so. Pharaoh has remained adamant in his refusal to meet the demands of Moses. The seeming conclusion of the interview is strengthened by the opening verses of the following chapter where the scene apparently changes and God speaks to Moses, informing him that the last plague would now be inflicted upon the Egyptians. After that catastrophic event, Pharaoh would allow the enslaved people to leave. At this climactic point, a discordant note instructing Moses to tell the Children of Israel that they should ask of their Egyptian neighbors "jewels of silver and jewels of gold," is again introduced into the narrative. As on previous occasions, the interjection of this theme that is out of harmony with the spirit of the occasion suggests an intrusion of unconscious material on the part of Moses himself although seemingly emanating from the Deity.

The apparent problem in the chronology of the narrative when the interview with Pharaoh seems to have been concluded and Moses is involved in a dialogue with the Deity may be understood on a different level. The finality of Pharaoh's remarks and his threatening tone may have caused a momentary psychological impasse in the mind of Moses. In a brief state of altered consciousness, he retreats from the situation to commune with God and thus gather renewed strength and resolution. At the same time, his repressed anger at the Egyptian ruler's harshly voiced refusal to meet his demands may have reactivated retaliatory impulses while in this trance-like state, leading to the demand for recompense from the Egyptians, "the jewels" (women), of which this oedipal father figure had deprived him when Moses had been forced to flee from Egypt, then as now, with his life in jeopardy.

Such an experience of communion with the Deity as is hypothesized here could have taken only an imperceptible moment in time. But since no distinction is made in the text between what was happening in outward reality and the inner experience, the result is a certain awkwardness in the sequence of events and a seeming break in chronology. Both situations must have been real for Moses though on different levels of reality.

A resolute leader now resumes his confrontation with Pharaoh, announcing the dread event of the tenth plague, the climax to the whole series of disasters brought about by the stubbornness of the ruler. God Himself would go forth at midnight and strike down the first-born of all Egyptians, even including the first-born of their cattle. In his dramatic declaration to Pharaoh, Moses allowed some of his own feelings to find expression. We are told at the end of the dire prediction, "And he went forth from Pharaoh in hot anger" (11:4–8).

The two opponents do meet one more time. During the night of this final catastrophe Pharaoh sends for Moses and Aaron urgently telling them and their people to leave Egypt forthwith (12:31). The carrying out of this threat which, according to the text, would bring death to every household in Egypt, is set against the background of elaborate instructions for the preparation of the Passover. Directions are given, first by God to Moses and Aaron, and then conveyed by Moses to the elders of Israel. Each household is to slaughter a lamb, one year old and without blemish. The blood from this sacrifice is to be spread on the doorposts of the houses where the Hebrews lived. This pascal lamb is then to be roasted and eaten by each family group, together with bitter herbs and unleavened bread, as a sacrificial meal. It was to be consumed in haste, preparatory for departure, "with your loins girded, your shoes on your feet, and your staff in your hand; and ye shall eat it in haste—it is the Lord's passover" (12:11).

We shall deal with this event mainly in relation to its psychological significance for Moses. This anthropomorphic view of God "going out into the midst of Egypt" on His errand of death must indeed encompass unconsciously the image of Moses himself at the height of his identification with God. In the course of the description given here by God to Moses, the text says, "And the blood [on the doorposts] shall be to you [the Hebrews] for a token upon the houses where ye are; and when I see the blood, I will *pass over* you, and there shall be no plague upon you to destroy you, when I smite the land of Egypt" (12:13) (italics added).

Surely God could know without the visible sign of blood where the Hebrews lived. The preceding plagues had also fallen on the Egyptians and spared the Hebrews without any signs to set one group apart from the other. The only exception was to note at times that the land of Goshen, the area where most of the Hebrews lived, would not be subject to the disasters. Why then, one must wonder, is this distinctive sign established for the tenth plague. The words "And when I see the blood, I will pass over you" clearly state that God Himself will use this evidence as a sign. The impression is that Moses again identifies with God but retains his human sensibilities, related here perhaps to feelings of narcissistic gratification in this most omnipotent of all acts.

A further, more realistic purpose, however, is also evident in the text. The words "and the blood shall be to you for a token" indicate that the occasion had to be dramatized for the people as an event in their history, never to be forgotten. They therefore had to play a role in it themselves. Indeed, the course of the narrative is interrupted to declare the importance of this occasion for future generations. The festival of Passover is solemnly established, to be observed each year with a symbolic repetition of the pascal ceremony and the sacrificial meal (Schlesinger 1972).

The first premonition of the tenth plague came at the very beginning of Moses' return to Egypt, when he himself was attacked by God, Who *sought to slay him* (4:24). As mentioned earlier in this study, he also was saved by a sacrifice involving blood, the circumcision of his son by his wife, Zipporah.

A unity is now established between the resolve with which Moses entered Egypt and the carrying out of this resolve at the point when he leaves the land. Unconsciously involved was the oedipal revenge that had to be fulfilled against the hostile father through the sacrifice of the son. The second part of the oedipal fantasy, the conquest of the woman, is symbolized in the act of spoiling the Egyptians, when the Hebrews *asked for* and received from them "jewels of silver and jewels of gold, and raiment" (12:35).

The individual oedipal fantasy can thus be detected in Moses as an undercurrent to the major theme, the liberation of his people. This situation has psychoanalytic validity, for the greatness of man and the strength of his deeds often have as their initial motive power the unfulfilled dreams and wishes and the angry hurts of the child.

The threat of the tenth plague is carried out. Thus the exodus takes place, an event regarded by many as the true beginnings of the Hebrews as a historic people.

The Flight

The final episode of the contest between Moses and Pharaoh, however, is not yet over. Pharaoh characteristically has a change of heart after the Hebrews leave. The cry goes up: "What is this we have done, that we have let Israel go from serving us?" "And the Egyptians pursued after them, all the horses and chariots of Pharaoh . . . and overtook them encamped by the sea" (14:5–9).

The idea is clearly conveyed that this dilemma of being caught between the waters and the pursuing Egyptians was purposely planned by God as a further opportunity of showing His power over Pharaoh. The text says, "And I will harden Pharaoh's heart, and he shall follow after them; and I will get Me honour upon Pharaoh, and upon all his host; and the Egyptians shall know that I am the Lord" (14:4). Two more times within a brief space the same motive is expressed again, ostensibly by God (14:17–18).

The Hebrews, however, respond to the situation with near-panic. "And when Pharaoh drew nigh, the children of Israel lifted up their eyes, and behold, the Egyptians were marching after them; and they were sore afraid; and the children of Israel cried out unto the Lord. And they said unto Moses: 'Because there were no graves in Egypt, hast thou taken us away to die in the wilderness?'" (14:10–11).

Moses answers the reproaches of the fear-stricken people like a true leader, speaking with unusual confidence and strength. He says, "Fear ye not, stand still, and see the salvation of the Lord, which He will work for you to-day; for whereas ye have seen the Egyptians to-day, ye shall see them again no more for ever. The Lord will fight for you, and ye shall hold your peace" (14:13–14).

And now occurs another of those puzzling nonsequiturs in the text that seem to indicate an omission of some kind. The narrative continues in quite another vein. "And the Lord said unto Moses: 'Wherefore criest thou unto Me? speak unto the children of Israel, that they go forward. And lift up thy rod, and stretch out thy hand over the sea, and divide it; and the children of Israel shall go into the midst of the sea, on dry ground'" (14:15–16).

Actually, Moses had responded to the exigency of the occasion with the strength needed to rally his people at this crucial time. Without his display of leadership, panic and disintegration could easily have resulted. Why then God's reproof to Moses, "Wherefore criest thou unto Me?" *These words must be a response to something other than the utterance just made by the leader to his people.* In reality, *it was the people who had cried unto the Lord*, not Moses. And it was the latter who answered them *as though he were God*. At this moment, prompted by the crisis at hand, Moses' identification with God must have been particularly strong. If, unconsciously, it was to his own miraculous powers that he was so confidently alluding when Moses called upon the people "to see the salvation of the Lord, which He will work for you today," an intrapsychic reaction was to be expected. Who was he to announce a miracle without God's preliminary instruction! It may have been in the reactive feelings of helplessness and inadequacy following on his daring that a silent call for help did indeed rise up within Moses. However, the situation was hardly the time for giving way to such feelings and they were quickly repressed. This repression finds a meaningful omission in the wordlessness of the text. Only in the response of God, the quick admonishment and the specific guiding instructions during the moment of confusion that must have followed, can we detect what may have preceded them within the heart of Moses.

One is reminded here of a previous situation, much less momentous, when Moses also makes a promise on his own authority that depends on God's compliance for fulfillment. It is when Moses promises Pharaoh that God will remove the frogs from Egypt on the morrow. There too we are told that *"Moses cried unto the Lord concerning the frogs which He had brought upon Pharaoh. And the Lord did according to the word of Moses"* (8:12–13) (italics added). But on this later occasion, when so much more was involved, God returns the responsibility to Moses, forcing both him and the people into active roles.

The announcement that the Children of Israel would "go into the midst of the sea on dry ground" is followed by the Deity with the words, "And I, behold, I will harden the hearts of the

Egyptians, and they shall go in after them; and I will get Me honour upon Pharaoh, and upon all his host, upon his chariots, and upon his horsemen. And the Egyptians shall know that I am the Lord" (14:17–18).

It is somewhat puzzling in our own time to reconcile the image of God with the seemingly insatiable need that the Deity manifests for honor and recognition as revealed in these final episodes of the exodus. But to impose our own concepts on the biblical world of three thousand years ago would hardly be valid. If God's declaration of His wish to impress the Egyptians with His might and power had been viewed as objectionable by the writer of the text, it would not have been recorded so openly.

It must have been of utmost importance to Moses himself that the God of Israel, with Whom he was so intimately associated, should be recognized and honored by Pharaoh and the Egyptian people. While the narcissistic needs of Moses would be gratified by this situation, much more was involved. The struggle was between the God of Israel and the polytheistic world represented by Pharaoh, the semidivine king.

The biblical view that it was the prerogative of the Deity to demand and expect honor and glory from His followers is evident throughout this body of literature. The prestige of the Children of Israel, the degree to which they would be respected and feared among the other nations would be influenced by the might and power of the Deity associated with them.

The God of the Hebrews was a strange and unfamiliar one to the Egyptians. Even to the Children of Israel He was still not altogether believable. Their escape from Egypt would have been meaningless on the larger stage of world history were it not for the role they were to play as bearers of the message associated with the One God. The Deity's need for honor and glory and His right openly to demand it can be understood as a requirement for the recognition of *His existence*, the God Whose name was *I AM* in contrast to the false gods of the Egyptians. The exodus was a struggle that had to come to a close, not with a whisper but with a mighty roar, the complete overwhelming of the enemy.

As with the story of the plagues, the miracle of the divided waters and the safe crossing of the Hebrews involve situations that have a basis in the potentially possible. Studies of wind and tides indicate that in the area involved a strong northeast wind together with an ebbing tide could have swept away the shallow waters of the *Sea of Reeds*, (a shallow extension of the Gulf of Suez) before an opposite current of air drove the waves back on their accustomed path (Driver 1911, 125). In regard to the route taken by the Hebrews, Albright (1942) says that in terms of his own Sinai expedition of 1947–1948 and based on recent archeological findings of ancient biblical sites, the course as described in Exodus was the only logical one the Hebrews could have followed (p. 96).

This momentous occasion in the history of a people concludes fittingly with the famous song of triumph (Exodus 15) following the crossing of the sea. This ode is especially associated with Miriam, the sister of Moses, who leads the other women in the exultant words of the song, accompanied by timbrels and dancing.

In referring to Miriam, the text describes her as the *sister of Aaron*, without mentioning her relationship to Moses. The omission seems rather obvious. It may indicate a dissociation of Moses from his personal family life, especially on this occasion when all his feelings were concentrated on the event taking place and in his total libidinal involvement with God and the people, Israel, as a whole. We may then have here another indication of how closely the text seems to reflect the mood and feelings of the hero.

The song, thought to be among the oldest of biblical writings, dating back to the thirteenth-twelfth centuries B.C. (Albright 1957, 14), expresses ecstatic feelings of deliverance and victory: "I will sing unto the Lord, for He is highly exalted; The horse and his rider hath He thrown into the sea." It describes the dramatic destruction of the enemy and the miraculous rescue of Israel: "They sank as lead in the mighty waters," but "Thou in love hast led the people that Thou hast redeemed." These are but a few excerpts from the lengthy song-poem.

The escape from slavery in Egypt, climaxed by the crossing of the sea, became one of the most important milestones of Hebrew biblical history, second only to the Covenant at Mount Sinai. It is memorialized at the annual festival of Passover, when every Jew is exhorted not only to remember the event but to think of himself as one of those who was personally delivered from the Egyptians at that fateful time (Schlesinger 1972).

Psychodynamics of Moses: Further Considerations

It is suggested here that the realistic task Moses assumed of confronting and challenging Pharaoh reactivated the oedipal situation of early life. The father figure was split into the powerful, oppressive image of the bad father, Pharaoh, and the idealized, omnipotent, good father—God. Significantly, the real parent, the Hebrew Amram, is not even mentioned in this important segment of the Moses saga except in a genealogical table. Moses was involved with the internalized father.

This splitting of the father image must have started at an early age. If, as suggested earlier, the family romance of Moses involved the fantasy of being the adopted son of Pharaoh's daughter, the Egyptian ruler would indeed be experienced psychically as the oedipal father, reinforcing the role commonly played by the head of state in the unconscious fantasy of his subjects.

The influence of Pharaoh on the fantasy life of the youthful Moses can be conjectured as centering on his omnipotence and his role as oppressor. Moses may have identified positively with the former aspect in wishful thinking and negatively with the latter image. He must have contrasted unfavorably the powerlessness of his own Hebrew father with the greatness and strength of Pharaoh, thus making Amram a denigrated figure, in part. The tendency of Moses to self-depreciation and to identify with the victim may have stemmed from such a source.

But there can be no doubt that Moses also had a strong positive identification with the father of his early childhood, a figure who generally remains a source of idealized strength and power (Jones 1912, 286). Moreover, the Levite Amram and his wife, Jochebed, who was also the sister of Amram's father, must have occupied a position of prestige among their own people, regardless of the low esteem in which the Hebrews were held in the larger social system. In their home it could be expected that the traditions of the patriarchal ancestors would be kept fresh in the memory of the family, thus making the *God of his fathers* an early influence in the life of Moses (Albright 1957, 241; Baron 1952, 34). Certain it is that without these positive ties to his family Moses could not have identified with his Hebrew brethren and his whole development as leader and prophet would not have taken place.

More significant and complex than the way Moses related to Pharaoh is the pattern of how he related to God. The unconscious mechanism of splitting the father figure into good and bad images protected Moses from excessive ambivalence toward the Deity by allowing a polarization of aggressive feelings onto Pharaoh, a suitable object for such emotions.

The most repetitive pattern we have noted was the way Moses oscillated in his feelings between omnipotence and inadequacy (Arlow 1951). There is a further quality that plays a significant part in the relationship between Moses and God. It involves an aspect of the superego that has tended generally to be overlooked in psychoanalytic writings by all but a few. I refer here to the supportive role played by the Deity toward His chosen prophet.

As shown in earlier chapters but revealed with special clarity in this period of the exodus, God treats Moses as a good psychotherapist might deal with a patient who is suffering from feelings of anxiety, inadequacy, and discouragement. God reassures, explains, builds up self-confidence, gives specific instructions in appropriate situations, and answers questions where clarification is requested, as in problems of identity regarding both God and Moses. He allows this son figure to share in the omnipotence of the Father, decreases anxiety by securing the help of Aaron, shows patience and forbearance in the face of discouragement on the part of Moses and his wish to retreat, and teaches him the techniques of dealing both with his own people and with Pharaoh. God understands the narcissistic needs of Moses, for after all a certain amount of narcissism is essential in the makeup of a prophet (Arlow 1951). Thus, He allows Moses the gratification of *being god* to Aaron and to Pharaoh. He reveals Himself to Moses by a special name, supposedly unknown even to the Patriarchs. At the same time, God holds the prophet firmly to the task at hand, admonishes, directs, and uses His authority to enforce action.

What, then, from a psychodynamic view of Moses himself does this aspect of the relationship with God signify? It indicates clearly that Moses experienced the Deity not only as a strict superego, the source of morality, of laws and commandments, but also as the *loving superego*, Who supports the ego and encourages its constructive development, both in the world of reality and in its conflicts with instinctual wishes and fears. In recent psychoanalytic writings, such as those by Shafer (1960, 163ff) and Sandler (1960, 155), it has been pointed out that although Freud, for theoretical and historical reasons, emphasized the prohibiting and censoring role of the superego, he also gave numerous indications of its function to protect and love. And indeed it is the concept of the comforting and protecting Father as well as the feared Authority that gives to religious life its particular strength (Freud 1928).

It was precisely during his periods of depression and discouragement that Moses was able to muster his ego strength by calling on the support of a loving superego. Without this kind of psychic resource, he could not have achieved the self-confidence that made his accomplishments possible.

Those who tend to see the religion of the Old Testament solely as the expression of a stern and forbidding Father religion miss this other aspect. The concept of a loving relationship between God and man is a basic element in the biblical theme. And although Freud (1928, 1930, 1933) tended to emphasize the negative aspects of religion, it was he who also caught the element of compassion in Moses, his hero, when he interpreted the Moses of Michelangelo as resisting the impulse to destroy the Tablets of the Law and keep them intact for his people (1914, 257–87).

In the popular fantasy, the figure of Moses does indeed stand out more vividly in his role as the powerful emancipator and stern lawgiver. Yet it was the feeling of compassion for his suffering brethren that motivated his great undertaking in the first place.

In the Wilderness

On the Way to Mount Sinai

 CHAPTER FIVE

IT IS DURING the many years of his leadership in the wilderness of the Sinai Peninsula that the personality of Moses is most fully revealed both in its towering strength and human weaknesses. It can hardly be questioned that this epoch of biblical history was of great significance both for the leader and the group as a time of growth and maturation, leading to influences that have endured in the history of Western culture for the past three millenia.

It seems almost anticlimactic to turn from this world-embracing concept to the group of slaves fleeing from Egypt in the latter part of the 13th century B.C. and to observe as an inauspicious beginning how quickly the exaltation stemming from their seemingly miraculous crossing of the Sea of Reeds gave way to murmurings and rebelliousness when they faced the privations of life in the desert.

It has been suggested that if this narrative were indeed a myth about *beginnings*, as some have claimed, of the kind used by other peoples to glorify the past, how differently the story could have been told! The humble origins of slavery and a raggle-taggle mob that escaped have been termed the "*inconvenience* of biblical tradition" and suggest to those who still doubt the historicity of the exodus that, given a choice, a more glamourous background for a people's history might have been invented (Hertz 1936, 395–96).

The story of the Children of Israel and their leader in the wilderness is indeed remarkably and convincingly human, even with all its miraculous aspects. It is also true that while much has been made of the unadmirable behavior of these escapees, there must have been a sufficiently strong core of positive elements that held them together throughout all the exigencies and made possible the formation of a people who contributed immeasurably to our own life and times. For in spite of his genius, Moses alone could not have accomplished what he did if his followers had not been basically responsive to his leadership.

With this perspective, let us now turn to the first adventure recorded in the Bible after the Children of Israel reached the freedom of the wilderness. It should be explained that this so-called wilderness was not a sandy desert, similar to the rolling dunes of the Sahara. It was a landscape of varied topography with valleys and mountains and riverbeds, the latter sporadically filled by brief, often torrential rainfalls. There was always vegetation of some kind, bushes and trees that could subsist with a scarcity of water. There were also occasional oases, the highly prized watering places much sought after and fought over by the wandering tribes with their herds of sheep and cattle (Driver 1911, 177ff).

It was through this territory, desolate but often awe-inspiring in its beauty, that the Children of Israel made their pilgrimage. They traveled for the first three days without finding water. The experience must have been a frightening one, ominous for the future. And when they finally sighted this precious commodity, their joy quickly turned to dismay, for it was not drinkable. The Bible says, "Therefore the name of it was called Marah [bitterness]. And the people murmured against Moses, saying: 'What shall we drink?' And he cried unto the Lord; and the Lord showed him a tree, and he cast it into the waters, and the waters were made sweet. There He made for them a statute and an ordinance, and there He proved them; and He said: 'If thou wilt diligently hearken to the voice of the Lord, thy God, and wilt do that which is right in His eyes, and wilt give ear to His commandments, and keep all His statutes, I will put none of the diseases upon thee, which I have put upon the Egyptians; for I am the Lord that healeth thee'" (15:23–26).*

Here we have a paradigm that sets the tone for the relationship between the Children of Israel and the Deity. It involves the conditional promise. If they will obey God's commandments, He will be with them and protect them.

In the biblical verses quoted above, however, the diseases that they are to be spared seem to have no connection with the immediate situation. This lack of sequence may be an example of how commonly shared experiences of the group are assumed to be understood without explicit verbal communication. In the minds of the recently escaped slaves from Egypt, polluted water may have been associated with the diseases that were brought about when the Nile River had been made undrinkable by the first of the ten plagues (7:20) (Hertz 1936, 274). Thus, it was necessary to allay their anxiety about the water at Marah. At the same time, the point was made that the same God Who had the power to cause disease was also the God of healing.

The attitude of the Children of Israel toward Moses is also revealed in the experience at Marah. The people "murmur" against Moses, saying, "What shall we drink?" Implicit in these words are not only feelings of dependency but also a tone of complaint and demand. Their question is not "What shall we *do*?" but rather "What shall we drink?" Thus, they do not face the problem in an adult way but express only a need, with underlying expectations and anger, placing the responsibility for their predicament entirely on Moses. During their period of slavery the Children of Israel had become accustomed to an authority outside themselves to make decisions for them.

Moses turns to God. His appeal has a different quality than that of the people toward their leader. Moses "cried unto the Lord." He neither murmurs nor complains but pleads for aid,

---

*All biblical references in this chapter, unless otherwise noted, are to the book of Exodus.

thus admitting his own inadequacy in this situation. There is a subtle but important distinction between a cry for help and the expression of an angry demand that a need be met.

Help is provided through the intervention of the Deity, but the method involved makes use of a natural phenomenon, a further aspect in the pattern that is to be followed of how God would perform His miracles for them. It is known that certain trees have the capacity to sweeten brackish waters.

From an objective viewpoint one might ask where this knowledge, suddenly made known to Moses by God, actually came from. It seems likely that the needed information may have existed in the mind of Moses from the time of his own earlier experiences in the wilderness. Since the theophany of the burning bush, when the spiritual life of the newly chosen prophet underwent a dramatic change, a certain shifting of psychic boundaries may have occurred (Kris 1952, 102, 312). Some of the resources of his ego may have been repressed in compliance with a more demanding superego, projected onto God. In the struggle between dependency and a longing for omnipotence, Moses may have had a defensive need to *forget and then receive anew* from God that which he had once learned himself. This psychic process would help to explain the close connection between some of the seemingly miraculous events that took place in the wilderness and the natural phenomena generally associated with them. In a state of crisis Moses may have tended to turn more readily to the Deity for help, as if not daring to depend wholly on himself. In this suppliant mood, the earlier knowledge could then have become available to him once more. Later situations of a similar nature also suggest certain inhibitions on the part of Moses about knowing the secrets of nature. Such knowledge could have been experienced by him as dangerously close to a hidden wish for a forbidden kind of power. There may have been a need to counteract any associations with concepts of magic, so much a part of the Egyptian cultural milieu.

The psychic struggle between feelings of dependency and the wish for omnipotence within Moses is subtly suggested in the wording of the conditional promise at Marah. In the verse beginning, "There *he* made for them a statute and an ordinance, and there *he* proved them" (italics added), the antecedent of the pronoun *he*, although capitalized in some versions of the Bible, is indefinite (15:25). There is ambiguity about who is doing the talking, God or Moses. First it seems as though *the man* is speaking. God is referred to in the third person, as *His* eyes, *His* commandments, *His* statutes, whereas in the second part of the verse, it is clearly God Himself Who is doing the talking, as He says, "for I am the Lord that healeth thee." (See full quotation above.)

This lack of clarity may express what is going on within Moses himself. As the water becomes drinkable, the leader's feelings of helplessness may have disappeared. He may have experienced a sudden resurgence of strength as a realignment of psychic forces took place. As Moses felt closer to the power of God, the boundaries between ego and superego could then have been merged and the repressed knowledge become available. The leader may then temporarily have felt God-like (Greenacre 1957; Lewin 1973, 317–18).

It should be noted that the Children of Israel are now addressed in the singular form, *thee* and *thou*, as in "If thou wilt diligently hearken to the voice of the Lord . . . I will put none of the diseases upon *thee*." Although this metaphor, which pictures the group as an individual in various relationships to the Deity, is not unusual in the biblical literature, its usage may here have specific meaning. Moses may unconsciously have shifted from one role to another in his identifications. At an earlier point in the Exodus narrative, there had been a reference to the Children of Israel collectively as "the son of God," in a context when Moses also experienced himself as the son of God, *symbolic of all Israel* (4:22–23). If, in the situation at Marah, the leader was momentarily identified with God, he could then be relating to the people *as if* they represented himself, again symbolic of the group, to whom he then related as the Deity. Such mechanisms of reversal and projection are common phenomena in psychoanalytic experience. Moses had strong identifications both with the Children of Israel and with God, a situation no doubt helpful to him in his dual roles as prophet and leader. However, the related task of maintaining a realistic sense of his own identity was thus made more difficult, as we shall have other occasions to observe. It was a price Moses had to pay for the flexibility of ego boundaries that gave him greater access to the fullness of his psychic powers, a condition often associated with gifted people of unusual creativity (Greenacre 1957).

The next significant episode involving food and water occurs in the Wilderness of Sin, one month after the departure from Egypt. But first there was a period of respite. The Bible says, "And they came to Elim, where were twelve springs of water, and three score and ten palm trees; and they encamped there by the waters" (15:27). This pleasant situation must have lasted several weeks. "And they took their journey from Elim, and all the congregation of the children of Israel came into the wilderness of Sin, which is between Elim and Sinai, on the fifteenth day of the second month after their departing out of the land of Egypt. And the whole congregation of the children of Israel murmured against Moses and against Aaron in the wilderness; and the children of Israel said unto them: 'Would that we had died by the hand of the Lord in the land of Egypt, when we sat by the fleshpots, when we did eat bread to the full; for ye have brought us forth into this wilderness, to kill this whole assembly with hunger'" (16:1–3).

A puzzling sequence now occurs. Instead of the leader's expected response to the angry words of the people, it is God Who intervenes, speaking to Moses himself. "Then the Lord said unto Moses: 'Behold, I will cause to rain bread from heaven for you; and the people shall go out and gather a day's portion every day, that I may prove them, whether they will walk in My law or not. And it shall come to pass on the sixth day that they shall prepare that which they bring in, and it shall be twice as much as they gather daily'" (16:4–5).

God here interrupts the confrontation between the people and Moses, presenting the leader with a plan so explicit that it must have been in readiness before in the mind of Moses himself. It is reasonable to assume that in the preceding period, at the oasis of Elim, the leader had thought about the problem of sustenance for his people in the harder days ahead. On the basis of his own lengthy experience in the wilderness, he would have been familiar with the substance later known as manna. It was formed from the juices of the tamarisk tree, which congealed and fell as white, frostlike grains on the early morning dew. When ground into flour or boiled, it provided a basic food. If, as assumed, this plan was prepared in advance, including the manner of its gathering, why does the Deity present it to Moses at the very moment when the leader is being challenged by the people?

Higher Biblical Criticism has its own explanations for the seeming lack of sequence, basing its reasoning on the theory that some of the verses were displaced (Driver 1911, 146–47).

Considering the text as it stands, however, we shall explore psychological aspects that may be involved. The accusations of the people against Moses were expressed in the harshest terms they had thus far used against him. The leader must have experienced considerable anxiety at this moment. Temporarily overwhelmed, he may have suffered not only a forgetfulness of previously acquired knowledge but also a characteristic inhibition of speech (Fenichel 1945, 181–82) (7). Moses then turned to God with a silent cry for help. The Deity responds by recalling to him the plan that had already been made. The text does not say whether Moses repeated to the people the message as he received it from the Deity. It may have been enough to have gotten this reassurance for himself. Both Moses and Aaron (his voice) now speak to the assembly. Their first words contain a denial that it was *they* who had brought the people out of Egypt. "And Moses and Aaron said unto all the children of Israel: 'At even, then ye shall know that the *Lord* hath brought you out from the land of Egypt; and in the morning, then ye shall see the glory of the Lord; for that He hath heard your murmurings against the Lord; and what are we, that ye murmur against us?'" Then Moses alone continues. "And Moses said: 'This shall be, when the Lord shall give you in the evening flesh to eat, and in the morning bread to the full; for that the Lord heareth your murmurings which ye murmur against Him; and what are we? Your murmurings are not against us, but against the Lord" (16:6–8) (italics added).

And now there is another puzzling transition. Moses tells Aaron to speak to the people and command their attention, for they are about to witness an unusual scene. "And Moses said unto Aaron, 'Say unto all the congregation of the children of Israel: Come near before the Lord; for He hath heard your murmurings.' And it came to pass, as Aaron spoke unto the whole congregation of the children of Israel, that they looked toward the wilderness, and behold, the glory of the Lord appeared in the cloud. And the Lord spoke unto Moses, saying: 'I have heard the murmurings of the children of Israel. Speak unto them, saying: At dusk ye shall eat flesh, and in the morning ye shall be filled with bread; and ye shall know that I am the Lord your God'" (16:9–12).

This is the same information Moses and Aaron had just given to the people. Is there a possible psychological explanation for this repetition or is it, as Higher Biblical Criticism claims, another example of displacement in the text?

It seems that the leader requires the supportive presence of the Deity, made manifest to the people, in order that his assurance of the promise made earlier would be believed. It is significant that when the Children of Israel are confronted with the evidence of God's presence, Moses is no longer in direct communication with the people, but having called on Aaron to be his spokesman, he is now in communion with the Deity. The information given earlier to the assembly by Moses is now repeated by God to the leader so that the entire assembly, aware of the Divine presence, might know the source of his authority.

The expression "they looked toward the wilderness" (16:10) is puzzling since they were already *in* the wilderness. It is possible that as Moses was speaking with the Deity, the prophet moved toward the outside of the camp where his personal tent was standing (Driver 1911, 146–47). If this movement was in the direction of the late afternoon sun, then as "the glory of the Lord appeared in the cloud," Moses himself may have been enveloped in the light of the setting sun, and as the people "looked toward the wilderness," he became indistinguishable from what appeared to them as the Deity Himself in this moment of revelation. It may have been at the receding figure of the leader that they looked, in the direction of the wilderness that they themselves would be following.

Let us present in summary significant details that support the above reconstruction. The changes in *who speaks to whom* throughout the episode cannot be wholly accidental. First, the people complain vehemently to Moses, harshly accusing him of bringing them into the wilderness to kill them with hunger. Moses is momentarily unable to respond. God then speaks to the leader, ostensibly a communication of which the people were not aware.

Moses and Aaron now address the people together, disclaiming responsibility for the situation but promising speedy fulfillment of their needs. Following this, Moses bids Aaron talk to the assembly and prepare them for what is to follow. Now the glory of the Lord appears in the cloud and God bids Moses tell the people, under these new circumstances, that which they had heard before from him alone. It is suggested here that the apparent nonsequiturs can be understood on the basis of the psychic processes taking place within Moses himself. In the fluctuating states of consciousness that seem to be occurring here, both the time sequence and space orientation are implicit in the textual content but presented with the lapses in coherence suggestive of the intermingling of preconscious and conscious material.

In the morning, the promise of bread was fulfilled. The Bible says, "And when the layer of dew was gone up, behold upon the face of the wilderness a fine, scale-like thing, fine as the hoar frost on the ground. And when the children of Israel saw it, they said one to another: 'What is it?'" [*Man hu?*] (16:14–15). From this, according to some scholars, the word *manna* was derived. Moses answers them in a matter-of-fact way: "It is the bread which the Lord hath given you to eat" (16:15). He then briefly repeats his instructions about how they are to gather it. He is once more their earthly leader, communicating with them in the ordinary way.

Each separate incident that deals with the complaints of the people to Moses about the needs of food and water conveys its own nuances of feelings and attitudes, as does the response of Moses to these situations. Yet certain familiar patterns are followed on both sides. The anger of the people is expressed in more strident terms on each successive occasion, and Moses reacts with increasing anxiety to their hostility.

The next setting for such a confrontation is Rephidim. It is in the vicinity of Mount Sinai, but its exact location is uncertain (Driver 1911, 155). The text says, "And all the congregation of the children of Israel journeyed from the wilderness of Sin, by their states, according to the commandment of the Lord, and encamped in Rephidim; and there was no water for the people to drink. Wherefore the people strove with Moses and said: 'Give us water that we may drink.' And Moses said unto them: 'Why strive ye with me? Wherefore do ye try the Lord?' And the people thirsted there for water; and the people murmured against Moses, and said: 'Wherefore hast thou brought us up out of Egypt to kill us and our children and our cattle with thirst?' And Moses cried unto the Lord, saying, 'What shall I do unto this people? They are almost ready to stone me'" (17:1–4).

Here the people not only *murmured* against Moses but they *strove* with him, a word suggesting more vigorous protest. Again, Moses faces an angry crowd making demands on him that he had no immediate means of fulfilling. It is understandable that the reactions of the leader to this situation would be feelings of inadequacy, anger, and fear. His response, "Why strive ye with me? Wherefore do ye tempt the Lord?" has puzzling aspects. He disclaims responsibility, implying again, as he must truly have believed, that he was only the instrument of God. The words *tempt the Lord*, in the sense of testing Him to prove His presence, reminded the angry crowd that they were dealing with a mightier power than the earthly leader whom they were assailing. At the same time, the words *me* and *Lord* in the above quotation give the impression of being synonymous. Moses may here be unconsciously retreating from feelings of helplessness to an association with the omnipotence of God.

Significantly, the demand of the people, "Give us drink," is in the plural form of the Hebrew verb *to give*, suggesting that more than one subject was being addressed. If Aaron is the other who was included, the text would more likely have stated so, as on many other occasions. The plural verb may signify that both Moses and the God he represented were being appealed to by the desperate people. They may have been responding unconsciously to his suggestion that at this moment he and God were indeed indivisible.

To a greater degree than in his struggles with Pharaoh, the reality of a multitude of people surrounding him and the immediacy both of their anger and their need placed the leader in a particularly threatening situation psychologically. He gives way to his feelings, crying out to God, "What shall I do unto this people? They are almost ready to stone me."

This is indeed the expression of a frightened and angry man, testifying movingly to his human estate. There is no indication in the text that Moses and Aaron had a bodyguard, although it seems likely that a small group of stalwart followers, probably led by Joshua, would be near them. However, these would hardly be adequate protection against a large, unruly mob. But it is also true that the respect and reverence of the people for Moses must have been very great and their dependence on him considerable. He must have appeared to them at times not only as the messenger and prophet of God but His very embodiment. He had been able to challenge and defeat Pharaoh himself, and the whole experience of the exodus was within an atmosphere of the miraculous in which Moses played the leading role. Perhaps it is not surprising then that they expected these miracles to continue without much effort on their part. Their attitude was much like that of children to a strong parental figure, the chief source of their security. They might complain to him as sons to a father. They might even entertain murderous impulses, but these people were not historically in the era of the primal horde, nor was Moses like the mythical father in *Totem and Taboo* (Freud 1912).

The controversial theory of Freud (1939, 52–54), that Moses was actually murdered in the wilderness by his own people on one of the occasions dealt with above, cannot be validated in Scripture (Jones 1957, 373) (8). In my own view, such an outcome does not seem psychologically convincing. For an event of this kind to have occurred and then been completely repressed would have been totally alien to the spirit of Scripture.

But sons have slain their fathers and groups have killed their leaders throughout the centuries. The erratic behavior of a few can sometimes turn the tide against the greater restraints of the many. The uneasiness of Moses when confronted by a dissatisfied crowd is understandable, not only in terms of reality but also on the basis of his own psychodynamics. Even though the leader declares that the people are ready to stone him, the expression may not have been intended literally. Nor was violence on his person ever threatened openly by any of the people.

As usual, the appeal of Moses to God for help is not in vain. As at the time of crisis in crossing the Sea of Reeds, God's instructions are immediate and specific, elements important to a man in a state of severe emotional tension. "And the Lord said unto Moses, 'Pass on before the people, and take with thee of the elders of Israel; and thy rod wherewith thou smotest the river, take in thy hand, and go. Behold, I will stand before thee there upon the rock in Horeb; and thou shalt smite the rock, and there shall come water out of it, that the people may drink.' And Moses did so in the sight of the elders of Israel. And the name of the place was called Massah [*to prove or test*] and Meribah [*to strive*] because of the striving of the children of Israel, and because they tried the Lord, saying: 'Is the Lord among us, or not?'" (17:5–7).

There are several elements in the above directives that sustain Moses and force him into action. Basic to the situation is his sense of the immediacy of God's presence as a source of help. Also involved is the mention of the rod, with its comforting association with God's powers, here transmitted symbolically to him. The command "Pass on before the people" may have the purpose of showing himself unafraid in front of them, thus reducing both their anxiety and his own. For their hostility must have stemmed chiefly from the fear that neither he nor the God he represented would be able to meet their life-supporting needs. Taking the elders with him would further reassure the people; their respected representatives would share the evidence of the good faith of Moses and of God. Moreover, their leader would be seen with the rod of God in his hand, the symbol of power. The words *and go* are also meaningful. Moses must have wanted greatly to put some distance between himself and the mob, with its unpredictable temper. And where does God direct him to go? To the place most closely associated with the presence of God, to Horeb, as Mount Sinai was also known. "Behold, I will stand before thee there upon the rock in Horeb."

Although not specifically stated, the implication of the biblical narrative is that the water flowed from Horeb down to the people at Rephidim. Since the relationship of these geographic points to each other is uncertain, it is difficult to know whether such a happening was realistically possible. (12) (Driver 1911, 157).

Travelers to this general area have brought back reports that dwellers in the wilderness make use of the technique of striking a stratified limestone rock, which will then give forth its concealed water through the porous cells (Keller 1964, p. 126). This knowledge Moses may have acquired from his own experience in the wilderness.

Why, however, the carefully worded information that God would stand before him on the holy mountain as the act of striking the rock was carried out? It is suggested here that the thought of striking the rock, especially at Horeb, must have been a frightening one to Moses. The metaphor of *God as a Rock*, whose strength and steadfastness could always be relied on, is a familiar figure of speech in the biblical literature. This object, therefore, could have symbolized God Himself. How then could Moses dare to strike the rock! If, however, this method was the only way of getting water for the people, the leader would be in a state of conflict, torn between a realistic need and his own inner resistance to such an act.

Only by the feeling that the presence of God was separate and apart from the physical aspect of the rock, and by using the holy rod, could Moses bring himself to perform the forceful gesture that in itself represented an act of aggression. Therefore the carefully worded instructions of God were needed. If God stood before him as Moses struck the rock, then the Deity and the symbol were separated from each other. Moses could thus be assured that he was not committing the unspeakable crime of striking God Himself, even in symbolic form.

And yet the experience must have left its mark on Moses and influenced the second occasion, many years later according to biblical chronology, when in a similar situation he again struck a rock for water, with quite different, indeed tragic, results. This well-known episode will be considered in a later chapter.

The Battle with the Amalekites

Immediately following the events at Rephidim, where the people "tried the Lord, saying: 'Is the Lord among us or not?'" the very next verse states, "Then came Amalek and fought with Israel in Rephidim" (17:8). The rabbis point out that this sequence indicates a connection between the two happenings, the attack by the Amalekites being a punishment for the lack of faith shown by the people.

It is not unusual for nomadic tribes to make war on each other for the possession of a watering place. The Children of Israel, having obtained water at Rephidim, now had to fight to protect this prize. Why then is this episode invested with meaning that seems to go beyond its practical importance, as the narrative suggests? Why do the Amalekites become the objects of hatred and lasting enmity?

The opposing forces meeting in combat are referred to as *Amalek* and *Israel*, suggesting a symbolic personalization of the two peoples. The Amalekites were descendents of Esau, the man destined to live by the sword. They represented the very opposite of what the Children of Israel were to prepare themselves for—a spiritual mission in the world. There had to be lasting enmity between the rule of uncontrolled aggression and the principle of sublimation as symbolized by the Israelites.

In a sense this struggle at Rephidim epitomizes the earlier conflict between Jacob and Esau. It was on his way back to the Promised Land, after his long exile, that Jacob wrestled with the angel and subsequently made peace with his brother Esau (Zeligs 1974, chap. 2). The Children of Israel, on their way to Mount Sinai, must also wrestle against their own aggressiveness here externalized in the Amalekites. The continuing enmity between Israel and Amalek symbolizes the eternal struggle between the forces of the id and the demands of the superego.

The role played by Moses in the battle of Rephidim completes the symbolism. "And Moses said unto Joshua: 'Choose us out men, and go out, fight with Amalek; tomorrow I will stand on the top of the hill with the rod of God in my hand.' So Joshua did as Moses had said to him, and fought with Amalek; and Moses, Aaron, and Hur went up to the top of the hill. And it came to pass, when Moses held up his hand, that Israel prevailed; and when he let down his hand, Amalek prevailed. But Moses' hands were heavy; and they took a stone, and put it under him, and he sat thereon; and Aaron and Hur stayed up his hands, the one on the one side, and the other on the other side; and his hands were steady until the going down of the sun. And Joshua discomfited Amalek and his people with the edge of the sword" (17:9–13).

The Children of Israel, whose rebelliousness not long before had aroused in their leader a fear for his very life, now looked up to this figure outlined against the sky, his two hands raised heavenward. He was in his own person *the banner of the Lord* (17:15), inspiring his people in this, their first test of strength in battle. They fought throughout the day, finally defeating their ruthless and experienced foes. That Moses was only human, that he was not God Himself, is expressed by his limited endurance. He had to be assisted by Aaron and Hur. This is a moving image of Moses, the symbol of both his spiritual leadership and his basic human dependency on others.

The episode is different also in that the Children of Israel take an active part in their own behalf. They transfer their conflict with Moses to a struggle in which they join with him against a common foe. Symbolically, the situation can be understood as an externalization of psychic forces—the ego, represented by the people, actively struggle with the aggressive forces of the id (Amalek), while gaining strength and resolution in looking upward at the encouragement given by the superego (Moses), who himself appeals to a higher superego.

The significance of this event is emphasized in the closing verses of this chapter. "And the Lord said unto Moses: 'Write this for a memorial in the book, and rehearse it in the ears of Joshua: for I will utterly blot out the remembrance of Amalek from under heaven.' And Moses built an altar, and called the name of it Adonai-nissi [*the Lord is my banner*]. And He said: 'The hand upon the throne of the Lord: the Lord will have war with Amalek from generation to generation" (17:14–16).

The strange expression in the above quotation is left grammatically incomplete as though suspended in midair. Evidently Amalek is that hand against the throne of the Ruler, a threat to God's purpose for Israel. The aggression that fights against spirituality is the force with which Israel must continue to do battle *from generation to generation* (Hertz 1936, 281; Zeligs 1974, chap. 2). Amalek symbolizes not only the forces in the external world that will strive continuously to defeat man's efforts to achieve a higher degree of spirituality, a mission that Israel had covenantally set for itself but also represents the destructive impulses from within that require a constant struggle to overcome. Thus, there will always be the *shadow of a hand* against the purity of the Throne. Perhaps the phrase in the biblical text is incomplete because the attainment of perfection in the nature of man can only be an ongoing effort but is never fully accomplished.

There is a seemingly contradictory note in the biblical text regarding Amalek. On the one hand, his memory is to be blotted out. At the same time; he is always to be remembered as the enemy to be hated and fought against (17:14–16). This contradiction is descriptive of the human condition. Man wishes to blot out his imperfections but can never fully succeed because of the very fact of his being human.

The image of Moses standing on a hilltop overlooking the battle of Rephidim is somehow reminiscent of the Moses of a later date, depicted in Deuteronomy 34, as he stands on a hill in Moab, overlooking the Promised Land after the final leave-taking from his people. Again it is they who would now take over the active role of the conquest of Canaan. At that time he is no longer within their vision. He must then serve as the internalized image of the collective superego of the group.

It is thus particularly fitting that the event of the battle of Rephidim should be "rehearsed in the ear of Joshua," who would now become the leader, and that it should be written as a "memorial in the book" (17:14).

The Covenant at Mount Sinai

The Birth of a People

 CHAPTER SIX

THE EXPERIENCE at Mount Sinai has remained an unforgettable event in the history of a people. The substance of what took place there, the nature of this remarkable contract between a people and its God, has been a subject of continuing interest and exploration, not only to biblical scholars and theologians, but to all for whom the Bible continues to exert its special kind of fascination.

Even for those whose education in this area has been limited to the Sunday-school story hour, the memory remains of the scene at Mount Sinai: smoke and fire issuing from the summit, the people huddled at its base, the earth quaking, while amidst thunder and lightning, the voice of the invisible God, invoked by Moses, proclaims the Ten Words.

There are no definitive answers to some of the controversial aspects of what really took place on that momentous occasion. That something of significance did occur, that the Children of Israel bound themselves in a covenant with their God, under the leadership of Moses, most scholars will agree. A tradition that has had such influence on Western culture for over three thousand years could hardly be without some basis in reality.

For a long time controversy over the geographic site of Mount Sinai was also widespread. However, archeological findings have confirmed in large part the basic correctness of the general route taken by the Children of Israel in their wanderings through the wilderness. Although a number of the exact sites of the various stopping places mentioned in the Bible are uncertain, Albright (1957) comments in this connection, "Many additional pieces of evidence for the substantial historicity of the account of the exodus and the wandering in the regions of Sinai, Midian, and Kadesh can easily be given thanks to our greatly increased knowledge of topography and archeology. We must content ourselves here with the assurance that there is no longer any room for the still dominant attitude of hypercriticism toward the early historical traditions of Israel" (p. 255). The traditional site of Mount Sinai in the south-central part of the peninsula is now accepted by many scholars.

The description of the locality by travelers and explorers corresponds well to the picturesque grandeur of Jebel Musa (Mount of Moses), a majestic peak rising over seven thousand feet above sea level. It forms the southeastern edge of an imposing mountain range that in its entirety is often referred to as Mount Sinai. Remarkably, another significant feature conforms to the biblical description. A wide plain, Er-Rahah (Palm of the Hand), descriptive of its flat, open area, slopes gently toward the mount. It is about one-and-a-quarter miles long and one-half mile broad, covering an area of about four hundred acres. Jebel Musa and the adjoining peaks gleam in the bright sunlight with the pink and reddish colors characteristic of syenitic granite.

Vivid reports of this sacred locality have been brought back, describing both its beauty and the favorable conditions that made it possible for a large number of people to remain in one place for almost a year. There is mention of "a fair abundance of perennial springs and streams" and in the adjoining valleys "enough herbage for the support of large flocks of goats and sheep" (Driver 1911, 183).

This part of the peninsula seems to be made up of both fertile areas and scenes of wildness, desolation, and grandeur. One writer says, "I have looked on scenery as strange, and on scenery more grand, but on scenery at once so strange and grand I have never looked and probably never shall again" (Goldman 1956, 103).

Our primary source of information about the events at Mount Sinai is, of course, the Bible itself. Exodus 19 begins, "In the third month after the children of Israel were gone forth out of the land of Egypt, the same day came they into the wilderness of Sinai. And when they were departed from Rephidim, and were come to the wilderness of Sinai, they encamped in the wilderness; and there Israel encamped before the mount" (1–2).*

Questions have been raised about the unusual sequence in these two verses. Logically, as Goldman points out, the statement should have reported the movement of the Children of Israel from Rephidim, where they were last stationed, to the new locality, Mount Sinai (Goldman 1956, 101). Instead, their arrival at the holy mount is stated first and the fact that they had set out from Rephidim follows. Moreover, the information that they reached Sinai and pitched their tents there is mentioned twice.

The amount of commentary and the variety of explanations that have been stimulated by even such minor details that the casual reader would hardly notice indicate the degree of interest and importance that every word of the text has had for biblical scholarship. Higher Biblical Criticism suggests that in the original document the order of the two verses was *doubtless* reversed or, in another opinion, represented a poorly edited composite (italics added) (Driver 1911, 168–69; Goldman 1956, 101).

Psychologically, the order of the verses is not hard to understand. First there is a triumphant announcement of the goal that has been reached. It is a topical sentence with the details following in the next verses. The words themselves are simple, almost matter-of-fact. Yet they have a lilting quality, the repetitiveness of a chant. There is an undercurrent of triumph, colored by a sense of the incredible having been achieved. Again they had made it, again they had reached their goal. But this time it was *arrival* rather than *departure*. It was the beginning of something rather than its successful conclusion. There was the breathlessness of anticipation, the apprehensiveness of the unknown. Having left Egypt in the middle of the first month and arrived at Mount Sinai on what was probably the first day of the third month, they had endured the hardships of the desert for six

---

*All biblical references in this chapter, unless otherwise noted, are to the book of Exodus.

weeks (Goldman 1956, 102). This was a comparatively short period of time, but in that new environment and way of life it must have seemed like the longest six weeks of their long sojourn in the wilderness. Could one have expected that such a moment of culmination, the journey from Egypt to Mount Sinai, would be stated in simple chronological sequence! Viewed in empathy with the probable feelings of Moses, the casualness of the reported arrival is belied by the verbal repetition.

It seems that the leader wasted no time in beginning his task. After the information that the people had encamped before the mountain, the text says, "And Moses went up unto God, and the Lord called unto him out of the mountain, saying: 'Thus shalt thou say to the house of Jacob, and tell the children of Israel: Ye have seen what I did unto the Egyptians, and how I bore you on eagle's wings, and brought you unto Myself. Now therefore, if ye will hearken unto My voice indeed, and keep My covenant, then ye shall be Mine own treasure from among all the peoples; for all the earth is Mine; and ye shall be unto Me a kingdom of priests, and a holy nation. These are the words which thou shalt speak unto the children of Israel.' And Moses came and called for the elders of the people, and set before them all these words which the Lord commanded him. And all the people answered together, and said: 'All that the Lord hath spoken we will do.' And Moses reported the words of the people unto the Lord" (19:3–8).

The immediate, positive response of the people to the words of Moses, even before they knew what the exact demands on them would be, shows their acceptance of the leader himself and their faith in him. It was he who had brought about their deliverance from Egypt and it was his guidance that sustained them through the hardships and dangers of their first six weeks in the wilderness. In spite of their "murmurings," the need for him and their belief in him as the powerful representative of God must have been very strong. That his presence was essential for their physical and spiritual survival must have been felt deeply and yet taken for granted, much as children do with parents.

The event of the covenant at Mount Sinai was a moment in time to which Moses had been directing the whole of his energies. All that preceded was but prologue to this climax. His personality was one of great responsiveness to the challenges of life, especially where these involved his people and his God. The first communication at Mount Sinai between the people and God, with Moses as intermediary, is already the statement of a covenant. But it could hardly be expected that this mission was completed. As a psychological necessity, something much more prolonged and dramatic could be anticipated.

This first exchange, God's expression of how He cared for Israel, the beautiful metaphor of the eagle's wings, is like the prelude to a musical composition. It conveys in profoundly moving and eloquent words, God's love for the people whom He thus chooses for special responsibility and privilege. The figure of speech portrays the care of the mother eagle for the young fledglings whom she will protectively carry on her back as a preparation for the time when they are strong enough to use their own wings. Although Moses supposedly lacks eloquence himself, it is through the words attributed to God that the verbal power of the man himself comes through, set free from its inhibitions through closer identification with the Deity. On whatever mystical terms God is understood, in the biblical terminology He speaks to man in language that is expressive of man himself. Thus it is *Moses* who conveys the moving message to the people even though it is portrayed in the words of God.

The leader now plays the role of intermediary between God and the Children of Israel in a new setting, an actual geographic locality especially associated with the presence of the Deity. Moses serves as messenger-prophet in a more literal sense, moving between God and the people. This situation must have placed unusual stress on him. Some of the minor inconsistencies in the text at this point may have been a consequence of the leader's state of mind, in terms of the frame of reference presented here.

One of these discrepancies involves the important communication (quoted above) that God directs Moses to bring to the Children of Israel. Yet the text tells us that this message is given to the *elders*, whom Moses evidently summons for this purpose (19:3). However, the response is made by *all the people*, who answered together and said, "All that the Lord hath spoken we will do" (19:8).

A simple explanation could be that the elders brought the message to the people and then conveyed their answer to Moses. However, the narrative does not project this image. We clearly have a united group giving a response to Moses himself. Why then this contradictory wording in the text?

Interpretations acquire added conviction as the same patterns of behavior are repeated in different situations. We shall see as the narrative develops that Moses seems to have been in conflict about whom to include in this first, more personal contact with God. Should only the elders share in the great revelation or should all the people participate?

Ambivalence regarding the role of the elders themselves may also have been involved. As indicated in other situations, Moses may have been reluctant to include them in his special relationship with God. By involving all the people, Moses would retain his unique position as intermediary, both with the Deity and the group as a whole.

Let us return to the beginning of this initial communication. The very first words that God addresses to Moses are: "Thus shalt thou say to the house of Jacob and tell the children of Israel." (19:3). Are the words "house of Jacob" just a poetic expression, a form of parallelism common to the biblical style, or do they convey some special meaning here? At this significant moment in his life, Moses' own sense of identity may have been involved. Who was he, at this point, in relation both to the Children of Israel and to God? At the very time when Moses is about to realize his long-cherished dream of uniting his people with God, he is reminded that they are indeed the house of Jacob, not just his own creation. Their origins were not in Egypt, nor with their liberation by Moses, but with the *fathers* of Israel, among them Jacob, the progenitor after whose sons the twelve tribes were named. And it was toward the land of their fathers, where the earlier covenants with God were made, that their direction was now set. A sense of the continuity of history is thus maintained.

The term *house of Jacob* may have further significance here. Rabbinic scholars have pointed out that this expression has a feminine connotation (Cohen 1947, 455). Although the word *house* is a common biblical metaphor for *wife* (Ginzberg 1909–1938, 5:191), the expression *house of Jacob* is found nowhere else in the entire Pentateuch (Hertz 1936, 291). The occasion on which it is now used must have been especially meaningful. Israel was about to enter into a new relationship with God, as *His betrothed* (Cohen 1947, 455).

After the response of the people that they would do all that God asked of them, the narrative states, "And Moses reported the words of the people unto the Lord" (19:8). The implication is that Moses, having first descended the mountain to convey the message to the people, now climbed its slopes again to report the answer to God. Upon hearing this confirmation, God reveals what is about to take place next. "And the Lord said unto Moses: 'Lo, I come unto thee in a thick cloud, that the people may hear when I speak with thee, and may also believe thee for ever.'" Following this dramatic announcement, Moses repeats almost the exact words he had said to the Deity in the preceding verse: "And Moses told the words of the people unto the Lord" (19:9). At this point Moses was still on top of the mountain, and no further communication had taken place with the people that could again be reported to God. Moreover, why did Moses have to report "the words of the people" to an omniscient Deity? Was he, in a moment of confused identity, projecting his own human limitations onto God?

The declaration God makes that He would manifest His presence before all the people may have had a profound effect on Moses. He must have known all along, deep within him, that such a phenomenon was bound to take place, that his personal experience at the burning bush would have to be reenacted in some way to include the people as a whole so that they, too, would be chosen for their mission. For had not God said at that time, "when thou hast brought forth the people out of Egypt, ye shall serve God upon this mountain" (3:12). The purpose of that prophetic promise had been as a reassurance to Moses himself that God had indeed sent him to Pharaoh to deliver His people.

In declaring the purpose of His coming manifestation, God says, "Lo, I come to thee in a thick cloud, that the people may hear when I speak with thee, and may also believe thee forever." It seems that an important aspect of the event would be to inspire greater trust in Moses on the part of the people so that his position of authority as messenger of God should never again be doubted. Thus, God will come *unto Moses* and speak *with Moses* so that all the people may see and believe. This great occasion, involving the people of Israel as a whole was here, in part, to be diverted to the needs of the leader himself, as unconsciously revealed in the wording of the text.

What was the need on the part of Moses to have his authority confirmed in so spectacular a manner at this point in his leadership? The situation seemed to be a repetition of that earlier experience at the burning bush. And yet the people had shown their confidence in him by the prompt and spontaneous acclamation that they were ready to follow the commandments of God.

Old fears and anxieties tend to be reactivated. The Children of Israel were about to witness the Divine Presence and to establish contact with Him. What might be the effect on them of such an experience? Would their earthly leader, who had at times seemed to them the very embodiment of God, now be diminished in their sight? Was it therefore necessary for God to assuage the anxiety of His prophet and speak supportive words?

It is at this point that the statement made earlier is repeated: "And Moses told the words of the people unto the Lord." A suggested interpretation is that Moses, his sense of identity and self-confidence now strengthened, and in gratitude for the Deity's promise of His appearance before the people, repeats their declaration of obedience to His commands. In such moments he is not only the representative of Israel; *he is Israel.* Their voice is his voice, and he speaks in identification with them. Such subtle shifts in identification, which seem to take place at times of deep emotional involvement, are reflected in ambiguities of the text. Higher Biblical Criticism, however, explains the repetition as a misplaced variant of the earlier verse. (Driver 1911, 182–83).

The anticipation of the momentous occasion may have created anxiety for Moses from another source. For the people to encounter God was to subject them to possible danger, a factor always present within the biblical frame of reference when the desired but feared presence of God is made manifest. The apprehension the leader may have felt on this level finds clear expression in the words of God Himself. Moses is given careful instructions about preparing the people for the coming event. "And the Lord said unto Moses, 'Go unto the people, and sanctify them today and tomorrow, and let them wash their garments, and be ready against the third day; for the third day the Lord will come down in the sight of all the people upon mount Sinai. And thou shalt set bounds upon the people round about, saying: Take heed to yourselves, that ye go not up into the mount, or touch the border of it; whosoever toucheth the mount shall surely be put to death; no hand shall touch him, but he shall surely be stoned, or shot through; whether it be beast or man, it shall not live; when the ram's horn soundeth long, they shall come up to the mount'" (19:10–13).

Moses adds one more instruction for the people in addition to those given by God. "And Moses went down from the mount unto the people, and sanctified the people; and they washed their garments. And he said unto the people: 'Be prepared against the third day; *come not near a woman*'" (19:14–15) (italics added).

One must wonder why the leader is here more concerned with this further aspect of sanctification than God Himself is. At the theophany of the burning bush, Moses was told to remove his shoes because the place on which he was standing was holy ground (3:5). Rabbinic interpretation of this command supports the psychoanalytic view that removing one's shoes has the symbolic connotation of sexual renunciation (Ginzberg 1909–38, 2:311). So even in this detail, the path of his personal experience was the one along which he led his people. Moses was here more demanding regarding sexual abstinence than God Himself, perhaps an expression of the severity of his own superego.

The meeting of the holy and ordinary, the sacred and the profane, could have been experienced by Moses as an act of brinksmanship. It brought man dangerously close to Divinity, an experience characterized by both ecstasy and dread. The three days of sanctification the people were to undergo was to put them in a frame of mind suitable for the coming experience. Physical cleanliness, the purification of the body, was a necessary condition for a spiritual encounter.

The biblical concept of holiness has meanings that go beyond the connotations of good and evil. One aspect has to do with *separation*, the setting apart of that which pertains to God, the sacred, and that which has to do with the ordinary life of man, the profane. As Pedersen (1926), explains it: "The profane is equivalent to what is normal, what belongs to daily life. . . . The more sacred the sphere the more does the profanation acquire the character of a debasement, a violation" (3–4:271). Thus, it follows that an unjustified intrusion of the profane into sacred territory involves the breaking of a taboo and is dangerous.

On the positive side, acquiring holiness means drawing closer to God. Rudolf Otto describes the essence of holiness, beyond that which has moral implications, as a *numinous* quality, the word stemming from the Latin *numen*, which refers to supernatural divine power. He sees the religious experience as involving a numinous state of mind, which is evoked in man when he undergoes a mystical sense of closeness with Deity, the sense of a presence, which inspires the most profound emotions of awe and reverence, and of *dread*, in a special sense that is different from the ordinary meaning of that word. This numinous experience is associated with what he calls the *mysterium tremendum*, a sense of overwhelming emotions in the face of that which is at the same time near but unknowable, close but transcendent (Otto 1923, chaps. 2, 3).

Yet holiness in the biblical frame of reference is within the reach of every man. To the degree to which he obeys the commandments of God he sanctifies the ordinary and imbues life with spiritual qualities. Thus, two aspects of the concept of holiness are involved in understanding the happening at Mount Sinai. By entering into a covenant with God, by promising to obey His commandments, the Children of Israel undertook to become a kingdom of priests and a holy nation. By an unusual experience of closeness with His presence, the emotional conviction of His reality was to be established as a lasting memory.

The biblical description of what occurs on the appointed day is a dramatic one. The people are gathered at the foot of the mountain where boundary signs have been set beyond which they were not to move on penalty of death. "And it came to pass on the third day, when it was morning, that there were thunders and lightnings and a thick cloud upon the mount, and the voice of a horn exceeding loud; and all the people that were in the camp trembled. And Moses brought forth the people out of the camp to meet God; and they stood at the nether part of the mount. Now mount Sinai was altogether on smoke, because the Lord descended upon it in fire; and the smoke thereof ascended as the smoke of a furnace, and the whole mount quaked greatly. And when the voice of the horn waxed louder and louder, Moses spoke, and God answered him by a voice. And the Lord came down upon mount Sinai, to the top of the mount; and the Lord called Moses to the top of the mount; and Moses went up. And the Lord said unto Moses: 'Go down, charge the people, lest they break through unto the Lord to gaze, and many of them perish. And let the priests also, that come near to the Lord, sanctify themselves, lest the Lord break forth upon them.' And Moses said unto the Lord: 'The people cannot come up to mount Sinai; for thou didst charge us, saying: Set bounds about the mount, and sanctify it.' And the Lord said unto him: 'Go, get thee down, and thou shalt come up, thou and Aaron with thee; but let not the priests and the people break through to come up unto the Lord, lest He break forth upon them.' So Moses went down unto the people, and told them" (19:16–25).

The sequence of events described above is quite puzzling. We are told that God comes down to the top of the mountain and calls Moses up. He is then instructed to go down and warn the people not "to break through unto the Lord to gaze" or many of them would perish. Moses reminds God that the people had already been warned not to go beyond the boundaries that had been set for them at the foot of the mountain. Nevertheless, God repeats His command, saying that Moses should come back with Aaron but the priests and the people should not break through.

The repetitive and sometimes contradictory instructions from God suggests a projection emanating from Moses himself. The conflict barely indicated earlier about who is to share with him the closeness of his own experience with the Deity comes out more clearly now. Should it be Aaron only? Are not even the priests to be allowed to come closer? If not, why the need for further sanctification on their part? And since the priests were already at the foot of the mount with all the people, what further steps to sanctify themselves could they take?

The basis of intrapsychic conflict is the existence of opposing wishes. Moses evidently did want others to share with him more fully the nature of his own experience with the Deity; that sharing was indeed the whole purpose of the Sinai event. But there must also have been a question in his mind, a doubt stemming in part from his own ambivalence, concerning who among his followers were qualified for a closer degree of intimacy. By making the wrong choices might he be exposing them to a dangerous proximity to the Holy One? Even the authorized bringing together of the holy and the nonholy involved the taking of risks. An error in the process could result in tragedy, as God himself repeatedly warned. If an offender should, even inadvertently, break through, he must not be touched but should be annihilated at a distance, either by being stoned or shot through, presumably with an arrow. Otherwise the contamination would be spread by contact with the illegitimately acquired holiness of the one who had thus sinned. The nature of holiness, as seen here, is a condition of both great privilege and great danger. Only those who are truly worthy and selected by God for this purpose can endure this special state of being which brings them close to the Deity.

The atmosphere in which the Ten Commandments was proclaimed was thus charged with dread and uncertainty. In such a setting elements of confusion and ambiguity are not surprising. These aspects in the narrative may be expressive of what was going on in the mind and heart of Moses himself at this crucial moment. For by what neat and structured process does one introduce a whole people to its God? There had been no precedent for such an event. The only experience that had some degree of similarity was his personal theophany at the burning bush.

The first communication between God and Moses before the assembled people, a group trembling with awe and apprehension in the dawning hour of morning, is described as follows: "And when the voice of the horn waxed louder and louder, Moses spoke and God answered him with a voice" (19:19).

We do not know the nature of this "voice" nor the words that Moses uttered, but it was he who initiated the communication—*Moses spoke*. It hardly seems possible, at this point, that the voice of Moses himself could be heard by the people in that tumultuous setting, amidst the thunder and lightning, the quaking of the earth and the sounding of the horn. The astonishing statement that God descended on Mount Sinai is mentioned twice (19:18, 20). Surprisingly, He now called Moses to come up. So Moses ascends the mount.

Let us assume that in this latter detail the reverse was true: that it was *Moses* himself who felt an imperative need at this crucial moment to consult God once more. When all seemed to be in a state of readiness for the divine revelation, it could have happened that Moses himself was seized with overwhelming feelings of anxiety. The situation may have been one of intolerable tension for him. On the one hand, he was answerable to the people for a divine manifestation. But could he be sure that he had read God's purpose and intent correctly? If not, and the confrontation did not take place, his authority in the eyes of the people would be badly shaken and the chief purpose of his mission endangered. At the same time, Moses would have to answer to God for the appropriate behavior of the people on this auspicious occasion of the meeting between them and the Holy One. Had the leader given the proper instructions to his people? Did they understand? Would they obey?

At this point, the impulse may have been to return to God for further instruction and reassurance. Moses calls to the Deity and then retreats to Him as an escape from a state of great tension stemming from his own self-doubt. As a further defense against awareness of these disturbing feelings, he projects the call as coming from God. Was it not more likely Moses himself who feared that the people might indeed break through against his orders and attempt to climb up the slope? If so, tragedy could result. Such apprehension on the part of the leader would reinforce the need of attributing to God the responsibility for repeating the prohibition.

The other aspect of his problem was *who could or should* share in the great privilege of coming closer to God and be witnesses for the people of God's presence among them? The Deity is also concerned with this problem. "And the Lord said unto him: Go, get thee down, and thou shalt come up, thou and Aaron with thee; but let not the priests and the people break through to come up unto the Lord, lest He break forth upon them.' So Moses went down unto the people and told them" (19:24–25).

In his dilemma, Moses falls back on the supportive figure of Aaron. Even the priests are to be excluded. The priests at this point in time, before the investiture of Aaron, may still have represented the first-born sons of the families rather than the tribe of Levi as a whole (Cohen 1947, 400). One wonders if Moses still had a special competitive feeling in relation to first-born sons. But even as far as Aaron is concerned, it is not stated at any subsequent time that the two brothers actually went up alone to the top of the mount. The negative aspects of the ambivalence thus win out in the end.

Moses delivers the message of warning to the people at the foot of the mount and is there with them when the Ten Commandments are proclaimed, beginning: "And God spoke all these words, saying: 'I am the Lord thy God, who brought thee out of the land of Egypt, out of the house of bondage'" (20:1–2).

In spite of the vivid details describing the scene, it is difficult to visualize what actually happened. There have been efforts at rational explanations regarding the spectacular phenomena manifested around Mount Sinai. Were the people witnessing a volcanic eruption? It has been determined that there are no volcanoes in that area, present or extinct. However, there have been numerous reports of violent thunderstorms in the area, whose reverberating crashes of sound echoing among the mountain peaks and flashes of lightning amid the darkness could indeed have been awe-inspiring to those accustomed to the flatness of the Egyptian delta. Some scholars view the description of those elemental forces as an expression of how the people themselves interpreted the scene before them, projecting onto its actual grandeur the added intensity of their excited fantasy. Throughout the biblical literature the elements of nature are utilized to express the moods of the people in regard to their feelings about God, Who manifests His power and presence through the natural phenomena He has created. As Pedersen explains it, "The dark cloud, the thunder and lightning, the trumpet-blast, the smoke, are all meant to express Yahweh's power over the world of nature" (Pedersen 1926, 3–4: 662).

If God could manifest His presence in a pillar of fire by night and a cloud by day, to accompany the Children of Israel through the wilderness, then the occasion at Mount Sinai called for a stronger, more vivid expression of that presence. How else could an invisible God appear to them except through the aspects of nature in her various moods! As another scholar observed, "The description given here of Jehovah's descent upon Sinai finds a parallel in many rhetorical passages of the Psalms and Prophets, and is doubtless to be explained similarly . . . it seems reasonable to regard the narratives recounting the delivery of the Law at Sinai as a dramatic picture, the details of which are not to be pressed. . . . Yet it is highly probable that in the locality where the events are placed, there really occurred natural phenomena which are reflected in the narrative. The literal truth was that God spoke to the heart of Moses; the poetic truth was that He spoke in thunder and lightning from the crest of Sinai" (Driver 1911, 177).

These attempts at rational explanations do not exclude the likelihood that something of significance did occur at Mount Sinai in which the people as a whole participated. As has been frequently pointed out, the tradition is too deeply rooted and has affected the history and destiny of Hebraic life too profoundly not to have a basis in reality.

There has been a certain discomfiture among scholars through the centuries at the contrast between the tumultuous setting in which the Ten Commandments were received and the quietness and solitude that must indeed have been the birthplace where this incomparable set of statutes was first brought into being by Moses, in hours of meditation and communing with the God he knew and loved. Martin Buber (1936) describes the dilemma in his own inimitable way:

> When those who have grown up in the atmosphere of the Bible think of the 'revelation upon Sinai' they immediately see once again that image which overwhelmed and delighted them in their childhood: 'the mountain burning with fire up to the heart of the heavens, darkness, cloud and lowering mist' (Deut. 4:11). We the late-born, oppressed as we are by the merciless problem of Truth, feel in our own minds a singular belated echoing of the protest which found its expression in the story of the Revelation to Elijah at Sinai (Kings I, 29:11ff.). The voice comes not out of the storm, not out of the fury and the fire, but in 'a small whisper'.

Interestingly, the rabbis of the Talmud were also discomfited by the spectacular setting in which the Ten Words were ostensibly delivered to the world. Although not disputing what they understood as the literal meaning of the narrative, they intuitively perceived that silence would have been a more comprehensible setting for that great event. In their discussions, fantasy often played a role. Thus, in contrast to the impressive display of mighty forces, they pictured another kind of background for this great happening. They imagined that it took place in an atmosphere of utter silence and was heard not only by Israel but by all the inhabitants of the earth. Hertz (1936) describes their fantasy: "As the Divine Commandments rang out from Sinai's height, no bird sang, no ox lowed, the ocean did not roar, and no creature stirred; all Nature was rapt in breathless silence at the sound of the Divine Voice asserting the supremacy of Conscience and Right in the Universe" (p. 400).

My own impression is that there may be a connection between those seemingly contradictory associations of sound and silence, between the loud reverberations of natural forces and the intervening periods of quiet. There must have come a time when the thunder ceased, when the lightning no longer flashed, when not even the ram's horn was heard. And in the ensuing silence, the quality of which was all the more dramatic because of the contrast with what had preceded, an absence of sound would have been almost palpably experienced by the hushed and trembling people as the eastern roseate light spread out in the areas beyond the heavy clouds still covering the mountain peak. Was it then that a voice rang out, "And God spoke all these words, saying: I am the Lord thy God"?

This time we are told that *God spoke*. Shortly before, as described above, *Moses spoke and God answered him by a voice* (20:1–3). As indicated, we do not know the nature of this voice, but it now uttered words in the language of men. By describing what was heard as *a voice*, the sense of mystery that appropriately belongs to this experience is retained. Mystery and a feeling of the incomprehensible are the very essence of a theophany. We cannot fully penetrate beyond that veil. The narrative makes it clear that the people experienced what they heard as the voice of God. And it is *what they thought and what they experienced* with which the biblical narrative is chiefly concerned. *People* are at the heart of the biblical story and it is *their perceptions and beliefs* about the nature of God that the narrative reflects.

The concept of the voice of God speaking through a prophet is not uncommon, although within the biblical frame of reference the prophet usually maintains his own sense of identity. The message is mediated through him as a person. However, the situation at Mount Sinai, one of such special significance for Moses personally, may have evoked in him a trancelike state, generally familiar in the field of religious phenomena. He could have delivered the Ten Words in a voice unfamiliar to the prophet himself and experienced both by him and the people as coming directly from God.

Moreover, Moses could not have forgotten that it was also in the silence of this same wilderness that he himself heard for the first time a voice calling, "Moses, Moses." And the voice said, "I am the God of thy father." It is from *the father* that the development of the superego, the voice of conscience, receives its main impetus. Psychoanalytically, the voice Moses heard then was the externalization of his own conscience, having its roots in the father. And now, in the extraordinary scene of the group experience, the conscience of a whole people is audibly evoked and recorded for all time in a covenant with the Father-God.

The people had spent the past three days in preparation for this event, cleansing themselves in body and spirit. Contrasts of silence and loud noise must have played a role from the beginning in this experience. It was in the silence of early dawn, first broken by the shattering sound of the horn that they had been summoned to the foot of the mount. "And it came to pass on the third day, when it was morning, that there were thunders and lightnings and a thick cloud upon the mount, and the voice of a horn exceeding loud; and all the people that were in the camp trembled. And Moses brought forth the people out of the camp to meet God; and they stood at the nether part of the mount" (19:16–17). In contrast to the sights and sounds around them, the frightened multitude must have stood in hushed silence, huddled together in the early cold and mist of that mountain air. Their eyes must have focused on the mountaintop, where a developing sunrise may have intermittently lighted up the summit of Jebul Musa, turning the ruddy granite into a fiery glow that contrasted with the morning clouds. To a people coming from the lowlands of Egypt, such a scene could indeed have left them struck with wonder and awe.

What the people were expecting to see would have some connection with what they perceived. The loud sounds of the ram's horn, or shofar, a signal of some momentous event about to take place, though not unfamiliar to them in other situations, still must have retained its power of evoking foreboding and alarm. Its exciting effects could unconsciously have been perceived as an externalization of their own rapidly beating hearts. Such emotions are greatly increased through mass communication, creating a kind of hypnotic group response. In the ensuing silence the voice of Moses himself would probably be carried to the receptive ears of the people, as "Moses spoke, and God answered him with a voice" (19:19).

This delineation, aimed at an empathic view of what might have taken place, is not an attempt to reduce this memorable scene to the level of a rational explanation. Biblical criticism in recent times has tended to give up such efforts, considering these phenomena as being beyond the bounds of what can be determined with certainty. But a psychological approach requires that the stimuli that may have influenced perceptions should receive recognition.

It was psychologically appropriate and necessary that the religious feelings of the people as a whole should be aroused, that as a group they should be initiated into a closer and more meaningful relationship with God, that they should stand on the edge of a great mystery and sense the Awful Presence of the Deity in the original meaning of those words.

That the point of tolerance had been reached, that the experience had truly penetrated into their minds and hearts, is made clear in what followed the pronouncement of the Ten Words. "And all the people perceived the thunderings and the lightnings, and the voice of the horn, and the mountain smoking; and when the people saw it, they trembled, and stood afar off. And they said unto Moses: 'Speak thou with us, and we will hear; but let not God speak with us, lest we die.' And Moses said unto the people: 'Fear not; for God is come to prove you, and that His fear may be before you, that ye sin not.' And the people stood afar off; but Moses drew near unto the thick darkness where God was" (20:15–18).

Now the communication is resumed between God and Moses. "And the Lord said unto Moses: Thus thou shalt say unto the children of Israel: Ye yourselves have seen that I have talked with you from heaven" (20:19). Having thus established His presence and authority, and moreover, His universality as One who spoke not only from Sinai but from heaven (Kaufmann 1960, 71), God now delivers to Moses a lengthy code of laws.

Several chapters are devoted to these statutes and commandments, which are known as the Book of the Covenant (20:19–23:33). They are concerned with matters both of religious ritual and situations involving moral and social behavior within a framework of civil and criminal law.

The biblical narrative does not give any details regarding the public reading of these laws except to say, "And Moses came and told the people all the words of the Lord, and all the ordinances; and all the people answered with one voice, and said: 'All the words which the Lord hath spoken will we do'" (24:3).

Following the affirmative response of the people, the ritual of the blood sacrifice is carried out. In a fashion that seems quite casual and taken for granted, we are told that Moses made a written record of the laws that had first been presented orally to the people. "And Moses wrote all the words of the Lord, and rose up early in the morning, and builded an altar under the mount, and twelve pillars, according to the twelve tribes of Israel. And he sent the young men of the children of Israel, who offered burnt-offerings, and sacrificed peace-offerings of oxen unto the Lord. And Moses took the blood, and sprinkled it on the people, and said: 'Behold the blood of the covenant, which the Lord hath made with you in agreement with all these words'" (24:4–8).

There is a confusing element in terms of the time sequence. Surely Moses did not write down all these laws during the one night and then rise up *early in the morning* and build the altar. It seems that details that are unimportant to the main concept are thus assumed to be understood without the need for verbalization.

The ritual as described above symbolizes the ratification of the covenant between the Children of Israel and God. Moses himself performs the priestly function. Israel and God are thus symbolically united by the sacrificial blood being sprinkled, first on the altar and then on the people.

While presented inauspiciously in the narrative, this aspect of the covenant rites has a good deal of significance. Such ceremonials, though varying in pattern, are characteristic of the ancient Orient, especially among Semitic peoples (Buber 1936, 115). Perhaps for this very reason it was assumed that a lengthy explanation of this part of the ritual was not necessary for recorded history.

The concept of covenant plays a basic role in the development of the Hebraic religion, as many scholars have noted. It involves a relationship freely entered into by both parties, a people and its God, expressing not only agreement regarding the acceptance of specific commandments on the part of the people but a total commitment to a certain way of life, dominated by moral and spiritual values. At Sinai the Children of Israel were not only *chosen* but exercised the right to choose.

There is a unique quality to the idea that morality is a covenant between God and man (Kaufmann 1960, 328). Psychoanalytically, this can be understood as an agreement between the ego and superego within the individual psyche. Obedience meant a state of psychic harmony; disobedience brought discomfort and suffering. Another aspect of uniqueness is the involvement of the group as a whole. Thus, the relationship of the individual to the group, under the aegis of a *collective superego*, marks a further step in this development.

There is a concluding episode to the covenant of Sinai that is presented almost as an afterthought and in a somewhat confusing manner. Actually, it is a significant part of the sacrificial ritual, involving an idealized version of the communal meal that traditionally followed certain types of covenantal rites among many peoples.

Even before the blood ceremonial at the altar takes place, God gives instructions concerning the event that is to follow. "And unto Moses He said: 'Come up unto the Lord, thou, and Aaron, Nadab, and Abihu, and seventy of the elders of Israel; and worship ye afar off; and Moses alone shall come near unto the Lord; but they shall not come near; neither shall the people go up with him'" (24:1–2).

Noticeable in the above are the elements of selectivity and exclusiveness. *All* the people had participated in what had gone before, the main events of the Sinai experience at the foot of the mount. A warning had already been issued several times that no one, on pain of death, was to go beyond the set boundaries. Now the conditions were to be somewhat relaxed and a special group was to be permitted to move farther up the mount. But although these chosen ones are invited to "come up unto the Lord," thereby implying closeness, they are then instructed "worship ye afar off", suggesting distance. Moreover, beyond the designated point, only Moses himself was to go on to the summit.

The wording of the text may be expressive of an old ambivalence within the leader himself, the wish both to share and not to share his special relationship with God. Further indicative of this conflict is the manner in which God addresses Moses while giving instructions relating to this event. First, the Deity speaks to him in the second person, saying, "Come up unto the Lord, thou and Aaron, Nadab, and Abihu, and the seventy elders of Israel." The text then abruptly changes to the third person as God continues, "and Moses alone shall come near unto the Lord; but they shall not come near."

Considered on the basis of how Moses himself may have felt, it might have been too blatant in terms of his own self-awareness had he heard God say, "And *you alone* shall come near unto the Lord." The third person here may have been used as a retreat on the part of the leader from too clear a confrontation with his own narcissism.

This entire episode has a particularly mystical quality. It involves an anthropomorphic view of the Deity to an unusual degree. "Then went up Moses, and Aaron, Nadab, and Abihu, and seventy of the elders of Israel; and they saw the God of Israel; and there was under His feet the like of the very heaven for clearness. And upon the nobles of the children of Israel He laid not His hand; and they beheld God, and did eat and drink" (24:9–11).

It is conceivable that this phenomenon may have been experienced by the group in a state of altered consciousness, understandable in those circumstances (Hertz 1936, 322). Buber (1936) describes what he thinks took place. He says of the elders and their vision of God: "They have presumably wandered through clinging, hanging mists before dawn; and at the very moment they reach their goal, the swaying darkness tears asunder (as I myself happened to have witnessed once) and dissolves except for one cloud already transparent with the hue of the still unrisen sun. The sapphire proximity of the heavens overwhelm the aged shepherds of the Delta, who have never before tasted, who have never been given the slightest idea, of what is shown in the play of early light over the summit of the mountains. And in seeing that which radiates from Him, they see Him" (pp. 116–18) (9).

The Hebrew word for *beheld (hazah)* is frequently used in the biblical literature of a prophet seeing a vision (Driver 1911, 254). Actually, the only specific detail of the appearance of God was in the statement that "there was under His feet the like of a paved work of sapphire stone and the like of the very heaven for clearness" (24:10) (Buber 1936). As Pedersen (1926) explains, even the more customary Hebrew word, *to see (ra-a)*, involves more than the visual sense, including a more total perception of all the senses (1–2: p. 100). And as Buber (1936) states, "Visions are subject to optical laws of their own" (pp. 116–18).

Traditionally, the offering of the sacrifice and the communal feast belong together, having an inherent unity that goes back to the totem meal of prehistoric times, as analyzed by Freud in *Totem and Taboo* (1912). At Sinai, the two parts are separated both in locality and by an interval of time. A psychological distance is thus suggested. The more customary sacrificial meal here turns into a *celestial* feast during which those involved *saw the God of Israel*. The visual incorporation of the Deity thus takes priority over the oral incorporation of the sacrificial animal, indicating a greater distance from the instinctual impulses, a higher degree of sublimation. The text says, "they beheld God, and did eat and drink," but no mention is made of any material substances that were consumed.

The statement "And upon the nobles of the children of Israel He laid not His hand" expresses a feeling of wonderment at the unexpected happening. They had dared to come closer to God and were not harmed. It was a spiritual achievement made possible through the leadership of Moses. It was a moment of harmony between ego and superego, on a level of group participation.

But even throughout this reaching, both literally and figuratively, for a higher concept of God, the elements of human struggle reveal themselves, especially as viewed in the personality of the leader. Moses is instructed by God, as noted above, that even this highly selected group is to remain at a distance. Moses alone could approach closer to God. Thus, he leaves his companions, accompanied only by Joshua. But the latter too is left behind as "Moses went up into the mount and the clouds covered the mount."

Joshua is the first to communicate with him again when the leader is on his way back, so it is assumed by critics that the younger man awaited him somewhere on the mountain slope

(32:17). However, it is realistically hard to think of him as remaining alone in that isolated area during the long period of the *forty days* that the leader was absent. One can only assume that this detail was not important to the narrative. From the viewpoint of the hero, Joshua was where Moses had left him. It seems the former knew nothing about what had happened among the people during the interval of Moses' absence (32:17). One consequence of this was to eliminate Joshua from the scene of the golden calf apostasy and thus free him from the responsibility and guilt in that tragic affair.

One must wonder why it was Joshua who accompanied Moses partway up the slope toward the summit even though earlier it had been indicated that Aaron was to come up with Moses (19:24). Perhaps, unconsciously, Joshua was less threatening as a rival sibling for God's love. Another reason may have been a more realistic one. Aaron was to be left behind to serve as an authority figure, a substitute for Moses himself. The concern of Moses for his people is expressed in the instructions he gives before leaving. "And unto the elders he said, 'Tarry ye here for us, until we come back unto you; and behold, Aaron and Hur are with you; whosoever hath a cause, let him come unto them'" (24:14).

The statement that Moses went up into the mount is made three times, two of them preparatory to the occasion when he finally remained there forty days and forty nights. This repetition must indicate its importance for the leader. The first time the expression is used occurs immediately after the elders have their vision of God. "And the Lord said unto Moses, 'Come up to Me into the mount, and be there. And I will give thee the tables of stone, and the laws and the commandments, which I have written, that thou mayest teach them'" (24:12). Moses then separates himself from the elders, but ostensibly still accompanied by Joshua. The second separation was from the latter, about whom we no longer hear. We are told, "And Moses went up into the mount, and the cloud covered the mount" (24:15).

Even after he is alone, it seems that Moses needs more time to prepare for this particular theophany. Perhaps he must learn to tolerate the experience of aloneness before facing the proximity of the Deity for such a long period. The text says, "And the glory of the Lord abode upon mount Sinai, and the cloud covered it six days; and the seventh day He called unto Moses out of the midst of the cloud" (24:16).

The perspective now changes as the description moves briefly from the top of the mount to the people at its foot. "And the appearance of the glory of the Lord was like devouring fire on top of the mount in the eyes of the children of Israel. And Moses entered into the midst of the cloud, and *went up into the mount*; and Moses was in the mount forty days and forty nights" (24:16–18) (italics added).

This shifting of scenes is significant of the two aspects from which this episode is presented, the viewpoint of Moses and that of the group. The leader separates himself, as if with difficulty, from his human companions and, by stages, moves closer to God. The Deity also is seen from two perspectives. Just a short time before, He had been experienced by the elders in a setting of unusual intimacy. Now He is beheld by the people as a distant and dreaded Being Who manifests Himself in a fiery cloud on the top of the mountain.

There must have been a significant association in the mind of Moses between his personal experience at the theophany of the burning bush and the later event, when he brought his people to Sinai. It was the coming together of two basic aspects of his own being, the realization of what must indeed have seemed to him like the *impossible dream*. On a symbolic level, he was returning *wandering children* to the Father, as he himself returned to Him at the burning bush. The role of intermediary must have evoked profound and deeply moving emotions in this great leader. His movements up and down the mountain slope may have been a symbolic expression of this role of reunification, the feeling that he was bringing together two parts of himself that at some earlier period had been torn asunder.

In the effort to achieve unity between his people and his God, Moses may have been trying, unconsciously, to bring about a lost harmony within himself, to undo the destructive effects of a long separation when, as a youth, he had yielded to the influences of Egyptian culture and become temporarily Egyptianized, if one presumes to read between the lines of the biblical narrative (Reik 1959, 16). Then came the moment of reunion, the returning of his people to the God of their fathers, for they too had been separated from Him during the many years of enslavement. Such an occasion required an adequate outlet for the feelings associated with profound religious emotions—anxiety, dread, anticipation, and a renewed sense of dedication to the will of God. It required, above all, a strengthened awareness of his own sense of self in a new and no doubt frightening situation.

The people, however, needed less persuasion to enter into the covenant than Moses did at his personal theophany. They had already seen the workings of the Deity in their escape from Egypt and how He had brought them to Himself on eagle's wings. Perhaps also, like children, they were ready to accept the Father without a full awareness of what their own share in that fateful partnership was to be.

This wish to reunite what has been separated, to make reparation, is to set in motion a process that helps to bring about a sense of psychic wholeness and harmony. The familiar metaphor describing one of the relationships between Israel and God is that of the bride meeting the bridegroom. Such a fantasy would have found fulfillment in the ceremony at Mount Sinai and in the people's response, "All that the Lord hath spoken we will do." It was a beginning as well as a culmination. The well-known medieval biblical commentator, popularly known as Rashi, says in this connection, "The Divine Presence went forth to meet Israel as a bridegroom goes forth to meet his bride" (Cohen 1947, 455).

There are other analogies and contrasts between the personal and the group theophanies. In both, God speaks out of the midst of fire, the first time in the awesomeness of a solitary experience in the silence of the wilderness, the second before a multitude in the dramatic setting of thunder, lightning, a quaking earth, and smoking fire rising from the mountain top.

Scholarly opinion in the school of Higher Biblical Criticism varies regarding the role of Moses as lawgiver and questions the origins and sources of the various codes of law found in the Pentateuch. For a long time the tendency was to deny the Mosaic background of the Ten Commandments and the Book of the Covenant. The former, some believed, was on too high a level of morality and culture than could be attributed to the time of Moses and his relationship with a group of newly released slaves.

And since many of the commandments in the Book of the Covenant dealt with agricultural, settled life in Canaan, it did not seem likely that the Children of Israel would receive such statutes in the desert, where they led a wandering life.

However, the picture changed when archeological findings yielded a number of legal codes from other ancient peoples in the Near East, making comparative studies possible. These showed that the moral concepts of the Ten Commandments were not at all alien to neighboring peoples. Similar statutes were a part of the culture of even earlier times than the 13th century B.C. The unique element contributed by the Hebrews lay in the fact that these moral principles were tied to religion. Their laws were God's commandments, an expression of His will. They therefore assumed an importance and sanctity that vitally influenced the whole of their lives. Also, in general the Hebrew laws found throughout the Pentateuch are characterized by a greater degree of humaneness and concern for the individual than the codes of the surrounding nations.

For a long time it was claimed that the ancient Code of Hammurabi was the basic source of the Mosaic civil law. A more recent view is that both systems, rather than stemming one from the other, are independent codifications of ancient Semitic common law, especially that which prevailed among the Northwestern Semites (Hertz 1936, 406).

Even some scholars of Higher Biblical Criticism, however, now think that the Ten Commandments basically, if not in the exact wording found in Exodus, could have been the work of Moses. Also attributed to him was the nucleus of the Book of the Covenant (Driver 1911, 415). That Moses was a great lawgiver can hardly be disputed. Tradition points too strongly in that direction. Moreover, he was trying to prepare his people not for a life in the wilderness but for a settled existence in the Promised Land. That Moses used creatively the concepts of his time, making them a vital part of social living, embodied in a covenant with God, is an expression of his genius and leadership in integrating ethical and social principles with faith in what became for him and his people a *living God*.

That the people of Israel could take the giant step from the worship of nature and its deities, so prevalent in the surrounding civilizations, to the concept of One God, invisible and incorporeal, is the basis of what established their uniqueness. That they retained a sense of wonder and awe in the face of the forces of nature is understandable. But that they saw these forces as a manifestation of the power of God rather than His actual embodiment was the giant step referred to. And that it was *One God*, Who manifested Himself through His handiwork, rather than a multiplicity of deities, is psychologically significant of the higher degree of integration of their own superego development, in which Moses played a dominant role.

The invisibility of God made intimacy with Him more difficult. People longed for signs of His presence. The symbolism of the Bible frequently uses natural phenomena for the manifestation of God's presence and as the instruments for carrying out His will. To expect a totally abstract and spiritualized concept of God in the world of that time, and indeed in our own world, is to deny the realities of how the human mind functions. The anthropomorphic aspects of God, used metaphorically, were essential in making Him a meaningful reality. The mystery that surrounded Him involved both nearness and transcendence. The genius of Moses helped to integrate these two aspects of God into a unified Whole.

The Golden Calf

Regression, Guilt, and Reparation

 CHAPTER SEVEN

ONE OF THE most memorable happenings associated with the period at Mount Sinai is the episode of the golden calf. The Bible tells the story with its customary brevity, in which every word, however, carries a dramatic impact. "And when the people saw that Moses delayed to come down from the mount, the people gathered themselves together unto Aaron and said unto him: 'Up, make us a god who shall go before us; for as for this Moses, the man that brought us up out of the land of Egypt, we know not what is become of him.' And Aaron said unto them: 'Break off the golden rings, which are in the ears of your wives, of your sons, and of your daughters, and bring them unto me.' And all the people broke off the golden rings which were in their ears, and brought them unto Aaron. And he received it at their hands, and fashioned it with a graving tool, and made it a molten calf; and they said: 'This is thy god, O Israel, which brought thee up out of the land of Egypt.' And when Aaron saw this, he built an altar before it; and Aaron made proclamation, and said: 'Tomorrow shall be a feast to the Lord.' And they rose up early on the morrow, and offered burnt-offerings, and peace-offerings; and the people sat down to eat and drink, and rose up to make merry" (32:1–6).*

It is clear that the people missed the presence of Moses and became anxious at his prolonged absence. He had been away forty days and nights. Regardless of the exact measure of time this biblical expression may denote, it is a long period to be without a leader whose presence must indeed have been essential to their feelings of security in the unfamiliar and desolate grandeur of that mountain wilderness. Moses and the God to whom the Children of Israel had recently pledged loyalty and obedience seemed to have abandoned them. At the very moment when they had declared their allegiance, the leader disappeared into the cloud at the summit of the mount and they were left alone. At this particular time, their emotional dependency on him was probably increased because of the shared experiences associated with the Covenant rituals in which he had played so vital a role.

There is no indication that Moses had prepared the people for his lengthy absence. It may be that he did not know himself how long he would be away. His parting message had been to the elders who had accompanied him and Joshua partway up the slope of the mountain for a special celebration and feast. "And unto the elders he said: 'Tarry ye here for us, until we come back unto you; and behold, Aaron and Hur are with you; whosoever hath a cause, let him come near unto them.' And Moses went up into the mount, and the cloud covered the mount" (24:13–14).

Why did the people then not turn to Aaron and Hur and ask them to take over the leadership as their concern over the absence of Moses increased? To the Children of Israel, however, the vanished leader must have seemed more than a man and thus could not be replaced by a mere mortal. They demand of Aaron, "Up, make us a god who shall go before us; for as for this Moses, the man that brought us up out of the land of Egypt, we know not what is become of him." The reference to "this Moses" and the need to delineate him as "the man who brought us

---

*All biblical references in this chapter, unless otherwise noted, are to the book of Numbers.

up out of the land of Egypt" suggests a dimming of memory regarding him, as though it was already difficult to distinguish the man from the legend. Their feelings of abandonment can be compared to those of children at the prolonged absence of the parent, the special person for whom they long. Their anxiety must have been intermingled with rage. They act out these feelings by seeking to satisfy both their need of Moses and at the same time show their defiance of him by disobeying his basic commandment in regard to the making and the worshipping of idols. The choice of Aaron for this purpose gave it greater authority. He was in the place of Moses and their act of rebellion took on further significance through his cooperation. They were forcing the substitute parent to rebel with them.

The expression "Up, make us a god" may imply a rebuke for the passivity of Aaron and his failure to recognize their need and do something about it, thus forcing the initiative on them. And indeed, if Aaron had been more in touch with the feelings of the people, whose restlessness must have taken some time to develop and to reach the point of tension where they demanded action, he might have forestalled what happened. Had he shown more signs of leadership, he might have reassured the people about Moses and his imminent return. They actually invite this kind of reassurance by their statement that they don't know what has become of him.

But Aaron does not protest or argue with them. Perhaps he was intimidated by the temper of the crowd. His response is certainly not a heroic one. In this first opportunity for real leadership, Aaron fails completely. He instructs them to "break off the golden rings which are in the ears of your wives, of your sons, and of your daughters, and bring them unto me." The people do so. Aaron melts down the gold and shapes it into a calf. It is the people, however, not Aaron, who express what the image means for them. "And they said, 'This is thy god, O Israel, which brought thee up out of the land of Egypt.'" In the very process of naming the object as their god and leader, the two being synonymous here, there is a sharing both of loss and reparation, resulting in comfort for their bereavement and hope for the future (Bleich 1976). Their request to Aaron for "a god who shall go before us" is clearly associated with "the man that brought us forth out of the land of Egypt," the leader of whom they said, "we know not what is become of him." They wanted the person whom they had lost returned to them. It seems evident then that they hailed the golden calf as *a substitute for Moses himself* (10). The boundary lines between the identity of Moses and of God may have been somewhat fluid for them at this time. It was the man who had made manifest for his followers, in varying degrees of reality, the presence of the invisible, incorporeal God.

It is *after* the people have designated the meaning of the image for them that Aaron responds. "And when Aaron saw this, he built an altar before it; and Aaron made proclamation and said, 'Tomorrow shall be a feast to the Lord.'" It would be hard to determine from this response what the golden calf represented to Aaron himself at this point. Perhaps he was not sure. Perhaps his only purpose was to appease the people. Unconsciously, however, the words "and when Aaron saw this" may have had the intent of diminishing his role in taking the initiative about what the molten figure stood for. A protective attitude toward Aaron is evident many times in the biblical narrative and can be understood as the positive aspect of the ambivalence Moses felt toward his older brother. Announcing "a feast to the Lord," as Aaron did, does not necessarily equate the image with the Deity.

It is clear that the people are satisfied by the response of Aaron. "And they rose up early on the morrow, and offered burnt-offerings, and brought peace-offerings; and the people sat down to eat and to drink, and rose up to make merry." The biblical text itself gives no indication that an orgiastic revelry took place at this time, as some biblical commentators have assumed and artists have depicted. To eat and drink and make merry is characteristic of celebrations in general, biblical ones included. The words "and rose up to make merry" do not particularly suggest a sexual orgy, nor would the biblical account have spared us the details had the latter taken place. One need not conclude from this interpretation that a high code of morality prevented the people from acting out their emotions in more sexualized fashion. Rather, it points to the nature of the feelings that animated them. *The people behaved as though a depression had been lifted, giving way to a hypomanic reaction.* The lost object, in the form of the golden calf, had been restored to them. The separation between the people and their leader was symbolically overcome. Moreover, they had accomplished this feat through their own initiative and by the sacrifice of their precious possessions. The need that prompted such efforts must have been very real.

The ceremonials of burnt-offerings and peace-offerings that the people observed were very similar to those carried out before under the guidance of Moses during the covenantal rites. In repeating these rituals were they again being obedient to the leader? Were they trying to recapture the spirit of that earlier occasion? Was it part of the effort to make good the loss? No one can speak with certainty about the unconscious fantasies that motivated the people. But it well may be that this seeming act of apostasy had some positive aspects.

What determined the choice of a calf for this occasion is uncertain. Higher Biblical Criticism has attempted a number of explanations regarding the significance of the golden calf from various historical and anthropological viewpoints. Some have suggested that the image of a bull in the temple of Memphis, revered as the incarnation of Osiris, and one in Heliopolis that represented the sun-god may have influenced the choice. Others reject this idea. More recent theories look to native beliefs among the Semitic peoples themselves for the origin of bull symbolism (Driver 1911, 347–48; James 1950, 32; Kaufmann 1960, 13–14; Pedersen 1926, 644). Albright (1957), the noted biblical scholar and anthropologist, is very firm, however, in his assertion that the concept of images as representative of God was basically foreign to the Mosaic religion from its beginnings (pp. 265–66). Buber relates the episode to the calf images that Jereboam, king of the northern state, set up in the temples of Dan and Bethel. Buber (1936) sees the latter, as does Albright, serving only as pedestals of a throne on which the invisible Deity could manifest His presence (pp. 147–48).

The calf was commonly used among the Israelites for sacrificial purposes. Psychoanalytically, the animal can be understood as a substitute for the first-born son, who belonged to God in a special sense (Reik 1931, 27ff; Zeligs 1974, 55). Elevating the calf to a place of worship can imply the symbolic triumph of the son over the father. The ambivalent feelings of the people thus find expression in degrading the figure of the father while at the same time honoring him (Freud 1912; Reik 1919, 318–61) (11).

It was Aaron who produced the golden calf. His role in the performance of sacrifices must have been an active one even before the formal institution of the priesthood. He may have had a close sense of identification with the helpless victims whom he prepared for the altar. The calf could have represented an aspect of Aaron himself, in the portrayal of an unconscious fantasy that had both a masochistic element and a counterwish that opposed it.

Aaron did not dare to compete with Moses on a more mature level. Thus, he did not present a real threat to the leader so that, as we shall see, Moses could more readily forgive him. Aaron's feelings, both of a positive or negative nature, are rarely revealed in the biblical narrative. The repressed sense of rebellion finding expression in his production of the calf must have touched a responsive chord in the people. Perhaps he intuitively understood what would satisfy them.

The excuse Aaron later gave Moses for his seemingly inexplicable performance is clearly an effort at self-extenuation. He says, "and I cast it [the gold] into the fire and there came out this calf" (32:24). The implication that he was not fully responsible for what emerged from the fire must have had an element of truth. Aaron's unconscious played a role in determining the shape that came out from the molten mass.

Moses first learns of the wrongdoing of the people from God Himself. "And the Lord spoke unto Moses: 'Go, get thee down; for thy people, that thou broughtest up out of the land of Egypt, have dealt corruptly; they have turned quickly out of the way which I commanded them; they have made them a molten calf, and have worshipped it, and sacrificed unto it, and said: 'This is thy god, O Israel, which brought thee up out of the land of Egypt'" (32:7–8).

By the expression *thy people*, as commentators point out, God dissociates Himself from them, and He too refers to Moses as the one who had brought them out of Egypt. But His rejection of the people whom He had so recently taken as His own has an intensity of anger that is rare in its openly anthropomorphic expression. "And the Lord said unto Moses: 'I have seen this people, and behold, it is a stiffnecked people. Now therefore let Me alone, that My wrath may wax hot against them and that I may consume them; and I will make of thee a great nation'" (32:9–10). The phrase "let me alone" seems particularly meaningful, as though God anticipates that Moses will try to stop Him, which is, of course, what happens. "And Moses besought the Lord His God, and said: 'Lord, why doth Thy wrath wax hot against Thy people, that Thou has brought forth out of the land of Egypt with great power and with a mighty hand? Wherefore should the Egyptians speak, saying: For evil did He bring them forth, to slay them in the mountains, and to consume them from the face of the earth? Turn from Thy fierce wrath, and repent of this evil against Thy people. Remember Abraham, Isaac, and Israel, Thy servants, to whom Thou didst swear by Thine own self, and saidst unto them: I will multiply your seed as the stars of heaven, and all this land that I have spoken of will I give unto your seed, and they shall inherit it for ever.' And the Lord repented of the evil which He said He would do unto His people" (32:9–14).

Thus, Moses intercedes vigorously for the Children of Israel. His arguments are on a remarkably realistic level in contrast to the emotional words of the Deity. Viewed as the externalization of an intersystemic conflict within Moses himself, the reality-oriented ego is here trying to contend with the punitive superego. The argument basically was "What would other people think if God carried out His threat to annihilate Israel?" This destructive impulse could indeed be attributed to Moses himself and projected onto God, as part of the leader's defensive struggle.

The intercession of Moses with God at this point is often compared to that of Abraham on the occasion of the imminent destruction of the cities of Sodom and Gomorrah (Gen. 18:20–33). But psychodynamically, important differences exist. In the latter situation, the Patriarch bases his argument on a plea for justice. Not all the people in the doomed cities were wicked. "Shall not the Judge of all the world do justly?" It was an appeal seemingly on a superego level (Zeligs 1974, 24–25). The rationale of Moses was in a more practical vein, stemming from the ego. Moses had to restrain his own turbulent emotions by a plea to his sense of reality.

His intrapsychic battle seemed to be won as he descended the slope with the stone tables in his hands. However, the scene that confronted him as he neared the foot of the mount powerfully arouses again the feelings of hurt, betrayal, and anger. How could he give the Tables of the Testimony to the people making merry before the pedestal of the golden calf! Moses did the only thing it was humanly possible for him to do. He hurled the tables to the ground, breaking them upon the rocks.

Was there a moment of hesitation before Moses released his hold on that precious burden? Who can say what went on in the mind and heart of the leader in that agonizing split second of time?

Freud's contention in analyzing the awe-inspiring figure of Moses by Michelangelo, which so captivated the master of psychoanalysis, was that the moment depicted in the statue was one of arrested motion (Freud 1914, 4:257–87). Freud maintains that it is necessary to imagine a preliminary movement to the one captured in the marble. He sees Moses as restraining the impulse to destroy the tables which were slipping from under his arm. He depicts the leader as impulsively beginning to rise from a resting position on beholding the scene below. The right hand, which had been helping to support the tables, suddenly relaxed its grip, clutching instead at the heavy beard in which his fingers are entwined as though to express the vehemence of his emotions. At the same time, his left foot is poised as if ready to impel the huge frame to a rising position. But this action is interrupted by a backward move of the right hand as it retreats in order to press the falling tables more securely against his body, at the same time drawing the thick strands of hair from the left side of the beard toward the right. It is this instant of reversed motion, when Moses prevents the tables from falling, that Michelangelo immortalized in unchanging marble, according to Freud's interpretation.

Moses is thus portrayed as having controlled his anger for the sake of preserving the sacred tables. Freud suggests that Michelangelo here deviates from the biblical text because of his own inner motives. Interestingly, the conclusion Freud draws is that the text being confused and contradictory, Michelangelo portrays his own concept of Moses, one superior to the historical or traditional one. He suggests that the sculptor depicts Moses both as a man given to moments of strong anger and one whose compassion was greater than his wrath. *This is indeed the biblical Moses himself* when evaluated in the totality of his behavior (12, 13).

Returning to the text, we find that the next response of Moses after breaking the tables was also one of swift action. "And he took the calf which they had made, and burnt it with fire, and ground it to powder, and made the children of Israel drink of it" (32:20). This drama of oral retribution is contained within the one verse. There is no indication of how Moses succeeded in carrying out this mass punishment or what the reaction of the people was, physically or psychologically.

We are told more in Deuteronomy at the time when Moses rehearses before the people the events of their history at the close of the long period of the wilderness wanderings. "And I took your sin, the calf which ye had made, and burnt it with fire, and beat it in pieces, grinding it very small, until it was as fine as dust; and I cast the dust thereof into the brook that descended out of the mount" (9:21). Here no mention is made of forcing the people to drink the polluted water. Perhaps at this later period of his life, Moses preferred not to remind them openly of that severe punishment, if indeed it was successfully carried out, an aspect to be considered further.

After this penalty has ostensibly been imposed, Moses turns to Aaron, saying, "'What did this people unto thee, that thou hast brought this great sin upon them?' And Aaron said: 'Let not the anger of my lord wax hot; thou knowest the people that they are set on evil. So they said unto me: Make us a god which shall go before us; for as for this man Moses, the man that brought us up out of Egypt, we know not what is become of him'" (32:21–23).

After hearing Aaron repeat the details of how the episode had occurred, Moses again directs his anger at the people. A harsher punishment now follows. "And when Moses saw that the people were broken loose—for Aaron had let them loose for a derision among their enemies—then Moses stood in the gate of the camp, and said: 'Whoso is on the Lord's side, let him come unto me.' And all the sons of Levi gathered themselves together unto him. And he said unto them: 'Thus saith the Lord, the God of Israel: Put ye every man his sword upon his thigh, and go to and fro from gate to gate throughout the camp, and slay every man his brother, and every man his companion, and every man his neighbor.' And the sons of Levi did according to the word of Moses; and there fell of the people that day about three thousand men" (32:25–28).

There are thus two punishments, taking place in sequence, for the same offense, a puzzling situation. Some biblical scholars suggest that the above verses are not in their original context and that they describe a punishment for some other act of rebellion against God, not for the worship of the golden calf (Driver 1911, 354). But no suggestion is given about what that other misdeed might have been or why the material was put in this particular place.

It seems that something was omitted from the text that might have explained the relationship between the two penalties. We shall try to reconstruct the scene on the basis of the available evidence and see if the pieces fit together.

The excuse Moses gives for his second, even more drastic action, is that "the people had broken loose." The usual interpretation is that they had belittled the true God by following in the pagan practices of their neighbors. But a further meaning may be involved in the confusing text at this point. The words "And when Moses *saw* that the people were broken loose" suggests that they were *still* in the throes of their wild celebration. But it is hardly likely that the people would have continued their boisterous behavior in the very presence of Moses. More probably, as they beheld their angry leader hurling the stone tables to the ground and then striding into their midst to knock down the golden image, all merriment would have ceased with a sudden, shocked return to a sense of reality.

Another alternative is that a *further breaking loose was now taking place*. If so, what might have stimulated this renewed outbreak of rebellion? In postulating the relationship between the two penalties that were inflicted, the time element between them—a factor not mentioned in the text—needs to be considered.

The first punishment involved the process of melting the statue, allowing the metal to cool, reducing the mass to powder, and pouring it on the water, before forcing the people to drink. What were the latter doing all this time? Did they remain there and look on, with a kind of fearful fascination, not realizing what the ultimate command would be? We are not told. My own hypothesis is that a new rebellion may have occurred at this point. Disbelief and horror must have seized hold of the people and they could have refused to obey. A scene of wild disorder may have followed as the people tried to escape, perhaps rushing to the gates of the camp.

"When Moses saw that the people were broken loose," he resorted to the severe measure described above, so that order could be restored. He may have feared a loss of control over the people and experienced a sense of helplessness and terror about his own powers as the leader. Moses therefore felt a strong need to reestablish his authority. The consequences, however, were that the people suffered more for their disobedience to Moses than for the apostasy, although the latter was a sin against God Himself. This aspect may have increased the feelings of guilt within Moses for the severity of his treatment. His defensiveness comes out clearly in the need to blame Aaron, "for Aaron had let them loose for a derision among their enemies." Moses here attributes the slaughter of the people as stemming directly from their apostasy rather than their subsequent disobedience to himself, as interpreted in this study. The need to repress awareness of this too great personal involvement may have led to the omission of the necessary connections in the text.

Again, as in his earlier exhortations with the Deity, Moses is fearful about the impression made on the surrounding peoples. One must wonder what "enemies" were observing the scene in that desolate mountain area. Were there, perhaps, a few wandering nomads watching from a distance? If so, would Moses, in the midst of his people, have been aware of them? Anxiety of this kind is an expression of one's own insecurity. It is true that a basic motivation of the leader was to exalt the "Name of the Lord" and to prove his God's superiority over the deities of the idol worshippers. But the overreaction in this area points to an increased personal uneasiness in Moses and indicates further his narcissistic identification with the God of Israel at this time, in terms of his own self-image.

The relationship to Aaron, as revealed in the above episode, is one of characteristic ambivalence toward his brother, expressed in hidden ways. Its eruption at this point and the need to repress it may have added to the distress of the leader. Even his openly worded reproach is comparatively mild considering the anger, hurt, and disappointment that Moses must have felt as he listened to Aaron's sorry tale of what had happened.

It can be assumed that there was significance to the specific nature of the command Moses gives the Levites who had responded to his call. They were the kinsmen closest to Moses himself and with whom he was probably most closely identified. He instructs them to "slay every man his brother, and every man his companion, and every man his neighbor," relationships in a descending order of closeness. Was the command presented in this way for the purpose of urging them to do their duty regardless of personal feelings? No doubt it was. But the admonition can also be understood as having unconscious meaning for Moses himself. If the repressed anger against his own brother, a feeling he could not acknowledge even to himself, needed a further outlet, it could find expression by displacement to his followers.

In Deuteronomy, when time has softened the disappointment and anger, Moses is able to speak more freely about that earlier situation. He says, "Moreover, the Lord was very angry with Aaron to have destroyed him; and I prayed for Aaron also the same time" (9:20).

The interpretation that Moses was personally involved in the order he gave to the Levites is strengthened by the otherwise puzzling words he addresses to them after they have carried out the command. "And Moses said: 'Consecrate yourselves to-day to the Lord, for every man hath been against his son and against his brother; that He may also bestow upon you a blessing this day'" (32:29). The underlying thought in this rather elliptical statement seems to be that those who are ready to sacrifice even sons and brothers in the service of God are worthy of a special relationship with the Deity.

Moses may here be expressing something related to an unconscious fantasy of considerable importance in regard to his own personal life. His sense of self-sacrifice and devotion to God and to the people as a whole may have demanded that he forgo the full satisfactions of family relationships. Thus, we hear almost nothing about his own two sons, very little about his wife, and even less about his parents. It was only through the special intervention of God, as it were, that he has Aaron with him (14:14). The clear implication is that no sacrifice is greater in proving one's devotion to God than to deny one's own family.

The apostasy of the golden calf seems to have struck at the heart of the leader on a deeply personal level. Its consequences can be more fully understood as part of the larger picture in the unfolding saga that now takes place.

Guilt and the Fear of Separation

The need for reconciliation follows immediately upon the tragic events of the golden calf episode. The function of forgiveness too rests with God. In the theophany that follows Moses again intercedes for his people. "And Moses returned to the Lord and said: 'Oh, this people have sinned a great sin, and have made them a god of gold. Yet now, if Thou wilt forgive their sin—; and if not, blot me, I pray Thee, out of Thy book which Thou hast written'" (32:32).

The first part of the sentence is left uncompleted—"If Thou wilt forgive their sin"—the assumption being that all would then be well and nothing further need be said (Hertz 1936, 360). But if not, then Moses himself does not want to go on living, asking to be blotted out from what is clearly meant as the Book of Life. Earlier, God had stated that even if He destroyed the people, He would still build a great nation for Moses himself (32:10). But that kind of solution was not acceptable to the leader.

God responds to the desperate words of Moses in a matter-of-fact way, saying, "Whosoever hath sinned against Me, him will I blot out from My book." But the Deity, it seems, was still not entirely appeased, for He adds, "'Behold, Mine angel shall go before thee; nevertheless, in the day when I visit, I will visit their sin upon them.' And the Lord smote the people because they made the calf, which Aaron made" (32:33–35).

Although these two verses are unclear in certain respects, several significant meanings can be gathered from them. First God creates more distance between Himself and the people, ostensibly as a sign of His displeasure. Not He but an angel will now lead them. But when He does visit them, He will visit their sin upon them. Aaron's share in the wrongdoing is diminished, the implication being that he only carried out the will of the people, "who made the calf, which Aaron made." And indeed Aaron's life was spared.

God declares that He Himself will punish the people as though ignoring the severe penalties that Moses had already meted out. The sense of guilt in Moses is thus decreased. The people, in fact, deserved *more* punishment, a fate which was still to come. Immediately following is the statement that God indeed "smote the people" but no details about what actually happened are given. Commentators conclude that the punishment referred to must have been that which Moses had already imposed. The leader may here have retreated from the responsibility of what he had done. It was God and not he who had dealt so severely with the wrongdoers. Elements of time and sequence here give way to psychological needs involving guilt and responsibility, an understandable situation during an altered state of consciousness. At the same time, since it was actually Moses who "smote the people," there is an unconscious identification here with the power of the Deity.

Ambivalence on the part of God is shown throughout the dialogue. The journey must continue, the task must be accomplished, but the hurt and disappointment are still there, within both God and Moses.

That the episode of the golden calf is not so readily forgiven comes out in what follows immediately at the beginning of the next chapter. "And the Lord spoke unto Moses, 'Depart, go up hence, thou and the people that thou hast brought up out of the land of Egypt, unto the land of which I swore unto Abraham, to Isaac, and to Jacob, saying: Unto thy seed will I give it—and I will send an angel before thee; and I will drive out the Canaanite, the Amorite, and the Hittite, and the Perizzite, the Hivite, and the Jebusite—unto a land flowing with milk and honey; for I will not go up in the midst of thee; for thou art a stiffnecked

The Golden Calf 175

people; lest I consume thee on the way.' And when the people heard these evil tidings, they mourned; and no man did put on his ornaments. And the Lord said unto Moses: 'Say unto the children of Israel: Ye are a stiffnecked people; for if I go up into the midst of thee for one moment, I shall consume thee; therefore now put off thy ornaments from thee, that I may know what to do unto thee.' And the children of Israel stripped themselves of their ornaments from Mount Horeb onward" (33:1–6).

There are several repetitions and inconsistencies in the above verses. Twice the Children of Israel are referred to as a "stiffnecked people." Twice there is a reference to the removal of their ornaments (33:3–6). In verse 4, the people perform this act voluntarily, ostensibly in response to the "evil tidings" that God would no longer lead them as before. In the next verse God instructs Moses to tell the Children of Israel to remove their ornaments, "that I may know what to do unto them," as though the Deity might forget the wicked deed they had done and needed this sign of their wrongdoing as a reminder. The act thus becomes a punishment rather than a spontaneous expression of repentance.

Higher Biblical Criticism points to these contradictory elements as *incontrovertible proof* that two sources have been put together by a redactor and thus contain inconsistences (Driver 1911, 358). We shall consider a psychological interpretation in an effort to understand these confusing aspects.

In the verses quoted above, the words of the Deity addressed to Moses are interrupted to relate an action on the part of the Children of Israel. "And when the people heard these evil tidings, they mourned; and no man did put on his ornaments" (33:4). The question arises: How did the people hear of the evil tidings? At this point Moses was still in the midst of his theophany. In the verses preceding this break in continuity, the impression is given that Moses, as well as his people, is the object of the Deity's anger. The use of the pronouns *thee* and *thou* heightens this personalized effect. God speaks in terms of "thou and the people thou hast brought up out of the land of Egypt" and again, "I will not go up in the midst of thee: for thou art a stiffnecked people; lest I consume thee in the way." Moses is here addressed as though he, in person, was an integral part of the

Children of Israel and thus equally responsible for their wrongdoing. And in a sense, this is how Moses himself must have perceived the situation.

However, after the statement "And when the people heard these evil tidings, they mourned; and no man did put on his ornaments," the tone of the Deity changes. There seems to be a softening or relenting in His anger. God now clearly distinguishes between Moses as leader and the group itself. *"And the Lord said unto Moses*: '*Say unto the children of Israel*: Ye are a stiffnecked people; for if I go up into the midst of thee for one moment, I shall consume thee; therefore now put off thy ornaments from thee, that I may know what to do unto thee'" (italics added). Moses is here addressed in his own person, as the intermediary between the Deity and the Children of Israel.

Returning to the question of how the people heard the evil tidings and thus carried out their gesture of mourning and repentance, the following interpretation is suggested: As Moses listened to the words of displeasure from the Deity, seemingly directed at him in so personalized a fashion, he must have felt deeply involved, both as an individual and in behalf of the group. The leader may have experienced strong emotions of guilt and grief. In his identification with the people, it may have been Moses himself who, hearing the evil tidings directly from God, removed his own ornaments in a gesture of repentance and mourning. Unconsciously, he projected onto the people an act carried out in their behalf. Thus, in his fantasy, or even in an altered state of consciousness, it is *the people* who remove their ornaments.

As in the situation described earlier relating to Exodus 19:8–9, Moses responds *as if he were Israel*. In some mystical sense there were moments, usually in situations of strong emotion, when—in the psyche of Moses—he and his people seemed to become a single entity. This tendency to merge briefly, either with the people or with the Deity, was a characteristic in the personality of Moses that manifested itself even more profoundly later in his life, indeed to the very end. Israel, in the metaphor of an individual, the son of God (4:22), and the leader, also His son, were from the beginning strongly identified in the heart of Moses.

The moving gesture of mourning symbolized by the removal of his ornaments seemed to bring about a psychic change in the relationship between Moses and the Deity. God now relents and makes a distinction between the leader and the group, thereby alleviating the former's sense of guilt. Significantly, several things that God said to Moses in the first part of the theophany are now repeated in the context that *the leader is to tell them to the group.* The term *stiffnecked* is repeated. The announcement that God would not go up in the midst of them for one moment lest He consume them is stated again. And now the instructions that the Children of Israel should put off their ornaments is carried out by them, not as a voluntary act but as a punishment. In a sense, by losing himself momentarily in identification with his people through an act of penitence, Moses finds himself again, a situation expressed in a renewed recognition by the Deity of his separateness as a person, his role as the leader.

A seemingly unrelated theme is now introduced into the narrative—the Tent of Meeting (Driver 1911, 358–60; Orlinsky 1954, 38–40) (14). The text says, "Now Moses used to take the tent and to pitch it without the camp, afar off from the camp; and he called it The tent of meeting, which was without the camp. And it came to pass, when Moses went out into the Tent, that all the people rose up, and stood, every man at his tent door, and looked after Moses, until he was gone into the Tent. And it came to pass, when Moses entered into the Tent, the pillar of cloud descended, and stood at the door of the Tent, and the Lord spoke with Moses. And when all the people saw the pillar of cloud stand at the door of the Tent, all the people rose up and worshipped, every man at his tent door. And the Lord spoke unto Moses face to face, as a man speaketh unto his friend" (33:7–11).

There is a psychological relationship between this theme and the material that precedes and follows it. We are told that God is disappointed with the Children of Israel and will no longer relate to them on the same basis of intimacy as before. He will send an angel to lead them. And then the information is given that Moses "used to take the tent and pitch it without the camp, afar off from the camp." This procedure is described not as an isolated incident but as a regular pattern of what took place. Why then is that familiar happening brought into the narrative at this particular time? The purpose may be to suggest that there is now a special meaning to the fact that Moses is separating himself from the Children of Israel. This behavior follows immediately on a similar action by the Deity, Who removes Himself psychologically by announcing that He will send an angel to lead them. Actually, neither act seems to involve any change on a reality basis. The mention of physical distance here suggests *emotional distance*, a form of representation found in dreams.

The words "And the Lord spoke unto Moses face to face, as a man speaketh with his friend" are a moving expression of the loving regard in which the Deity held Moses. Although clearly a figure of speech, the words portray an unusually vivid anthropomorphic image in which man and God meet on a basis resembling equality. Coming so soon after God's anger concerning the golden calf debacle, this moving scene of warmth and reassurance is especially meaningful.

In the preceding theophany, Moses had tried to make peace with God, both on his own behalf and for his people. Although some degree of success seems to have been attained, the relationship clearly had not returned to its previous, more favorable status. And now suddenly God Himself takes the initiative. He comes to Moses and speaks beautiful words of warmth and friendship that convey a special quality of closeness and intimacy. Moreover, the Children of Israel are also involved. They stand far off, "every man at his tent door," and "all the people rose up and worshipped," even as the Deity was honoring their leader with His presence. Moses is now closely identified with the Deity. The greatness of the one envelops the other.

This theophany can be seen as having a strong wish-fulfilling aspect. It comes at a time and in a fashion that may have met a special need on the part of Moses for reassurance that God had indeed forgiven him for the golden calf catastrophe. His presence within The Tent of Meeting, physically removed from the camp of the people, helped to identify the leader as a separate person yet in association with his followers.

The distance between Moses and his people is not presented as an insuperable gap. We are told that after communicating with God in the Tent, "Moses would return unto the camp" (33:11).

The Golden Calf   179

But even after this comforting, fantasy-like theophany, it seems that the anxiety of the leader was not yet fully assuaged. In a further dialogue with the Deity, Moses returns to the matter that now most concerns him. "And Moses said unto the Lord: 'See, Thou sayest unto me: Bring up this people; and Thou hast not let me know whom Thou wilt send with me. Yet Thou hast said: I know thee by name, and thou hast also found grace in My sight. Now, therefore, I pray Thee, if I have found grace in Thy sight, show me now Thy ways, that I may know Thee, to the end that I may find grace in Thy sight; and consider that this nation is Thy people'" (33:12–13).

Moses seems not to have heard God's earlier words: "and I will send an angel before thee" (33:2). The tone of his complaint, "Thou hast not let me know whom Thou wilt send with me," suggest either that the term "an angel" is too indefinite to satisfy him or else that God's reply did not provide the answer he was looking for. The Deity responds to him again, this time with a more definitive and comforting answer. "And He said: 'My presence shall go with thee, and I will give thee rest'" (33:14). Commentators have been puzzled by the use of the word *rest* in this context. But if the problem was an inner one, caused by the turmoil of anxiety and doubt, then the term is appropriate. If God was with him, his anxiety would be alleviated.

Moses, however, still does not seem to be fully convinced. He repeats his request with greater urgency. "And he said unto Him: 'If Thy presence go not with me, carry us not up hence. For wherein now shall it be known that I have found grace in Thy sight, I and Thy people, from all the people that are upon the face of the earth?' And the Lord said unto Moses: 'I will do this thing *also* that thou hast spoken, for thou hast found grace in My sight, and I know thee by name'" (33:15–17) (italics added).

The word *also* does not fit into this context, leading scholars to wonder what it might refer to. My own interpretation is that the Deity here *anticipates a further wish* on the part of Moses, one that the leader finds it difficult to express. All Moses can do, therefore, is to repeat the earlier plea that conceals this more secret thought. God encourages him by indicating in advance that He will *also* grant that yet unspoken request in addition to the promise already given: "My presence shall go with thee, and I will give thee rest." Moses now dares to give utterance to the underlying wish. "And he said: 'Show me, I pray thee, Thy Glory'" (33:18).

This was indeed a strange and unusual request. He seems to be asking for some kind of visual manifestation of God's presence, a puzzling and daring thing to do in the light of his own concept of God's invisibility and incorporeality. The expression "God's glory" has a mystical connotation, an indefinable significance (15). Heschel (1956) maintains that it expresses the *presence* not the *essence* of God (p. 82). But since the Deity had already assured Moses of His presence, the *glory* Moses asked to see must indeed signify something more, an aspect that may have been too hidden and sacred for mortal man to know.

Understandably, Moses would have hesitancy in voicing such a request. He claims special privilege because God knows him by name and pleads, "Now therefore, I pray Thee, if I have found grace in Thy sight, show me now Thy ways, that I may know Thee, to the end that I may find grace in Thy sight; and consider that this nation is Thy people" (33:13). This all sounds a bit confusing, like a man asking for a personal favor that he is not sure he has the right to ask. The confusion manifests itself in the circular reasoning: if Moses has found grace in God's sight, he should be allowed to know God better in order to find grace in His sight. The meaning probably is in order to find *more grace* in His sight, a situation that would be made possible by the greater knowledge of God. The clause "And consider that this nation is Thy people" seems unrelated at first glance but is meaningful. Moses is making a personal request on the basis that he is the leader of a people chosen by God. If he is to induct them into a fuller knowledge of the Deity, he himself must be more fully prepared. The same reasoning emerges again, indirectly, when he says, "If Thy presence go not with *me*, carry *us* not up hence" (33:15) (italics added), indicating in the singular and plural use of the pronouns, his interrelatedness with the group. What happens to him, he implies, is also important for the people as a whole. Although this argument is undoubtedly true, the underlying wish behind these verses is of a deeply personal nature. What is taking place here is a moving and dramatic expression of a human being's intense effort to achieve a closer personal experience with

God in a mood of both longing and fear. The moment must have been one of great psychological stress, accompanied by the attempt to restore his own sense of worthiness through a further manifestation of God's love.

The Deity's response is as enigmatic as the request of Moses. "And He said, 'I will make all My goodness pass before thee, and will proclaim the name of the Lord before thee; and I will be gracious to whom I will be gracious, and will show mercy to whom I will show mercy'" (33:19).

The two parts of the reply seem to be somewhat disparate, but they balance each other. First, God equates His glory with His goodness, thus transposing any suggestion of a physical aspect into a moral quality. Since one's name, in biblical thinking, is related to one's essence (Pedersen 1926, 3–4: 644), by proclaiming His name before Moses, God again emphasizes His moral attributes. His name (I AM) which declares His existence, is indeed the same as His presence. In psychoanalytic terms, the presence of God, here symbolic of the superego, is in itself a manifestation of the moral qualities for which He stands.

On a more mystical level, God is experienced by man beyond the sum of His moral qualities. But in this indefinable area the Deity seems to be as evasive about disclosing further His divine nature as Moses is in finding words for his question. Furthermore, God also makes clear the independence of His actions. He Himself will determine who shall be the recipients of His graciousness and His mercy.

One gets the impression that even to this favored son God deems it best not to yield entirely to the suppliant's wishes. The veil of mystery must not be opened too far. Thus, God both acquiesces and refrains from acquiescing, an attitude that anticipates and prepares for that which is about to take place.

In the first part of His response God agrees to the request of Moses, saying, "I will make all My goodness pass before thee." At the same time, as though to counterbalance this degree of fulfillment, He declares, "I will be gracious to whom I will be gracious."

God's need to assert His freedom of choice might be clarified if seen from the viewpoint of Moses himself. If the leader felt guilty in making a request that at heart had a deeply personal basis, he would be reassured if God responded not to this seemingly unworthy motive but because the Deity Himself, out of His graciousness and mercy, *chose* to do so.

God now relates to his beloved prophet in the language best understood by man—the symbolism of the physical senses. But caution is maintained. "And He said, 'Thou canst not see My face, for man shall not see me and live.' And the Lord said: 'Behold, there is a place by Me, and thou shalt stand upon the rock. And it shall come to pass, while My glory passeth by, that I will put thee in a cleft of the rock, and will cover thee with My hand until I have passed by. And I will take away My hand, and thou shalt see My back; but My face shall not be seen'" (33:20–23).

The problem of how Moses could satisfy his need without penetrating into that which is forbidden to man was to be solved in an intriguing manner. However, it should be noted that this experience is recorded *not as it took place but as God described how it would take place.*

The situation is indeed a strange and mystical one, even for Moses. It provides for the immediacy of God's presence in a vividly anthropomorphic fashion but at the same time expresses God's transcendence, that which is beyond man's reach. Even at this moment, when the psychological needs of Moses seem to have been unusually great, he neither expects nor wants the ultimate barrier between the human and the Divine to be let down. *For no man could see God's face and live.*

Where could this unusual theophany have taken place? In the course of it, the action moves from some point on the "rock," presumably Mount Sinai, to a cleft in that rock. "And the Lord said: 'Behold, there is a place by Me, and thou shalt stand upon the rock.'" Evidently, therefore, Moses was not on the rock to begin with.

The dialogue between the leader and God follows the description of the Tent of Meeting and the purpose it served (33:10–12). So ostensibly, the theophany begins there. But how does Moses get from the tent to the mount? Does he walk or is he transported in the same way that he is brought from the rock to the cleft? In a mystical experience of this kind such details can be expected to remain ambiguous and, indeed, to be regarded as immaterial.

My own hypothesis is that this entire theophany took place within the Tent of Meeting itself, while Moses was in an altered state of consciousness. It is not hard to visualize the leader entering the tent in a mood of unease, with great longing to find comfort in the closeness of God's presence. He passes easily into a state of psychological receptivity most conducive to achieving this end. The repressed wishes come to the surface and are experienced in a dreamlike state.

The longing for a relationship with a parental figure is often expressed symbolically in imagery that centers around bodily contacts that stem from the hidden memories of infancy. These generally have sexual connotations, although the wishes involved may not be primarily sexual. Thus, the symbolism of Moses standing in a cleft of the rock could suggest various expressions of such unconscious wishes. There is the imagery of the whole body as phallus, belonging to the Father, being a part of the Father, and in contact with the Mother Earth. He is covered with the hand of the Father, a gesture that protects him from the ambivalence of that same parental figure, who is both loving and awesome, desired and dreaded, and whose face one dare not behold. Only the *back* could be seen as a child might see the back of the father in a repressed memory of an intrusion into the parental bedroom.

Or, on another level of experiencing, the cleft might symbolize a projected feminized image of Moses himself, from the period of the negative oedipal phase of development, in which the boy turns from the mother with a longing to take her place with the father. In a further condensation of meaning, such as occurs in dreams, there is the fantasy of the child returning to the womb of the mother so that he can learn the secrets of what goes on in the relationship between the parents. The curiosity *to see* and *to know* that lead to the acquisition of knowledge comes from such primitive sources, as Freud has pointed out. All of these universal, unconscious fantasies that find expression in such symbolism as described above may stem from one basic wish—the longing to break through the isolation of the human spirit by contact with a comforting presence, especially in a time of anxiety and stress. It is again the small child reaching out for the familiar parental figure.

The psychological aspects of this theophany are highly reminiscent in tone and content of the one at the burning bush, which marked the beginning of Moses' mission. On both occasions there are elements indicating associations with early infantile experiences that remain repressed in the unconscious and seek discharge in dreams and dreamlike states. Both times Moses exhibits the same quality of persistence in the way he argues with God, as if there is a repeated need for reassurance in order to overcome some doubts about either himself or the Deity. Thus, at the burning bush, Moses keeps questioning God's choice of him as the deliverer of his people from Egypt, pleading, "'Who am I, that I should go unto Pharaoh and that I should bring forth the children of Israel out of Egypt?' And He said: 'Certainly I will be with thee'" (3:11–12). Then, also, the presence of God was the most important element in the situation. The leadership of Moses cannot be effective apart from that close sense of relationship with God. If then, following the golden calf apostasy, God threatens to withdraw His presence, though only to a greater distance, Moses can no longer consider either himself or his people as *chosen*. Thus, he pleads in the later theophany, "For wherein now shall it be known that I have found grace in Thy sight, I and Thy people? Is it not in that Thou goest with us, so that we are distinguished, I and Thy people, from all the people that are upon the face of the earth?" (33:16). The special mission of this people was to make known to the world the glory of God. If the Deity withdrew His presence, the people would no longer have any motivation for their task. Just as Moses had needed God's presence to bring the people out of Egypt, so now he required the same condition of His nearness to lead them to the Promised Land.

At the burning bush the matter of a name arose also (3:13–14). Then Moses wished to know God by name. Now, he points out that *God knows him by name*, a sign of special intimacy (Pedersen 1926, 3–4: 644). At that earlier time Moses was concerned that the Children of Israel might not believe him to be the appointed messenger of God. Now it was a more individual problem that confronted Moses. He felt that he had to understand more fully the nature of God, perhaps in order to feel better qualified as the leader of a people who had received the Covenant at Mount Sinai. He needed the Deity as a model on which he could pattern his own character and behavior so he in turn could serve as a model for the Children of Israel.

In conflict with the wish to know God is the danger of coming too close to Him. The Children of Israel had earlier expressed this kind of apprehension at the time when God proclaimed the Ten Words in their hearing. They pleaded with Moses to serve thereafter as their intermediary (20:15–16). Now the leader himself shared this dread, although on a different level, when he wanted to know God even more than had already been granted to him.

The episode of the golden calf, coming as it did so close on the spiritually moving events of the revelation and the Covenant, must have been a shattering experience for Moses. His moment of fulfillment, so long anticipated as the reward for all the travail that preceded it, had provided only a brief period for rejoicing. In that instant when the outraged leader beheld the scene at the foot of the mount and flung the stone tables to the ground, a profound state of shock must have occurred. And as suggested earlier, also shocking to him may have been the extreme severity with which he himself had punished the people. In other situations of rebellious behavior on their part, it was God Who generally assumed the punitive role, thus providing a protective shield for Moses. Now it was the leader himself who directly carried out the heavy penalties. The repressed emotions associated with these events may have been reflected in what was now taking place in the relationship between Moses and God. The leader had to go through a soul-searching experience. Was he truly following in the ways of God? To what degree did the Deity think it necessary to punish? How much could He forgive? If only Moses knew God better, he would understand more clearly how to lead his people along the path God wished them to follow. The leader needed to feel the nearness of God and be reassured about the goodness of God, perhaps as a defense against his own sense of isolation and doubts about his own goodness in relation to his people.

Renewal of the Covenant

It is not until the next theophany that God more fully keeps the promise made earlier to Moses in the words "I will make all

My goodness pass before thee, and will proclaim the name of the Lord before thee" (33:19). Moses is instructed to return to the mount once more. "And the Lord said unto Moses: 'Hew thee two tables of stone like unto the first tables, which thou didst break. And be ready by the morning, and come up in the morning unto mount Sinai, and present thyself there to Me on the top of the mount. And no man shall come up with thee, neither let any man be seen throughout all the mount; neither let the flocks nor herds feed before that mount.' And he hewed two tables of stone like unto the first; and Moses rose up early in the morning, and went up into mount Sinai, as the Lord had commanded him, and took in his hand two tables of stone. And the Lord descended in the cloud, and stood with him there, and proclaimed: 'The Lord, the Lord God, merciful and gracious, long-suffering, and abundant in goodness and truth; keeping mercy unto the thousandth generation, forgiving iniquity and transgression and sin; and that will by no means clear the guilty; visiting the iniquities of the fathers upon the children, and upon the children's children, unto the third and fourth generations'" (34:1–7). Thus God makes known His moral nature and the implications that flow from it (16).

Moses accepts God's revelation by an act of worship. "And Moses made haste and bowed his head toward the earth, and worshipped" (34:8). He then pleads on behalf of the people for that which he had before primarily asked on a more personal basis—God's presence among them. It is now in identification with his people that he prays. "And he said: 'If now I have found grace in Thy sight, O Lord, let the Lord, I pray Thee, go in the midst of us; for it is a stiffnecked people; and pardon our iniquity and our sin, and take us for Thine Inheritance'" (34:9). God responds with a depth of feeling that equals Moses' own. "And he said: 'Behold, I make a covenant; before all thy people I will do marvels, such as have not been wrought in all the earth, nor in any nation; and all the people among which thou art shall see the work of the Lord that I am about to do with thee, that it is tremendous. Observe thou that which I am commanding thee this day; behold, I am driving out before thee the Amorite, and the Canaanite, and the Hittite, and the Perizzite, and the Hivite, and the Jebusite. Take heed to thyself, lest thou make a covenant with the inhabitants of the land whither thou goest, lest they be for a snare in the midst of thee. But ye shall break down their altars, and dash in pieces their pillars, and ye shall cut down their Asherim. For thou shalt bow down to no other god; for the Lord, whose name is Jealous, is a jealous God; lest thou make a covenant with the inhabitants of the land, and they go astray after their gods, and do sacrifice unto their gods, and they call thee, and thou eat of their sacrifice; and thou take of their daughters unto thy sons, and their daughters go astray after their gods, and make thy sons go astray after their gods'" (34:10–16).

It is clear that the warning which follows the promise introduces a renewal of the Covenant and that both are an aftermath of the golden calf apostasy. That was a sin which must not be repeated. The temptations would be much greater when the Children of Israel were in the Promised Land, exposed to close contact with their pagan neighbors. Except for some differences in wording, the laws that God now gives to Moses are basically the same as those contained within the more comprehensive set of statutes that had been delivered to the people on the first occasion of the covenantal rites (20:19–23:33) (Driver 1911, 364).

Psychologically, it seems reasonable to assume that the important aspects to emphasize at the time of the renewal were the warnings against idolatry and a repetition of the laws dealing with worship and ritual, as an antidote to the kind of temptation that had brought about the recent catastrophe. It was hardly necessary to repeat all the statutes of moral and social behavior concerning how the people were to deal with each other. These laws were already in their possession, having been written down by Moses himself in the so-called Book of the Covenant. It was in relation to God that the people had erred, and it was in this area that the laws were repeated (Hertz 1936, 366).

The restoration of the Ten Commandments themselves constituted a separate action. There are some interesting differences between the first time they came into being and the second time. The earlier occasion had a kind of pristine glow about it. Never again would there be such a time when the Deity Himself pronounced the Ten Words before the people. That was a unique happening, memorable and unrepeatable. Nor did it need to be repeated. It had already become a part of the traditions of the Children of Israel.

Moreover, the first time that the actual recording of the Ten

Words took place, God had assumed full responsibility for the task. "And the Lord said unto Moses: 'Come up to Me into the mount, and be there; and I will give thee the tables of stone'" (24:12). In another reference to this act, just as Moses was about to descend from the mountain after the first forty days and forty nights, the text says, "And He gave unto Moses, when He had made an end of speaking with him upon mount Sinai, the two tables of the testimony, tables of stone, written with the finger of God" (31:18). And at still another point, the narrative states, "And the tables were the work of God, and the writing was the writing of God, graven upon the tables" (32:16).

On the second occasion, however, Moses is instructed to perform part of the task himself. "And the Lord said unto Moses, 'Hew thee two tables of stone like unto the first; and I will write upon the tables the words that were upon the first tables, which thou didst break" (34:1).

No reason is given for this change in procedure. What might have been going on within Moses himself at this time? The leader may now have wished to perform this part of the work himself. It would be an opportunity to share in the restoration of that which he had himself destroyed—an act of reparation. Did this mood then go even further and extend to the writing also? In terms of the text as it stands, there is an element of ambiguity regarding who actually did the writing, God or Moses. The text says, "And he was there with the Lord forty days and forty nights; he did neither eat bread, nor drink water. And *he* wrote upon the tables the words of the covenant, the ten words" (34:28) (italics added).

Grammatically, the antecedent of the pronoun *he* is Moses. Yet earlier the statement is clearly made that God Himself would write the Ten Words on the tables (34:1). Although the biblical narrative is often seemingly unconcerned about the antecedents of pronouns, psychologically, the possible meanings in terms of the specific situation should be considered. Moses at this time was in a state of exaltation to a degree unusual even for him, as a subsequent event will indicate. In his theophany with God, the leader had achieved what he had hoped for and more. The Deity had shown him special favor by revealing *all His goodness* in a truly dramatic fashion. God has also agreed to be with Moses and the Children of Israel on their way to the Promised Land. The covenant had been reestablished. Throughout all these experiences, which lasted a long period of time, Moses had not partaken of nourishment and was thus in a physiological state that tended to heighten psychic awareness. It is in the afterglow of these emotional excitations, as Moses is about to descend from the mount and meet his people that the simple statement is made, "And he wrote upon the tables the words of the covenant, the ten words" (34:28). In such a mood of oneness with God, the distinction between himself and the Deity may have been briefly suspended. The *he* that did the writing therefore could have been either God or Moses, for the two were momentarily one in the consciousness of the leader.

When this important event is recapitulated in Deuteronomy, a clear distinction is made. It is *Moses* who hews the tables of stone and *God* Who does the writing. Moses says, "At that time the Lord said unto me: 'Hew thee two tables of stone like unto the first, and come up unto Me into the mount; and make thee an ark of wood. And I will write on the tables the words that were on the first tables which thou didst break, and thou shalt put them in the ark.' So I made an ark of acacia-wood, and hewed two tables of stone like unto the first, and went up into the mount, having the two tables in my hand. And He wrote on the tables, according to the first writing, the ten words, which the Lord spoke unto you in the mount out of the midst of the fire in the day of the assembly; and the Lord gave them unto me. And I turned and came down from the mount, and put the tables in the ark which I had made; and there they are, as the Lord commanded me" (Deut. 10:1–5).

Thus, Moses recollects that the Ten Words were indeed written by the finger of God. No other way would have been comprehensible to him in that process of recall. Another puzzling inconsistency, however, is present in this retelling. The narrative in Exodus makes no mention of the ark at the time when the Ten Commandments are reproduced. It is only later, when the actual work of the Tabernacle is described that the text says, "And Bezalel made the ark of acacia wood" (37:1). Yet as Moses *remembers it*, he himself made the ark.

Over the long period of years between the events he described and the later period of recall, Moses may have remembered very clearly those aspects that he felt were important for the people to know—that God Himself wrote down the Ten Words that provided the basic religious and moral guide for the Children of Israel. Regarding other details, Moses may have wished to have as much of a role in this significant event as possible. This wish may have been father to the thought and influenced the recollection. Moses is convincingly human in his errors, in spite of the greatness of his accomplishments.

One of the most quietly dramatic and profoundly significant images of Moses depicted in the Bible is that of the leader returning from the heights of Mount Sinai with the new Tables of the Testimony in his hands (Arlow 1961). He had spent a long period on the mountaintop in a state of fasting (34:28). He had experienced the closeness of God as never before. He had learned the attributes of Godliness more fully. It was a Moses of greater strength who came down from the mount.

The mood of quiet exaltation in which Moses returned to his people is expressed in a striking figure of speech. The Bible says: "And it came to pass, when Moses came down from mount Sinai with the two tables of the testimony in Moses' hands, when he came down from the mount, that Moses knew not that the skin of his face sent forth beams while He talked with him. And when Aaron and all the children of Israel saw Moses, behold, the skin of his face sent forth beams; and they were afraid to come nigh him. And Moses called unto them; and Aaron and all the rulers of the congregation returned unto him; and Moses spoke to them. And afterward all the children of Israel came nigh, and he gave them in commandment all that the Lord had spoken with him in mount Sinai. And when Moses had done speaking with them, he put a veil on his face. But when Moses went in before the Lord that He might speak with him, he took the veil off, until he came out; and he came out; and spoke unto the children of Israel that which he was commanded. And the children of Israel saw the face of Moses, that the skin of Moses' face sent forth beams; and Moses put the veil back upon his face, until he went in to speak with Him" (34:29–35).

At first Moses himself was unaware of the radiance that emanated from him, but the people saw it and were afraid to come near. Evidently that mysterious aura was akin to the holiness of God, a holiness that evoked the dread of the sacred. Aaron and the leaders of the congregation approached first. As Moses spoke with them and nothing untoward happened, all the Children of Israel came near and Moses gave them the commandments he had received from God. By this time the leader must have known what had frightened them, and when he was done speaking, he put a veil on his face.

Medieval artists and sculptors have often depicted Moses with horns protruding from his forehead, as did Michelangelo in his famous statue. This concept stemmed from an early Latin translation of the Bible, the Vulgate, in which the Hebrew word for *horn*, meant here in the sense of *rays* (of light), was translated literally (Hertz 1936, 368; Rosenfeld 1951).

There is a special, almost indefinable quality to the description of the returning Moses, the tables of the Law in his hands and an unusual radiance on his face. The wording of this biblical passage gives the effect of a certain awkwardness, like a halting sense of speech, which in its own way adds to the poignancy of the situation. It seems to be expressive of the man himself, who is relating an incredible experience. Moses gives the impression of being in a certain state of depersonalization, as though the man who had gone up the mount was talking about another person, the new spiritual Moses who came down from the mount. There is a repetitiveness of significant phrases, as though the words had to be repeated in order to be believed. Three times the expression "the skin of Moses' face sent forth beams" is mentioned, as if with a sense of awe and disbelief. And three times it is noted that the veil is put on and taken off as the occasion required. The word *Moses* is used ten times in the seven verses under consideration, even when a pronoun would have seemed more appropriate. Thus, in the expression "when *Moses* came down from mount Sinai with the two tables of testimony in *Moses*' hand" (34:29) (italics added) the name is clearly redundant. It does, however, strengthen the effect that Moses is talking about another Moses.

The feeling of depersonalization is augmented by the state of the leader's unawareness—"Moses knew not that the skin of his face sent forth beams." This lack of self-consciousness may have been indicative of his increased spirituality. And yet the awesome effect on the people must have impressed itself strongly on Moses himself, bringing him back to a greater awareness of reality.

The dual role of Moses as a man of God and a leader of his people is beautifully expressed in the metaphor of the veil. We are told that the two occasions on which Moses customarily removed the veil was when he communicated with God and at the times when he conveyed to the people the commandments he had received from Him. As leader, Moses also had to be in contact with the people and concerned with the reality aspects of their lives. The veil that he put on his face can be understood as symbolizing the reality-oriented part of the ego covering the intensity of his spiritual self, that aspect of him that was closest to God (Freud 1923, 48).

The episode of the golden calf, in terms of its effect on Moses, can be understood as an ordeal whose chastening aftermath led to a strengthening and deepening spirituality on the character of the leader and, through him, on his people as a whole.

Reparation: Construction of the Sanctuary

The Children of Israel remained in the area of Mount Sinai for almost a year (Num. 10:11–12). After the sobering experience of the golden calf episode, the people showed their renewed devotion to God in the building of the sanctuary. It was an opportune time for a return to the Deity by way of activities that engaged both their hearts and their hands. The construction of the Tabernacle and its consecration is the subject of the following chapter. For our purpose here, we need refer only to the attitude of the people in relation to this undertaking. It must have had a strengthening and unifying effect on the group. Much time, effort, and emotional involvement clearly went into this task, adding purpose and animation to the lives of the participants.

The actual work of construction took four months and was completed nine months after the date of their arrival at the sacred mount (40:17). Then came the impressive consecration ceremonials and the installation of Aaron as the High Priest (Lev. 8–10). This span of time, therefore, was a highly meaningful and colorful one for the group as a whole, a period filled with new religious zeal and purposeful activity in which all participated.

The people gave every indication of wholehearted involvement in the building of the Tabernacle. The text says: "And they came, every one whose heart stirred him up, and every one whom his spirit made willing, and brought the Lord's offering, for the work of the tent of meeting, and for all the service thereof, and for the holy garments. And they came, both men and women, as many as were willing-hearted and brought nose-rings, and ear-rings, and signet-rings, and girdles, all jewels of gold; even every man that brought an offering of gold unto the Lord" (35:21–22).

It is significant that there is an absence of coercion regarding individual participation in this group project. Several times the statement is repeated indicating the voluntary nature of the appeal. "And they came, every one whose heart stirred him up, and every one whom his spirit made willing." This recognition of the individual's right to freedom of choice, even in an activity that involved the interests of the group as a whole, is a remarkable phenomenon in that far-off day. It is expressive of a basic concept that takes cognizance of man's relationship to God on a twofold basis, as an individual and as the member of a group.

The wholehearted response of the people was stimulated, no doubt, by the very fact of its voluntary nature. The undertaking provided an opportunity for them to express their religious feelings in a personal way. It is true that they had also volunteered to give their precious possessions for the making of the golden calf. In both instances the need was the same—a wish for leadership from a higher authority that would give them a sense of security and direction. The need was the same, but the path over which it led under the guidance of Moses was happily different.

For a long time the Children of Israel had been the recipients of God's special concern. Now the human need to show both their gratitude for His saving acts and to perform reparation for their wrongdoing was open to them. At the completion of the project we are told, "According to all that the Lord commanded Moses, so the children of Israel did all the work. And Moses saw all the work, and behold, they had done it; as the Lord had commanded, even so had they done it. And Moses blessed them" (39:42–43).

The period at Mount Sinai was also a time when the people were organized with a kind of semimilitary precision, preparatory to their forward march to the conquest of the Promised Land. God said to Moses, "Take ye the sum of all the congregation of the children of Israel, by their families, by their fathers' houses, according to the number of names, every man by their polls; from twenty years old and upward, all that are able to go forth to war in Israel; ye shall number them by their hosts, even thou and Aaron" (Num. 1:1–3). Thus, everyone had a place where he belonged, from the primary unity of the family to the tribe. The basic structures for the making of a people were established during the months in the vicinity of Mount Sinai. Individual and group behavior was regulated in the areas of social relationships, moral laws, and religious ceremonials.

The departure from Mount Sinai took place at a specified time and in a specified way. "And it came to pass in the second year, in the second month, on the twentieth day of the month, that the cloud was taken up from over the tabernacle of the testimony. And the children of Israel set forward by their stages out of the wilderness of Sinai; and the cloud abode in the wilderness of Paran" (Num. 10:11–12).

The description conveys an image of orderliness and discipline in contrast to the informal encampment close to a year ago, when the wanderers reached that same area. The conglomeration of loose tribes had become a people. But a long time was to elapse before their initiation into peoplehood was to develop through a slow transformation into a cohesive group with its own unique identity and way of life.

The Tabernacle

A Sanctuary in the Wilderness

 CHAPTER EIGHT

THE TWO BASIC areas of achievement attributed to Moses relate to his work as the great liberator and the great lawgiver. The diverse abilities needed for these tasks indicate the complexity and genius of the man who undertook them. He had the ability both to formulate plans in solitude and to carry them out in action with the people.

Moses understood that the Covenant was only a charter, as it were, for a way of life that required a social structure to give cohesiveness and organization to the group. The next logical step was to make plans for a place of worship, where the people could regularly maintain their relationship to the Deity through the cultic observances of ritual and worship that would be most meaningful to them. This project required both time and solitude.

The planning of the Tabernacle took place in the quietness of the mountaintop at Sinai during those fateful forty days and nights that precipitated the episode of the golden calf at the foot of that same mount. The leader may have found respite in turning his thoughts and psychic energies from the overwhelming emotions and physical stresses associated with the events of the Covenant to the structured tasks of setting up plans and specifications for the Tabernacle. As time went on, Moses may have become so involved with the task before him that he lost sight of what his lengthy absence might mean in the lives of the people below. Or perhaps he was not fully aware of their emotional dependence on his very presence among them in spite of their ambivalent feelings.

Instructions for the building of the Tabernacle and its sacred objects are given with remarkable detail in the directives delivered by God to Moses. Seven full chapters (25–31)* are devoted to these plans and a further lengthy description (chapters 35–40) largely similar in content, is recorded once more as the work is carried out.

The project is to begin with an offering by the people. "And the Lord spoke unto Moses, saying: 'Speak unto the children of Israel, that they make for me an offering; of every man whose heart maketh him willing ye shall take of them: gold, and silver, and brass; and blue, and purple, and scarlet, and fine linen, and goats' hair; and rams' skins dyed red, and sealskins and acacia wood; oil for the lights, spices for the anointing oil, and for the sweet incense; onyx stones, and stones to be set, for the ephod, and for the breastplate. And let them make Me a sanctuary, that I may dwell among them. According to all that I show thee, the pattern of the tabernacle, and the pattern of all the furniture, even so shall ye make it.'" (25:1–9). A detailed description of the plans then follows.

The actual work of construction, however, is delayed by the unhappy episode of the golden calf. It is after the second stay of Moses on the mount and his return with the renewal of the Covenant and the forgiveness of God for the sin of the people that the work began.

As described in the latter part of the previous chapter, the people cooperated in a willing spirit to build the house of wor-

---

*All biblical references in this chapter, unless otherwise noted, are to the book of Exodus.

ship. The work was done on a voluntary basis. In one respect, however, all were equally responsible. For the regular maintenance of the daily Tabernacle service, a tax of one-half shekel, a silver coin, was imposed on every male adult. The democratic aspect of this communal duty is made clear in the commandment: "The rich shall not give more and the poor shall not give less, than the half shekel, when they give the offering of the Lord, to make atonement for your soul" (30:15).

The Tabernacle consisted of an inner sanctum, the Holy of Holies, where the Ark was kept, and an adjoining larger area, the Holy Place, which housed the altar of incense, the sevenbranched candelabrum, and the table with the showbread.

The sanctuary proper stood in an enclosure called the court of the Tabernacle. In common with portable tents of worship, characteristic among Bedouin tribes of early times, the sanctuary was constructed so that it could be transported from place to place as it accompanied the Children of Israel in their wanderings (Albright 1957, 266; Cross 1947; Orlinsky 1954, 38–40).

The biblical description of the Tabernacle and its objects provides new insights into the background of the cultural life of the Children of Israel at this time. In spite of the years spent in slavery and, for the most part, outside the mainstream of Egyptian culture, they were indeed a part of the civilization of their time, a theme to which we shall return later.

The building of the Tabernacle reveals a knowledge of craftsmanship and a feeling for beauty. However, some critics point out that in spite of the details, certain aspects of the construction are ambiguous and seem unrealistic (Driver 1911, 426). But it should be remembered that the motive was to record a meaningful historic and religious experience, not to provide a blueprint for architectural purposes.

The structure was rectangular in shape with characteristics of both a building and a tent. There was a framework of acacia wood. The outside covering is described as a "tent over the tabernacle," woven of goats' hair and consisting of eleven curtains fastened together with loops and brass clasps so as to form a unified, protective whole for the structure beneath. As additional insurance against the hazards of the weather, there were two more layers, one of red ram's skin and the other probably of sealskin. These were all held down by cords fastened to pegs driven into the ground in the manner of a tent.

The inner curtains, ten in number, were of fine linen embroidered with figures of cherubim and dyed in bright colors of violet, purple, and scarlet. These were stretched across a network of gold-covered acacia wood, so arranged that the ten pieces formed a single, unified covering, "that the tabernacle may be one whole"(26:6).

The Holy of Holies, which occupied the far end of the structure, faced eastward. It was in the form of a perfect cube, being fifteen feet in length, width, and height. The adjoining area, the Holy Place, extended for twice the length. It was separated from the Holy of Holies by a curtain, or veil, made of fine embroidered linen, the material and design matching those of the surrounding walls of the Holy Place. This curtain was fastened with golden clasps to four pillars of gilded acacia wood set in silver bases.

The court of the Tabernacle was a rectangular space measuring one hundred fifty feet in length from west to east and seventy-five feet from north to south. It was enclosed by hangings of white linen fastened to sixty acacia pillars decorated with silver capitals and set in bronze bases seven-and-a-half feet apart. An entrance in the middle of the eastern wall, thirty feet in width, was covered with a screen or curtain, of fine embroidered linen, attached to four pillars.

Within the Holy of Holies was the most sacred object in the Tabernacle, the Ark of the Covenant, which contained the stone tablets of the Ten Commandments. It is significant that in the directives given by God to Moses, the construction of the Ark was the first matter to be considered, indicative of its importance. The Ark was an oblong box made of acacia wood and overlaid with pure gold, both without and within. It was equipped with gold rings at the four corners through which gilded poles of acacia wood could be inserted for the purpose of transportation. A slab of pure gold across the top was known as the *mercy seat.* From its opposite sides rose the figures of two cherubim made of pure beaten gold. They faced each other across the mercy seat, their wings forming an arch overhead, the whole symbolizing the

Throne of God. The Ark was the sole object in the Holy of Holies. This inner sanctum was open only to the high priest, who was permitted to enter it once a year, on the Day of Atonement.

Within the Holy Place there were several distinctive objects that played an important role in the daily rituals of the sanctuary. Directly in front of the curtain that led to the Holy of Holies stood the small altar of incense, also made of acacia overlaid with pure gold. It was about three feet in height and one-and-a-half in length and width. Its four corners were ornamented with horns similar to those on the large altar in the courtyard. Incense was offered on the small altar twice a day, in the morning and at night, by the priests who alone were allowed to enter the Holy Place. On the north side stood the table of the Presence, constructed of the same materials of wood and pure beaten gold. It measured three feet in length, one-and-a-half in width, and a little over two feet in height. On every sabbath day, twelve loaves of freshly baked bread of fine wheat flour were placed on this table in two rows of six each, as an offering of the Children of Israel, representative of the twelve tribes. The old loaves could be eaten only by Aaron and his sons and were to be consumed in a holy place. Near the showbread there was a golden cup containing pure frankincense and other small utensils used in the performance of the rituals (Lev.24:7).

Opposite the table of the Presence, on the south side, there was the beautifully wrought candelabrum with its seven branches, three on each side of the central stem. It was made of pure beaten gold, decorated with designs of almond blossoms. In its cupped openings, pure olive oil was to burn continually, day and night. The observance of these rituals was one of the important obligations of the priests.

The only part of the sacred precincts open to the laymen was the large court of the Tabernacle. In its center, a sloped ramp led to the altar of burnt offerings, where the sacrifices were made. It was a hollow receptacle built of acacia wood overlaid with bronze. Its measurements were seven-and-a-half feet in length and width and four-and-a-half in height. There were horns on the four corners. A fugitive from justice could, under certain conditions, claim asylum by running to the altar and clasping these horns.

In the area between the altar and the sanctuary proper stood a large bronze laver supported on a bronze base. It held the water needed by the priests in the performance of their ritual ablutions (*EJ* 1972, 15:679–88; Hertz 1936, 326–36).

Preparations for the attire of the high priest were made with the same concern for detail that went into the construction of the sanctuary. There is an unusual note of warmth in the words relating to Aaron and his sons when God says to Moses: "And bring thou near unto thee Aaron thy brother, and his sons with him, from among the children of Israel, that they may minister unto Me in the priest's office, even Aaron, Nadab and Abihu, Eleazar and Ithamar, Aaron's sons. And thou shalt make holy garments for Aaron thy brother, for splendour and for beauty" (28:1–2).

The nearness of God (His presence) was repeatedly sought after by Moses for himself and his people. Now he was enjoined to bring Aaron and his sons closer to himself, in preparation for bringing them closer to God. That Moses had to be told to do so suggests both a human need and wish for closeness on the part of Moses himself and at the same time a conscious effort to overcome the tendency to emotional distance that was more characteristic of him in family relationships. Aaron must have represented both a rival sibling and a longed-for father figure. As high priest, he would be in a situation uniquely conducive to both roles of this ambivalent relationship. It was Moses himself who established the authority of the high priesthood. At the same time, as the chief figure responsible for the observance of religious ritual, Aaron was clearly in a father role. So in a sense Moses makes the brother into a father but one over whom he himself had authority.

That Moses wished the high priest to symbolize the glory and splendor befitting a representative of God is clear in the kind of garments prescribed for Aaron. First, there was a basic tunic, or coat, reaching to the feet and having long sleeves. It was made of fine linen as were the breeches beneath it, which came to the knees. These simple garments were worn by all the priests. Then came the more distinctive articles of attire for the high priest alone. Over the tunic there was a sleeveleess blue robe made of wool. Its hem was fringed with richly colored balls, woven of fine wool in the shape of pomegranates. These alternated with small golden bells that tinkled in response to the movements of the wearer. Their function, it is believed, was to make known to the congregation in the court that the high priest was performing his duties within the sanctuary (Hertz 1936, 346). Over this blue robe came the *ephod.* How it is worn is not described in the text. The customary view is that it was a short, vestlike garment held up by two shoulder straps. On each of these there was an onyx stone in a gold setting, inscribed with the names of the tribes of Israel, six on each side. The ephod was made of fine linen colored blue, purple, and scarlet, interwoven with gold threads. It was fastened around the waist with a woven band of the same materials. Some scholars however maintain that the ephod was worn *below* the waist, somewhat in the fashion of a short skirt, the woven band forming the *top* of the ephod rather than the bottom, and with the breastplate *above* the ephod rather than upon it (Driver 1911, 300 f.; 312-13; Hertz 1936, 340-341; *EJ* 1972,13:1063-68.)

The most striking article in the attire of the high priest was the breastplate, a rectangular piece suspended from the shoulder straps of the ephod by golden chains. It was made of the same materials as the ephod. The cloth was doubled over so as to form a pouch. On the surface of the breastplate, in gold setting, there were four rows of precious stones, three in each row, representing the twelve tribes of Israel. Each stone was of a different kind and color and was engraved with the name of the tribe for which it stood. Hidden within the breastplate were the *Urim* and *Thummim,* articles of a rather mysterious nature whose appearance is not described in the Bible. They were used for the purpose of trying to determine the will of God in regard to certain actions, a procedure known as the casting of lots. Some think that the entire breastplate, which was called the *breastplate of judgment,* was somehow involved in the process, and others believe the ephod itself also played a role. The general opinion is that the *Urim* and *Thummim* were marked stones of some kind. Upon his head, the high priest wore a tall crownlike turban with a plate of pure gold across the forehead which was engraved with the words *Holy to the Lord.* Finally the work is completed and a pleased leader bestows his blessing on the people (39:42–43).

As with so much of the biblical subject matter, there has

been a good deal of controversy among scholars about the degree of historical validity concerning the Tabernacle. Higher Biblical Criticism tended toward the view that the entire story of the sanctuary in the wilderness is the product of a later period, stemming from exilic or postexilic times, and was inserted into the narrative by the priestly school of writers in order to give Mosaic authority to the concept of centralized worship in Jerusalem, the importance of which they were trying to impress on the people. Their theory was that the construction was an idealized image modeled after the Temple of Solomon. They point out that the specifications of the Tabernacle and its objects are often unclear, with important details omitted. They suggest that certain aspects as presented are unrealistic. How, they questioned, could the light, portable framework support the many heavy curtains that covered the structure? Where, they wondered, did all the costly material come from that went into the making of the sanctuary and its furnishings? They were also skeptical about the capacity of the recently freed slaves to carry out the skilled craftsmanship involved in the work (Driver 1911, 426–32).

It should be remembered, however, that the state of civilization in these arts was very high in Egypt, and the Hebrews must have learned a good deal while living among them for so long. Before their enslavement there was a period of freedom during which a number of Jacob's descendants must have learned the arts and craftsmanship of the surrounding culture, and some had become experts in the various fields. The text specifically refers to two of these, Bezazel and Oholiab. The former was named by God to direct the work, the text pointing out his special talents: "And He hath filled him with the spirit of God, in wisdom, in understanding, and in knowledge, and in all manner of workmanship. And to devise skillful works, to work in gold, and in silver, and in brass, and in cutting of stones for setting, and in carving of wood, to work in all manner of skillful workmanship. And He hath put in his heart that he may teach, both he and Oholiab, the son of Ahisamach, of the tribe of Dan" (35:31–34). It should be also recalled that the Hebrew slaves are believed to have been engaged in the building of entire cities, such as Pithom and Rameses, where many kinds of skills must have been involved.

As for the materials that went into the making of the sanctuary and its objects, according to the biblical narrative they derived from the spoils carried away by the escaping slaves. Also, more could be purchased from passing caravans. The Children of Israel were not compeltely isolated during the period of the wilderness.

An element in the narrative confusing to some scholars is the fact that the term *Tent of Meeting* is used in connection with *two* structures, the simple tent "pitched afar off from the camp" (33:7–11) to which Moses retreated and the elaborate Tabernacle, set in the center. Higher Biblical Criticism suggests that only the former is the authentic Tent of Meeting in the wilderness. But the traditional viewpoint is that both tents, the one pitched outside the camp, which preceded the construction of the Tabernacle, and the latter, in the midst of the encampment with the various tribes arranged in orderly fashion on the four sides, had a role in the life of the Children of Israel (Hertz 1936, 361).

Modern research tends to support the latter view. Archeological and historical studies have confirmed the fact that portable tents of worship similar to the one under discussion were in use for centuries among the Bedouin tribes of Arabia even in pre-Islamic times. Albright (1957) remarks concerning the Mosaic background of the Tabernacle and its objects, "it is captious to refuse them [the Tabernacle and the Ark] Mosaic date, since they were completely foreign to sedentary Canaanite practice and since they are known to have persisted for some time after the conquest of Palestine. The archaeologist no longer has any difficulty in proving the antiquity of many details in the description which is given in the Priestly Code" (p. 266; Buber 1936, 148–49; Cross 1947; Driver 1911, 426–32; Orlinsky 1954, 38–40).

Yehezkel Kaufmann (1960) says in this respect, "The idea that the tent is a reflex of the Second Temple is a baseless contention of modern criticism" (p. 238, n.13). And Martin Buber (1936) observes, "The view that the Ark is of Mosaic origin is again being accepted. Between Moses and Samuel, in whose early days we already find the Ark in the full light of history despite the fact that the narrative of its capture contains legendary elements, no other period can be thought of in which this, the greatest symbol in the Israelite faith, can have been introduced. It is 'a genuine migrating sanctuary.' Archaeological and ethnological findings have confirmed its period" (pp. 148–49). Even Driver (1911), the well-known scholar of modern criticism, observes, regarding the opinion of his colleagues: "however, it is acknowledged that traditions of the ceremonial objects as described in the wilderness Tabernacle go back a long way, before the period of Solomon" (p.431).

Indeed to view the planning and construction of the Tabernacle as a later insertion is to ignore the psychological reality of the text itself. It is alive with a vitality that can spring only from the genuineness of its origins and the deep emotional involvement of both the group and the leader who produced it.

The consecration of the Tabernacle and the installation of the priesthood was the next important event. Aaron was to be consecrated as high priest, a hereditary role that would be passed on to the eldest son. These events are described in the book of Leviticus (8–10).

The dedication ceremonies took seven days. During that time Aaron and his sons were required to remain within the precincts of the Tabernacle, probably in order to maintain their priestly sanctity, which had been established through various rituals of ablutions, the donning of priestly garments, and anointment with oil, all performed under the directives of Moses. On the eighth day, the newly consecrated priests were ready to enter upon their duties in behalf of the congregation. Aaron was now authorized to speak to the people and instruct them in the sacrifices they were to offer. He does so and and the people participate accordingly.

Everything seemed about to draw to a happy conclusion. The text says: "And Aaron lifted up his hands toward the people, and blessed them; and he came down from offering the sin-offering, and the burnt-offering, and the peace-offering. And Moses and Aaron went into the tent of meeting, and came out, and blessed the people; and the glory of the Lord appeared unto all the people. And there came forth fire from before the Lord, and consumed upon the altar the burnt-offering and the fat; and when all the people saw it, they shouted, and fell on their faces" (Lev. 9:22–24).

The Tabernacle   205

And then, suddenly, at the very height of this joyous occasion, tragedy struck. In the words of the text: "And Nadab and Abihu, the sons of Aaron, took each his censer, and put fire therein, and held incense thereon, and offered strange fire before the Lord, which He had not commanded them. And there came forth fire from before the Lord, and devoured them, and they died before the Lord" (Lev. 10:1–2).

So tragic an event on such an important occasion could be regarded only as an expression of displeasure on the part of the Deity and attributed to the wrongdoing of the victims. Yet the exact nature of this wrongdoing is obscure. "Strange fire," according to some commentators, refers to unconsecrated fire (Hertz 1936, 445). The altar had been consecrated, and the sanctity of its flames might have been violated by the unauthorized contact with the fire in the censers of the two youths.

The statement that they "offered strange fire, which He had not commanded them" contains the essence of the sin. However, the very ambiguity of the text suggests that an underlying meaning may be involved. Did the error lie in the nature of the fire itself, its *strange*, or *alien*, quality, or was it strange in the sense that it *did not belong* to the order of the ritual as Moses had planned it? In terms of the latter explanation, an expanded text could read: "[They] offered strange fire, which He had not commanded them [to bring]." The wrongdoing would then refer to the act itself, which in turn would render the flames in the firepans unsanctified, or strange. Talmudic rabbis suggest this possibility, that the two had acted on their own initiative (Ginzberg 1909–1938, 3:188–189).

In a further effort to find a rationale for what had occurred, commentary in the Talmud suggests that the downfall of Nadab and Abihu was brought about by their arrogance and that the youths were motivated by jealousy toward their elders, Moses and Aaron. Thus, the underlying theme of a father-son conflict is suggested (Hertz 1936, 445; Rubinstein 1968, 102). The rabbis may here be intuitively indentifying with the unconscious of Moses himself. The four sons of Aaron, in their new priestly garments, were participating in the dedication ceremonies. A sudden burst of flames that consumed the sacrificial animal on the altar signified to the awed observers the presence of the Diety and His acceptance of the sanctuary as a place of sacrifice and worship. It was a high moment in the celebration. If, at this inopportune time, Nadab and Abihu approached the altar with their own fire-pans, probably unexpectedly, Moses may have reacted with feelings of surprise and displeasure at what must have seemed to him arrogant behavior. What occurred immediately after would then be interpreted on a cause-and-effect relationship.

Realistically, however, the actual happening could easily have been accidental. The young men might have been in a state of fatigue on this final day of a week-long series of rituals during which they had not been permitted to leave the precincts of the Tabernacle for fear of contaminating their newly acquired sanctity as priests. They might have been confused about the sequence of events in this unfamiliar procedure and thus have approached the altar at the wrong time. In this uneasy state of mind, the two might not have noticed that the fire, momentarily quiescent, was about to spring up again. Or perhaps there was a sudden flare-up from their own fire-pans that touched off the oil with which they had been anointed. Moreover, the preparation of sacrificial animals would have involved contact with fat and blood, substances that could easily have caught fire from a flying spark. Inexperience in the total situation would have increased the chances for an accident of the type that occurred.

The fact that there is no foreshadowing of this tragic event strengthens the possibility that the above explanation is plausible. Earlier, Moses had been instructed by God with the words, "And bring thou near unto thee Aaron, thy brother, and his sons with him," naming the four young men (28:1). Evidently the event that now occurred had not been anticipated then, even by an all-knowing God. It seems unlikely that on such an occasion, when they themselves were being elevated to the priesthood, the sons of Aaron would be in a mood to rebel against the directives of Moses or to cause discomfort to their father.

How does Moses actually respond to this sudden and unexpected catastrophe? "Then Moses said unto Aaron: This is it that the Lord spoke, saying: 'Through them that are nigh unto Me will I be sanctified, and before all the people will I be glorified" (Lev. 10:2). The loss of the two young men should be accepted as a form of sacrifice in the sanctification of the altar. The bereaved father is thus indirectly admonished not to give way to unseemly grief on an occasion that was meant for a joyous glorification of God. We are told, "And Aaron held his peace."

There is a special pathos to this story as far as Aaron is concerned. On the very day of his greatest glory, when he was about to acquire a new role, which would make him more of a person in his own right and not just a shadowy figure at the side of Moses, he is struck a crushing blow.

As for Moses, his dominating concern of the moment is that the holiness of the sanctuary and of the priesthood should not be impaired through defilement by the presence of death within the sacred precincts. Strict ritual laws governed the burial rites, especially those involving the priestly family. Thus, neither Aaron nor the two remaining sons, Eleazar and Ithamar, were even allowed to participate in the task of removing the bodies from the Tabernacle grounds. Nor were they permitted to observe the usual rituals of mourning, such as letting the hair of their heads go loose or rending their clothing, as was customary among the laymen. To do so would have impaired the dignity of their priestly status. The eyes of the whole congregation were on them, and the people would be influenced by their behavior. Neither could they leave the tent of meeting to attend the burial service, for as Moses said, "'The anointing oil of the Lord is upon you.' And they did according to the word of Moses" (Lev. 10:7).

The first response of the leader to his brother regarding this tragic event, although probably intended to help him accept the will of God, clearly expressed the belief that the Deity demanded special sacrifice from those whom He brought close to Himself. It was a belief that Moses had long held in regard to his own personal life. Now that Aaron too had been especially favored by the Deity, shouldn't he also be expected to show his greater devotion to God by accepting this loss with grace?

The feeling that a sacrifice was expected of Aaron suggests a wish that he too should be subject to some of the same deprivations that Moses himself had experienced. Thus, unconsciously, it was a hostile wish.

What might have aroused such an emotion on this occasion? For the first time Aaron in a sense eclipsed his brother in the eyes of the people as he appeared before them in the magnificent apparel of the high priest and assumed the duties of that role. It would be understandable if, at that moment, Moses experienced a reactivation of childhood sibling rivalry. The unacceptable thought is then projected onto the Deity as a demand for sacrifice on the part of Aaron.

There was another potential source for evoking sibling rivalry at this time. How must Moses have felt as he prepared the sons of his brother for the priesthood? Thoughts of his own offspring, Gershom and Eliezer, could not have been entirely absent from his mind. The latter are given no share in the sanctification ceremonies or a role in the functioning of the Tabernacle. Their existence is simply ignored, a situation that in itself is a form of death. By their very absence the sons of Moses could also be understood as a form of sacrifice.

But paternal longings, so significant a part of human family ties, cannot easily be denied. These feelings may have found some expression in Moses through identification with Aaron's role as father and by taking over, vicariously, the latter's sons, whom he was now initiating into the priesthood. Here too, however, ambivalence may have manifested itself. Aaron had been generously blessed with four sons. Now they were reduced to two, the same number as those of Moses, a situation that made unconscious identification with his own offspring easier. On the positive side of the ambivalence, Moses must also have suffered the pain of losing the two young priests, his substitute sons as well as the sons of his brother.

Here again the Talmudic rabbis seem to echo the unconscious of Moses, in that he might have been threatened by the sudden elevation in status of his older brother. They suggest that the sorrow that befell Aaron on this occasion was for the purpose of teaching a lesson in humility. At the very time he was being elevated to the proud position of high priest, a father role to the people, his glory was diminished as a biologic father. As if to compensate for this depreciation of Aaron, legend also presents him in numerous stories as a model of humility (Ginzberg 1909–1938, 3:182–184, 328f.; 6:81).

Folklore response to the death of the two youths has it that their garments remained untouched by the flames, and some versions of the story declare that even their bodies were left intact.

It is said that two thin lines of flames issued from the Holy of Holies, then parted into four, two each entering the nostrils of the victim, causing death. Thus, the holy priestly attire was spared. Furthermore, other opinions maintained that the two young men "in their love and affection for God, were willing to die in body, that they might live before the Lord" (Ginzberg 1909-1938, 6:75). This belief helped to ameliorate the harshness of the punishment, which must unconsciously have been perceived as excessive. Also, by differentiating the manner of death that overtook Nadab and Abihu from that of the sacrificial animal on the altar, a defensive need to disguise the similarity between the two burnings may unconsciously have been at work. Unlike the pagan gods, the God of Israel did not demand human sacrifices.

However, the oldest son did stand in a special relationship to the Deity. This concept finds expression in the commandment, "Sanctify unto Me all the first-born, both of man and of beast, it is mine" (13:2). This statute can be understood as a form of tribute to God, a symbol of submission to the Heavenly Father by the earthly one, who had produced a son, thereby rivaling the Creator Himself. Moreover, the first-born male unconsciously represented an oedipal interloper to his father for he had *opened the womb* of the mother, briefly passing through the same area that had hitherto belonged exclusively to him. Among the Hebrews, animal sacrifice became a substitute for human sacrifice, the original meaning of which was repressed. However, the significant words of Moses to Aaron, "This is it that the Lord spoke, saying: 'Through them that are nigh unto Me will I be sanctified,'" although intended on a sublimated level, contain an undertone of the repressed.

The commandment of Exodus quoted above continues to be fulfilled in Jewish tradition through a special ritual. The first-born son is redeemed from service to God through the payment of a small fee to the priesthood, a ceremony known as *Pidyon Haben* (redemption of the son). For the people of Israel as a whole, the tribe of Levi was elected by God as the group dedicated to His service and charged with duties relating to the functioning of the Tabernacle. From the family of Aaron and its descendents came the special branch of the priesthood that was endowed with the sacred tasks of performing the rituals associated with the religious practices of the sanctuary. Thus, Moses carried out his goal of establishing orderly ways of worship and sacrifice, making possible the expression of religious feelings and needs on the part of the people, which brought them into closer communion with God.

Further Hardships in the Wilderness

Maternal Aspects in the Personality of Moses

 CHAPTER NINE

IN THE PERIOD following the departure from Mount Sinai an increasing spirit of discontent and rebelliousness seemed to pervade the people, leading to a number of tragic events as we shall see. One must wonder what special factors, if any, stimulated their mood and behavior.

During the preceding months, the most momentous event in their lives, that which gave lasting meaning to the exodus itself, had taken place—the Covenant with God at Mount Sinai. It was to be regarded in future millenia as the most significant occurrence in shaping their history as a people. The period spent at the foot of the holy mountain was also the time when the Tabernacle and its sacred furnishings were brought into being by the united efforts of the group. Why then was the temper of the people now so prone to dissatisfaction and unruliness?

In little more than a year the Children of Israel had moved from a degrading position of slavery, with its hard labor and cruel punishments, to the status not only of freedom but of being chosen by God to become a "kingdom of priests and a holy nation" (Exod. 19:6). This was indeed a dramatic uplifting from the lowest rung of the ladder to the highest in things of the spirit. Yet there was now an increase in discontent leading, in a crescendo of crises, to the punishment of wandering in the wilderness for a generation.

Life during the encampment at Mount Sinai must have been easier than traveling through the wilderness. That long stay of almost a year would have been possible only where there was a plentiful supply of water and the earth produced a certain abundance of vegetation. We know from studies of that area this was indeed so (Driver 1911, 183).

It may be that the change from the more comfortable, seminomadic life at the foot of Mount Sinai to the resumption of their wanderings in the unfamiliar and dreary terrain through which they were now moving affected the mood of the people and stirred up depressive and angry feelings. A similar sequence had taken place shortly after the exodus, when they left the pleasant oasis of Elim and expressed their discontent in the Wilderness of Sin (Exod. 16:1–3).

The self-image of the Children of Israel also may have been different now. Did they perhaps feel that since they were a people chosen by God their lot should henceforth be an easier one? Such attitudes of being special, for one reason or another, are not uncommon, among either individuals or groups.

A further aspect may be involved. It often happens that human beings who have been ill-used for a long time and have had to suppress their anger and rebelliousness, or indeed were too hopeless even to have awareness of such feelings, react to an improved situation in certain ways that are psychologically understandable, though on the surface they do not appear so. The new sense of self-worth is manifested by giving vent to emotions more freely and finding release for long-pent-up angers. This phenomenon is especially noticeable in therapeutic situations. Having gained some measure of self-confidence from the relationship with a helping person, patients will often go through a period of *acting out* their destructive feelings, both as a form of discharge and in order to test the person in authority, as if to see if he or she will really tolerate their *badness*, thus showing that he or she *cares*. Only after going through that process can they develop along more positive lines. Similarly, the Children of Israel often had to test their leader and through him God as well. Thus, their complaints and "murmurings" increased, with Moses as the inevitable target. He had proved at Mount Sinai how close he was to God. The demands that he exercise his awesome power in order to satisfy their needs and gratify their wishes were easily aroused. Failure on his part to make use of the omnipotence with which they endowed him in their fantasy could be experienced by the people either as indifference to their deprivations, or even more significantly, as a sign that he lacked these powers.

In the complexity of the human psyche, other factors may also have played a role. During the years of oppressive slavery under harsh taskmasters the people were forced to work within a frame of reference that had now become outworn. Instead of building cities that others would inhabit, they had to learn how to build a community for themselves in which obedience to God's moral laws and religious precepts were to be the guiding principles. It is understandable that the change from being treated as beasts of burden, with no power of making decisions for their own lives, to the sudden lifting of the chains would bring about some confusion in their outlook, their expectations, and their behavior.

The attitudes described above find expression shortly after the departure from Mount Sinai. In a curiously enigmatic fashion, the first three verses of Numbers 11* set the tone for what follows. Without specifying any of the details, the general statement of a catastrophe that took place is recorded: "And the people were as murmurers, speaking evil in the ears of the Lord; and when the Lord heard it, His anger was kindled; and the fire of the Lord burnt among them, and devoured in the uttermost part of the camp. And the people cried unto Moses; and Moses prayed unto the Lord, and the fire abated. And the name of that

---

*All biblical references in this chapter, unless otherwise noted, are to the book of Numbers.

place was called Taberah [burning] because the fire of the Lord burnt among them" (11:1–3).

These opening statements, with their theme of wrongdoing, punishment by the Deity, and intercession by Moses, presented in a framework of isolation and ambiguity, are like the prelude of a morality play that is to be enacted

But why the highly elliptical nature of these statements? What is being left out here and for what reason? What "evil" did the people speak "in the ears of the Lord?" Why did they bypass Moses, their usual intermediary, and dare to approach the Deity Himself for this purpose? God had never been very tolerant of "murmurers," as they should have known.

The nature of the people's unhappiness becomes clear very shortly. The text goes on to say, "And the mixed multitude that was among them fell a-lusting; and the children of Israel also wept on their part, and said: 'Would that we were given flesh to eat! We remember the fish, which we were wont to eat in Egypt for nought; the cucumbers, and the melons, and the leeks, and the onions, and the garlic; but now our soul is dried away; there is nothing at all; we have nought save this manna to look to'" (11:4–6).

It seems that the "lusting" was initiated by a "mixed multitude," generally interpreted as non-Israelite strangers, such as malcontents and prisoners of war, who had taken advantage of the exodus to join the escapees from Egypt (Hertz 1936, 614). These less desirable classes, the text implies, stirred up the spirit of rebellion, whereupon "the children of Israel also wept."

And now, at this point when the people were complaining about the monotony of their diet, the manna, which was so depreciated, is described with a degree of detail that suggests considerable interest in this food. "And the manna was like coriander seed, and the appearance thereof was the appearance of bdellium. The people went about, and gathered it, and ground it in mills, or beat it in mortars, and seethed it in pots, and made cakes of it; and the taste of it was as the taste of a cake baked in oil. And when the dew fell upon the camp in the night, the manna fell upon it" (11:6–9) (Driver 1911, 153-54).

This is a vivid, realistic account of a basic activity in the daily lives of the people, the ingathering and preparation of food. It is presented in a matter-of-fact way, with no indication that the tasks involved were burdensome. The final product is even made to sound inviting, "And the taste of it was as the taste of a cake baked in oil." It may be that the purpose of these verses was to emphasize that it was not *need* but so-called *lust* that drove the people to rebelliousness and therefore proved that they were worthy of punishment. We are also reminded with what ease the manna was obtained, how it fell from heaven as it were, provided by the God to Whom they were now complaining.

The unhappiness of the people is further depicted. "And Moses heard the people weeping, family by family, every man at the door of his tent; and the anger of the Lord was kindled greatly; and Moses was displeased" (11:10–11). This description has strong emotional overtones. Curiously, while God was *angry*, Moses was only *displeased*. The leader must have gone among the people to observe their discontent and clearly was profoundly affected by the scene. He may have felt their silent reproaches, or heard their actual ones, even as he witnessed their tears.

Moses probably felt responsible for the unhappiness of the people. They undoubtedly blamed him, and its seems that he accepted their reproaches as deserved. This situation may have reduced him to feelings of helplessness because he could not meet their wishes. Instead of being omnipotent as they expected, he must have seen himself as impotent in their eyes. Thus, they had deemed it necessary to speak directly into "the ears of the Lord."

Weeping seems a strange reaction to the grievance about a monotonous diet. This behavior is more descriptive of a depressive mood rather than an angry one. The people speak longingly of Egypt, Mother Egypt, and her opulent breasts, of which they have been deprived. It may be that they were now in a regressive state, wanting the comforts of the mother rather than the *words* of the Father, which they had received at Mount Sinai. The resumption of the pilgrimage through the barren landscape may have been an unhappy reminder of their separation from the green fields of Egypt where they had had at least the opportunity of growing their own food. The good aspects of the mother were here fondly recalled, while the suffering of their enslavement at her hands was repressed. It is not surprising that "the anger of the Lord was kindled greatly" at this ungrateful people.

But the milder emotion of Moses himself, who was only *displeased*, is puzzling, particularly so when he turns to God and expresses himself with a great intensity of feeling that goes considerably beyond displeasure. "And Moses said unto the Lord, 'Wherefore has Thou dealt ill with Thy servant? and wherefore have I not found favour in Thy sight, that Thou layest the burden of all this people upon me? Have I conceived all this people? Have I brought them forth, that Thou shouldst say unto me: Carry them in thy bosom, as a nursing-father carrieth the sucking child, unto the land which Thou didst swear unto their fathers? Whence should I have flesh to give unto all this people? for they trouble me with their weeping, saying: Give us flesh, that we may eat. I am not able to bear all this people myself alone, because it is too heavy for me. And if Thou deal thus with me, kill me, I pray Thee, out of sight; and let me not look upon my wretchedness'" (11:10–15).

These are strong words coming from the man of "slow tongue." They express despair rather than merely displeasure. And underneath the despair, a good deal of anger can be discerned, not only toward the people but toward God, Who had placed this burden on him. Such feelings in relation to the Deity, however, are unacceptable and so are projected to God Himself. Thus, whereas "the anger of the Lord was kindled greatly," Moses dared express only the milder emotion of displeasure, even though the object of that feeling is ambiguous. The unhappiness of the people had evidently stirred the leader to compassion. Was he therefore displeased because God was angry at the Children of Israel, whereas he himself identified with their plight? Should God not have provided them with what they desired, as Moses himself clearly wished to do, had he the power?

The question arises about why Moses felt the deprivation of the people so deeply. At this point they were not actually suffering from hunger or thirst. They complained only of being tired of the unchanging fare of manna and looked back longingly to an earlier period of illusory good, when their oral wishes were recalled as having been gratified. Moses did not feel threatened by them physically in this situation as in others. Why could he not have ignored their somewhat childish dissatisfaction and tears?

There must have been a deep wish within Moses to gratify the people. His inability to do so would then have made him feel powerless. His protestation about *not* being the "nursing-father" who had conceived and brought forth all these *children* is indeed significant. It may be an effort to deny what Moses must really have profoundly felt—a deep maternal feeling for his people, which intensified his sense of impotence and a longing for power so that he could then feed them all at the breast as a loving mother should.

The overreaction of Moses to the complaints and weeping of the people and the symbolic language in which he expresses his emotions offer a clue to the unconscious factors at work. The maternal aspect in the character of Moses, which played a role in making it so difficult to endure the tears of *his children*, is basic to our understanding of his personality. Moses was following a pattern reflected in the nature of the Deity Himself. In the graphic disclaimer, "Have I conceived all this people? Have *I* brought them forth?" (italics added), the pronoun *I* in the Hebrew is in the so-called emphatic position. The implicatoin is that *not he but God Himself is the nursing-father of all this people*. Was it not the Deity Who had redeemed them from slavery and brought them to Mount Sinai for a spiritual rebirth, to be *His* people, Moses is suggesting. And indeed the God of biblical tradition has important aspects of the maternal figure subtly integrated into His character qualities (Barag 1946; Ticho 1972) (17). It was the frustration of such feelings within Moses himself that must have contributed to his conflictful state at this time as on other similar occasions.

This maternal quality in the character of the leader could have stemmed from several sources (Patai 1967). It has been noted that creative people tend to have greater capacity for identification with both parental figures (Greenacre 1963, 19–20). However, Moses gives evidence of an undue degree of frustration in not being able to live up to his idealized image of the combined parental figures. Such reactions, especially in relation to the mother imago, may originate in the early mother-child relationship, which influences the later image of the oedipal father. As one psychoanalyst described this type of development, "But the lineaments that his [the oedipal father] image bears are those that belonged to that of the pre-oedipal mother." Along the lines of Freudian thought, he adds at another point, "For it is within the recesses of the ego ideal that infantile omnipotence can find a lodgement and a hiding place." He then goes on to make the meaningful statement, "It is in the unconscionable demands made by the perfectionist ego ideal that one has, I believe, one element in that existential despair so feelingly described by Kierkegaard" (Evans 1972; Zeligs 1960).

In the complaint of Moses that he cannot bear the burden *alone*, he expresses a sense of isolation both from the people and from God. The feelings of inadequacy and anger resulting from his frustration temporarily separate him from the basic source of his strength, a sense of closeness to the Deity, bringing about the kind of aloneness that could easily lead to despair. It was fortunate that Moses was not able to tolerate for any length of time this sense of separation from God. In his very expression that he cannot bear the burden alone, Moses has already broken through the barrier of that aloneness and is asking for help.

There is an understandable relationship between the two complaints that Moses presents before God. First, he is not able to provide meat for all the people, and is troubled by their weeping. Second, he cannot bear alone the burden of caring for them. It is an expression of a sense of responsibility for their needs and a feeling of inadequacy in fulfilling them.

God hears the words of anger and despair uttered by His beloved prophet and tries to ameliorate the situation along the particular lines suggested by Moses himself. "And the Lord said unto Moses: 'Gather unto Me seventy men of the elders of Israel, whom thou knowest to be the elders of the people, and officers over them; and bring them unto the tent of meeting, that they may stand there with thee. And I will come down and speak with thee there; and I will take of the spirit which is upon thee, and will put it upon them; and they shall bear the burden of the people with thee, that thou bear it not thyself alone'"(11:16–17).

Having set forth the plan for one aspect of the complaint, God then deals with the other matter, which seems at the moment to be of even greater urgency. He does so in the manner of an exasperated parent who, even as he yields to demands for gratification by rebellious children, also promises punishment.

"And say thou unto the people: 'Sanctify yourselves against tomorrow, and ye shall eat flesh; for ye have wept in the ears of the Lord, saying: Would that we were given flesh to eat: for it was well with us in Egypt; therefore the Lord will give you flesh, and ye shall eat. Ye shall not eat one day, nor two days, nor five days, neither ten days, nor twenty days; but a whole month, until it come out of your nostrils, and it be loathsome unto you; because that ye have rejected the Lord who is among you, and have troubled Him with weeping, saying: Why, now, came we forth out of Egypt?'" (11:18–20).

It is difficult to distinguish here God's feelings from those of Moses himself. Clearly, the Deity too has been troubled by the weeping of the people and declares that they have rejected Him, Who was among them, even as Moses must have felt.

Why then, at this point when God shares his feelings and is so supportive of him, does Moses suddenly express doubt about the power of the Deity to carry out His promise? "And Moses said: 'The people among whom I am, are six hundred thousand men on foot; [18] and yet Thou hast said: I will give them flesh, that they may eat a whole month! If flocks and herds be slain for them, will they suffice them? Or if all the fish of the sea be gathered together for them, will they suffice them?'" (11:21–22).

One can only conjecture here the conflicting thoughts and emotions of the leader. Was there a resurgence of unconscious competitiveness with God, Who was about to fulfill the wishes of the people for meat, something that Moses himself had wanted so much to do but had not the power to accomplish? Or was Moses unconsciously projecting his own impotence onto the Deity? The miraculous feat that God promised seemed, momentarily at least, impossible to Moses, thus indicating some confusion between his own identity and that of God's. But the moment of doubt evidently passed quickly, as seen in God's response, "And the Lord said unto Moses: 'Is the Lord's hand waxed short? now shalt thou see whether My word shall come to pass unto thee or not.'"(11:23).

First, God's plan for anointing seventy elders is carried out. The text says: "And Moses went out, and told the people the words of the Lord: and he gathered seventy men of the elders of the people, and set them round about the Tent. And the Lord came down in the cloud, and spoke unto him, and took of the spirit that was upon him, and put it upon the seventy elders; and it came to pass, that, when the spirit rested upon them they prophesied [literally, "spoke in ecstasy"], but they did so no more"(11:24–25).

Two elements in this episode are of special interest in regard to the behavior of Moses. God grants his request to have others who would lend him support in his tasks of leadership. But this wish for help, expressed with so much emotion, does not seem to endure very long. The seventy elders on whom the spirit of Moses was so impressively bestowed do not maintain their exalted state for any length of time. The text says, ". . . when the spirit rested upon them, they prophesied, but *they did so no more*" (italics added). The brief episode has a perfunctory character, as though mechanically carried out. Moses "gathers" the men and "sets" them round about the Tent, almost as if they were inanimate objects. God speaks only to Moses and takes of "the spirit that is upon him and puts it upon the others." Their "prophesying" sounds more like a hypnotic trance and has no lasting power. It can be inferred that, after all, Moses was not so eager to share his special relationship with God in this manner. Perhaps he felt that when God "took of his spirit" and bestowed it on the elders, less remained with him. This description also indicates that their power was of a secondary nature, having come only indirectly from God through the person of Moses himself. Thus, from the beginning, this particular wish of Moses was ambivalent.

A further related incident is of interest here. Not all of the seventy men had responded to the call. The Bible says, "But there remained two men in the camp, the name of the one was Eldad, and the name of the other Medad; and the spirit rested upon them; and they were of them that were recorded, but had not gone out unto the Tent; and they prophesied in the camp. And there ran a young man, and told Moses and said: 'Eldad and Medad are prophesying in the camp.' And Joshua, the son of Nun, the minister of Moses from his youth up, answered and said: 'My lord Moses, shut them in [restrain them].' And Moses said unto him: 'Art thou jealous for my sake? would that all the Lord's people were prophets, that the Lord would put His spirit upon them!' And Moses withdrew into the camp, he and the elders of Israel" (11:25–28).

How does one explain this reaction of Moses to the news that two of the men, who were also appointed to be among the elders but failed to come to the Tent of Meeting, were nevertheless also seized by the spirit and prophesied in the camp? Their power thus exceeded even those of the elders who had been directly subjected to the influence of the sanctification. Moses' rebuke to his two devoted followers who were zealous to protect the undivided authority of the leader seems contrary to the above interpretation that Moses was reluctant to share his unique role with God. His pious wish that all the Lord's people should be prophets can be understood as a *reaction formation* to the underlying, contradictory wish, unacceptable to his superego, that he alone should retain the position of being special. His words of reproach to the two younger men, Joshua and the nameless other, are also intended unconsciously for himself.

The promise of God to gratify the craving of the people for meat is now fulfilled, together with the punishment that follows. "And there went forth a wind from the Lord, and brought across quails from the sea, and let them fall by the camp, about a day's journey on this side, and a day's journey on the other side, round about the camp, and about two cubits above the face of the earth. And the people rose up all that day and all night, and all the next day, and gathered the quails; he that gathered least gathered ten heaps; and they spread all abroad for themselves round about the camp. While the flesh was yet between their teeth, ere it was chewed, the anger of the Lord was kindled against the people, and the Lord smote the people with a very great plague. And the name of that place was called Kibroth-hattaaveh [the graves of lust], because there they buried the people that lusted"(11:31–34).

The impression is given that the plague started immediately, even as the people had begun to eat. Yet earlier God had predicted that they would eat meat for a whole month until it became loathsome to them. Again, only conjecture about this seeming contradiction is possible here. Both the prediction and how the actual event took place find expression in words of intense anger. These feelings can be attributed to Moses himself and defensively projected onto God. The initial threat, at the moment of its utterance, may have served as a discharge for the overwrought emotions of the leader. He was saying in effect, "Give them what they want until it hurts." What actually occurred may have resulted from reality factors. It is possible, as some commentators have suggested, that the people in their greed may have eaten the quails in too great quantity or without sufficient cooking or curing. It may also be that the fatigue associated with the capture of the birds predisposed the people to illness. The text says that the quails "fell about a day's journey on this side, and a day's journey on the other side," and that the time spent in gathering them was two days and an intervening night, so that "even he that gathered least gathered ten heaps." Hysterical factors, too, may have played a role, the sick reactions of a few setting off similar responses among others, with the whole situation being aggravated by a sense of guilt and the awareness of the leader's displeasure. He whom they had rejected by complaining directly to God had been vindicated both by the miraculously arriving birds and the impressive ceremony of the sanctification of the elders. It could be said that they were not able to enjoy their ill-gotten gains. And indeed the whole tone of the narrative is strongly slanted toward gluttony and its punishment, while at the same time there is a contradictory impression of genuine suffering and unhappiness on the part of the people. These two aspects may reflect the ambivalent feelings of Moses himself in regard to the situation.

It is certainly not insignificant that in an earlier episode (Exodus 16) quails were also available to the people. At that time, according to the text, "the quails came up, and covered the camp"(16:13). Evidently the people did not have to journey any distance to reach them, thus being spared the fatigue of doing so. Nor were the Children of Israel on that occasion accused of lust or threatened with punishment.

The different interpretation of the two events may have been primarily in the psychological state of the leader himself. On the earlier occasion, the intrapsychic situation of Moses suggested that he *shared* in the omnipotence of God, thus gaining strength for his feelings of inadequacy in this way rather than yielding to anger and despair as in the later episode. Perhaps Moses expected the people to be able to endure the privations of life in the wilderness with greater fortitude after their consecration at Mount Sinai. His expectations of them as well as of himself must have been unrealistically high.

It might be relevant to summarize here the psychodynamics of Moses as interpreted in the context of this biblical chapter. The complaints and tears of the people move the leader to feelings of frustration and inadequacy because he cannot fulfill their wishes. He feels rejected by them and suffers a loss of self-esteem. His anger toward them is diverted to the Deity, Who had burdened him with this ungrateful people. He is now emotionally isolated both from his followers and from God, an unbearable situation leading to despair.

In the metaphor of the nursing-father, the hidden role of Moses as a maternal figure emerges. Thus, he is both father and mother, in identification with God, Who brought forth the Children of Israel out of Egypt and made them His own.

God agrees to meet the expressed wishes of Moses, arranging for the seventy elders to be sanctified and promising also to provide meat for the people. In a state of isolation and confusion Moses expresses doubt about the ability of God to accomplish the latter feat. For a moment his sense of earth-bound reality took precedence over the mystical acceptance of God's omnipotence. We do not know what fleeting unconscious fantasy may have provoked this disavowal, which indicated a *forgetfulness* of God's identity. Perhaps there was a brief resurgence of early oedipal competitiveness in a reaction to his own feelings of impotence because he himself could not satisfy the wishes of the people.

In the sanctification of the elders, Moses goes through a ritual of mystical reunion both with God and with the representatives of the people. Though it has a somewhat formalistic aspect, the ceremony may have served to restore the prestige of Moses in the eyes of the people and to break down his feelings of isolation in relation to both them and the Deity. The intrapsychic harmony of the leader is restored. He no longer feels alone and has no further need to have the elders share his burden. The narcissistic injury of his inadequacy as witnessed by the people is further nullified by the seemingly miraculous arrival of the quails, a manifestation of God's power, with which Moses was closely identified.

Thus, we see in this chapter the concern of Moses for the people and his unhappiness at not being able to gratify their wishes. The desire to feed and nurture *his children* highlights the *motherly* aspects of his personality. At the same time, Moses himself manifests a human need for nurturance and support on his own behalf. He turns to God in his distress, expressing toward the Deity the same emotions of displeasure and frustration as those displayed by the people toward him. God in turn assumes the motherly role toward Moses, trying to comfort and sustain him while at the same time also fulfilling the more fatherly function of disciplining the unruly Children of Israel. These processes take place in a setting resembling the familial situation.

Out of the learning experience in the wilderness grew the increased maturity of both the people and the leader, revealed with particular clarity in Chapter 11 of Numbers. The introjective-projective patterns that Moses utilizes in his communications with the Deity are part of a complex intrapsychic mode of functioning, with mystical aspects beyond full psychoanalytic analysis.

Moses and His Siblings

Rivalry and Love

 CHAPTER TEN

THE PERSONAL LIFE of Moses in relation to his family is rarely mentioned during the period of the wilderness. In the time of general unrest following the departure from Mount Sinai, an unusual occurrence takes place (Numbers 12).* Moses is drawn into an involvement with his two siblings, Miriam and Aaron. The episode begins abruptly and develops with dramatic intensity, reaching a definitive conclusion through the intervention of God.

"And Miriam and Aaron spoke against Moses because of the Cushite woman whom he had married; for he had married a Cushite woman. And they said: 'Hath the Lord indeed spoken only with Moses? Hath He not spoken also with us?' And the Lord heard it.—Now the man Moses was very meek, above all the men that were upon the face of the earth.—And the Lord spoke suddenly unto Moses, and unto Aaron, and unto Miriam:

---

*All biblical references in this chapter, unless otherwise noted, are to the book of Numbers.

'Come out ye three unto the tent of meeting.' And they three came out. And the Lord came down in a pillar of cloud, and stood at the door of the Tent, and called Aaron and Miriam; and they both came forth. And He said: 'Hear now My words: If there be a prophet among you, I the Lord do make Myself known unto him in a vision, I do speak with him in a dream. My servant Moses is not so; he is trusted in all My house; with him do I speak mouth to mouth, even manifestly, and not in dark speeches; and the similitude of the Lord doth he behold; wherefor then were ye not afraid to speak against My servant, against Moses?' And the anger of the Lord was kindled against them; and He departed. And when the cloud was removed from over the Tent, behold Miriam was leprous, as white as snow; and Aaron looked upon Miriam; and behold, she was leprous. And Aaron said unto Moses: 'Oh my lord, lay not, I pray thee, sin upon us, for that we have done foolishly, and for that we have sinned. Let her not, I pray, be as one dead, of whom the flesh is half consumed when he cometh out of his mother's womb. And Moses cried unto the Lord, saying: 'Heal her now, O God, I beseech Thee.'

"And the Lord said unto Moses: 'If her father had but spit in her face, should she not hide in shame seven days? let her be shut up without the camp seven days, and after that she shall be brought in again.' And Miriam was shut up without the camp seven days; and the people journeyed not till Miriam was brought in again. And afterward the people journeyed from Hazeroth, and pitched in the wilderness of Paran" (12:1–16).

This brief episode constitutes the entire chapter and seems to have a character of its own. Yet in a curious way it echoes some of the underlying emotions associated with the events that immediately preceded it. In chapter 11 we are told at the very beginning that "the people spoke evil in the ears of the Lord," and He was angry with them because of it. And now, more specifically, it is Miriam and Aaron who speak evil of Moses, and again God is angry.

The reasons given by the sister and brother of Moses for their displeasure against him are along two different lines that seem to bear no relationship to each other. And yet they are stated *as though* there was a connection. The first mentioned is that they did not like his having married a Cushite woman; second, they rebelled against the idea that God revealed Himself *only* to Moses. "Hath He not spoken also with us?"

Scholars have been puzzled by the seeming disparity between the two complaints and concluded that these represented two variants of the same story (James 1950, 37–38). There is, however, a common element between them. *Jealousy* could underlie both causes for the discontent of Miriam and Aaron. In the first situation this feeling, directed against their sister-in-law, whose identity is presented so ambiguously, has to be disguised, since it was morally and socially unacceptable. The cause for the second complaint is clearly jealousy of the special relationship that Moses has with God, from which the siblings feel themselves unfairly excluded. The inherent connection between the two presenting complaints is covertly expressed by their being mentioned together. The wife of Moses may have been experienced as a rival by both Miriam and Aaron in their respective relationships with Moses. The unconscious fantasies associated with that form of competitiveness was of a more forbidden nature than the sibling rivalry for love of the Father, which was on a more sublimated level.

Biblical commentary has not been able to establish whether "the Cushite woman" refers to Zipporah, the daughter of Jethro, whom Moses had married some years before in Midian, or whether he had made a second marriage, with the implication that his first wife was no longer alive, although her death is not recorded in the Bible. It is suggested by some scholars that the term Cushite may come from *Cushan*, a synonym for Midian, and thus refers to Zipporah. Others think that the more usual meaning of the word, *Ethiopian*, suggests a second marriage of Moses with a woman from that area (Hertz 1936, 618).

As will be recalled, there was a period of separation between Moses and Zipporah before she was reunited with him in the wilderness. The original plan had been for the wife of Moses and their two sons to accompany him to Egypt when the newly chosen prophet had decided to return there on his mission of rescue. And indeed they did depart with him. But while the family was resting at a lodging place, probably at the very borders of Egypt, the bizarre incident occurred in which the life of Moses was threatened by God Himself. Zipporah saves her husband by circumcising one of her sons in a strange ritual described earlier (chap. 3).

From that point on, the woman is not mentioned again until much later, after the exodus had already taken place and the Children of Israel were about to enter the area of Mount Sinai. We are told then that Jethro, hearing of the events regarding Moses and his people, paid his son-in-law a visit, bringing back with him Zipporah and the two sons of Moses, Gershom and Eliezer (Exod.18:1-7). Only then do we learn that the family of Moses had been sent back to Midian on the earlier occasion referred to above, ostensibly for their safety. Even now no reason is openly given for this action, the text simply stating that *he had sent her away* (Exod. 18:2).

The period of time since their reunion could not have been much more than a year. She was returned to him shortly before the Children of Israel encamped at Mount Sinai, where they remained for about that length of time. The event we are now concerned with occurred not long after the resumption of the journey toward the Promised Land.

During this brief time it is hardly likely that Zipporah died and Moses married again, moreover, a stranger from Ethiopia. It is more plausible that Miriam, having met Zipporah scarcely a year before, had not really accepted her during those past months, either as a member of the group or a sister-in-law. She may truly have perceived her as a stranger and thus doubly resented her as the *other woman* in Moses' life.

If, as manifested in the events of the preceding chapter (Num. 11), the spirit of dissension was rife throughout the camp, Miriam's latent dissatisfaction, held in abeyance before this, may have been stimulated by the contagion of the general discontent. The term *Cushite woman* seems to be used here in a derogatory sense. By avoiding her name and referring instead to her ethnic background, they deprive her of individuality and emphasize her alien status. There is, however, a puzzling aspect when this same appellation is repeated in the seemingly factual statement, "for he had married a Cushite woman" (12:1). The impression is given that this was a recent event. Since further evidence is lacking for such an unexpected happening, it can be assumed that the information thus proffered is for the benefit of the reader who may not have been familiar with the facts of his earlier life. Psychologically, such a reminder may be expressive of Moses' own attitude, the feeling that for him too this marriage emotionally belonged to the past and he had to be reminded of its continued existence in the present.

This same impersonal tone in presenting information as if for the enlightenment of the reader only is significant of the way in which the reunion of Moses and his family was recorded in Exodus (18:1-6). Jethro introduces himself, Zipporah, and her two sons, as though he didn't expect them to be remembered and they had to be identified anew. "And Jethro, Moses' father-in-law, took Zipporah, Moses' wife, after he had sent her away, and her two sons; of whom the name of the one was Gershom; for he said: 'I have been a stranger in a strange land'; and the name of the other was Eliezer; 'for the God of my father was my help, and delivered me from the sword of Pharaoh.'" This seems a strange occasion for such a recollection concerning the birth of the sons and the meaning of their names. What purpose could this belated explanation serve? It must have been a reminder that Moses had a family that he had left behind him in Midian. Then Jethro introduces the little group once more, this time, directly to Moses: "And he said unto Moses: 'I thy father-in-law Jethro am coming unto thee, and thy wife, and her two sons with her.'"

The response of Moses, however, acknowledges only the presence of Jethro. "And Moses went out to meet his father-in-law and bowed down and kissed him; and they asked each other of their welfare; and they came into the tent" (Exod. 18:7). Not only is Zipporah ignored, a situation that might be explained on the basis that it would not have been seemly for Moses to show public interest in a woman, but his sons too are treated in the same way. The omission of any feeling on his part in what should have been a joyous reunion is striking even in terms of the restraint with which familial expressions of affection are dealt with in the life of Moses.

In contrast to the lack of attention to his immediate family, the meeting between Moses and Jethro is marked by a high degree of hospitality. The warmth of their greetings and the recounting by Moses of all that had happened to him and to his people since he had left the house of his father-in-law are related with great feeling. Jethro responds with equal enthusiasm, acknowledging the greatness of the God of Moses and offering sacrifices in His name. Then a feast is held in which Aaron and all the elders of Israel participate. But throughout not a word is said about how Moses felt on beholding his wife and sons again (Exod.18:8–12).

One can assume that the leader would not allow himself the privileges and pleasures of the ordinary man. He may have felt that all his energies and thoughts belonged to God and to his people, Israel. The concentration of interest is now expressed toward a father figure, as a displacement perhaps for the warmth he had to withhold from his wife.

In relation to his sons, the mystery is even greater. Did they too, as well as Zipporah, now belong to a past that seemed remote to him in terms of feelings as well as time? So much of significance had taken place since he had last seen them. Did they belong to a phase of his life that he might indeed have *wanted* to forget, when he was a stranger in a strange land? Was this why the meaning of their names is here brought into the context, an unconscious, perhaps disturbing reminder of the conflicts of his earlier life before his existence had been imbued with a new purpose and meaning at the theophany of the burning bush?

One can only conjecture about such feelings on the part of Moses, but silence does indeed sometimes speak louder than words. It is unusual in Scripture for the relationship between a man and his sons to be so ignored. For better or worse, it is generally given some expression in the text. The need in Moses to keep this area repressed must have been very strong. Gershom and Eliezer are never mentioned again in connection with any event in the life of their father and are only referred to once more, for genealogical purposes in a part of Scripture quite remote from Exodus—(1 Chron. 23:14–16).

A puzzling feature of this family reunion is its *locale*. We are told that it took place where Moses was encamped, at the "mount of God," (Exod 18:5). But the Children of Israel were still at Rephidim on this occasion (Exod. 19:1). Hertz suggests that since Moses had earlier gone ahead to Mount Sinai when he struck the rock to obtain water for the people, he might have remained there (Hertz 1936, 288). But this explanation is plainly conjectural. My own interpretation is that the expression *mount of God* is used here in a symbolic sense. It occurs also at the time Zipporah is sent away from Moses, or rather, simply vanishes wordlessly from the narrative (Exod. 4:26–27). Moses then meets Aaron as predicted by God. The text states that the two brothers meet at the "mount of God," a geographic impossibility since Moses is ostensibly at the very borders of Egypt when the reunion takes place. In both of these instances, when the wife of Moses disappears and when she is returned to him, *the mount of God* may symbolize the *presence* of God, Whose will dictated both events. Moses required God's permission to enjoy the privileges of the marital state. During the period of the struggle with Pharaoh in Egypt, the leader had to devote his full energies to the task at hand, and thus family life had to be temporarily renounced. That Moses may have had some conflict about this renunciation is indicated by the repression with which this whole matter is treated. Evidently he did want his wife and sons with him in Egypt, for he brings them to the very borders of that land before they silently disappear.

But even on the happier occasion when Moses is reunited with them—at the "holy mount," that is, with the consent of God—some element of conflict must have remained, explaining the inhibition of his feelings when he greets his wife and sons. Nevertheless, Moses must have accepted the responsibilities of his family life and probably shared a tent with his wife, at least part of the time. Zipporah was thus both accepted and ignored.

Miriam may have intuitively sensed the emotional estrangement between Moses and Zipporah and thus was emboldened to add her own disparagement of the "Cushite woman." Curiously, there is an extrabiblical legend to the effect that Miriam was angry with Moses because he did *not* avail himself of his connubial rights and by this abstinence set himself above her and Aaron by being more righteous in this respect than they (Ginzberg 1909–1938, 3:256). Thus, through a reversal of the real situation the reality of Miriam's jealousy is denied. We have here another example of how intuitively and, in this case, defensively the fantasy of the people responded to the stimulus of the biblical story. Moreover, in contrast to the *meekness* of Moses, so extolled in relation to this episode, the legend points to his pride in being overly righteous.

The treatment of the marriage of Moses as though it were a new or recent event may be subtly expressive of a situation in which there is a *renewal* of the marital relationship of Moses and Zipporah. The element of newness also may suggest a continued failure on the part of Miriam and Aaron to accept Zipporah and even a possible resistance on the part of Moses himself to doing so. A relationship that does not become an accustomed one by merging into the social background retains an uncomfortable aspect of newness. Another legend about Miriam states that she was once instrumental in bringing about the remarriage of her parents, Amram and Jochebed, who, according to the story, had been separated after the decree of Pharaoh concerning the death of infant sons. The result of their reunion was the birth of Moses. On this basis, therefore, Miriam may have regarded herself as responsible for his very existence. He may indeed, in unconscious fantasy, have been her oedipal child, and she in turn probably occupied a corresponding role in his own fantasy life as the mother-sister who had saved him from death in his infancy, when he was hidden in the reeds along the banks of the Nile.

Zipporah may have been the object of a general lack of warmth among the people as a whole as well as by Miriam, who was the real mother figure for the group. The new arrival had been spared all the dangers of the period in Egypt preceding the exodus, the tribulations of the early desert wanderings, and indeed the entire experience of slavery endured by the others. Miriam, on the other hand, had been in the center of the travail from the beginning. After the return of Moses to Egypt she was the only woman who could claim a close relationship to the great leader and prophet. Suddenly Zipporah appears on the scene. Understandably, Miriam must have felt displaced.

Even before this event Miriam may have experienced feelings of being unrecognized and neglected by her younger brother. Whereas Aaron shared a good deal of reflected glory at the side of Moses, she herself had played no significant role since her song and dance of rejoicing after the crossing of the sea in the flight from Egypt (Exod. 15:20). The presence of Zipporah may therefore have accentuated her sense of loss, both in the personal life of Moses and in the lack of special recognition from the Deity, a privilege that Moses alone seemed to enjoy. In the sibling rivalry of the latter situation Miriam clearly does not want to compete with her admired brother but only to be loved equally by the Father, a form of justice frequently demanded by sisters and brothers in the family situation.

That Miriam was the main offender in this little family drama is made clear by the fact that she is mentioned first and is the only one who is punished. Perhaps she involved Aaron in an effort to have someone share the guilt. Miriam's ability to incite Aaron with her own feelings of resentment against Moses is also not difficult to comprehend. Aaron had shown himself throughout as a person yielding easily to influence under pressure and failing to emerge as a real personality in his own right. He might also have been tempted to ally himself with Miriam in a wish for greater closeness to this mother-sister figure, in whose affections he probably took second place to the younger brother. Moreover, repressed attitudes of resentment and jealousy toward Moses must certainly have existed, although the positive feelings for him, sublimated perhaps in a fatherly, supportive attitude and a shared sense of glory, must have prevailed most of the time. The role of being a partner to Moses, frequently standing at his side, may also have made him perceive Zipporah as someone who might come between him and the great leader despite the realistic differences in their relationships with him. Perhaps of even greater import may have been Aaron's devotion to Miriam, which finds moving expression in his compassion when she is struck down with the dread disease of leprosy and the intensity of his plea to Moses that her health be restored.

Miriam's feelings of jealousy are so understandably human that one must wonder why God was moved to such anger and imposed a punishment so severe. Perhaps it was because she *acted out* her negative feelings. For Miriam and Aaron "spoke against Moses," ostensibly to others, or the knowledge of this behavior would not have been known. Coming from personalities so close to the leader himself, even the slightest suggestion of disapproval or criticism might have had a demoralizing effect among the people, especially in the generally prevailing mood of discontent. Such an influence was dangerous and had to be quickly suppressed. That it should emanate from two people whose loyalty and support should have been unquestioned added to the enormity of the offense. But this episode proves again how genuinely human are the people of the biblical world and how similar to ourselves in their emotional reactions.

It will be recalled that the preceding chapter (Num. 11) begins with the statement, "And the people were as murmurers, speaking evil in the ears of the Lord; and when the Lord heard it, his anger was kindled." Behavior of this kind, therefore, was regarded as abhorrent to the Deity. Viewed as a projection of Moses himself, this abhorrence indicates his sensitivity to this form of aggression. When the verbal attack was directed against his own person and came from those nearest to him in family ties, the hurt must have been especially great. Perhaps he felt particularly defenseless because of his own tendency to inhibition in speech. Therefore Moses could not defend himself directly. Another would have to do so. And who could that Other be but God Himself! The strong and moving words with which the Deity intervenes in behalf of His chosen prophet can be understood as reflecting the intensity of Moses' own involvement. They are ringing words that have resounded through the ages and made clear for all time the place of Moses as the foremost prophet of God for the Hebrew people. Though quoted at the beginning of this chapter, they bear repetition here: "And the Lord spoke suddenly unto Moses, and unto Aaron, and unto Miriam: 'Come out ye three unto the tent of meeting.' And they three came out. And the Lord came down in a pillar of cloud, and stood at the door of the Tent, and called Aaron and Miriam; and they both came forth. And He said: 'Hear now My words: if there be a prophet among you, I the Lord do make Myself known unto Him in a vision, I do speak with him in a dream. My servant Moses is not so; he is trusted in all My house; with him do I speak mouth to mouth, even manifestly, and not in dark speeches; and the similitude of the Lord doth he behold; wherefore then were ye not afraid to speak against My servant, against Moses?' And the anger of the Lord was kindled against them" (12:4–9).

The word *suddenly* in the above quotation comes somewhat as a surprise. It expresses a sense of immediacy, as though no further delay could be tolerated in righting the wrong that had been done. This single unexpected word may be indicative of the intrapsychic conflict going on in Moses himself at this time. The effort to resolve it came through identification with God as his protector. Moreover, how profoundly special Moses felt in relation to the Divinity, a position that no one must challenge, is also revealed here more fully. It was this relationship that made it possible for him to carry on the heavy burdens of his great task.

In connection with this situation of overt sibling rivalry the biblical text points out a certain quality in Moses. "Now the man Moses was very meek, above all the men that were upon the face of the earth" (12:3). This verse has become well known for several reasons. It is an unusually clear-cut characterization of the great man in a literature that tends to portray personality through action rather than descriptive phrases. *Meakness* in the Hebrew word signifies *humility* and is not inconsistent with strength of character (James 1950, 37–38).

This verse has also been used by some biblical critics as evidence that Moses himself could not have been the author of such a passage for he would not have written about himself in this laudatory way (Archer 1964, 234). Without entering into this controversy one can nevertheless observe that this kind of reasoning involves a projection of modern values and judgments onto an ancient time when authors wrote anonymously for the most part. They could thus express with ingenuous sincerity what they really felt. There is certainly an element of exaggeration in the statement that Moses was meek "above all the men that were upon the face of the earth." It is possible that this form of expression was typical of those times, just as at a later period Solomon is described as "the wisest of all men" (1 Kings 3:12). As indicated in that latter situation, such descriptive phrases also can be understood as serving an unconscious purpose (Zeligs 1974, 268). Moses may have felt a special responsibility to cultivate a sense of meekness, or humility, in order to avoid undue pride about his relationship with God. The prophet could have developed this attitude in an effort to counteract motives of another kind—the hidden wish to be special and the secret pride that would go with such a relationship.

The punishment for Miriam that follows God's reprimand, as related in the quotation given earlier, is indeed dramatic. It is

Aaron who responds first to the climactic situation. He appeals to Moses directly rather than to God, thus acknowledging the role of his brother as intermediary and addressing him humbly as "my lord." His words of penitence and plea for forgiveness make Aaron more of a real person than ever before. The fact that he pleads in behalf of another, for evidently he himself had been spared, adds to the quality of compassion in his appeal.

The immediate response of Moses to Aaron's appeal was an impassioned plea on his own part: "Heal her now, O God, I beseech Thee." Both brothers seems to be in a state of shock at the suddenness and severity of the punishment. But the Deity is more deliberate in His reply. Miriam, it seems, had sinned against God Himself by her offense against His servant. However, the punishment was to be tempered with mercy. His reply too has a tone of deep emotion. "And the Lord said unto Moses: 'If her father had but spit in her face, should she not hide in shame seven days? Let her be shut up without the camp seven days, and after that she shall be brought in again.' And Miriam was shut up without the camp seven days; and the people journeyed not till Miriam was brought in again" (12:14–15). It was customary for lepers to be housed outside the camp because the disease was considered contagious.

One could theorize that the sudden affliction of Miriam could be understood as a psychosomatic response to a highly traumatic experience. Skin eruptions are a common expression of emotional disturbance. But the reality factor is not as significant as the meaning that the episode had psychologically for the people involved.

As suggested above, viewed from the psychodynamics of Moses himself, the character quality of meekness can be understood here as a reaction formation to its opposite, which is pride. Moses was too proud to defend himself. Doing so would have meant an acknowledgment that he had been personally offended by Miriam and Aaron on a level that he must have felt should have been beneath his notice. Therefore, he retreats from the ordinary human relationship of being a brother to the elevated position of the prophet of God. The reaction is a defense against his vulnerability as a human being. It is not Moses the brother whom they have offended but the servant of God, and thus the Deity Himself must defend him. However, not only pride must have been involved but to an even greater degree an underlying attitude that he was not entitled to deeply personal feelings in regard to family.

God's response to the plea of Moses is somewhat puzzling in terms of the continuity of the text "And the Lord said unto Moses: 'If her father had but spit in her face, should she not hide in shame seven days?'" The reason for which her father might have administered such a punishment is not stated. It was an avoidance that Moses had also utilized, as though to verbalize the act would have caused shame to the leader. God shows this same regard for the feelings of his prophet. The discontinuity in the text thus suggests a repression and displacement of feelings. Miriam deserved to be shamed and humiliated by her father because she had shamed and humiliated a brother-father figure. The attitude of Moses toward her is that of an offended parent, and it may be that all he really wanted to do was to shame her by spitting in her face, evidently a customary method of expressing anger and contempt to someone guilty of an offense.

Did the outbreak of leprosy represent the harsher wish of the unconscious? The boundary line between aggressive wishes stimulated by a need to repair a damage to self-esteem and the actual behavior in the modifying light of reality comes through in the change from the first penalty imposed on Miriam to the considerable easing of that punishment following the plea of Moses. God is not only the punitive superego but also functions as the reality-oriented ego, in empathy with the psyche of Moses.

The statement that the people waited seven days for Miriam before continuing their journey indicates that the group too regarded her with deference and could forgive her shortcomings.

This brief vignette in the personal life of Moses is meaningful in terms of his own character and that of his siblings. It expresses the importance that the biblical literature gives to ethical and moral values in human relationships and how these are reinforced by direct commandments from the Deity. At the same time, the accompanying stream of unconscious content contains in hidden form the roots of behavior, an understanding of which is now more accessible to us.

The episode reveals a defensive need on the part of Moses to maintain self-esteem through a certain image of himself, leading to a reaction-formation of meekness against pride. It shows his need to be *special* in relation to God but also expresses, on a manifest level, a compassionate love for Miriam and regard for Aaron. Miriam's conflicting feelings of rivalry and love concerning her younger brother, her wish to share equally in the love of the Father, the involvement of Aaron in this emotional conflict and the evocation in him of deep concern and affection for his sister are common human experiences that bring the biblical personalities closer to us.

One might ponder the nature of the psychic reality concerning the intriguing description of the encounter between God, Moses, Aaron, and Miriam. Although theophanies are part of the fabric of biblical narratives, this particular one has a certain element of uniqueness. It involves two people outside the tent, while Moses remains within. Moses within the tent was Moses in the presence of God and thus especially prone to altered states of consciousness. Was he then in identification with the Deity, voicing what seemed to him the righteous anger of God, words audible to the two offenders outside? Certainly any conscious deception would have been alien to the character of the leader.

Theophanies, however, belong to the category of the mystical and the mystifying. Perhaps what is important is that the narrative conveys its message with dramatic intensity, elevating the hero and punishing the wrongdoers.

The Report of the Spies

Conflict Between Faith and Fear

 CHAPTER ELEVEN

THE EPISODE to be considered here represents a turning point in the history of the Children of Israel in the wilderness, leading to a lengthy sojourn of the biblical forty years in that desolate territory before entering upon their conquest of the Promised Land.

In the familiar story, twelve men are sent ahead to bring back a report about the land, its topography, the inhabitants, the strength of its cities, and the produce of its soil. After forty days, they returned. What they told the people was a mixture of good news and bad. They brought back some of the fruits of the land, such as pomegranates and figs. Especially impressive was a cluster of grapes so large, the story goes, that it had to be carried on a pole between two men.

All the scouts talked glowingly about the fertility of the land, declaring that it flowed with milk and honey. But at this point the mood of their recital changed. They went on to say, "the people that dwell in the land are fierce, and the cities are fortified, and very great; and moreover we saw the children of Anak there [19]. Amalek dwelleth in the land of the South; and the Hittite and the Jebusite, and the Amorite, dwell in the mountains; and the Canaanite dwelleth by the sea, and along by the side of the Jordan" (13:28–29).*

Of the twelve men only two, Caleb and Joshua, were in favor of attempting the conquest of the land. The other ten advised against it, saying that the Children of Israel were not strong enough to attack the walled cities and overcome its formidable inhabitants.

There are some strange contradictions in the report of the scouts. On the one hand, they speak enthusiastically of the produce of the soil and exhibit proof of its fertility. At the same time, they declare that it is "a land that eateth up the inhabitants thereof" (13:32), the meaning of which is not elaborated. Immediately following is the statement, "and all the people that we saw in it are men of great stature . . . and we were in our own sight as grasshoppers, and so we were in their sight" (13:33).

If it is a land flowing with milk and honey, if the earth is fertile and the people strong, how then could this country be described as "one that eateth up the inhabitants thereof"?

On the one hand, the deep awe with which the wanderers of the wilderness beheld the settled life in Canaan and its inhabitants of great stature, and on the other, the low sense of self-esteem with which they saw themselves come out vividly in the revealing words, "and we were in our own sight as grasshoppers, and so we were in their sight." It is psychologically sound that they should see themselves *first* in their own eyes as grasshoppers and *then* project this feeling on others. It is evident that the returned scouts were in an ambivalent frame of mind about their experiences. As the following interpretation will suggest, their presentation was interwoven with images stemming from underlying fantasies of a frightening nature, probably stimulated by their fears.

In dream symbolism, insects often represent siblings, thus reducing these rivals for parental affection to insignificance as a way of expressing aggressive and contemptuous feelings toward

---

*All biblical references in this chapter, unless otherwise noted, are to the book of Numbers.

them (Freud 1900, chap. 9). The unconscious fantasy here utilizes the same imagery as the dream. But the wishful thinking is reversed by self-contempt, with the aggression turned against themselves. It is the scouts who see themselves as insects in the scornful eyes of those who already possess the motherland. Their fear is aroused by the prospect of entering into battle with the giant father-brothers. Added to the reality situation is the unconscious guilt that must have been aroused by the motive for their spying, the intent to take possession of the *mother* by force.

Was there also, unconsciously, a fear of the fertile mother herself, growing out of envy by these long-deprived children of the wilderness as they beheld her more fortunate sons living off the land? The desire to be fed by the mother, to find a substitute for the fleshpots of Egypt (symbolically the mother's breasts) would be associated with aggressive wishes to take possession of that prize by force, a wish followed by fear of retaliation. Thus, there is a reversal in the fantasy of being fed by the good mother. She becomes a hostile figure who devours those who try to approach her with aggressive intent. This is the mother of the repressed infantile unconscious, with the *vagina dentata*, onto whom is projected the cannibalistic impulses of the nursling at the breast. (Fenichel 1945, 79ff.). Thus, the Promised Land becomes one that "eateth up its inhabitants." The luscious grapes that the scouts brought back became the sour grapes of denial, envy, and fear.

Only Joshua and Caleb, whose faith in the Father was strong, could deal with those fears. And indeed, the sin of both the other scouts and the Children of Israel who were influenced by them was in their lack of faith in God and in Moses. The easy suggestibility of the people, their emotional response to the fears and anxieties communicated to them by those who brought the reports, indicate mass hysteria, a condition that made impossible a rational evaluation of the factors involved or, more important for them, the capacity of listening to Moses and of being guided by him (Freud 1922, chap. 9).

At this point the Children of Israel may have been more afraid to leave the familiar hardships of the desert than to face the unknown dangers of invading Canaan. The text says: "And all the congregation lifted up their voices, and cried; and the people wept that night. And all the children of Israel murmured against Moses and against Aaron; and the whole congregation said unto them: 'Would that we had died in the land of Egypt! or would that we had died in this wilderness! And wherefore doth the Lord bring us into this land, to fall by the sword? Our wives and little ones will be a prey; were it not better for us to return into Egypt?' And they said to one another, 'Let us make a captain, and let us return into Egypt'"(14:1–4).

Their half-hearted declaration that they should go back to Egypt can also be understood as a hostile rejection of Moses. They did not urge *him* to lead them back but said, "Let us make a captain, and let us return into Egypt." It was Moses who had led them away from a familiar motherland, whose fleshpots they now glamorized in memory, and toward the frightening, devouring mother who "eateth up its inhabitants."

The response of the two leaders to the outcry of the people is equally dramatic. "Then Moses and Aaron fell on their faces before all the assembly of the congregation of the children of Israel"(14:5). Adding to this picture of despair, Joshua and Caleb, the *good* scouts, "rent their clothes," the expression of a great calamity.

And indeed, this outburst of desperation on all sides is understandable. After all they had been through, after all they had endured in the wilderness, in the face of their hopes and promises, to be confronted with such a formidable prospect as presented by the demoralized scouts was too much for these weary pilgrims.

The despair of Moses must have been increased by his failure to stem the tide of their hysterical outbreak. Joshua and Caleb try to do so. "And Joshua the son of Nun and Caleb the son of Jephunneh, . . spoke unto all the congregation of the children of Israel, saying: 'The land which we passed through to spy it out, is an exceeding good land. If the Lord delight in us, then He will bring us into this land, and give it unto us—a land which floweth with milk and honey. Only rebel not against the Lord, neither fear ye the people of the land; . .the Lord is with us; fear them not.' But all the congregation bade stone them with stones, when the glory of the Lord appeared in the tent of meeting unto all the children of Israel"(14:6–9).

The above quotation states a highly significant happening in a surprisingly matter-of-fact fashion. When they are reminded "the Lord is with us," the people respond by a threat of violence to Caleb and Joshua, and then, suddenly, within the space of the same sentence, we are told that "the Lord appeared in the tent of meeting unto all the children of Israel."

Moses must indeed have needed the supportive presence of God in that critical moment. But though the Deity appears "unto all the children of Israel," the theophany evidently takes place in the tent, alone with Moses while the people waited outside. The dialogue between God and Moses is a lengthy one, significant of the importance of the problem at hand.

"And the Lord said unto Moses: 'How long will this people despise Me? and how long will they not believe in Me, for all the signs which I have wrought among them? I will smite them with the pestilence, and destroy them, and will make of thee a nation greater and mightier than they' (14:7–12). And Moses said unto the Lord: 'When the Egyptians shall hear—for Thou broughtest up this people in Thy might from among them—they will say to the inhabitants of this land, who have heard that Thou Lord art in the midst of this people. . . . Because the Lord was not able to bring this people into the land which He swore unto them, therefore hath He slain them in the wilderness. And now, I pray Thee, let the power of the Lord be great, according as Thou hast spoken, saying: The Lord is slow to anger, and plenteous in lovingkindness, forgiving iniquity and transgression, and that will by no means clear the guilty; visiting the iniquity of the fathers upon the children, upon the third and upon the fourth generation. Pardon, I pray Thee, the iniquity of this people according to the greatness of Thy lovingkindness, and according as Thou hast forgiven this people, from Egypt even until now'"(14: 13–19).

God responds to the plea of Moses. "And the Lord said: 'I have pardoned according to thy word. But in very deed, as I live—and all the earth shall be filled with the glory of the Lord —surely all those men that have seen My glory, and My signs, which I wrought in Egypt and in the wilderness, yet have put Me to proof these ten times, and have not hearkened to My voice; surely they shall not see the land which I swore unto their fathers, neither shall any of them that despised Me see it . . . tomorrow turn ye, and get you into the wilderness by the way to the Red Sea'"(14:20–25).

God's pardon does not exclude punishment for the guilty. Even after His anger has been ameloriated by the intercession of Moses, the displeasure of the Deity continues to find vehement expression. "And the Lord spoke unto Moses and unto Aaron, saying: 'How long shall I bear with this evil congregation, that keep murmuring against Me? . . .Say unto them: As I live, saith the Lord, surely as ye have spoken in Mine ears, so will I do to you: your carcasses shall fall in this wilderness, and all that were numbered of you, according to your whole number, from twenty years old and upward, ye that have murmured against Me, surely ye shall not come into the land . . .save Caleb, the son of Jephunned, and Joshua, the son of Nun. But your little ones, that you said would be a prey, them will I bring in and they shall know the land which ye have rejected. . . . After the number of the days in which ye spied out the land, even forty days, for every day a year, shall ye bear your iniquities, even forty years, and ye shall know My displeasure'"(14:26–34).

With these impassioned words, the Deity repeats His disappointment and indignation at the people's lack of faith in Him. There is indeed an unusual amount of repetitiveness in this lengthy speech, only part of which is quoted above. The Deity seems to be giving voice to the feelings of Moses himself, the leader who had brought his people thus far, to the very borders of the Promised Land, only to have them retreat in fear from the attempt to accomplish the long-cherished goal

But the whole people is not to be rejected. Those old enough to be responsible for their lack of faith, twenty years of age and over, would not be granted the privilege of entering the Promised Land. After their deaths, a younger, more courageous generation would take their place. These latter would indeed fulfill God's plan to conquer and settle the land He had sworn to give them.

The question again arises about how one is to comprehend this kind of phenomenon, this discourse, as it were, between Moses and God. Over it is cast the glow of that mystical quality that pervades the entire relationship between this man and his God.

From the limited view of a psychoanalytic approach, we see Moses in an encounter with his externalized superego, engaged in a struggle between two conflicting emotions. On the one side is anger and disappointment in his people who, at this crucial moment, were proving themselves unworthy of his hopes and plans for them. Did he perhaps have a fleeting wish that they might indeed all disappear and that God would magically provide a new and better following for him? However, the more mature part of the self intervenes.

It is Moses who has to restrain the wrath of God, here the projected, severe superego. He does so by repeating the beautiful and moving words which the Deity Himself had proclaimed as part of His covenant with Israel at Mount Sinai (Exod. 34:6–7). Moses now reminds God of the qualities He had earlier ascribed to Himself in relation to Israel, His lovingkindness and forgiveness. The punitive aspect of the psyche is thus moderated through standards established earlier by the ego ideal, whose strictness is here balanced by compassion. God is ego ideal as well as superego.

As Moses faces the people once more, they listen with the attention they had refused to give him earlier. The words "and they mourned greatly" express sadness and contrition. Clearly, the intervention of God Himself, as they experienced it, must have led to this drastic change of attitude. The narrative says, "the glory of the Lord appeared in the tent of meeting unto all the children of Israel" (14:10). Presumably, the Divine Presence was manifested in the customary manner of a cloud hovering over that sacred spot where Moses alone could enter. The people must have waited outside in a mood of silent apprehension, wondering what terrible penalty would be meted out to them. Perhaps the prospect of a lifetime in the wilderness was more frightening to them than fighting formidable enemies. Perhaps they now wished to redeem themselves from the sin of their lack of faith. So, like impulsive children, they plunge from one act of rebellion to another. They decide to go forward immediately and begin the battle. The text says, "And they rose up early in the morning, and got them to the top of the mountain, saying: 'Lo, we are here, and will go up unto the place which the Lord hath promised; for we have sinned.'" (14:40). Moses, however, warns them to desist, declaring that their efforts would be in vain for God would not be with them. But as if determined to prove themselves, as if caught in a kind of counterphobic state, in its own way as hysterical as their first response, again they do not listen. The people surge forward up the mountain leading to the enemy. Moses and the Ark of the Covenant remain behind. As predicted, the Children of Israel suffer a severe defeat at the hands of the Amalekites and the Canaanites and are driven back to the place from which they started.

The reality factor in this episode of the twelve scouts is not hard to understand. The Children of Israel were not ready, within such a short space of time, to change from a psychology of slavery to that of conquering warriors prepared to invade and take possession of a land like Canaan, with its settled population and fortified cities. They needed more time than Moses himself had fully understood, supported as he was by his intense faith in God.

Over and over again, one is impressed with the psychological validity of the biblical narratives and the integrity with which they are told. The motive is certainly not the glorification of a people's history or its heroes but rather the recounting of the moral and spiritual struggles in the framework of their relationship with God and the events of history in this developmental phase of their peoplehood.

Certain aspects of the episode under consideration have the characteristics of a dream or fairy tale in terms of its symbolism. There is a trip into a new and magical land by twelve men who had known the hardships both of slavery and of life in the wilderness. It starts out as a wish-fulfilling dream with a view of the harvest-laden fields and the fruitbearing trees in this fertile country with its settled homes and fortified towns, so different from the vast and desolate spaces they had come from. As with Alice in Wonderland, to their excited imagination everything is either magnified or reduced in size as their emotions rise to ecstatic heights or fall in fear and despair. The Promised Land lay before them like a table overflowing with plenteous food, but they were like hungry children who dared not reach out their hands toward it. For guarding the table were giant figures, whereas they themselves became small and insignificant as grasshoppers, fearful for their lives.

The symbolism, the contradictions, and the conflicting emotions are expressed in a fashion that suggests a certain fluidity of psychic structure, allowing an easy accessibility to unconscious fantasy. Perhaps in those far-off days when this literature was produced the human psyche functioned more naturally in a world where reality and fantasy were closer together than in our own time. Although human nature, in many ways, has remained remarkably the same throughout the last three millenia or more, subtle changes brought about by cultural factors may have separated for us, to a greater degree, the sense of reality from the world of fantasy. If so, one of the difficulties in reading the biblical narrative is the tendency to use our own measuring rods of logic and reason in trying to understand the patterns of expression characteristic of those ancient times.

However, when defensive needs were not involved, the style of writing could be wholly on a rational level, free from obscurities. Such is the dialogue between Moses and God in this particular episode. Their exchanges are of exceptional length and intensity of feeling but forthrightly expressed on both sides. Moses had no need to be defensive through ambiguity. He was able to accept his feelings of both anger and compassion. Though these emotions were, in part, projected onto the Deity, Moses uses this mystical relationship in a constructive rather than defensive manner. As intercessor, he here plays the role of the reality-oriented ego in dialogue with God, the superego, Who is threatening total punishment.

Much in the way of control and understanding were required of Moses at this time. He had to curb his own impatient spirit and postpone the longed-for accomplishment of his goal to a distant time. Through this interchange with God, the leader finally arrives at a necessary compromise between his own wishes and a sense of reality. The people were to go through a long period of strengthening, but the goal was to be steadfastly maintained. Moses' plea not to destroy the people was presented on the basis both of reality factors and in terms of the ego ideal that God Himself had enunciated at Mount Sinai. The so-called secondary process of thinking was largely involved rather than the dreamlike state so often found in other theophanies. The man and the Deity speak with each other in the manner God Himself described on another occasion: "With him do I speak mouth to mouth, even manifestly and not in dark speeches"(12:8). The ego, superego, and ego ideal function together to reach the solution of a problem. To say this, however, is to present only a skeletal image of the human psyche, apart from the living radiance of the spirit of Moses, which transcends our psychological evaluation.

The episode of the twelve spies exemplifies in dramatic fashion an important phase in the psychic developmental life of the Children of Israel during the period of the wilderness. The anxiety they experienced at the prospect of invading the Promised Land can be understood symbolically as a regression to the pre-oedipal period of the child, where the fear of the destructive mother figure is even more terrifying than that of the oedipal father and his fantasied threat of castration. It is in the overcoming of these unconscious infantile fantasies that maturation takes place and the more reality-oriented ego progresses toward maturity. On numerous occasions throughout the biblical narratives, this struggle between the problems characteristic of the pre-oedipal stage of the child is regressively experienced by the Children of Israel as a people during their stay in the wilderness, a terrain that can indeed symbolize the frightening mother with her threats of starvation and lack of water.

The Sinai experience, within this symbolic structure, is a covenant with the father and the effort to overcome the dread of the oedipal dilemma by promising obedience to his commandments. In return, there would be the reward of entering the Promised Land and the fulfillment of adult satisfactions. But psychic development does not occur in a straight line and, as we shall see in the next chapter, the image of the cannibalistic mother plays an even more terrifying role as punishment for defying the authority of the father.

Moses Faces the Revolt of Korah

A Crisis in Leadership

 CHAPTER TWELVE

THERE WERE MANY episodes of complaints and "murmurings" by the Children of Israel against their leader, Moses, during the period of the wandering in the wilderness. However, the so-called revolt of Korah has its own special characteristics and significance. The other situations were marked by the rebelliousness of the people as a group, without specific leaders being mentioned. The motivating factors were largely occasioned by the hardships and deprivations of desert life. In the revolt of Korah a new and more threatening element was introduced—the struggle for power involving the very leadership of Moses.

Jealousy toward a leader and the wish to displace him is as old as humanity itself. In the above situation, however, not only was the leadership in jeopardy but also the principles and goals for which he stood.

Korah, the main leader of the uprising, was a Levite of high standing, a close relative of Moses, their fathers having been brothers, the sons of Kohath (Exod. 6:18–21). Also participating in the uprising were Dathan and Abiram, leading men of the tribe of Reuben. As descendants of the oldest son of Jacob, they must have felt especially displeased that they were not given greater recognition on the basis of their family status. Commentators have noted that in the organized line of march that the tribes followed in their pilgrimage the Reubenites and the Levites were side by side, thus providing opportunities for the two groups to exchange grievances and perhaps conspire together against Moses and Aaron (Hertz 1936, 639).

Biblical scholars differ about the specific causes of this revolt, a situation that is not surprising, since the text itself is ambiguous and confusing concerning the details. Higher Biblical Criticism hypothesizes that several different rebellions were originally involved, one of these being a protest of the Levites against the greater privileges of the priestly class, the house of Aaron. Another cause of dissension, they believed, was the opposition of the lay people concerning the special status of *all* the clerical elements (*IB* 1953, 2:220; *Peake's* 1953, 261ff.) A further viewpoint is that the most significant aspect of the revolt was a struggle for power against the leadership of Moses himself, a kind of continuing underground turbulence now reaching a peak of intensity after the debacle following the report of the spies who had brought back discouraging views about the possible conquest of the Promised Land (Orlinsky 1954, 40). And indeed, the emphasis in the biblical narrative is largely on the personalities involved.

In rabbinic tradition and legend the figure of Korah came to symbolize the rebel who stirs up controversy solely for personal motives but uses the argument of the true demagogue that he is fighting for the rights of all the people (Hertz 1936, 638). Buber (1936) also feels that "the historical nucleus of the story of Korah and his band . . . does not appear to have been a protest against any clerical class, but was directed against the special status of Moses in person"(pp. 182–83). Another writer points out that this was the only instance recorded where the motives of Moses were impugned (James 1950, 39).

Regarding this episode, the text says, "Now Korah . . . with Dathan and Abiram . . . took men; and they rose up in the face of Moses, with certain of the children of Israel, two hundred and fifty men; they were princes of the congregation, the elect men of the assembly, men of renown; and they assembled themselves together against Moses and against Aaron, and said unto them: 'Ye take too much upon you, seeing all the congregation are holy, every one of them; and the Lord is among them; wherefore then lift ye up yourselves above the assembly of the Lord?'" (16:1–4).*

Although a Levite himself, Korah purports to speak here as a protagonist of *all* the people in decrying literally the holier-than-thou attitude, as he saw it, of Moses and Aaron (Rubinstein 1968, 117ff.).

Moses responds to this accusation of self-aggrandizement with intense emotion. The text says, "And when Moses heard it, he fell upon his face" (16:4). This response was a characteristic reaction on his part to moments of great stress, probably expressing a prayerful appeal to God for help. Then, recovering his equilibrium, the leader faces his adversaries. "And he spoke unto Korah and unto all his company saying: 'In the morning the Lord will show who are His, and who is holy, and will cause him to come near unto Him. This do; take you censers, Korah and all his company; and put fire therein, and put incense upon them before the Lord tomorrow; and it shall be that the man whom the Lord doth choose, he shall be holy; ye take too much upon you, ye sons of Levi; is it but a small thing unto you, that the God of Israel hath separated you from the congregation of Israel, to bring you near to Himself, to do the service of the Tabernacle of the Lord, and to stand before the congregation to minister unto them; and that He hath brought thee near, and all thy brethren the sons of Levi with thee? and will ye seek the priesthood also? Therefore thou and all thy company that are gathered together against the Lord—; and as to Aaron, what is he that ye murmur against him?'" (16:5–11).

The first part of the last verse quoted is left incomplete. It is not difficult to conjecture what Moses may have decided to leave unsaid. The following is suggested: "Therefore thou and all thy company that are gathered together against the Lord" *will feel the displeasure of the Lord and the punishment that will be meted out to you.* It would have been a prediction that committed God to a certain

---

*All biblical references in this chapter, unless otherwise noted, are to the book of Numbers.

act in the future that the Deity Himself had not foretold or authorized. Moses therefore interrupted himself in the impulse to utter the threat and so left it unfinished. The concluding part of the verse refers to Aaron only. Its clear implication is that Aaron is only an instrument of the Deity and thus not to be held responsible for the high position conferred upon him. Moses excludes a specific reference to himself, with the assumption that rebellion against him is equivalent to rebellion against God.

The accusation of personal ambition with which they had reproached him Moses returns upon their own heads, thereby pinpointing the real cause of their discontent. At stake were the hierarchical laws regarding the special duties and privileges of the priesthood, headed by Aaron and his sons, who were thus set apart from the rest of the Levites. The latter were assigned to the less prestigous tasks associated with service in the Tabernacle. They were not permitted to come near the altar and its sacred vessels except in the act of transporting them, and then only after the priests themselves had covered these holy objects with the appropriate cloths. Thus, they had no share in the actual performance of the worship ritual, which was conducted only by the priestly family (4:13; 15:20).

Although Korah had not voiced the specific cause for his discontent, Moses must have been well aware of it. The test he imposes on the rebel leader and his followers is indeed one that has to do with service at the altar, a ritual hitherto restricted to the priests. There is no indication whether the two hundred fifty men who accompany Korah are Levites or laymen or included both groups. They are described as leaders and men of renown. Certainly Dathan and Abiram were not of Levitic families. The test suggested by Moses, therefore, must be a response to the argument of Korah that "all the congregation are holy, every one of them." He asserts that God Himself would show who was to have the privilege of being close to Him in the service of the Tabernacle. The authority of Moses was bestowed on him by God, and it was to that source the leader turned for vindication. Realistically, the covenant at Mount Sinai, which Korah tried to use as a basis for his rationalization, involved a *process of becoming*. The Children of Israel could achieve the status of a "kingdom of priests and a holy nation" only through their own development in time by obedience to God's laws (Buber 1936, 190).

Moses turns his attention next to Dathan and Abiram. Although the text gives the impression that the three instigators had approached him together, Moses now had to send for the other two. Hertz suggests that they may have retreated to the background while the outraged leader was addressing Korah (Hertz 1936, 640). But the two refuse to respond in person, a further insult to the authority of Moses. The reply they sent back is an arrogant one: "and they said: 'We will not come up; is it a small thing that thou has brought us up out of a land flowing with milk and honey, to kill us in the wilderness, but thou must needs make thyself also a prince over us? Moreover, thou has not brought us into a land flowing with milk and honey, nor given us inheritance of fields and vineyards; wilt thou put out the eyes of these men? We will not come up'" (16:12–14).

There is a taunting and sarcastic quality in the reference to Egypt as a land flowng with milk and honey. Thus, Moses is reproached not only for failing to bring them into a good land but also for *taking them away* from one. In blatant disregard for the truth, they put on him the onus for not leading them into Canaan.

It is likely that the two Reubenite leaders would not have dared to utter such words to Moses face to face and thus, in cowardly fashion, did so by proxy. The expression, "wilt thou put out the eyes of these men" is a puzzling one. Some commentators interpret it as meaning that Moses was blinding the people to the truth in that he had not kept his promises to them (Hertz 1936, 640). But the specific reference to "these men" must be to the messengers who brought back the insulting reply. In view of the taunting quality of the message, the motive seems more likely to have been a further attempt to arouse the temper of the leader. Let Moses take out his anger on the hapless messengers, the words suggest, since the real culprits refused to come up. The latter must have known full well that the moral character of the leader would forbid such a discharge of his anger, and so he would be left helpless in his wrath or commit an unjustified act of violence.

Moses was indeed angry, but the distraught leader had other resources. The text says, "And Moses was very wroth, and said unto the Lord: 'Respect not Thou their offering,'" insisting that he had not done harm to any of his detractors (16:15). With that, he dismisses the subject of Dathan and Abiram, turning again to Korah, the chief figure in the revolt. He repeats the challenge made before, that Korah and his followers should appear before the tent of meeting on the morrow, with their firepans and incense. Aaron would also be there. God would then make known who was to serve Him.

The men assemble at the appointed time. The "princes of the congregation, the elect men of the assembly," their fire-pans glowing and redolent with incense, are about to take upon themselves the sacred privilege of the priestly service. They are at the very door of the tent of meeting and close behind them a large audience of witnesses, the people of Israel, summoned by the confident Korah, all waiting to see the outcome of this challenge to the authority of Moses.

The sight must have stirred the leader to feelings of overwhelming anxiety and wrath toward the whole, seemingly faithless multitude for whom he had labored and sacrificed so much. And then it happened quite suddenly: "and the glory of the Lord appeared unto all the congregation. And the Lord spoke unto Moses and unto Aaron, saying: 'Separate yourselves from among this congregation, that I may consume them in a moment.' And they fell upon their faces, and said: 'O God, the God of the spirits of all flesh, shall one man sin, and wilt Thou be wroth with all the congregation?'" (16:19–22). Thus Moses intercedes again for his people.

One can picture that scene—the ambitious ones, ready with their fragrant, glowing fire-pans, and those who watched, the whole assembly of the Children of Israel, suddenly stricken with fear at the sight of the glory of the Lord before the door of the Tent of Meeting. Perhaps they could also witness Moses and Aaron as the two "fell upon their faces" in a posture of worship and prayer. It is likely that the poignant words of their leader, asking that the people be spared, were audible to the throng and had a profound effect.

On an intrapsychic level, in terms of Moses himself, it can be said that the angry and punitive superego, here projected onto the Deity, is modified and subdued by the realistically oriented ego. If Moses himself, for a fleeting moment had wished that the whole ungrateful congregation should be consumed, the emotion quickly passes. Again, only the guilty and those associated with them were to be punished. The authority of the leader and the laws he established had to receive strong reinforcement at this time in the minds of the people. Otherwise, the cohesiveness of the group would be further shaken and the whole purpose of their historic destiny endangered.

The narrative moves quickly toward the denouement: "And the Lord spoke unto Moses, saying: 'Speak unto the congregation, saying: Get you up from about the dwelling of Korah, Dathan and Abiram.' And Moses rose up and went unto Dathan and Abiram; and the elders of Israel followed him. And he spoke unto the congregation, saying: 'Depart, I pray you, from the tents of these wicked men, and touch nothing of theirs, lest ye be swept away in all their sins.' So they got them up from the dwelling of Korah, Dathan, and Abiram, on every side; and Dathan and Abiram came out, and stood at the door of their tents, with their wives and their little ones. And Moses said: 'Hereby ye shall know that the Lord hath sent me to do all these works, and that I have not done them of mine own mind. If these men die the common death of all men, and be visited after the visitation of all men, then the Lord hath not sent me. But if the Lord make a new thing, and the ground open her mouth, and swallow them up, with all that appertain unto them, and they go down alive into the pit, then ye shall understand that these men have despised the Lord.' And it came to pass, as he made an end of speaking all these words, that the ground did cleave asunder that was under them. And the earth opened her mouth, and swallowed them up, and their households, and all the men that appertained unto Korah, and all their goods. So they, and all that appertained to them, went down alive into the pit; and the earth closed upon them, and they perished from among the assembly. And all Israel that were round about them fled at the cry of them; for they said: 'Lest the earth swallow us up.' And fire came forth from the Lord and devoured the two hundred and fifty men that offered the incense" (16:23–25).

Here, in terse language, the shocking fate of the rebels against the authority of Moses is depicted. As in other situations, it would be futile and beyond the purpose of this study to attempt any rational explanation of these catastrophic events.

Earthquake and fire can be natural disasters; but that these should occur at the very time and place called for in the exigencies of the story is indeed a part of the mystery. One might conjecture that such catastrophes did occur and were witnessed by the Children of Israel during their long sojourn in the wilderness and in the course of time became associated in their traditions with the acts of rebellion that also must have taken place. Unusual events of nature were generally viewed as signs of Divine intervention.

A number of psychoanalytic implications emerge from the specifics of this narrative. The verbal imagery of the earth opening her mouth and swallowing up the people, a metaphor used twice in succession, is indeed a vivid image of the preoedipal, cannibalistic mother, an unconscious fantasy from infantile life (Fenichel 1945, 63ff.; Lewin 1973, 129ff.). The unusual feature, as one commentator observed, is not the earthquake itself but the closing of the yawning gap afterward, like the jaws of a huge mouth springing closed, for indeed, "the earth closed upon them" (Cohen 1947, 881). In his psychoanalytic studies of rabbinic legends, Rubenstein (1968) observes that the fear of the primitive image of the mother is more decisive in that literature than the dread of the oedipal father (p. xiv).

The fire that follows immediately after the earthquake, consuming the two hundred fifty men, can be understood as the symbol of Divinity in its masculine form. Thus, both earth and fire, preoedipal and oedipal parental images, are involved in destroying the *rebellious children.*

Dathan and Abiram, who complained that Moses had deprived them of a land flowing with milk and honey (symbolically, the mother's breasts) had taunted him by calling an evil mother good. As Martin Buber (1968) says in another connection that is equally applicable here, "The punishment speaks the language of the sin" (p. 27). Those who now attacked the *good mother* (Moses) were punished by the *bad* one, here clearly personalized as the earth opening her mouth and swallowing them. An ironic aspect enters into this situation. A lack of courage had prevented the people from entering the Promised Land, because it had been described as one that "eateth up its inhabitants." Now the wilderness itself proved to be such a land in an almost literal sense.

This episode provides another instance of how the symbolism of the biblical text, its choice of language and metaphor, seems to express so precisely the moods and feelings of the hero himself in terms that are appropriate to the situation and to his personality. That is indeed a mystery about which we can only hypothesize.

With the special sensitivity to cosmic forces often characteristic of gifted people, Moses may have anticipated the nature of the "uncommon death" that he predicted for the rebels. He may have perceived on a sublimal level some disturbance of a physical nature in the atmosphere, some uneasiness of the earth's surface, which then served as a stimulus for his prediction. A preoedipal fantasy of his own may thus have been reactivated and then found unconscious expression in the wording and imagery of the narrative. His own intense feelings must have found an outlet in those explosive forces of nature that seemed magically to respond to his call.

The specific fate of the chief rebel, Korah, remains somewhat of a mystery. We are told that all the men that "appertained unto Korah" were swallowed up, together with Dathan and Abiram (16:32), but in a somewhat ambiguous fashion the person of Korah himself is not mentioned there. Even when the leaders of the revolt are named, Korah is included in some instances and at other times he is omitted (16:23–27). An element of uncertainty about how to treat the chief rebel seems to have been involved. It is noted in a later chapter of Numbers (26:10) that Korah did indeed go down into the pit with Dathan and Abiram. We are then further informed that the *sons* of Korah were spared in the debacle.

One must wonder why these facts were reported only at a later time and almost as an aside, in connection with a genealogical census. It may be that Korah was a person about whom Moses had strong personal feelings of an ambivalent kind. Both stemmed from the same family of Levites and had the same grandfather (Exod. 6:18–21). The two must have known each other from their youth and grown up together in a milieu where kinship ties were strong. Thus Korah, a man of strength and a leader in his own right, may have been a figure with whom Moses could unconsciously have identified. He would then have been especially sensitive to the challenge of this man, particularly the accusation discrediting Moses' own integrity. Moreover, the competitiveness of Korah may have touched off unconscious feelings of guilt in Moses because of his own inner struggles of a similar nature.

Conflicting feelings stemming from these sources may have interfered in any clear-cut decision about whether or how to punish Korah. The uncertainty about his fate has encouraged extrabiblical legends in which that archvillain undergoes both types of punishment, being consumed by fire as he is swallowed up by the earth (Rubenstein 1968, 121–22).

A repressed element of compassion in Moses about the act of destroying Korah may have found expression in saving the sons. Descendants of the sons of Korah are mentioned again in the Bible (I Chron. 6:22) as leaders of song in the sacred service, appointed by David. A number of psalms also are credited to their authorship.

The earlier episode about the report of the spies has close psychological connections with the revolt of Korah that follows. At that time also Moses was confronted by a rebellious people who defied his authority. Then, also, God appears before the Tent of Meeting before the whole congregation of Israel and threatens total destruction (14:6–9).

Fear of the hostile mother dominates the earlier episode. In the event dealt with in this chapter, anger at the authority of Moses and Aaron as the favored sons of God, a form of sibling rivalry, is the underlying theme. The same personalities, Dathan and Abiram, are associated in legend with the two Hebrews fighting each other in Egypt at the time when Moses tried to intervene and was met with the scornful words: "Who made thee a ruler and a judge over us?" (Exod. 2:14). The same motif of sibling rivalry and jealousy again brings these two brothers of the house of Reuben on the scene together with Korah, a rival cousin from the family of Levi itself, joined in rebellion against the two chosen by God, Moses and Aaron. Like a great extended family, the Children of Israel in the wilderness have to go through stages of development in their relationship with each other and with parental images. Of particular significance, as suggested by the strength of its repression, is the relationship of Moses to *sons*, a subject that is treated in very obscure and indirect ways throughout his life history. As has been noted, his own sons receive only scant attention. They are obliterated by being ignored, a psychological form of annihilation. Two of the four sons of Aaron are destroyed by a mysterious fire from heaven, but the other two are spared (Lev. 10:1-3). And now the sons of Korah are allowed, unobtrusively, to survive in a situation where their demise was to be expected. As in the hidden traditions of his patriarchal past, Moses too had a father-son conflict, as these studies have indicated. But this kind of ambivalence is so forbidden that it cannot find a path to conscious awareness. Both the hostility and the compassion seek an outlet through indirection.

The rebellion of Korah and his followers was memorialized in an unusual and somewhat puzzling fashion. The text says: "And the Lord spoke unto Moses, saying: 'Speak unto Eleazar the son of Aaron the priest, that he take up the fire-pans out of the burning, and scatter thou the fire yonder: for they are become holy; even the fire-pans of these men who have sinned at the cost of their lives, and let them be made beaten plates for a covering of the altar—for they are become holy, because they were offered before the Lord—that they may be a sign unto the children of Israel.' And Eleazar the priest took the brazen fire-pans, which they that were burned had offered; and they beat them out for a covering of the altar, to be a memorial unto the children of Israel, to the end that no common man, that is not of the seed of Aaron, draw near to burn incense before the Lord; that he fare not as Korah, and as his company; as the Lord spoke unto him by the hand of Moses" (17:1-5).

It is significant that the first problem to occupy the attention of Moses after the tragic events of the day should be a ritual matter concerning holiness. The fire-pans had become holy because they were used to offer burning incense to God, even though the act was performed unlawfully by those not belonging to the priesthood. This concern of Moses for maintaining the purity of the Tabernacle service, for safeguarding its holiness, clearly indicates that the accusations of Korah and the others attributing motives of personal privilege to the leaders were unwarranted. By this act of concern for the holiness of the fire-pans, Moses shows how vital he considered the separation of the sacred from the profane, or ordinary. This principle of separation was the basis on which the priesthood was to be set apart even from the rest of the Levites, the lesser body devoted to the service of the Tabernacle.

What was done with the fire-pans is also of interest psychologically. They were made into a covering for the altar "that it may be a sign unto the children of Israel," that is, a reminder of the rebels who had defied the laws of holiness. The wrongdoers were themselves consumed by fire. They became the sacrifice, but the fire-pans, the instruments of their offering, acquired inadvertently the quality of holiness that their owners had aspired to. These objects now achieve the distinction of covering the altar itself. Thus, in a sense, the wish of the men who died is realized through that which had been an extension of themselves. Their lives would be memorialized, not only as rebels, according to the avowed purpose of Moses, but also as those who had wished to be closer to God. Although their struggle had been colored by personal motives, it had nevertheless been in a cause related to the service of the Deity. And perhaps Moses himself was, in part, performing an act of reparation by transforming the fire-pans into a covering for the altar. By this symbolic act, he was granting to his opponents the opportunity for atonement. Their very act of rebellion undergoes a spiritual transformation. Those who had rebelled against the laws of holiness were now permitted to come closer to God.

The Aftermath

The spirit of rebellion, however, had not been entirely laid to rest. There was an unexpected aftermath to the tragic events of the previous day. The text says, "But on the morrow all the congregation of the children of Israel murmured against Moses and against Aaron, saying: 'Ye have killed the people of the Lord!'" (17:6).

These words of reproach are significant. The reference must be not only to the Levites who were involved but also to the others, in the same sense that Korah had declared, "all the congregation are holy, every one of them" (16:3).

Even the "uncommon death" of the rebels thus fails to subdue the spirit of the people. Through their own initiative they express feelings of outraged justice against what seemed to them unwarranted harshness on the part of their leaders. The sense of the elect that Moses had instilled into them during the momentous experience at Mount Sinai may be having its repercussions here. Their response to the events of the previous day could be reflecting the teachings of the leader himself, an acceptance of their own value as a people chosen by God. The innate strength of the Children of Israel is seen in the reproach quoted above. If they had been completely submissive to the controls imposed on them by Moses, they would hardly have been suited for the task of fulfilling a spiritual mission in the world.

What happens next is one of those strange and mystical phenomena, not unique in the experience of Moses, but difficult for the modern mind to comprehend. Even before Moses himself could react to the outcry of the people or ask for divine help, there is sudden intervention by the Deity. The text says, "And it came to pass, when the congregation was assembled against Moses and against Aaron, that they looked toward the tent of meeting; and behold, the cloud covered it, and the glory of the Lord appeared. And Moses and Aaron came to the front of the tent of meeting. And the Lord spoke unto Moses, saying: 'Get you up from among this congregation, that I may consume them in a moment.' And they fell upon their faces" (17:7–10).

A situation of crisis quickly develops, with consequences that seem out of proportion to the actual degree of rebellion. For there is no indication that the people were about to express their anger against the leaders in any other way except verbally. They uttered no threats nor did they encroach on the sacred area of the Tabernacle, as Korah and his followers had attempted to do the day before. The closest the people came was to "look toward the tent of meeting."

Significantly, this time, when God threatens to destroy the whole congregation, Moses does not intercede for them as had happened the day before. The progress of events seemed to overtake him. A plague had already begun and was spreading rapidly among the people. A quick decision on the part of the leader was necessary to deal with the situation. Moses hurriedly instructs Aaron what to do. "And Moses said unto Aaron: 'Take thy fire-pan, and put fire therein from off the altar, and lay incense thereon, and carry it quickly unto the congregation, and make atonement for them; for there is wrath gone out from the Lord: the plague is begun.' And Aaron took as Moses spoke, and ran into the midst of the assembly; and behold, the plague was begun among the people; and he put on the incense, and made atonement for the people, and he stood between the dead and the living; and the plague was stayed. Now they that died by the plague were fourteen thousand and seven hundred, besides them that died about the matter of Korah. And Aaron returned unto Moses unto the door of the tent of meeting, and the plague was stayed" (17:11–15).

The anger of the Deity is described by Moses in unusual terms: "there is a wrath gone out from the Lord; the plague is begun." *Wrath* seems to take on a personalized aspect, like a dissociated specter that is immune to verbal intercession. As Hertz (1936) puts it, "Wrath is spoken of as a Divine messenger that is to execute God's punishment on the guilty. It goes forth to kill, and slays as it proceeds" (p. 643).

One is reminded here of the daemonic aspect of God, as experienced by Moses many years before, when he himself was attacked by the Deity, who sought to slay him at the inn, on the very borders of Egypt, when Moses was about to begin his mission (Exod. 4:24–26). Similarly, this same quality of sudden, unexpected wrath attacks the people and is again appeased by an act of atonement, a service that Zipporah had performed in the earlier episode involving Moses. But this time the consequences are more serious. According to the text, fourteen thousand seven hundred die before the plague is stopped. Biblical numbers often have a symbolic and mystical significance. Fourteen is twice seven, a number especially associated with the cultic aspects of religious life in the Bible.

The fire-pan with its burning incense plays a role once more, this time through the legitimate offices of Aaron, whose priestly authority is thus impressed upon the people. In an unusually dramatic role, he runs with his fire-pan to a point where, standing between the living and the dead, he stops the plague in its tracks.

Let us attempt to understand this episode on the basis that it was provoked by some happening in reality that followed the protest of the people. The leader must have been emotionally and physically exhausted from the events of the previous day and unprepared for this aftermath. It may have been deeply discouraging to him that the unusual power he had displayed in calling forth God's punishment on the culprits in so dramatic a fashion had not succeeded in subduing the people.

Overcome by feelings of anger, helplessness, and guilt, Moses *may have wanted* to punish the whole assembly, to make them feel the full force of his displeasure. In the state of altered consciousness, which was in part a response to intolerable stress, a dissociated part of his own psyche takes over, as happens in a dream. He could then, in fantasy, enact the scene of destruction while the observing part of his ego looked on with horror. Having lost control over an aspect of himself, he projects this behavior onto the Deity, whose anger must be appeased through a propitiatory act, for the situation was now beyond an appeal to reason. Moses quickly instructs Aaron what to do.

Reality and fantasy must both have played a role in the situation. A certain amount of hysteria probably manifested itself among the people, who must also have been in a state of shock from the traumatic events of the preceding day. Hysteria in a crowd can be very contagious and assume bizarre forms, spreading with the rapidity that Moses attributed to the plague but which is much more understandable as a hysterical phenomenon.

The presence of Aaron running among them with the gleaming, fragrant fire-pan must have been reassuring to the people and brought them out of the mass hysteria. Admittedly, this reconstruction, while bringing some rationale to the text, faces the uncertainty with which reason must stand on the edge of mystical experience.

After the emergency is over, Moses, in a calmer mood, seeks other ways to restore the confidence of the people and gain their acceptance of the hereditary nature of the priesthood through the house of Aaron. The communication with God is also resumed in more familiar patterns. The Deity now instructs Moses to ask the Children of Israel for a representative from each of the twelve tribes to bring him a rod with the individual's name inscribed upon it. Aaron's rod would represent the tribe of Levi. Moses placed all the rods in the Tabernacle before the Ark, as God instructed. Moreover, the Deity says, "And it shall come to pass, that the man whom I shall choose, his rod shall bud; and I will make to cease from Me the murmurings of the children of Israel, which they murmur against you" (17:20). Then we are told, "And it came to pass on the morrow, that Moses went into the tent of testimony; and behold, the rod of Aaron for the house of Levi was budded, and put forth buds, and bloomed blossoms, and bore ripe almonds. And Moses brought out all the rods from before the Lord unto all the children of Israel; and they looked, and took every man his rod" (17:23-24).

The rod of Aaron, however, remained in the Tabernacle, or as it is called in this narrative, the tent of testimony, so that it would be a reminder to the people of God's choice. The budding rod was a phallic symbol of regenerative power, significant of the hereditary rights and privileges of the priesthood as bequeathed from father to son in the house of Aaron.

The Children of Israel were now so subdued and frightened, they cried to Moses, "Behold, we perish, we are undone, we are all undone. Every one that cometh near, that cometh near unto the tabernacle of the Lord, is to die; shall we wholly perish?" (17:27-28). It was a cry of despair that received no direct reply. But the following chapter is devoted to instructions by the Deity to Aaron setting forth the duties and obligations of the house of Aaron in regard to the sanctuary and also the tasks and responsibilities of the Levites, carefully delineating the rights and privileges of the former from those of the latter. Through specific knowledge of the laws, the anxiety of the people could be diminished.

The revolt of Korah represented the most severe test of strength in the leadership of Moses against a would-be usurper who was skillful enough to involve the group as a whole. At stake was the very existence of the Children of Israel as a nation destined for a spiritual force in the world.

The personality of Moses as revealed in the intensity of his anxiety and concern about the outcome, attests to his humility and inner doubts about his own strengths in the face of this formidable opposition. His decision to put everything on the line, as it were, in predicting dramatic happenings that would prove God was on his side must have required tremendous faith and courage both in himself and the Deity. In a sense, Moses was also putting God to the test. If he, Moses, was truly the chosen leader, the Deity Himself would have to demonstrate that fact to the people. His leadership had to be vindicated both for himself and in the eyes of the Children of Israel.

Why Did Moses Strike the Rock?

The Role of Unconscious Fantasy

 CHAPTER THIRTEEN

WHY WAS MOSES not permitted to enter the Promised Land? Surely it seems that he, of all people, most deserved this fulfillment. As with other problems that evoke deep human feelings relating to questions of justice, of reward and punishment, the Bible frequently gives no clear-cut answer in regard to specific situations. The general principles of morality are laid down with great definiteness, as in the Ten Commandments. But the behavior of the Deity Himself is often a source of bewilderment and frustration even to His most faithful followers.

Martin Buber (1968) epitomizes this enigma by saying, "man must not subject God to the rules of logic" (pp. 196–97). *Man's behavior*, however, must be subjected to the rules of the *psychologic*, that is, a study of the underlying motivations of his conduct.

A dramatic episode in the latter days of the life of Moses leads to the sad consequences referred to above. He was not to have the privilege of entering the Promised Land. Although the leader would bring his people to its borders, he himself was to die in the wilderness. This situation developed out of one of the hardships of desert life, a scarcity of water. It was reminiscent of what had happened at Rephidim many years before, according to biblical chronology (Exod. 17:1–7).

It will be helpful to recapitulate here some aspects of that previous experience as interpreted in chapter five of this volume. The text concerning it is as follows: "And all the congregation of the children of Israel . . . encamped at Rephidim; and there was no water for the people to drink. Wherefore the people strove with Moses, and said: 'Give us water that we may drink.' And Moses said unto them: 'Why strive ye with me? wherefore do ye try the Lord?' And the people thirsted there for water; and the people murmured against Moses, and said: 'Wherefore hast thou brought us up out of Egypt, to kill us and our children and our cattle with thirst?' And Moses cried unto the Lord, saying: 'What shall I do unto this people? they are almost ready to stone me.' And the Lord said unto Moses: 'Pass on before the people, and take with thee of the elders of Israel; and thy rod, wherewith thou smotest the river, take in thy hand, and go. Behold, I will stand before thee there upon the rock in Horeb; and thou shalt smite the rock, and there shall come water out of it, that the people may drink.' And Moses did so in the sight of the elders of Israel. And the name of the place was called Massah [trying] and Meribah [strife], because of the striving of the children of Israel, and because they tried the Lord, saying: 'Is the Lord among us, or not?'" (Exod. 17:1–7).

Two aspects in the above passage are especially relevant to our present study. One is the reaction of Moses to the aggressive demands of the people. He clearly feels frightened, powerless, and dependent on God for leadership. The other element is the instruction that God gives Moses, telling him to strike the rock, a command directly opposite to the one now given at Kadesh, where he is told to *speak* to the rock and it would give forth its water.

It can be assumed that Moses had some understanding of the natural process that causes porous limestone rock to give forth its water when struck a heavy blow (Keller 1964, 126). This knowledge could have been gained earlier during the time spent in crossing the wilderness after his flight from Egypt and while among the Bedouin Midianites, when he was a member of the household of Jethro. What, however, might have stood in the way of his immediately attempting this solution?

As discussed in relation to the earlier event, striking the rock must have had an unconscious, symbolic meaning for Moses that made it difficult for him to perform this act. The concept of God as a Rock, strong and steadfast, is a figure of speech frequently found in the biblical literature. Its popularity in the later writings of the prophets and in the Psalms stems from the time of Moses. One biblical scholar comments on its use in Deuteronomy 32, known as the Song of Moses. He says, "Nine times in the course of this single hymn is repeated this most expressive figure taken from the granite crags of Sinai and carried hence through psalms and hymns of all nations" (Hertz 1936, 896-97). The origin of this symbol is thus related to Mount Sinai, itself a massive rock. Indeed, the closest Moses came to experiencing the presence of God had been from a cleft in that sacred mountain (Exod. 33:18–23).

In the realm of unconscious fantasy, the symbol can assume a reality of its own. The rock, especially in the area of the holy mountain, could have represented the Deity Himself. As Ernest Jones (1912) points out, the definitive characteristic of a symbol is its connection with unconscious representations. As he puts it, "The process of symbolization is carried out unconsciously, and so the individual is quite unaware of the fact that he has employed one at all, since he takes the symbol for the reality" (p. 97).

Awe and wonder at the grandeur of nature are often associated with deep religious feelings in the biblical literature. (Otto 1923, 146). In the impressive environs of the Sinai wilderness, to the responsive heart of Moses, the concept of the rock as Deity may have taken on a mystical significance, the full extent of which he was not aware. Striking the rock could thus have become a form of aggression against God Himself.

But if this method was the only way of getting water for the people, Moses would be in a state of conflict, torn between a sense of reality and his own resistance to an act that unconsciously had a special meaning for him. In that earlier experience at Rephidim, specific directions from God had been necessary, not only for the purpose of defining the task in a time of confusion but also as indicating permission to perform the deed. God says, "Behold, I will stand before thee, there upon the rock in Horeb." This was an odd form of reassurance. Moses' concept of God did not generally require this kind of physical proximity. But if we assume that the act of striking the rock was unconsciously associated with anxiety, then the closeness of God's presence would help to alleviate this feeling. As suggested in connection with that episode, if God was felt as an actual presence, the rock would lose its symbolic significance, for the Deity would then be experienced on a level of consciousness that would make the symbolism of the rock unnecessary for that specific occasion. The puzzling biblical verse, "Behold, I will stand before thee, there upon the rock in Horeb," would be understandable within this context.

Some scholars believe that the later incident at Kadesh, with which we are now primarily concerned, is just another version of the previous happening at Rephidim and Mount Horeb (Driver 1911, 158). There are, however, significant differences between the two. Moreover, the people must have suffered from a lack of water on more than one occasion.

The time of this second episode is many years later. Yet the earlier experience may have left its mark on Moses. There must also have taken place a deepening and mellowing of his religious spirit. The thought of striking the rock would thus have been even more abhorrent to him.

The biblical narrative regarding this event begins as follows: "And the children of Israel, even the whole congregation, came into the wilderness of Zin in the first month; [of the fortieth year of wandering] and the people abode in Kadesh; and Miriam died there. And there was no water for the congregation; and they assembled themselves together against Moses and against Aaron. And the people strove with Moses, and spoke, saying: 'Would that we had perished when our brethren perished before the Lord! And why have ye brought the assembly of the Lord into this wilderness, to die there, we and our cattle? And wherefore have ye made us to come up out of Egypt, to bring us into this evil place? This is no place of seed, or of figs, or of vines, or of pomegranates; neither is there any water to drink'" (20:1–5).*

These reproaches of the people against their leaders expressed not only need but considerable anger. Masochistically, they declare that it would have been better for them to have perished with their brethren "before the Lord," indirectly implying that the God of Moses, Who had not spared their relatives on a number of other occasions, could hardly be expected to save those who had thus far survived. At the same time, they proudly present themselves as "the assembly of the Lord," who were thus worthy of better treatment. It was Moses and Aaron who had brought them into this "evil place" that was such a contrast to the delights of the land that had been promised them.

As had happened before in such situations, Moses was unable to respond to this diatribe (14:5; Exod. 15:24). He tended to become speechless, overwhelmed with emotions, when strongly berated by the people. He and Aaron retreat to the Tent of Meeting, where God now gives them specific instructions about how to deal with the crisis. "And Moses and Aaron went from the presence of the assembly unto the door of the tent of meeting, and fell upon their faces; and the glory of the Lord appeared unto them. And the Lord spoke unto Moses, saying: 'Take the rod, and assemble the congregation, thou, and Aaron thy brother, and speak ye unto the rock before their eyes, that it give forth its water; and thou shalt bring forth to them water out of the rock; so thou shalt give the congregation and their cattle drink.' And Moses took the rod from before the Lord, as He commanded him. And Moses and Aaron gathered the assembly together before the rock, and he said unto them: 'Hear now, ye rebels; are we to bring you forth water out of this rock?' And Moses lifted up his hand, and smote the rock with his rod twice; and water came forth abundantly, and the congregation drank, and their cattle. And the Lord said unto Moses and Aaron: 'Because ye believed not in Me, to sanctify Me in the eyes of the children of Israel, therefore ye shall not bring this assembly into the land which I have given them.' These are the waters of Meribah,

---

*All biblical references in this chapter, unless otherwise noted, are to the book of Numbers.

where the children of Israel strove with the Lord, and He was sanctified in them" (20:6–13).

There is no consensus among scholars about the real nature of the sin Moses committed. The impression conveyed by the narrative and accepted by the casual reader is that Moses did wrong both in addressing the people so angrily and in striking the rock instead of speaking to it as commanded by God. The fact that he struck the rock twice, also suggests a loss of control. Talmudic opinion, in the main, tends to agree with this commonsense interpretation (Ginzberg 1909–1938, 3:312).

The text itself, however, seems to avoid a direct statement about the specific nature of the wrongdoing of Moses. Other instances of this avoidance are even more apparent when the unhappy incident is mentioned again. On three separate occasions in his later discourses to the people (Deut. 1:37; 3:26; 4:21), Moses refers sadly to his not being permitted to enter the Promised Land, and each time he gives the same reason in almost identical words: "the Lord was angry with me for your sakes"; that is, because of how the people had behaved. He thus blames them for his responses. The great leader here reveals a common human weakness that makes him all the more believable as a genuine human being.

We return to the intriguing question: in what did his wrongdoing consist? For indeed, the act of striking the rock and speaking angrily to the people do not in themselves seem sufficiently serious to merit the severe rebuke and punishment that followed.

The nearest the text comes to a definitive answer to this question is in the words, "Because ye believed not in Me, to sanctify Me in the eyes of the children of Israel, therefore ye shall not bring this assembly into the land which I have given them" (20:12). Clearly, in some way, the offense involved the Deity Himself.

Reference to the nature of the guilt is brought up again a little later in the same chapter, at the time of the approaching death of Aaron. God says, "Aaron shall be gathered unto his people; for he shall not enter the land which I have given unto the children of Israel, because ye rebelled against My word at the waters of Meribah"(20:24). And in regard to Moses himself, when he is allowed to view the Promised Land from a distant mountaintop in Moab, God explains once more why the two leaders were excluded from entering Canaan: "because ye rebelled against My commandment in the wilderness of Zin, in the strife of the congregation, to sanctify Me in the waters before their eyes" (27:14).

Both these times, the *disobedience* is equated with *rebellion*. This rebellion stemmed from a lack of faith in God—"ye believed not in Me." This disbelief must have consisted of a doubt on the part of Moses that water could be brought forth from the rock by the power of the word alone, even though that word had the authority of the Deity behind it.

This was not the first time that Moses had faltered in his belief that God could meet the needs of the people in ways that clearly went beyond the bounds of natural forces. The earlier situation had occurred at the time when God declared to Moses that He would provide meat for the entire host of the Children of Israel (Num. 11). On that occasion, however, although Moses was rebuked by the Deity with the words "Is the Lord's hand waxed short?" he was not punished. Significantly, that breach of faith had not affected the leader's behavior *in the eyes of the people*, as had occurred at Kadesh. Moreover, the feeling had been expressed openly and thus was not repressed, as on this second occasion.

This lurking doubt in the power of God, deep within the heart of Moses, must have been generated, in part, by an unconscious *wish to rebel*, a reactivation of competitive feelings against the oedipal father of his childhood. To rebel is to defy authority. *It is an act of will*. Thus, it suggests more than an expression of anger and a loss of self-control. What could have been involved was the emergence of a *counter-will*, an unconscious, unverbalized intent to defy the Father. Freud explains the counter-will as stemming from an *antithetic idea*. He says that it is dissociated from the conscious intention. When it comes to carrying out the conscious intention, the counter-will takes over, often to the surprise of the individual himself (Freud 1893a, 5:38–44). Elsewhere, he comments, "antithetic ideas arise in us in a marked manner when we feel uncertain about whether we can carry out some important intention" (Freud 1893b, 92–95).

In regard to Moses, the counter-will was set up against the

superego command to speak to the rock and must indeed have been influenced by doubt about the outcome, the lack of faith for which God reproached him.

The conditions denoting indecision about what he would actually do were inherent in the very wording of the command as received by Moses. "And the Lord spoke unto Moses, saying: 'Take the rod, and assemble the congregation, thou and Aaron thy brother, and speak ye unto the rock before their eyes, that it give forth its water'" (20:7–8). If Moses was to speak to the rock, why did he need to take the rod with him? Perhaps having the rod in his hand may have been intended to serve as a source of strength and reassurance, a symbol both to himself and to the people that he was endowed with the authority to act as the representative of the Deity. Did it become, instead, a stimulus for rebellion, the rod of God being used for the leader's own unconscious purpose?

The situation at Kadesh was a particularly complex one. The intrapsychic conflict with which Moses was struggling stemmed from several sources impinging on each other. It was for the very purpose of avoiding an aggressive act toward the Deity that Moses was reluctant to strike the rock, although that method had proved successful on an earlier occasion. A logical alternative, it then seemed, was to speak to the rock instead. Such an approach would represent a desired sublimation of forbidden aggressive impulses. Certainly this resolve, coming in the form of a command from the Deity, was also an expression of the will of Moses, a conscious intention of what he planned to do.

But the hoped-for solution had the characteristics of a *compromise-formation*, unconsciously containing within itself another form of aggression, even more serious in nature than that which it sought to avoid—competitiveness with the Deity (Freud 1924, 2:32–33).

In the biblical tradition, God had created the whole world through the power of *the word* (Gen. 1). Would not a command issued to the rock, such as, "Pour forth your water!" have a connotation of God-like omnipotence? At the time of the exodus, Moses had to await guidance from God before causing the waters of the sea to divide (Exod. 14:15-16). Significantly, God's command that Moses speak to the rock gives no instructions about the exact words to be uttered. For the man with the slow tongue, indicative of inhibition, the fantasy of the magical power of words, common to childhood, may have retained its significance in the unconscious to an undue degree. The intensity of his wish to be powerful could have taken on forbidden aspects of competitiveness for which the inhibition would have served as a defense against aggression and a wish for omnipotence (Freud 1926, 14–15). Perhaps it was because of this disability that he could not respond to the verbal attacks of the people when these were especially violent. It was this same sense of verbal inadequacy, it will be recalled, that had led to his pleading many years before, at the theophany of the burning bush, to be excused from the mission ordained for him, saying, "Oh Lord, I am not a man of words, neither heretofore, nor since Thou has spoken unto They servant; for I am of slow speech and of slow tongue" (Exod. 4:10). It is at this point that God gave him Aaron, a supportive *alter ego*, to act as his voice. The underlying wish for omnipotence, against which Moses was so strongly defending himself, is also partially satisfied. God said, "and he shall be to thee a mouth, and thou shalt be to him in God's stead" (Exod. 4:16). At a later time, (see chapter 4) when Moses was commanded to appear again before the Egyptian ruler after the first rebuff, he said to God, "'Behold, I am of uncircumcised lips, and how shall Pharaoh hearken unto me?' And the Lord said unto Moses, 'See, I have set thee in God's stead to Pharaoh; and Aaron thy brother shall speak unto Pharaoh, that he let the children of Israel go out of his land'" (Exod. 6:30; 7:1–2).

In both these situations the complaint of weakness in speech was met with permission for Moses to play a God-like role, first to Aaron and then to Pharaoh. The tendency to verbal inhibition is thus clearly related to a wish for omnipotence. Only with God's express permission could Moses be powerful in the use of words.

It might be noted that during all the periods of crisis through which the Children of Israel passed, from the time of the plagues in Egypt to the exigencies in the wilderness, when saving acts were performed for the people, these miracles were never brought about by direct verbal command on the part of Moses over the forces of nature. They occurred following his prophetic words expressing the will of God (Kaufmann 1960,

82f.). Thus, speaking directly to the rock would have been a significantly new element in the situation. Even though he would be acting as the agent of God's will, the underlying wish for omnipotence could have changed the meaning of the situation for him. The leader was faced with an insoluble dilemma. In terms of his unconscious conflict, he either had to commit an act of aggression by striking the rock, unconsciously symbolic of the Deity, or be competitive with Him in the wish for omnipotence through the power of speech.

The situation at Kadesh differed from the earlier experience in another important respect. Then only the elders had been present (Exod. 17:6). Now the whole congregation was to witness this happening, significant of the power of God. Moses and Aaron are clearly instructed to assemble *all* the people and are told, "speak ye to the rock *before their eyes*, that it give forth its water" (20:8) (italics added).

Viewing this directive as emanating form the unconscious of Moses himself, it may give further evidence of the personal element involved. Moses wanted all the people to witness this manifestation of power, perhaps as a compensation for the sense of inadequacy he had experienced when exposed to their humiliating accusations. The derogatory terms in which they had made their demands must have touched to the quick this area of vulnerability—his tendency to feel verbally powerless.

A further aspect must have influenced the final outcome, this time one that stemmed from a sense of reality. Suppose he failed before that entire assembly because he had used the untried method of speaking to the rock! He would have to face the scorn and derision of the people, perhaps even the danger of personal violence. And beyond that there was the possibility that his leadership would be undermined and the whole purpose of the larger undertaking come to naught.

When the actual moment came, when Moses found himself standing beside the rock, facing the taunting multitude, his conflicting feelings must have reached a state of unbearable tension. No doubt he felt that it was they, the people, who had placed him in this untenable situation. The release of his pent-up feelings came in an outburst of anger: "and he said unto them: 'Hear now, ye rebels; are we to bring you forth water out of this rock?' And Moses lifted up his hand, and smote the rock with his rod twice; and water came forth abundantly, and the congregation drank, and their cattle" (20:10–11).

Several meanings seem to be concentrated in the one explosive sentence uttered by Moses. Hertz (1936) interprets it as, "*Can we bring you forth water from this rock?*" and says concerning it, "In that moment of irritation and gloom, Moses gives expression to doubt in front of the masses as to the fulfillment of God's power" (p. 656). Martin Noth (1968) describes the verse as "an expression of embarassment and doubt with a reproachful address to *the rebels* whose behavior has caused that embarrassment and that doubt" (p. 146).

Clearly, Moses feels that *he* was being tested as well as God, which was undoubtedly true. The implication of his reproach seems to be that an impossible task was being asked of him. The leader's own faith to achieve such a miracle must have faltered at that point. Since he felt unable to obey God's commandment, he may have *anticipated the possibility of failure* in getting water for the people. Therefore, as a protective measure but without awareness of what he was doing, he was preparing them in advance for an unfavorable outcome. The words "Ye rebels, are we to draw *you* forth water out of this rock?" (italics added) suggest that they were unworthy of such a miracle because they were rebellious, that is, lacking in faith. He was, in effect, accusing the people of the very sin with which God subsequently confronted the leader himself.

The text specifically states that Moses struck the rock twice. Perhaps the real need to draw forth the water made this repetition necessary. It seems more likely, however, since he evidently struck the rock in rapid succession, half-expecting that nothing would happen, that Moses needed a further outlet for his feelings of frustration and rage. After the second blow, "water came forth abudantly, and the congregation drank, and their cattle." Now came the significant words: "And the Lord said unto Moses and Aaron: 'Because ye believed not in Me, to sanctify Me in the eyes of the children of Israel, therefore ye shall not bring this assembly into the land which I have given them.' These are the waters of Meribah [strife], where the children of Israel strove with the Lord, and He was sanctified in them" (20:11–12).

There is a striking contradiction in these verses. First we are told that God reproached Moses and Aaron for having failed to sanctify Him in the eyes of the people and immediately after that, the words "and He was sanctified in them."

Something of significance seems to have been omitted here. What has been left out can be understood as representing a repression on the part of Moses, the substance of which would explain the contradiction referred to. In the words "These are the waters of Meribah, where the children of Israel strove with the Lord," Moses himself is directly identified with God since it was actually the *man* with whom the people were striving. Therefore, the pronoun in the second part of the verse, "and He was sanctified in them," may also refer to Moses.

The sudden gushing forth of the waters must have been unexpected for Moses himself. He had been in a mood of defeatism and anger, feeling that *he* did not deserve a miracle, especially through an act of disobedience. The words he had addressed to the people he must unconsciously have experienced as being directed to himself by the Deity: "You rebel, am I to draw *you* forth water from this rock!" And the appropriate response, according to the conscience of Moses, should have been, "No, Lord God, I do not deserve it." But nevertheless, "the water came forth abundantly."

The leader must have experienced a sudden change of mood, a deep sense of relief. He was still powerful with the rod of God! The responsive shouts of joy and appreciation from the multitude that must have followed would indeed have been like the proverbial balm to his troubled spirit. The disbelief and anger in the sea of faces surrounding him had suddenly changed. Now there must have been awe and reverence instead. *He was sanctified in their eyes*, as if he were, indeed, the very embodiment of the Lord!

But other feelings quickly take over. In the words of reproach that follow immediately, God confronts Moses not only with a lack of faith but with its consequences: "Because ye believed not in Me, *to sanctify Me in the eyes of the children of Israel*" (italics added). And that indeed must have been the crux of the matter. Moses had failed to give due honor to God *in the eyes of the people*. As the rabbis point out, if the leader had produced water from the rock by the power of the word alone, the accomplishment would have redounded to the greater glory of the Deity Himself through the man who spoke in His Name (Ginzberg 1909–1938, 3:312).

The ego can be caught off guard by persistent wishes of unconscious fantasies that seek realization. In the very moment when Moses should have been exalting God in his heart he may have felt instead a narcissistic gratification, an all too human emotion. This brief self-indulgence is quickly repressed. The only indication in the narrative of its existence is the contradiction, which states first that Moses failed to sanctify God in the eyes of the people and follows it with the words "and He [*he*] was sanctified in them." After that passing moment of self-exaltation, Moses must have been assailed by feelings of guilt. He had fallen short of his own ego ideal in several respects. First, the leader had acted out his aggression and struck the rock after having planned to speak to it instead. Also, by his angry words of reproach he must have evoked feelings of guilt in the people, together with doubt about whether the miracle would actually take place. Then, against this background of uncertainty, came the gushing forth of the waters, making Moses appear especially great *in their eyes* as well as in his own. It may have been in response to this sense of awe in the people that Moses felt himself sanctified in them.

Nachmanides, the noted medieval commentator, touches on this point. He thinks that the wrongdoing of Moses lay in the words he used, for these implied that Moses and Aaron rather than God were to perform the miracle (Cohen 1947, 902–03). For the grave sin of usurping God in the eyes of the people, even momentarily, for being competitive with God Himself, the punishment of not being allowed to enter the *mother-land* was meted out. Indeed, the original rivalry between son and father is in relation to the mother.

Striking the rock served a further unconscious purpose. The conflict was terminated in an outburst of anger against the people, as noted above. This reaction not only helped to alleviate his tension but also changed the focus of his thoughts and feelings. Instead of speaking to the rock as intended, Moses turned his attention to the multitude before him. Since his verbal anger was directed against them, it can be assumed that the blows he struck the rock also served as an expression of his rage toward them. Thus, instead of being the filial son, relating to the Father-God and obeying His commandment, Moses became the father himself, chastising his rebellious children. In this situation, the rock would have lost its symbolic significance as the Deity, becoming instead, an object for the displacement of his anger against the people. The originally feared impulse, aggression against God, was thus, in a sense, avoided. But as is generally true in a compromise-formation, the warded-off impulse finds another pathway for gratification (Freud 1926, 44–45). Not only was the aggression satisfied but the narcissistic wish also finds an outlet. In the relief and exultation of the success that followed upon striking the rock, the fantasy of feeling God-like found expression. This forbidden wish-fulfillment had to be repressed and denied. But the immediate announcement of the punishment that would follow indicates an awareness of guilt and the return to a sense of reality in terms of his own identity. The omission in the text referred to above could be replaced by an expanded version of God's reproach to Moses, as follows: "You failed to sanctify Me in the eyes of the people because you yourself wished to be sanctified in them, in My stead."

The role of Aaron in this situation is a characteristic one. He too suffered the penalty of dying in the wilderness. Commentators have wondered about the nature of *his* guilt. Perhaps Aaron's sin was one of omission. *He did nothing*. Probably, under the circumstances, that was all he could do. God's commandment concerning Aaron came through Moses. "And the Lord spoke unto Moses, saying: 'Take the rod, and assemble the congregation, thou, and Aaron, thy brother, and speak *ye* unto the rock before their eyes that it give forth its water; and *thou* shalt bring forth to them water out of the rock; so *thou* shalt give the congregation and their cattle drink'" (20:7-8 (italics added). It cannot be accidental that the commandment to assemble the people and speak to the rock uses the plural form of the pronoun, *ye*, thus including Aaron, whereas in the positive results that are to follow, providing water for the people, the singular form, *thou*, is used twice, thus disregarding Aaron. He is allowed to share in the responsibilities but not in the reward. Again, the tendencies in Moses that make him so understandably human unconsciously manifest themselves. He could not permit the brother to share his own special relationship with the Father. Aaron, however, had to be involved in this event. It would have been unthinkable to have allowed him in the privilege, denied to Moses, of entering the Promised Land.

And now we come to another aspect of this psychologically important event in the personal life of Moses. It is significant that the situation about the scarcity of water follows immediately on the statement that Miriam had died at Kadesh. The text says, "And the children of Israel, even the whole congregation, came into the wilderness of Zin in the first month; and the people abode in Kadesh; and Miriam died there, and was buried there. And there was no water for the congregation" (20:1–2).

The relationship between cause and effect is frequently established in this literature through the use of sequence (Pedersen 1926, 1–2, 115). Thus, the implication is that *because* of the death of Miriam there was no water for the congregation. There is indeed a psychological connection between the two happenings. Symbolically, the loss of Miriam was experienced as that of a mother figure and her nurturing breast. Water is as basic to life in the desert as milk is for the infant. Yet the Bible does not even record that the people mourned for her. In contrast, when Aaron died shortly thereafter, the event is treated in a much more expansive fashion, occupying eight verses (20:22–29). Moreover, we are clearly told, "And when all the congregation saw that Aaron was dead, they wept for Aaron thirty days, even all the house of Israel" (20:29).

This contrast may reflect the attitude of a patriarchal society in which the importance of women, in both their nurturing and sexual roles, is repressed, thus minimizing on a certain level the conflicting emotions relating to mother and wife. Unconsciously, this repression increases the affects associated with these relationships.

How does Moses himself react to the death of Miriam? No mention is made of a sense of grief on his part either. Characteristically, he did not allow himself to experience feelings of this kind on a personal basis, especially in family relationships. That aspect of his life tended to be ignored even beyond cultural conditioning. Psychologically, this renunciation favored a deeper relationship to God and a strengthening of his role as leader of *all* the people (Freud 1922, 122–23).

We shall assume, however, that the death of Miriam was not an unimportant event for her brother Moses. She had been a mothering figure to him in his infancy. She had endured with him the perils of the escape from Egypt, had led in the rejoicing at the crossing of the Sea of Reeds, had participated in the hardships of the wilderness, and gloried in the covenant at Mount Sinai.

Losing the mother may reactivate the oedipal hostility toward the father by evoking a repressed childhood image of him as a rival for her love and attention. This psychic process of loss and resentment may have taken place within the people as a whole. The fact that no public mourning for her is recorded and may indeed have been kept to a minimum suggests that there was little opportunity for catharsis. Feelings of grief and anger would then remain unabated, with increased ambivalence toward the father figure. Unconsciously, the people may have blamed Moses for this loss. Their complaint about the lack of water may have taken on a greater degree of animosity under these circumstances. Moreover, Moses himself may have had similar feelings toward the Father-God Who had done this to him.

A rabbinic legend intuitively picks up the underlying theme of Miriam as the group mother and a source of nurturance. It says that after Rephidim, for as long as Miriam lived, the Children of Israel never lacked water. A well magically accompanied them. "This well," says Ginzberg, "was in the shape of a sieve-like rock, out of which water gushed forth as from a spout. It followed them on all their wanderings, up hill and down dale. Wherever they halted, it halted too, finally settling opposite the Tabernacle. Thereupon the leaders of the twelve tribes would appear, each with his staff, and chant these words, 'Spring up, O well, sing ye unto it; nobles of the people digged it by direction of the lawgiver with their staves.' Then the water would gush forth from the depths of the well." When Miriam died, so says the legend, the well dried up (3:53).

Interestingly, in this postbiblical fantasy, the leaders of the tribes are able to accomplish what Moses could not. Although carrying their staves, they *spoke* to the "sieve-like rock" and the water came forth. Here, the rock can be understood as symbolic of a combined parental figure, both father and mother. This image is conceptualized even more clearly in Deuteronomy, as part of the Song of Moses referred to earlier (32:18). The leader, in his final words, warns Israel about her conduct in the future and predicts her unfaithfulness, saying, "Of the Rock that begot thee thou wast unmindful./And didst forget God that bore thee" (Patai, 20). Hertz comments concerning these lines, "A figure as bold as it is beautiful. God is represented as a Father, to whom Israel owed its existence as a people; and, at the same time, as a Mother, travailing with her infant, and forever watching over it with tender affection" (Hertz 1936, 899). Moses too must have identified with both these roles and some of his character traits can best be understood in that context.

The legend about Miriam's well may also have served the purpose of subtly indicating the positive approach that Moses should have used in his own experience with the rock, thus gently reproving him for his aggressive act. That he learned the lesson is indicated by a later happening. The people were then on the eastern border of Moab, in the wilderness of the Arnon River gorge. Evidently they were in need of water but this time we hear no complaints. They moved on to a place called Beer (a well). The text says, "that is the well whereof the Lord said unto Moses: 'Gather the people together, and I will give them water.' Then sang Israel this song, 'Spring up , O well, sing ye unto it'" (21:16-18). This verse is the source of the later legend quoted above. Here the water is supplied by supplication and through the efforts of the people themselves, under the immediate direction of God, with Moses serving only to "gather the people together."

The symbolism of the rock as the mother's breast comes through in another legend, which states that after the blow struck by Moses, blood flowed from the rock instead of water. Moses complains to God but is rebuked for striking the rock instead of speaking to it as commanded. Moses is reminded by the Deity that during the period in Egypt when Pharaoh ordered all male children to be destroyed, many women hid their newborn infants. An angel was sent to care for them and gave each child two smooth pebbles, one of which provided milk, the other honey (Ginzberg 1909–1938, 2:257). Thus, through the good offices of an angel, God plays the role of the nurturing mother offering her breasts to the abandoned children. The clear inference of the legend is that, in striking the rock at Kadesh, Moses was symbolically drawing blood from the maternal bosom, showing anger and a lack of faith in God, here the maternal provider. The primitive aspect of the fantasy points to its preoedipal source in the unconscious of the people from whom it stemmed. It seems that they intuitively understood a deeper source of man's common anger, which may go back to the time of the frustrated nursling who bites the mother's breast. In this folktale, the people are identifying with the Children of Israel at this point and blaming the leader even as he was blaming God.

Underlying biblical tradition, one can discern the profound influence of the mother image subtly merged into the figure of the Father-God (see chapter 9). In the above legends, the rock symbolizes the combined parental figure, whereas Moses is given the role of the rebellious child, who thus deserves punishment. The opportunity to make the most of a revered leader's moment of weakness is here fully utilized by his followers. Actually, the fantasies present in reverse the role generally played by Moses. His tendency was to take on the responsibilities of both father and mother to the Children of Israel, here also modeling himself on his concept of God.

Frequently, a series of events occurring simultaneously play a part in bringing about psychic conflict. Thus, a further element may have been involved in the situation at Kadesh. The people were now fairly close to the Promised Land, whose conquest was about to begin. Even before the episode relating to the rock Moses must have felt, somewhere deep within him, that for reasons he could not comprehend he would not have the privilege of entering that land. Psychoanalytically, the implication is that Moses was forbidden by his own superego to do so, a taboo that may have been rendered more threatening by the imminent approach of the tribes to Canaan. The conflict about striking the rock, against the background of the latter situation, could have reactivated an oedipal rebellion stemming from the past, now directed against the Father-God, Who had also deprived him of Miriam, a mother figure. Since this area of conflict belonged to the unconscious, Moses could not have any awareness of the real reason behind the prohibition, which was projected to God.

The Talmudic rabbis, in their own need for explanations, suggested that the theme of a heroic leader and a favored son of God, who was himself subject to a punishment so severe, pointed to a lesson in divine justice for the benefit of the people (Ginzberg 1909–1938, 3:313–14). However, a feeling must have persisted that an element of mystery surrounding the situation remained. Something about the disparity between the punishment and the crime was puzzling on a rational level.

Legend tries to deal with this elusive factor. It portrays God as having decreed long before that Moses was to die in the wilderness and then used the offense at Kadesh as a rationalization to justify the penalty. But, so the story goes, God was more explicit with Moses himself. The leader is told that his glory would hardly be enhanced if he were the one to bring a new generation into the Promised Land while those of his own age group, whom he had led out of Egypt, were buried in the desert. As a consolation, Moses was told that after the Ressurection, he himself would bring those disinherited ones into the motherland (Ginzberg 1909–1938, 3:313–14).

Although obviously intended to be comforting, the myth suggests that Moses may have been suffering from a sense of guilt, familiarly known as the guilt of the survivor, because he had outlived so many of his peers. Besides himself, only Caleb and Joshua were left of that earlier generation (4:28–38).

Rabbinic legend also says that Moses pleaded with God to ascribe a definite reason that would explain why he was being punished. Otherwise posterity would associate him with those others whose sins of disobedience and rebelliousness had brought about their deaths in the wilderness (Ginzberg 1909–1938, 3:313–14). What is suggested here is a wish on the part of the rabbis to deny that the sin of Moses was indeed also one of rebelliousness against God and thus subject to the same punishment that the others had received. By the specific nature of the request attributed to Moses, that a reason for his punishment be stated, the rabbis were intuitively indicating an awareness that the leader, in his protest and denial, suffering from an unconscious sense of guilt, was in need of a more satisfactory answer than he himself could find. God granted this request and it was recorded in Scripture several times that the offense for which Moses was prohibited from entering the Promised Land was his transgression at the rock in Kadesh, where he failed to sanctify God in the eyes of the Children of Israel. This explanation did indeed contain the kernel of the truth.

Some commentators observed that the Bible purposely withheld the exact nature of the sin for which Moses was not permitted to enter the Promised Land. The real reason was to remain unknown, they maintained, as part of the mystery surrounding this great figure, even as the exact site of his grave is unknown.

However, the deeper psychological aspects could not be fully grasped because its nature was hidden in the unconscious. Moses, struggling with competitive feelings toward the Father-God, could not take possession of the motherland, a situation involving unconscious incestuous fantasies (Feldman 1955; Zeligs 1960, 287–310; 1974, chap.1).

Final Years in the Wilderness

Adversities and Triumphs

 CHAPTER FOURTEEN

THE EVENTS recorded in the latter part of the book of Numbers consist of a series of experiences that take place in the last few years of the wilderness wanderings. In these events, the Children of Israel themselves play the major role, with Moses remaining more or less in the background as far as his personal feelings and conflicts are involved.

The transition of the main role from the leader to the group at this point is psychologically understandable. Moses has brought his people close to the end of their journey. He now withdraws to a greater degree. One can visualize him at this time, occupying himself with the preparation of the final discourses that he will deliver to the people in the memorable words recorded in Deuteronomy. The Children of Israel themselves must take over the stage preparatory to the coming loss of their lifetime leader.

The series of dramatic events with which these narratives deal give some indication of the prevailing state of mind among the Children of Israel preliminary to their assuming the responsibility for entering upon the conquest of the Promised Land.

There was still much they had to learn about their own areas of weakness and of strength.

The Detour around Edom

The people have now resumed their journey toward the borders of the Promised Land. The most direct route would have been through Edom, which lay to the south-southeast of the Dead Sea (then known as the Salt Sea).

Significantly, the lesson learned so painfully and at such cost in the recent experience when Moses struck the rock instead of speaking to it was now put to use. The hope was to take a direct route through Edom. But the Children of Israel avoided aggressive action as a means of accomplishing this aim. Instead, they tried to use the power of persuasion. "And Moses sent messengers from Kadesh unto the king of Edom: 'Thus saith thy brother Israel: Thou knowest all the travail that hath befallen us; how our fathers went down into Egypt, and we dwelt in Egypt a long time; and the Egyptians dealt ill with us, and our fathers; and when we cried unto the Lord, He heard our voice, and sent an angel, and brought us forth out of Egypt; and, behold, we are in Kadesh, a city in the uttermost of thy border. Let us pass, I pray thee, through thy land; we will not pass through field or through vineyard, neither will we drink of the water of the wells; we will go along the King's Highway, we will not turn aside to the right hand nor to the left, until we have passed thy border.' And Edom said unto him: 'Thou shalt not pass through me, lest I come out with the sword against thee'" (20:14–18).* The Children of Israel continue their plea, but Edom arrays itself in force against them, so Israel turns away. They must now take a circuitous route around the borders of Edom.

The next significant event along this journey took place at Mount Hor, the exact location of which is uncertain. It was there that the death of Aaron took place.

The text says, "And the Lord spoke unto Moses and Aaron in mount Hor, by the border of the land of Edom, saying: 'Aaron shall be gathered unto his people; for he shall not enter into the land which I have given unto the children of Israel, be-

---

*All biblical references in this chapter, unless otherwise noted, are to the book of Numbers.

cause ye rebelled against my word at the waters of Meribah. Take Aaron and Eleazar his son, and bring them up unto mount Hor. And strip Aaron of his garments, and put them upon Eleazar his son; and Aaron shall be gathered unto his people, and shall die there.' And Moses did as the Lord commanded; and they went up into mount Hor in the sight of all the congregation. And Moses stripped Aaron of his garments, and put them upon Eleazar his son; and Aaron died there in the top of the mount; and Moses and Eleazar came down from the mount. And when all the congregation saw that Aaron was dead, they wept for Aaron thirty days, even all the house of Israel" (20:23–29).

An element of pathos underlies this narrative in spite of its factual tone, or perhaps because of it. The very lack of openly expressed grief in a situation where this emotion would be appropriate has the effect of understatement that seeks to deny that which cannot be denied. Although it is in character with the personality of Moses that feelings of grief regarding familial matters should be restrained, there is an undue element of what seems like unfeelingness in the way this episode is described. Although Aaron is an old man and his tasks have been duly accomplished, his death is presented as a punishment for the disobedience he is said to have shared with Moses at Kadesh, when the latter struck the rock. Tradition seeks to rationalize this seeming injustice by the dictum, "Whoso joins a transgressor is as bad as the transgressor" (Ginzberg 1909–1938, 3:314). This rabbinic response suggests an identification with the feelings of Moses himself. Did the thought of his own approaching death and the reason given for it weigh so heavily on his mind that he needed someone to share the guilt and the punishment?

One can visualize the people below watching silently as the three familiar figures move up the mountain slope and disappear into the mists "in the sight of all the congregation." It was evidently understood that Aaron was departing from their lives. There could not have been any surprise when only two came back and, moreover, they beheld Eleazar dressed in the garments of the high priest.

We are not told whether Moses spoke any final words of comfort or consolation to his brother or if the two embraced at that last moment. We do not know what father and son said to one another in the sad leave-taking. The traditional farewell blessings a father customarily bestowed on his sons are not mentioned. The death of Aaron conveys a greater sense of loneliness than that of Moses himself, who was actually alone when his end came.

Moses removes the priestly garments from Aaron one by one and puts them on Eleazar in the manner prescribed by God. That task must have been a painful one. It was he who had clothed his brother in the insignia of the high priest. Now he was transferring this position of authority from father to son, who thus receives his power directly from Moses as representative of God.

The very brevity and austere wording of this whole scene has a dramatic impact on the reader. The biblical setting presents only three stark figures etched against a background of mountain wilderness. What they felt is left to the imagination.

There are puzzling aspects about this whole procedure. We do not know why Aaron had to go to his death dressed in the ceremonial robes. Or why it was necessary for him to be divested of those garments in piecemeal fashion, an added humiliation for a man about to die. Nor do we know why the investiture of Eleazar had to take place in the solitude of the mountaintop instead of the court of the Tabernacle, before the whole congregation, where Aaron had been consecrated.

This transfer of authority from father to son in the manner that it occurred must also have been painful to the younger man, especially at the moment of his father's death.

The directives for the procedure as carried out ostensibly came from God Himself. There was no precedent to follow, since Aaron was the first to occupy that high office. Certainly the manner in which Eleazar was initiated set no pattern for the future. One can conclude that the feelings and motives of Moses himself unconsciously motivated the scene that was enacted. It was not unusual for him to attribute to the Deity wishes and acts that stemmed from his own unconscious but which he could not acknowledge as part of himself.

The role Moses performs is a characteristic one. He takes the active part while Aaron is the passive object. Eleazar too, in that stressful experience, must have felt keenly the real source of the authority with which he was being invested.

Aaron's role as passive object in this situation is subtly indicated from its beginning. The announcement of his death is made by God to *both Moses and Aaron*. But the actual words are addressed *only to Moses*, while the other stands by silently as his fate and the manner in which it is to be carried out is pronounced. "And the Lord spoke with Moses and Aaron in mount Hor, by the border of the land of Edom, saying: 'Aaron shall be gathered unto his people. Take Aaron and Eleazar his son'" (20:23–26) (see full quotation above). It may have been important to the younger brother that Aaron should be cognizant of the fact that Moses was carrying out the command of God in this painful matter and not acting on his own initiative. As for Aaron, not a word, either of protest or appeal, not even a sign of resigned acceptance is uttered by him whose fate is thus revealed. One is struck by the difference in the way Moses himself at a later time meets the announcement of his own death. He responds with an emotional plea to be granted the privilege of setting foot in the Promised Land. The appeal is denied, but the effort had been made (Deut. 3:23–27).

It is not surprising that Talmudic rabbis, so intuitively sensitive to the undertones of the biblical text, identify with Moses in that they too seem to forget Aaron was also present at God's announcement. They discuss the theme of how Moses faced the problem concerning the best way to inform his brother of his impending death. They fantasize also how he tried to comfort Aaron with such words as the following: "'And now I pray that my death were as thine. For when thou diest, I bury thee, but when I shall die, I shall have no brother to bury me. When thou diest, thy sons will inherit thy position, but when I die, strangers will inherit my place.' With these and similar words, Moses encouraged his brother, until he finally looked forward to his end with equanimity" (Ginzberg 1909–1938, 3:320–27).

In touching on these personal relationships, so ignored in the biblical text itself, rabbinic wisdom both conceals and reveals the areas of conflict within Moses that apparently were involved in the sad drama he enacted. One Talmudic opinion was that Moses feared the people might deify Aaron, who was much beloved by them. It is said that for a similar reason Moses himself was buried in an unknown grave on a mountaintop. Did he perhaps desire that Aaron should share a fate like the one he anticipated for himself? There are no exact laws of science to measure what goes on in these shadowy areas of the human heart. One can only theorize on the basis of what is plausible as patterns of behavior repeat themselves in significant situations. Moses clearly had to struggle with competitive feelings both as a sibling and as a father because he had to guard jealously his position of being *first* in God's favor.

In what he was now doing Moses was exposing both Aaron and Eleazar to the full force of a painful experience where a son was blatantly displacing a father about to die. Nor could this happening have been easy for Moses either. It was as though he compulsively had to act out a ritual commanded by God without any awareness of its unconscious significance.

Moses, who had felt the need to forgo the gratification of a close relationship with his own sons because of his ambivalent feelings, saw Aaron retaining the joys of fatherhood and having the satisfaction of knowing that a son would succeed him as high priest. Did his brother's happier situation in this respect accentuate his own sense of deprivation and motivate the leader's behavior at this point when the succession was about to take place? At another time too, when Aaron and his sons were involved, a joyous occasion had been changed into one of grief. As will be recalled, at the consecration of the Tabernacle his two older sons, Nadab and Abihu, were consumed by "strange fire" near the altar, just after Aaron had been initiated into his high office. Then, Aaron was even forbidden by Moses to show any expression of sorrow, because such behavior would have marred the sanctity of the occasion. Now again, the manner of Eleazar's investiture could only have added to the trauma of the father's demise.

What the terse language of the Bible leaves out the expansive interpretations of the rabbis and the popular fantasies of the people fill in. Feelings and motivations are poured back into the bare outlines of the text, and the characters assume more real and lifelike proportions. Moses is now permitted the grief that the biblical narrative did not allow him. Thus, legend has it that "the weeping and mourning of Moses and Eleazar for Aaron made all the rest of the people do the same" (Ginzberg 1909–1938, 6:113). Was it perhaps the reverse that was true?

The negative side of the ambivalence, however, is also openly brought to the surface in the Haggadic amplifications. It was conjectured that the secrecy in which the death of their high priest and the transfer of authority to Eleazar took place could well have aroused the suspicion of those who were not friendly to the leader. Legend has it that some accused him of doing away with Aaron out of jealousy because the people loved the older brother more than they did him. Others fantasized that it was Eleazar who performed the wicked deed in his impatience to take his father's place. In these wildly imaginative folktales the kernel of truth regarding human motivation, especially as pertaining to Moses himself, can be discerned.

Aaron was one hundred twenty-three years old when he died in Mount Hor (33:30). Tradition depicts him as a man who loved peace and strove unceasingly to restore good relationships between people and in helping them attain a state of harmony with God through obedience to His commands. Was there a rabbinic effort here to compensate for, or to negate, the biblical verdict that Aaron had been guilty of an act of disobedience against the Deity, the reason given for his not being permitted to enter the Promised Land?

Although the connection is not overtly made, there is no difficulty in understanding why the highly esteemed virtue of being a peacemaker was so lavishly bestowed on Aaron. He had spent his life in obedient service to Moses, rarely asserting his own opinions or wishes. Even in the episode of the golden calf he was responding largely to the demands of the people rather than acting on his own initiative. Although Aaron was originally called upon to be the "voice" of Moses because of the latter's "slowness of tongue," in actuality it is Aaron who becomes the silent and shadowy figure standing mutely, for the most part, beside his brother.

In contrast to the sternness and sense of justice that the people saw in Moses, whose beneficence was more subtly concealed, they probably responded with greater warmth to the less threatening and more compliant personality of Aaron, who, like themselves, was subject to the authority of the leader. They intuitively rationalized Aaron's weaknesses, turning them into virtues. Thus, Aaron was seen as valuing peace above all else, as the explanation of why he always deferred to his brother.

The Destruction of Hormah

The thirty days of mourning for Aaron, ostensibly spent at the foot of Mount Hor, being over, the Children of Israel resumed their journey toward Canaan. But the Canaanites who dwelt in the southern part of that land, in the area now known as the Negev, heard of their approach and made a preventive attack on them, taking some of the Children of Israel captive. The text goes on to say, "And Israel vowed a vow unto the Lord and said: 'If Thou wilt indeed deliver this people unto my hand, then I will utterly destroy their cities.' And the Lord hearkened to the voice of Israel, and delivered up the Canaanites; and they utterly destroyed them and their cities; and the name of the place was Hormah" (21:2–3).

Some scholars point out that this episode involved geographic features that would have made it unrealistic for the Canaanites of this particular locality to have come into conflict with the Children of Israel at this time. The former were considerably farther north of where the Children of Israel apparently were encamped. Hertz (1936) suggests that this event actually refers to an earlier experience regarding Hormah, which took place many years before, when the Children of Israel first left Kadesh-barnea and moved northward toward the southern borders of Canaan, a direction that would have afforded them a direct route to the Promised Land (p. 659). At that time the decision was made to send scouts for the purpose of spying out the territory. The disheartening report they brought back changed the course of history for the Children of Israel. Their failure in courage led to God's pronouncement that they would have to wander in the wilderness for forty years. The crestfallen people then declared their belated intention to proceed with the original plan of conquest. In spite of Moses' command to the contrary, they persisted in their unauthorized effort to go up into the hill country and fight the Canaanites. Bitterly defeated, the Children of Israel were driven back to Hormah, the place from which they had evidently started and which they must have conquered earlier, since they had advanced from that point.

It has been suggested that the term *Hormah*, which means *utter destruction*, refers to an entire area rather than just the city and was named thus as descriptive of its condition after the first conquest by the Children of Israel thirty-eight years earlier (Hertz 1936, 623). However, since the exact locations of both Hormah and Mount Hor are uncertain, there is no necessity to assume that this second encounter with the Canaanites of the south could not have taken place as described.

In their vow to God the Children of Israel refer to themselves in the symbolism of an individual, thus emphasizing their unity of purpose. "If Thou wilt indeed deliver this people unto *my* hand, then *I* will utterly destroy their cities" (italics added). God responds in similar fashion: "And the Lord hearkened to *the voice* of Israel" (21:2–3) (italics added). In subtle fashion, the earlier experience at Hormah, when they also acted in unison but *in defiance of their leader* is thus recalled. But now they are responding in a different attitude, determining first that their action would be approved by the Deity. Therefore, the consequences also are different.

The unhappy event associated with Hormah so many years before is now brought into a relationship with the more successful outcome, accentuating the triumph of the present over the past. The Children of Israel demonstrate that they have achieved to a greater degree the maturity necessary for the conquest of the Promised Land. A sense of history, an awareness of change, seems to be one of the underlying motivations in this account of the pilgrimage, especially during these latter years. But as so frequently happens in the progress of both individuals and nations, a movement forward is often followed by a regression, as the next happening will relate.

The Brazen Serpent

The Children of Israel now continue their wearisome journey around the borders of Edom. The biblical narrative says succinctly, "And they journeyed from mount Hor by way of the Red Sea, to encompass the land of Edom" (21:4). The "Red Sea" here refers to the Gulf of Aqaba, the eastern arm of the larger body of water.

Ancient Edom stretched from the southern tip of the Dead Sea to the port of Ezion-Geber (Elath) on the northern shore of the Gulf of Aqaba. Much of its winding borders were through hot, rocky, desert areas, difficult to traverse. Edom was a mountainous land, dominated by the impressive height of Mount Seir, which rose five thousand feet into the air. It is associated in the Song of Moses with the presence of God, Who is described as accompanying Israel on its journey from Mount Sinai (Deut. 33:2).

But evidently the Children of Israel were not particularly grateful either to God or to Moses on that particular occasion. It was a tiring pilgrimage, and they grew impatient. Had they been allowed to take a direct route eastward across Edom, they would have been spared what must have seemed to them unnecessary hardship. Again, the old familiar refrain is heard by their leader: "Wherefore have ye brought us up out of Egypt to die in the wilderness? For there is no bread and there is no water and our soul loatheth this light bread'" (21:5). At the same time that they complain about the lack of bread they also express loathing for the bread they have. Clearly, the chief reason for this outburst, as the narrative states, was that "the soul of the people became impatient because of the way" (21:4).

Having recently shown their prowess by defeating the Canaanites from the south and having also dedicated the victory to God in the form of a *herem*, or sacrifice, the Children of Israel may have been less inclined to endure the subsequent privations that faced them. Perhaps they felt that they now deserved better at the hands of God and of Moses.

The punishment for their complaints comes swiftly, as if expressing the impatience of the weary leader himself. "And the Lord sent fiery serpents among the people, and they bit the people; and much people died. And the people came to Moses and said: 'We have sinned, because we have spoken against the Lord, and against thee; pray unto the Lord, that He take away the serpents from us.' And Moses prayed for the people. And the Lord said unto Moses: 'Make thee a fiery serpent, and set it upon a pole; and it shall come to pass, that every one that is bitten, when he seeth it shall live.' And Moses made a serpent of brass, and set it upon the pole; and it came to pass, that if a serpent had bitten any man, when he looked unto the serpent of brass, he lived" (21:4–9).

The snake has long been an object of ambivalence, evoking feelings both of dread and fascination, not only among individuals but in the mythologies and cultic practices of primitive religions. It was regarded among the ancients as possessing magical powers that could both destroy and heal. Among the Egyptians, the serpent represented the world of darkness and death (Frankfort 1948, 18, 132). But, at the same time the sacred serpent is also depicted as guardian and protector, having special health-giving and healing powers. (*EJ* 1972, 5:958–9) (21).

In the Bible the snake generally appears in an unfavorable light, as the enemy of man, a view first presented in the familiar story of the Garden of Eden. As a symbol common in dreams, the snake represents the male organ. As such, it is the source of life but in its orgiastic capacity can be experienced as a temporary death. The feelings of both reverence and dread that it calls forth are thus readily understood. The concept of the healing qualities of the snake, its life-giving powers, is expressed in the insignia of the medical profession, the staff of Asculapius, a rod entwined with a snake, and the caduceus, with two snakes around its staff.

It is not altogether surprising, therefore, that the serpent that bit the Children of Israel in the wilderness should have been used symbolically to effect their cure also, a procedure that may have worked through the power of suggestion. If the snakes that bit the people were not actually poisonous in the first place, the resulting deaths may have been caused by mass hysteria and could then be cured by mass suggestion.

The explanation offered by the Talmud concerning this phenomenon is psychologically sound. It says that the cure was effected not by the magical properties of the serpent image but by the upward gaze of the people, which directed their thoughts and feelings toward the Almighty (Hertz 1936, 660). This idea embodies the concept of sublimation, a process in which instinctual energy is transformed into psychic power, which finds an outlet along paths more socially acceptable. The people had sinned by complaining about the lack of oral gratification and other physical discomforts. They were cured through repentance and faith.

The Children of Israel now resumed their journey. The trek toward the south had brought them all the way to Ezion-Geber, at the tip of the Gulf of Aqaba. After circling the southern border of Edom, they were finally able to turn their faces northward, in the direction of the Promised Land.

The account in Deuteronomy (2:1–18), in line with its own purposes, gives emphasis to somewhat different aspects of this part of the journey. It states that the wayfarers were now able to take a shorter route across the eastern portion of Edom, around the foothills of Mount Seir, the area inhabited by the children of Esau. Once more they are instructed by God through Moses, on how to behave on this detour through a land belonging to kinsmen: "Ye are to pass through the border of your brethren the children of Esau that dwell in Seir; and they will be afraid of you; take ye good heed unto yourselves therefore; contend not with them; for I will not give you of their land, no, not so much for the sole of the foot to tread on; because I have given Mount Seir unto Esau for a possession. Ye shall purchase food of them for money, that ye may eat; and ye shall also buy water of them for money, that ye may drink" (Deut. 2:4–6).

When the narrative continues after the episode of the brazen serpent, the Children of Israel are somewhere on the highlands along the eastern border of Edom. The crossing of the Zered River, actually a dry wadi part of the year and a torrential stream during the rainy season, had special significance. It joined the Dead Sea at its most southeastern point and formed the boundary between Edom and the neighboring kingdom of Moab, which lay directly to the north.

The long years of wandering in the wilderness were now nearly over. A turn in their fortunes awaited the weary pilgrims. Again, the people were warned: "Be not at enmity with Moab, neither contend with them for I will not give thee of their land for a possession" (Deut. 2:9).

The approach along the eastern border of Moab was on the plateau that forms a large part of that territory now known as Transjordan. It is several thousand feet above sea level, much of it sloping down steeply along the western side to the plains of the

Jordan Valley below. Eastward, the land merges into the highlands of the Arabian Desert.

By keeping to the east of Moab the Children of Israel avoided not only the well-fortified cities and highways of the interior but also the deep gorges with their steep hillsides that divided the land in the western section.

East of the Jordan

In this period of history the lands east of the Jordan were highly populated, enjoying large areas of fertile territory. They were well watered by numerous perennial rivers that had their source in the eastern highlands of the Arabian Desert. These streams flowed in a more or less zigzag direction toward the west, emptying at various points into the inland waterways that formed the eastern border of Canaan—the Sea of Galilee, the Jordan River, and the Dead Sea. The three most important of these rivers, mentioned at various times in connection with biblical events, were the Yarmuk, which was the largest, the Jabbok, and the Heshbon.

These rivers and their tributaries cut deeply through the earth, forming canyons that divided the land into distinctive segments, making travel and communication difficult, especially between the cities on the highlands and the settlements in the Valley of the Jordan below. There was a striking contrast between the green fields and pastures watered by the rivers and the dry, rocky areas of the desert lands that lay farther to the east. The deep gorges and their steep cliffs added to the unusual scenic beauty of the topography (Glueck 1946, 83–125).

This was the impressive territory where the Children of Israel were to make their first conquests before crossing the Jordan. Indeed, some of them were to remain there as permanent settlers.

But the wayfarers pursuing their weary journey along the hot, rocky desert road east of Moab were still unaware of what lay before them. They finally pitched their tents on the northern bank of the Arnon River, probably having crossed that body of water at a shallow point. There the happy experience referred to earlier awaited them. In the words of the Bible, "And from thence to Beer [well]; that is the well where the Lord said unto Moses 'Gather the people together, and I will give them water.' Then sang Israel this song: Spring up, O well—sing ye unto it —/ The well which the princes digged/ Which the nobles of the people delved/ With the sceptre, and with their staves'" (21:16–18).

Some commentators have suggested that this episode more likely refers to an old well that had been in existence before, which the people unearthed and cleaned out.

The Arnon River formed the northern boundary of Moab at that time, separating it from the kingdom of the Amorites. As on previous occasions with other rulers, the Children of Israel sent messages to Sihon, king of that land, asking for permission to cross peaceably through his territory. They promised to go along the King's Highway without trespassing upon fields or availing themselves of water from the wells except as those commodities might be bought and paid for. But Sihon responded by coming out and attacking Israel. Of the ensuing battle, the text says, "And Israel smote him with the edge of the sword, and possessed his land, from the Arnon unto the Jabbok even unto the children of Ammon; for the border of the children of Ammon was strong. And Israel took all these cities; and Israel dwelt in all the cities of the Amorites, in Heshbon, and in all the towns thereof. For Heshbon was the city of Sihon, the king of the Amorites, who had fought against the former king of Moab, and taken all of his land out of his hand, even unto the Arnon" (21:24–26).

This conquest was a significant victory for the Children of Israel. It had been achieved over forces that recently had successfully defeated Moab and wrested considerable land from that kingdom all the way back to the Arnon River. It is not surprising that the new conquerors were in a mood to give voice to their gladness. The narrative here indulges in a song of victory, referring first, in a historical vein, to Sihon's earlier conquest, expressed in a popular ballad of that day, and then triumphantly surpassing that event with their own victory over the previous conquerors (21:27–30).

Their next adventure was the conquest of Bashan, which lay to the northeast of Sihon's territory. The king of that land was

Og, said to be the last of the legendary giants, the Raphaim. A graphic detail about him is related in Deuteronomy. "For only Og king of Bashan remained of the Raphaim; behold, his bedstead was a bedstead of iron; is it not in Rabbah of the children of Ammon? Nine cubits was the length thereof, and four cubits the breadth of it, after the cubit of a man" (Deut. 3:11).

The victories over the two Amorite kings, Sihon and Og, and the conquest of their towns and villages, initiated a great change in the lives of the Children of Israel. Their nomadic way of life was over. The wanderers of the wilderness were deeply impressed with the greenness and fertility of the lands around them and the great rivers that made those favorable conditions possible.

These countries east of the Jordan were noted for their grain-producing areas, their tall trees, and fine pasturelands, on which cattle and sheep of superior quality could be raised. The territory known as Gilead, a scenic area of highlands and deep canyons, was famous for its forests, orchards, and vineyards, as well as for its fine pastures. From certain of its trees came the so-called balm of Gilead, a medicinal substance, much valued not only throughout Canaan but also in more distant lands. In later days the prophet Jeremiah refers to it when bewailing the sorrows of his people, crying out, "Is there no balm in Gilead; is there no physician there?" (8:22). Although the term *Gilead* was often used regarding East Jordan as a whole, it referred more specifically to the area between the Yarmuk and the Jabbok rivers.

It is not surprising that the Children of Israel were reluctant to leave these lands that they had conquered. The tribes of Reuben and Gad, who owned a great number of cattle, were especially attracted by the fine pastures and wanted to remain. Their leaders came to Moses and asked permission to make their permanent homes east of the Jordan. A lengthy discussion ensued during which Moses reminded them of the catastrophe that had followed many years before, when the scouts, who had been sent to bring back a report concerning Canaan, discouraged the people about continuing with their conquest of the Promised Land. Was Israel to be deterred again from its purpose? But the leaders of Reuben and Gad and part of the tribe of Manasseh assured

Moses that their intention was to cross the Jordan with their kinsmen and help to conquer that land. Only then, when the other tribes were established in Canaan, would they return to the East Jordan. In the meantime they would build settlements there, fortify the cities, and settle their families in safety and security.

On these terms Moses agreed. The tribes of Reuben, Gad, and a large part of the tribe of Manasseh settled in the hill country and cities of the former Amorite kingdoms. These areas stretched from the Arnon River all the way to Mount Hermon in the north.

The kingdom of the Ammonites lay to the northeast of Moab and the territory of the Amorites. It was another country against which the people of Israel were forbidden to make war, as Moses recalls in his Deuteronmic Discourse: "the Lord spoke unto me, saying: 'Thou art this day to pass over the border of Moab, even Ar [city of Aroer?]; and when thou comest nigh against the children of Ammon, harass them not, nor contend with them; for I will not give thee of the land of the children of Ammon for a possession'" (2:17–19).

Israel was now encamped upon the Plains of Moab, an open area immediately to the north of the Dead Sea, east of the Jordan. Opposite them was the town of Jericho, fated to be their first conquest on the other side of that river.

The Plains of Moab are of special significance in the history of the Children of Israel. Its eastern border is fringed by a mountain range from the loftiest peak of which, Mount Nebo, Moses would behold the Promised Land, upon which he was never to set foot. And on that same lonely mountaintop he would one day, in the not too distant future, meet his destined end.

The Story of Balaam

The Paradoxical Prophet

 CHAPTER FIFTEEN

AT THIS POINT in the biblical narrative an unusual story is introduced. It concerns a pagan seer, or prophet, named Balaam, who was thought to be endowed with special powers to bless or to curse. Balaam's reputation had reached all the way from his home in Mesopotamia to the distant land of Moab, whose ruler, Balak, was feeling threatened by the presence of the Children of Israel encamped on the northern border of his kingdom. He sends messengers to Balaam asking that he come to Moab and curse the Children of Israel for him, hoping thus to nullify their military might.

The character of Balaam and his adventures on this exploit has provided a challenging area for a variety of scholarly interpretations. The opposite ways in which he was viewed are themselves of interest. Some of the rabbis of Talmudic days rated him highly, whereas others held him and his prophetic powers in low esteem. At a later date he was favored in Christian literature because it was believed that some of his oracles predicted the coming of Jesus (24:17).*

---

*All biblical references in this chapter, unless otherwise noted, are to the book of Numbers.

Balaam has been described as "one of the most enigmatic characters in the Bible." According to biblical criticism, "the tradition about him is both ancient and reliable." The view is expressed that the inconsistencies in the prose narrative may go back to real or apparent contradictions in the original body of tradition "as suggested by the archaic elements in the language and content of the oracles he pronounced" (*EJ* 1972, 119–124).

During the Middle Ages, Balaam was often portrayed as a comic figure in the morality dramas of that period, especially in the well-known episode with the talking donkey. But on the other hand, some scholars regarded him as a respected visionary and prophet.

Let us see what we can gather from the biblical material itself. The text says, "And Balak the son of Zippor saw all that Israel had done to the Amorites. And Moab was sore afraid of the people, because they were many; and Moab was overcome with dread because of the children of Israel" (22:2–3).

The king sends ambassadors of high estate to the home of the seer, bearing the following message: "Behold, there is a people come out of Egypt; it covers the face of the earth; and they abide over against me. Come now therefore, I pray thee, curse me this people; for they are too mighty for me; per-adventure I shall prevail, that we may smite them, and that I may drive them out of the land; for I know that he whom thou blessest is blest, and he whom thou cursest is cursed" (22:5–6).

Balaam, however, stalls for time. "And he said unto them: 'Lodge here this night, and I will bring you back word, as the Lord may speak with me'" (22:8).

The very fact that Balaam was undecided must be accounted to his credit, since the messengers had come with promise of monetary rewards. Although the act of uttering a curse in this ritualistic fashion was not expected to involve his personal feelings, Balaam evidently did have some compunctions about the matter. To curse a whole people from whom one had suffered no harm, just for the sake of material gain, may have aroused uneasiness. Although Balaam evidently had faith in his own efficacy to bless or to curse, it is clear that he also felt himself bound to a higher authority regarding the use of those powers.

The text implies that the Deity to whom Balaam refers for

guidance is the same as the God of Israel. No explanation is given about how this faith was acquired by a pagan seer. It has been suggested that since Mesopotamia was the original home of Abraham himself, Hebraic concepts of God could not have been altogether unfamiliar in that area.

We are told that God does indeed come to Balaam that night, as expected. Talmudic commentary has observed that even Moses did not have such immediate accessibility to the presence of the Deity (Rubenstein 1968, 154–55). In the manner of the God of Israel He begins by making an investigation. God asks a question, thus putting responsibility first on the person seeking help. "What men are these with thee?" He inquires. Balaam explains who his guests are and why they have come. God listens and then makes His decision. He tells Balaam quite definitely, "Thou shalt not go with them; thou shalt not curse the people for they are blessed" (22:9–12).

This confrontation with the Deity can be understood psychologically as a projection of Balaam's own superego. The seer decides to act on its clear message. He will not go to Moab.

The ambassadors return to Balak with the disappointing reply. But the king refuses to accept a negative response. He sends a second delegation, men of even greater prestige, with offers of even higher rewards. "And they came to Balaam and said to him: 'Thus saith Balak the son of Zippor: 'Let nothing, I pray thee, hinder thee from coming unto me; for I will promote thee unto very great honour, and whatsoever thou sayeth unto me I will do; come therefore, I pray thee, curse me this people'" (22:16–17). "And Balaam answered and said unto the servants of Balak: 'If Balak would give me his house full of silver and gold, I cannot go beyond the word of the Lord, my God, to do anything small or great. Now therefore, I pray you, tarry ye also here this night that I may know what the Lord will speak unto me'" (22:18–19).

God again is conveniently available to Balaam and comes to him once more that night. This time the Deity takes a more moderate position. He says, "If the men are come to call thee, rise up, go with them; but only the word which I speak unto thee, that shalt thou do" (22:20).

From the viewpoint of Balaam's own conscience there is now

a crack in the firmness of his previous resolution. The opportunity to put off a final decision signifies that a door is being left open for temptation. He has taken a step closer to the forbidden deed. A situation for conflict is thus created.

There is validity here to the Hebraic concept that man is given a certain freedom of choice even after knowing the path he should follow. But he must also bear the consequences of that choice.

The lively incident that follows, involving an angel and the talking donkey, exemplifies with remarkable precision, from a psychoanalytic viewpoint, the seer's conflict with his superego. The text says, "And Balaam rose up in the morning, and saddled his ass, and went with the princes of Moab. And God's anger was kindled because he went; and the angel of the Lord placed himself in the way for an adversary against him" (22:21–22).

There is clearly inconsistency here in the way God behaves. First, Balaam is instructed not to go with the messengers. Later, God tells him to go but to speak only what he is told. Then, when the seer does go, God is angry. No explanation is attempted in the text regarding this obvious contradiction.

The Deity's anger here can be understood as a projection of Balaam's own feelings. The seer was *angry with himself* because he had yielded to his baser impulses instead of holding firm to the more commendable decision that had been the first response to his voice of conscience. The profound inner uneasiness is then projected onto the dramatic figure of the angel of the Lord who blocked his path.

The role of the talking donkey, seen as amusing by many but on another level quite touching and certainly meaningful, adds a vivid and unusual atmosphere to the story. "Now he was riding upon his ass, and his two servants were with him. And the ass saw the angel of the Lord standing in the way, and went into the field; and Balaam smote the ass, to turn her into the way. Then the angel of the Lord stood in a hollow way between the vineyards, a fence being on this side, and a fence on that side. And the ass saw the angel of the Lord, and she thrust herself unto the wall, and crushed Balaam's foot against the wall; and he smote her again. And the angel of the Lord went further, and stood in a narrow place, where there was no place to turn either to the right hand or to the left. And the ass saw the angel of the Lord, and she lay down under Balaam; and Balaam's anger was kindled, and he smote the ass with his staff. And the Lord opened the mouth of the ass, and she said unto Balaam: 'What have I done unto thee that thou hast smitten me these three times?' And Balaam said unto the ass: 'Because thou hast mocked me; I would there were a sword in my hand, for now I would have killed thee.' And the ass said unto Balaam: 'Am I not thine ass, upon which thou hast ridden all thy life long unto this day? Was I ever wont to do so unto thee?' And he said: 'Nay.' Then the Lord opened the eyes of Balaam, and he saw the angel of the Lord standing in the way, with his sword drawn in his hand; and he bowed his head, and fell on his face. And the angel of the Lord said unto him: 'Wherefore hast thou smitten thine ass these three times? Behold, I come forth for an adversary, because thy way is contrary unto me; and the ass saw me, and turned aside before me these three times; unless she had turned aside from me, surely now I had slain thee, and saved her alive.' And Balaam said unto the angel of the Lord: 'I have sinned; for I knew not that thou stoodest in the way against me; now therefore, if it displease thee, I will get me back.' And the angel of the Lord said unto Balaam,: 'Go with the men; but only the word that I shall speak unto thee, that thou shalt speak.' So Balaam went with the princes of Balak" (22:22–35).

This experience of Balaam can be understood as having occurred in a dreamlike state. The interpretation here is that there are two possibilities about the scene of the action. One is that the phenomenon actually took place on the narrow path as described. Such paths were characteristic of the countryside, especially where vineyards were planted. When Balaam started out, it was probably early in the morning. He may not yet have been fully awake and was very likely in a doubtful state of mind about the rightness of the errand on which he had embarked. As a seer, he would be particularly prone to altered states of consciousness, with ready access to underlying fantasies (Greenacre 1957, 60–65; Kris 1952, 312–14).

The other possibility is that this entire episode could have taken place as *an early morning dream before Balaam actually left his bed*. The conflict about whether he should go evidently had not been satisfactorily resolved the night before and may thus been continued in a dream during the early hours of the morning. Unresolved problems, colored by anxiety, are known to strive for solutions in this manner. The text says, "Balaam arose early and saddled his ass," performing this menial task himself, although one would have expected a servant to do so since two accompanied him on the way. Thus, in the dream Balaam becomes the chief actor, a role appropiate to a problem-solving attitude. Being stopped on a narrow path is a symbolic expression of conflict. Balaam is not only hindered in his progress toward a forbidden goal but also suffers the trauma of having his foot crushed against the wall, a symbolic castration.

There are other details in the narrative that suggest dreamlike qualities (22). Although we are told that the messengers from Moab returned with Balaam, the impression is given that he was quite alone when the remarkable phenomenon took place. A sense of isolation as far as human companionship is concerned seems to pervade the entire scene. One is aware only of the seer, the donkey, and the angel. The princes of Moab aren't mentioned again until after the conflict is resolved and Balaam is instructed to continue the journey. Then we are told, "So Balaam went with the princes of Balak" (22:35). Where were they while all the action was taking place? And where were the two servants? If they were on the scene, why didn't they offer help with the seemingly recalcitrant donkey?

Within the dream setting every element has significance. One must ask what purpose was served by the presence of the two servants? Realistically, this detail is understandable. Balaam was a man of means. But the biblical narratives, similar to dreams in this respect, do not bother to mention irrelevant factors. What functions, then might these two have served in the dream? They play no role in the action itself. Nor are they mentioned again.

It is suggested here that the two servants can be understood as shadowy aspects of Balaam's own psyche which find graphic representation in the figure of the angel and the donkey. In this little intrapsychic drama, these two elements in the dream play the roles of the superego and the id. The functions they perform are in the service of the ego.

The angel with the drawn sword in hand, blocking the narrow path, is a clear representation of the superego. Balaam is being stopped in his tracks by his own conscience. He is unaware of the presence of the angel at first, because the conflict has not yet reached consciousness.

In terms of the biblical setting the role of the donkey is more unusual, although animals in helping roles are commonly found in other forms of literature, such as myths and fairy tales. The donkey here represents the instinctual forces of the id, whose first responsibility is to preserve life. Usually regarded as an obstinate and stupid animal, the donkey here is obstinate in a good cause, concern for her master.

It is known that genetically the superego has a deep instinctual relationship with the id, growing out of the developmental conflict between them. The id therefore can, under certain circumstances, be in closer touch with what is happening within the superego than the conscious part of the personality itself (Freud 1923, 53).

Psychologically, it is not surprising that the donkey speaks. Its voice is the externalized voice of Balaam himself from a part of the psyche that has indeed been with him all his life, as the donkey has. Balaam doesn't seem surprised by the phenomenon, another characteristic of a dreamlike state.

The animal is evidently a female, being referred to in the text as "she." This element also must have significance. Through the condensation of meanings characteristic of dreams, the donkey can be understood as both the projected feminine aspect of Balaam's own personality and the original object of this identification, the mother. In typical maternal fashion she tries to protect Balaam from the threatening father figure. It is the father from whom a preponderant part of the superego is formed, especially in a partriarchal society.

As a professinal seer, who was called on to bless or to curse without emotional involvment on a personal level, Balaam may have tended to repress his own feelings. The she-donkey, through her reproaches for his cruel treatment, arouses his compassion, thus moving him away from his preoccupation with a wholly self-centered goal. It was when he admitted her loyalty to him all his life, thus acknowledging his wrongdoing in striking her, that "the

Lord opened the eyes of Balaam, and he saw the angel of the Lord standing in the way, with the sword drawn in his hand." His own life is saved through an awakened sense of guilt about his unkindness toward the donkey. In this chastened frame of mind Balaam is more open to the warning voice of the angel.

The Meeting with Balak

Balak goes out to the border of Moab to meet his guest. He reproaches Balaam with the words, "'Did I not earnestly send unto thee to call thee? wherefore camest thou not unto me? am I not able indeed to promote thee to honour?' And Balaam said unto Balak: 'Lo, I am come unto thee; have I now any power at all to speak anything? the word that God putteth in my mouth, that shall I speak'" (22:37–38). Thus, Balaam tries again to prepare the king for what was coming.

The ritual of sacrifices preparatory to the divination is duly carried out. At Balaam's direction, seven altars are built and on each one a bullock and a ram are offered up. Balak is then told to remain by the burnt-offering while the seer retreats to another hill, saying, "peradventure the Lord will come to meet me; and whatsoever He showeth me I will tell thee" (23:3).

The king had brought Balaam to a high point of the hill, and according to the text, "He saw from thence the utmost part of the people " (22:41). The sight of the tents of Israel spread in a vast and orderly array on the plains beneath him, with the Tabernacle in the center, must have taken Balaam by surprise. It conveyed a message of discipline under God, the very essence of what the angel with the drawn sword must have meant to him. The seer may have experienced a strong sense of identification with the Children of Israel at that moment and with the God they worshipped.

Regardless of any scholarly uncertainties concerning when and by whom the inspired oracles of Balaam were produced, they are indeed convincingly expressive of the mood that must have animated the man who uttered them. Only a person truly *possessed of the spirit* could have pronounced those beautiful incantations. According to Albright (1957), these poems stem from the thirteenth-twelfth centuries B.C., which places them in a period appropriate to the era involved (p. 14).

The Oracles of Balaam consist of four parts, interspersed by the continuing narrative. Only a few excerpts will be quoted here. The text says, "And the Lord put a word in Balaam's mouth, and said: 'Return unto Balak, and thus shalt thou speak.' And he returned unto him, and lo, he stood by the burnt-offering, he, and all the princes of Moab. And he took up his parable and said: From Aram Balak bringeth me,/ The king of Moab from the mountains of the East:/ 'Come, curse me Jacob,/ And come, execrate Israel.'/ How shall I curse, whom God hath not cursed?/ And how shall I execrate, whom the Lord hath not execrated?/ For from the top of the rocks I see him,/ And from the hills I behold him; Lo, it is a people that shall dwell alone,/ And shall not be reckoned among the nations./ Who hath counted the dust of Jacob/ Or numbered the stock of Israel?/ Let me die the death of the righteous,/ And let mine end be like his!'" (23:7–10).

"And Balak said unto Balaam: 'What has thou done unto me? I took thee to curse mine enemies, and behold, thou has blessed them altogether'" (23:11).

Balaam reminds the king that he could only speak what God put into his mouth. But Balak would not be put off. He urges the soothsayer to try again, bringing him to another hill from which he could not see so clearly the full expanse of Israel's encampment but only the outermost part. Sacrifices were repeated but to no avail. Balaam's ecstatic pronouncements and the glorious future he envisions for the Children of Israel are repeated more glowingly, much to the king's disappointment and anger.

After the second oracle, Balak pleads in despair, "'Neither curse them at all, nor bless them at all.' But Balaam answered, and said unto Balak: 'Told I not thee, saying: All that the Lord speaketh, that I must do?' And Balak said unto Balaam: 'Come now, I will take thee unto another place; peradventure it will please God that thou mayest curse me them from thence.' And Balak took Balaam unto the top of Peor, that looketh down upon the desert" (23:25–28).

Once more the seven altars were built and the sacrifices

performed. This third time, however, Balaam does not even retreat to a solitary point on the hill as before. Then he had been merely an instrument for God's message. Now his whole being is given over to ecstatic inspiration, resembling more closely the true Hebrew prophet. The text makes this change in attitude clear. We are told, "And when Balaam saw that it pleased the Lord to bless Israel, he went not, as at the other times, to meet with enchantments, but he set his face toward the wilderness. And Balaam lifted up his eyes, and he saw Israel dwelling tribe by tribe; and the spirit of God came upon him. And he took up his parable, and said: 'The saying of Balaam the son of Beor,/ And the saying of the man whose eye is opened;/ The saying of him who heareth the words of God./ Who seeth the vision of the Almighty,/ Fallen down, yet with opened eyes;/ How goodly are thy tents, O Jacob,/ Thy dwellings, O Israel!/ As valleys stretched out,/ As gardens by the river-side;/ As aloes planted of the Lord,/ As cedars beside the waters;/ And his king shall be higher than Agag,/ And his kingdom shall be exalted./ . . . Blessed be every one that blesseth thee,/ And cursed be every one that curseth thee" (24:1–9).

The emotions of the king are understandable. "And Balak's anger was kindled against Balaam, and he smote his hands together; and Balak said unto Balaam: 'I called thee to curse mine enemies, and behold, thou hast blessed them these three times. Therefore now flee thou to thy place; I thought to promote thee unto great honour; but, lo, the Lord hath kept thee back from honour.' And Balaam said unto Balak: 'Spoke I not also to thy messengers that thou didst send unto me, saying: If Balak would give me his house full of silver and gold, I cannot go beyond the word of the Lord, to do either good or bad of mine own mind; what the Lord speaketh, that will I speak? And now behold, I go unto my people; come, and I will announce to thee what this people shall do to thy people in the end of days'" (24:10–14).

Even though dismissed by the king, Balaam now acts of his own accord. He was not yet through with the harried ruler of Moab. Uninvited, and in spite of the king's anger, Balaam goes on to complete his prophecy with a fourth oracle. He predicts the triumph of Israel over her enemies, including the downfall of Moab.

It should be noted, however, that as the degree of his enthusiasm for Israel and its God increases, there appears to be a growing sense of secret gratification in frustrating and humiliating the Moabite king. In effect, while blessing Israel, he curses Balak and his people, as though the conflicting need to obey one authority had to be balanced by the need to defy another, the process of blessing had to be weighed against the act of cursing, a kind of evenhandedness characteristic of the obsessive-compulsive personality.

Although his encounter with Balak ends with the words, "And Balaam rose up and went and returned to his place; and Balak also went his way" (24:25), and although the soothsayer had said earlier, "And now, behold, I go unto my people" (24:1), it seems that he did not return directly to Mesopotamia. He is next found in the camp of the Midianites. It is there that Balaam comes to an unexpected end. The text states, as though in passing, that Balaam was slain by the soldiers of Israel during a battle with the Midianites. "And they slew the kings of Midian with the rest of their slain . . . Balaam also the son of Beor they slew with the sword" (31:8).

Was this strange denouement just an ironic twist of fate or did it have some significance for the narrative? The question arises of what the recently inspired prophet, filled with ecstasy about the greatness of Israel and its God, was doing among its enemies? And why was he killed by the soldiers of Israel?

The assumption by some commentators that Balaam was a Midianite is disputed by more recent scholarship (*EJ* 1972, 42: 122). And indeed the biblical text states clearly that he came from the town of "Pethor, which is by the River" [Euphrates] (22:5) (Hertz 1936, 669).

Perhaps the sequence of events as presented in the narrative can provide a clue to the puzzle of his presence among the Midianites. Immediately following the encounter between Balak and Balaam, in the course of which the Children of Israel are so eloquently glorified, a most inglorious aspect of their behavior is portrayed.

The text says, "And Israel abode in Shittim and the people began to commit harlotry with the daughters of Moab. And they called the people unto the sacrifices of their gods, and the people did eat and bowed down to the gods. And Israel inclined himself unto the Baal of Peor" (25:1–3). Peor! The very height from which Balaam had pronounced one of his blessings.

The kind of cultural contamination that Moses feared and abhorred above all else now threatened his people. The cultic fertility rites of their pagan neighbors involved sexual orgiastic practices. They believed that through imitative magic, following the example of the sexual life of their gods and goddesses, they could bring about more abundant harvests. Such rites were the very antithesis of what Moses had taught them. The God of Israel transcended nature in all its aspects. His Oneness was an inseparable attribute of His divinity.

The demoralizing behavior of the men of Israel is dramatized through a particularly shameful episode involving one of them. In the words of the text: "And behold, one of the children of Israel came and brought unto his brethren a Midianitish woman in the sight of Moses and of all the congregation of Israel while they were weeping at the door of the tent of meeting" (25:6). We are not told why the people were weeping, but evidently it was because a plague had broken out among them as a punishment for their wrongdoing (25:8–9) (Hertz 1936, 681).

The culprit involved in the above incident is first referred to just as a "man of Israel." Only later do we learn that the guilty one was Zimri, the son of Salu, "a prince of a father's house among the Simonites." His paramour was Cozbi, the daughter of Zur: "he was head of the people of a father's house in Midian" (25:14–15). Although the wrongdoer's identity was known, emphasis is placed first on the act itself rather than the person who committed it. He who had done this heinous thing was "a man of Israel" and thus in a collective sense all were guilty. All those who had committed harlotry with the daughters of Moab must have felt *there but for the grace of God go I*. And indeed they were asking for such grace at that very moment. Significantly, the misconduct of the men of Israel is first depicted in the metaphor of an individual: "And Israel joined himself unto the Baal of Peor." This use of the singular form to signify a whole people is not unusual in biblical phraseology. Here it expresses the oneness of the group and the communal responsibility that goes with this togetherness.

But although there was a collective accountability, the individual was also answerable for his own conduct. The deed committed by the "man of Israel" could not go unpunished. This task of retribution was undertaken by one Phinehas, the son of Eleazer, a grandson of Aaron, thus one of the nephews of Moses. Phinehas went into the tent where the couple was lying and with one fierce thrust of his spear pierced both of them through their bodies (25:7–8).

Although so graphically depicted, this account of the crime nevertheless presents some puzzling aspects. Would a man commit the forbidden act of bringing a "Midianitish woman" into the sanctified precincts of the Hebrew encampment for such purposes so openly and flauntingly "in the sight of Moses and of all the congregation of Israel"? Sexual misconduct is more likely to be carried out secretly, under fear of discovery. It seems more reasonable to assume that the presence of the woman was reported to Moses, who reacted with a sense of outrage. The dramatic quality of the recounting may reflect the intensity of the leader's response.

A further puzzle arises. There seems to be some confusion throughout this episode between the terms, *Moabites* and *Midianites*, although they are unmistakably two distinctive peoples. First we are told that the men of Israel were led astray by the "women of Moab," on whose borders the Israelites were encamped. But it was a Midianitish woman whom Zimri brought into the Hebrew encampment as his paramour. And it was the Midianites whom God subsequently directed Moses to punish. "And the Lord spoke with Moses, saying: 'Harass the Midianites, and smite them; for they harass you, by their wiles wherewith they have beguiled you in this matter of Peor, and in the matter of Cozbi, the daughter of the prince of Midian, their sister, who was slain in the day of the plague in the matter of Peor'" (25:17–18).

The home territory of the Midianites was south of the land of Moab, along the eastern shore of the Gulf of Aqaba. Talmudic commentary suggests that these migratory people may have been allies of Moab at this time and thus had pitched their tents along the northern border of that land. No mention is made of such an alliance, although there is a statement earlier in the narrative about the Moabite king consulting the elders of Midian regarding the problem of the Children of Israel poised on his border (22:4); (23).

We are not told how Balaam came to be found in the Midianite camp, hobnobbing with its leaders. When the seer left Balak, he was said to be going back *to his place*, which was in Mesopotamia, to the north (24:25).

On his return journey the pagan seer may have undergone a sudden change of heart. He was leaving Moab empty-handed and with the angry words of Balak ringing in his ears. His earlier feelings of ecstasy when in communion with God must have quickly evaporated. What was Israel to him or he to Israel that he should bless her so profusely! Typical of certain obsessive-compulsive personalities, Balaam may have been caught up in a pattern of doing and undoing. He may now have felt a compulsion to return to the foes of Israel and attempt to undo the effects of his earlier act of obedience to the Deity. In the beginning of this adventure, on the way to Moab, Balaam had undergone an experience of spiritual change, prompted by the warning of the angel with the drawn sword. Now, on the journey back, the pagan seer may have gone through a regression, retreating to the negative aspect of his ambivalence in regard to what he should or should not have done. It was evident from the beginning that Balaam was easily swayed in his position from one side of a question to the other.

After the battle during which Balaam was slain, the men of Israel returned triumphantly from the scene laden with the spoils of war and bringing with them as captives the women and children of Midian. Moses, who had gone to meet the returning victorious soldiers, was stirred to passionate anger when he beheld these strangers about to be led into the Hebrew encampment. Were not these women the very ones who had brought degradation and punishment on Israel! What further licentiousness might not their presence evoke? The text says, "And Moses was wroth with the officers of the host . . . And Moses said unto them: 'Have ye saved all the women alive? Behold, these caused the children of Israel, *through the counsel of Balaam*, to revolt so as to break faith with the Lord in the matter of Peor, and so the plague was among the congregation of the Lord'" (31:16) (italics added). He then orders all women and male children to be destroyed.

One wonders why the male children were selected for destruction while the girls were allowed to live? There is an old saying that one does not look for logic in certain kinds of narrative. The underlying concept behind this adage is that the reasoning in such situations often lies in the unconscious and therefore does not make sense in terms of rational thinking.

While the importance of keeping his people free from the demoralizing influence of pagan neighbors is understandable, there is a clear impression that the severity of the leader toward the Midianites went beyond even God's commandments. The Deity had said, "Harass the Midianites" (24:17–18) and again, just before the battle, "Avenge the children of Israel of the Midianites" (31:1–2). Neither expression conveys the degree of harshness with which the enemy was met, resulting in the slaying of every adult male, according to the narrative, and the death of captive women and children.

A puzzled commentator says in this respect, "The war against the Midianites presents peculiar difficulties. We are no longer acquainted with the circumstances that justified the ruthlessness with which it was waged, and therefore we cannot satisfactorily meet the various objections that have been raised in that connection" (Hertz 1936, 704). The *circumstances*, however, may have been chiefly within the unconscious of Moses himself, in which reality and fantasy may have been intermingled. This situation is reminiscent of the severity of the punishment which Moses is said to have inflicted upon the people after the apostasy of the golden calf (Exod. 32:19–28). There, also, the degree of punishment and the numbers involved may have reflected the anger of Moses expressed in terms of the fantasied retribution rather than the less dramatic reality of what actually took place.

The underlying evidence of the text points to a further explanation of Balaam's relationship with the Midianites and his death while among them. Haggadic literature is fond of contrasting Moses, the prophet of Israel, with Balaam, the pagan seer (Ginzberg 1909–1938, 6:125). The rabbis intuitively suggest that Balaam represented the opposite of Moses, his very counterpart, an opinion with which a scholar of our own times, Richard Rubenstein (1968), concurs (pp. 54–55). That is a concept we shall now explore.

There are indications that Balaam had meaning for Moses on a deeper level than the leader of Israel himself could have been fully aware of. He could indeed unconsciously have experienced the pagan soothsayer as a personification of what he most hated and rejected in himself, his own despised image. Therefore, Balaam had to be annihilated as violently as Moses wished to annihilate what he wanted to be rid of within himself.

What influences in the life of Moses could have stimulated this kind of projection? Our fantasy life is largely colored by earlier experiences. Like Balaam, Moses too had once "tarried" among the Midianites. Similar to a composite figure in a dream, Balaam may have represented to Moses not only an aspect of himself, but also the ambivalently loved father figure, Jethro, in whose household he had once found refuge. From the retrospect of later years Moses could have experienced the Midianite priest as having instigated his daughters, women of Midian, to behave seductively toward their guest, even as the leader of Israel now accused Balaam of doing in regard to the women of Midian with the men of Israel. Did Moses feel that *he* had been seduced into a marriage that had become burdensome to him? Was the parting with Zipporah not altogether unwelcome when she disappears silently from the scene at the time Moses is about to reenter Egypt on his task of liberation? (See chapter 3.) She is brought back to him after the exodus, when Jethro visits Moses in the wilderness. It was a reunion about which he again was silent, although there was a warm reception for Jethro himself. The later criticism of Miriam and Aaron about the alien background of his wife, which is understood here as referring to Zipporah, may also have contained a reflection of Moses' own attitude.

This rejection of the Midianite woman as an alien influence, however, in spite of Jethro's expressed admiration for the God of Israel, may have been associated in the mind of Moses with an even more significant factor. There is much to suggest that following his experience at the burning bush the newly elected prophet of Israel underwent a change in his attitude toward sexuality, resulting in a high degree of sublimation. Devotion to God and to the task of freeing his people now become the dominating influences in his life. But strong instinctual feelings cannot altogether be abolished, bringing about conditions for unconscious conflict and the need for further defenses, such as denial and projection, as we shall see.

While the story of Balaam seems to have an entity of its own, the Talmud astutely attributes its authorship to Moses together with the rest of the Pentateuch (Ginzberg 1909–1938, 6:134; Pfeiffer 1941, 41). The rabbis sensed that unless the material had significance in relation to the leader of Israel, it would hardly have been included in the most sacred portion of the Bible.

This Talmudic association of Balaam with Moses is consistent with the frame of reference of the present study, which views the material in identification with the hero, Moses himself. Psychoanalytically, Balaam can be understood as representing a dissociated part of the ego of Moses, split off from the rest of his psyche, a process often found in dreams, myths, and fairy tales (Rank 1909, 75f). This mechanism allows the free expression of wishes and fantasies rejected by the more reality-oriented part of the personality.

Balaam was peculiarly suited to become the object of projections stemming from the past of Moses. The pagan seer came from Mesopotamia, the original home of the forefathers of Israel, whose God he is said to have worshipped, though evidently on his own level of comprehension. Legend even associates him with Abraham, who also turned from the worship of idols to the true God, but the folktale hastens to point out the virtues of the Hebrew patriarch in contrast to the faults in the character of Balaam (Ginzberg 1909–1938, 6:126).

The physical separation of the story of Balaam from the mainstream of the narrative helps to maintain the denial of its relationship to Moses, thus aiding in the defensive nature of its underlying meaning. Moreover, on this different level of consciousness, inconsistencies and ambiguities in the story do not require logical explanations. Unconscious processes have a logic of their own, largely of a symbolic nature or based on association of ideas. Thus the episode of the talking donkey and the angel blocking the way speak a language of their own. The indefiniteness of the locale where the war with the Midianites took place can be understood in terms of its significance for Moses himself. The home territory of the Midianites on the eastern shore of the Gulf of Aqaba is related to his past experience with this people and is fused with the more immediate situation of their presence on the borders of Moab as allies of Balak, the king.

Other unrealistic aspects relating to this war are also more understandable within the given frame of reference. The total annihilation of the males, although the Midianites remained a living entity in later history, the destruction of their cities and encampments, the number of women captives brought back, and the huge amount of spoils taken by the men of Israel, all may have a degree of subjectivity stemming from the mind of Moses himself. Of importance was the wish to overcome the foreign influence which the Midianites now symbolized for him, especially in regard to sexuality. The order that all the women captives "that had known man by lying with him" (31:17) should be slain suggests a need to purge himself of repressed sexual impulses that had once brought about his own union with a Midianite woman, similar to the feelings that led the men of Israel to downfall with the women of Midian and Moab. The small boys who were to be destroyed may unconsciously have symbolized, as they often do in dreams, the phallus of the father, thus also representing rejected sexuality in Moses himself. Was he, moreover, unconsciously acting out the role of Pharaoh in regard to male children, although with a different intent? Was Moses here substituting a sense of omnipotence for the sexuality he was relinquishing?

The Midianites as a foreign sexual influence that had to be expurgated is further manifested in the unusually lengthy process of purification commanded by Moses for both the men of Israel returning from the war and all the people and objects they brought back with them before they could be admitted into the sacred encampment of the Children of Israel (31:19–24).

Apart from the accusation voiced by the leader of Israel following the battle with the Midianites, there is no direct indication in the text that the pagan seer actually played the role among the Midianites ascribed to him. References concerning him at this point in the narrative consist of only two brief statements. First there is the announcement that Balaam was killed by the soldiers of Israel (31:8). Later comes the brief justification for this act, that the women of Midian had been influenced to seduce the men of Israel through the "counsel of Balaam," (31:16) an explanation for which the reader is totally unprepared.

The contradictory image which the figure of Balaam has evoked, its enigmatic character, is more readily comprehended when viewed as an aspect of Moses himself. Balaam may have been an actual personality who was indeed summoned by Balak to curse his enemies, a procedure not unusual in those times. Mesopotamia, Balaam's home territory, was noted for its seers. Fantasy can make use of reality to meet psychological needs when suitable objects are available. This form of mental functioning was not unusual for Moses, judging from his boyhood "family romance" (see chapter 1).

Viewed on a reality basis, Balaam is an understandable human being, neither saint nor villain but with much to his credit. It could not have been easy to resist the temptations of riches and honor or to face steadfastly, even defiantly, the anger of a frustrated king. He struggles with his conscience and for a while at least, reaches a higher level of being.

The war with the Midianites is associated in the text with the coming death of Moses himself. "And the Lord spoke unto Moses, saying: 'Avenge the children of Israel of the Midianites; afterward shalt thou be gathered unto thy people'" (31:1–2). The news that during the battle Balaam was also slain, together with the kings of Midian, is stated so inauspiciously as to seem merely incidental. Its significance for Moses is thus denied.

There must be meaning in the connection of the two events—the conquest of the Midianites and the death of Moses. The symbolic significance of the Midianites can be understood as a foreign body within the psyche of Moses himself as well as within his people. Balaam and the kings among whom he was slain may have represented hostile father figures related to the oedipal conflict. Before his own death, Moses had to overcome the wishes related to this conflict, now projected upon Balaam and the Midianites, the pagan element he hated in himself and feared for his people, associated, as it was, with apostasy and sexual orgy. In destroying Balaam the soldiers of Israel, carrying out the unconscious wishes of their leader, were also destroying a rejected part of Moses himself, a necessary step before the leader could meet the wholly spiritual Father-God in the last theophany, death itself. It seems likely that the Book of Balaam, as this narrative was also known, was indeed written by Moses, making use of either a real or a legendary figure.

How does one explain the estimable qualities that Balaam displays? These, too, can be understood as aspects of Moses himself. Repressed wishes of a positive nature, but that one feels unworthy of fulfillment for oneself, may be projected onto another person and unconsciously gratified through identification with the latter (Freud, A. 1946, 133). Hidden behind the figure of Balaam, Moses, the man of "slow tongue," may have been released from his tendency to inhibition in speech and able to express with passionate fervor his love for the Children of Israel, his faith in their historic destiny, and God's protection of them from their enemies. From the heights of Peor, in the presence of Balak, the Children of Israel are blessed through the very instrument chosen to curse them. Legend says that the power of Balaam's voice carried as far as sixty miles (Ginzberg 1909–1938, 6:133), symbolic, perhaps, of the power of release from the inhibition of this faculty within Moses himself.

As in the Song of Moses (Deut. 32:1–43), to be discussed in the following chapter, the leader of Israel, more accustomed to command than to praise, may have needed a protective shield before he could express his positive feelings for his people, truly regarded by him as "the congregation of the Lord" (31:16).

The fact that the story of Balaam is given so much space in the sacred literature attests to its importance in the biblical theme. He represents not only an aspect of Moses himself but also of the Children of Israel as a whole, in their continuing struggle to rise above the pagan beliefs and practices of their neighbors to the newer ways of life and thought compatible with the covenant of Mount Sinai.

The Balaam episode can be understood as representing a stage of development in which the Deity was largely experienced as projected conscience. For Moses himself God was the Deity Who transcended the world of nature and Who made ethical demands on people to control their own instinctual desires. The conquest of the Promised Land by the Children of Israel had to be accompanied by a corresponding movement in their developmental progress along ethical and religious grounds. Balaam can be understood as symbolizing the projection of regressive forces within themselves, a threat which had to be removed.

The Moses of Deuteronomy

The Final Tasks of Leadership

 CHAPTER SIXTEEN

THE MOSES OF Deuteronomy is very much the same personality with whom we have become familiar in the earlier narratives of his leadership. This consistency in his character traits and patterns of behavior is psychologically convincing in its validity. The events narrated in Deuteronomy contribute an essential, integral part of the continuing story of the leadership of Moses and the Children of Israel whom he led. It leads to the definitive conclusion that lends meaning and substance to the whole, not only in terms of the group history but in its underlying symbolic and psychological significance.

As with so much of biblical scholarship, the book of Deuteronomy has been the subject of widely differing opinions regarding its authorship, its dates of composition, and the historical milieu that influenced its style and content. In recent decades there has been an upsurge of interest among scholars regarding these matters. The traditional viewpoint that Moses himself was the author of a large part, if not most, of Deuteronomy, an opinion formerly limited to religious orthodoxy, has been gaining a greater degree of interest and acceptance by scholars who use the same methods of modern critical analysis utilized by their colleagues who hold opposing views (Baron 1952, 42–43; Craigie 1976; Driver 1903, 21; *EJ* 1972, 5:1574–83; Hahn 1954, xi–xii; Hertz 1936, 937–41; *IDB* 1976, 230. For the interested layman, a brief account of biblical exegesis regarding Deuteronomy will be presented in chapter 18 (see also, chap. 20).

The approach in the present study will continue to follow the same pattern as before, giving priority to the psychological significance of the text as it stands. The hypothesis we continue to explore is the extent to which the material reflects the thinking and feeling of Moses himself. It is concerned not only with the manifest content of the text but especially with the underlying, or latent, meanings, the stream of unconscious fantasies that frequently accompany conscious thought. Arlow (1961) says in this connection, "The intrusion of unconscious fantasy thinking into conscious mental experience is well known to us . . . this tendency plays a role in the structuring of perception and in the interpretation of external reality."

A distinctive feature of Deuteronomy is that it is written in the first person, the leader directly addressing his people. It consists of three lengthy discourses, a poem known as the Song of Moses, and the Blessing of the Tribes. The time is the fortieth year of the wanderings of the Children of Israel in the wilderness. The place is the Plains of Moab, directly across the Jordan River from the city of Jericho, the point at which they are to cross over to begin their conquest of Canaan. It is the farewell address of Moses to his people.

The whole tone, mood, and purpose of this remarkable book is in harmony with the personality and life situation of the great leader himself. He must have given considerable thought to the event of his final leave-taking. All of his passionate concern for his people and their future destiny as a "kingdom of priests and a holy nation" (Exod. 19:6) rises to a crescendo in these discourses.

The direct form of address is wholly appropriate to the occasion. It would be difficult to see how any other approach would have served the purpose as effectively. Deuteronomy provided the last opportunity for Moses to impress on his people the teachings of the past forty years in the wilderness. They had achieved physical freedom through the memorable events of the exodus. Their liberation of the spirit had been carried forward in the hardships and triumphs of life in the wilderness and the experience at Mount Sinai. The testing of courage in conflict had been faced in the battles east of the Jordan.

The Children of Israel were now confronted with the imminent loss of their leader. It was an occasion fraught with strong emotions, both for Moses and for those who were to go on without him. As in later years, when Israel was exiled to many lands, and the Book had to replace the Temple and the motherland, so now the laws and commandments of Moses, associated with the God in Whose name they were given, had to replace the actual presence of the man who for so long had been the living representative of God in their midst.

The word *Deuteronomy*, which means *Second Law*, as translated from the Greek, was earlier known as *Mishnah Torah*, the *Repetition of the Law*. But Deuteronomy is not just a rehearsal of what had been given before. Many of the precepts and commandments it contains are not found in the earlier books of the Pentateuch (Archer 1964, 245). Nor are historical events reviewed there narrated with exactly the same details and given the same emphasis as before.

The very differences in the retelling, such as would normally take place in the narration of an event at a later time, make these recollections more credible. Perfect recall is not usually an attribute of the human mind.

Wish-fulfilling tendencies can color memories and present past events more as one had hoped they had really happened. A leader talking to his people near the close of his life would have different needs and feelings in his relationship with them than in the original situations. The remarkable aspect of this experience in rehearsing the past is the authenticity with which the material comes through and the degree of correspondence with the original events. The impression conveyed in the discourses is that Moses spoke spontaneously. His words were impassioned and eloquent as never before. However, it can be assumed that he had recorded the outstanding events as they occurred and had this written material available. But surely he did not need much refreshment of memory. What he had experienced with his people must indeed have been a living part of him.

The purpose of these addresses was not only to revitalize the memories of the people concerning those eventful forty years but also to provide the framework for a renewal of the Covenant. That which was emphasized and that which was muted in tone was determined largely by the purpose that motivated the entire proceedings.

The content of Deuteronomy was thus fitted to its own special situation and to some of the subtle changes in the personality of the leader himself in those latter days of his life. His vital and creative spirit is seen in new dimensions as Moses tries to prepare both his people and himself for their separate destinies—they to the new life that awaited them in Canaan, and he to his lonely death on a mountaintop in Moab.

Throughout Deuteronomy, Moses shifts the primary emphasis from his own relationship with God to the task of strengthening the bonds of his people with the Deity. The leader would not be present much longer to be their spokesman and intermediary. His final task was to make God a living reality in their lives. The rehearsal of the laws and commandments was to play an important role to that end. Equally significant was the colorful fabric into which those laws and precepts were woven, the historic events and experiences of the past forty years, now brought back to them dramatically that they might form a lasting memory and tradition.

Underlying the entire book of Deuteronomy one senses a deep concern within the leader regarding the problem of how his people would meet the new challenges of their lives. It is the kind of feeling a parent might have when contemplating the future of his progeny without his guiding presence. Moses evidently had some doubt about the capacity of the people to carry out the tasks before them. In a sense, this feeling of anxiety can be seen as a recapitulation of his personal experience, so long ago, at the theophany of the burning bush, when he had felt self-doubts about his own ability to perform the mission to which God was calling him. Repeated persuasion and commands on the part of the Deity had been required to convince Moses that he could do so. The essence of that theophany can be summed up briefly in the exchange that then took place. "And Moses said unto God:

'Who am I, that I should go to Pharaoh, and that I should bring forth the children of Israel out of Egypt?' And He said: 'Certainly I will be with thee'" (Exod. 3:11–12). The faith of Moses in himself depended on the strength of his relationship with God. And now it was the task of the leader to bolster that same kind of faith in the Children of Israel, the sense of the presence of God in their midst. Moses had been with his people to lead them out of Egypt. Now they themselves had to undertake the conquest of the Promised Land. The time of their adolescence as a people was over. The challenges and rigors of adulthood now faced them. The same mingling of hope and distrust that Moses had once experienced concerning his own powers he now sensed in his people. The path to confidence had to be the same—a renewal of their faith in God. This strengthening could be brought about through a rehearsal of past events in which God had made His presence felt. The responsibility on their side was to obey the laws and commandments of the Covenant and do so without the personal guidance of their leader.

Significantly, although a large part of Deuteronomy is made up of laws and commandments that Israel is to observe, the injunction to *love* God is interspersed throughout the discourses. Obedience should spring from the heart through devotion to the Deity. This aspect of love as a commandment is a unique development in the history of religion (Hertz 1936, 770).

Moses seems to be fully aware of the temptations and pitfalls that will await the people as they enter into a new phase of their existence. He utilizes every resource at his command to prepare and strengthen them, painting vivid verbal images of both rewards and punishments or, as expressed in the covenant pattern characteristic of those times, in the colorful array of blessings and curses consequent on the degree of faithfulness to the commandments of God. The intensity of the leader's feelings, the strength of his motivations, have not diminished in the closing years of his life but have indeed grown stronger as the time for the actualization of his goal approaches.

The Thirty-Eight Years of Silence

Although Deuteronomy itself is a review of the past in terms of the events that have taken place, the specifics of how and where the forty biblical years were spent is not altogether clear. With the exception of this final year before they enter upon the conquest of Canaan, the experiences of the Children of Israel in the wilderness, as recorded in the narratives, have all taken place in the first year and a half or so after the exodus. The intervening stretch of time is so lightly passed over that the casual reader is scarcely aware of this lapse. The thirty-eight years of silence are referred to by the medieval scholar, Ibn Ezra, as a "blank page in the Book of Numbers (Hertz 1936, 655).

The fact that chronology was not totally unimportant to the narrator is clearly manifested by the exactness with which the time is noted on occasions of significant events. The precise date of the escape from Egypt, which determined the future observance of the Passover festival, is carefully stated. The first Passover eve observances were on the fourteenth day of Nisan, the exodus taking place on the fifteenth (Exod. 12:51). Also significant in terms of the time noted were the early days in the wilderness, when anxiety about survival was probably at its height and the people's faith in the leadership of Moses and the God he professed was being tested. Thus, they "thirsted" for the "first three days" in the wilderness, only to come upon bitter waters at Marah. There they witnessed the power of Moses, who sweetened the water with the branch of a tree, as instructed by God. The arrival of the wanderers at the first large oasis, Elim, was noted in the text, but it is their departure from that pleasant spot, again to face the unwelcome hardships of the wilderness, that is specifically recorded: the fifteenth day of the second month (Exod. 16:1). They had endured their first month in the wilderness.

The arrival of the Children of Israel at the foot of Mount Sinai took place on the first day of the third month after the exodus (Exod. 19:1). Their period of encampment at the holy mount lasted ten months and nineteen days, their departure taking place on the twentieth day of the second month in the second year after they left Egypt (Num. 10:11). Evidently, when a specific time was regarded as being of historic importance, careful note of it was given. Otherwise, the passage of time was largely ignored, probably lost in the sameness of events day after day, and the unchanging problems and hardships of life in the wilderness.

These hardships and problems, especially during the period of adjustment, are indeed dealt with in specific episodes early in the wanderings. However, they are associated more with place than time, the geographic localities at which they occurred being noted or the number of days they were on the march from one camping site to another. Most of the experiences recorded occurred on the way from Mount Sinai to Kadesh, thus taking place in the early part of the second year.

In Deuteronomy 1:2 Moses states that this journey takes eleven days, but this information may have been given as a statement of what it *should* take under normal conditions. The purpose of this comment, it has been suggested, was an implied reproach reminding the Children of Israel that they themselves had been at fault for the much longer period it had taken to cover that territory (Hertz 1936; 737).

It was from Kadesh that Moses sent spies to traverse the land of Canaan and bring back a report about the conditions that would face the Children of Israel in their attempt at conquest. This report and its consequences proved to be a turning point in their history. With the exception of Caleb and Joshua, the report of the spies was discouraging. They talked fearfully about walled cities and giant inhabitants, arousing fear to the point of hysteria among the people. Because of their lack of faith and courage, God condemned them to wander in the wilderness for forty years. During this life span, the older generation would perish and a new generation, braver and bolder than their fathers, would undertake the task.

Overwhelmed by this judgment, the Children of Israel decided that they would attempt the attack after all, and against the warning of Moses not to do so, for God would not be with them in this undertaking, they storm up the mountain slope to meet the Canaanites, are badly defeated and driven back to their starting point. They are now ready to obey God's commandment to reverse their steps: "tomorrow turn ye and get you back into the wilderness by the way to the Red Sea" (Num. 14:1–25). They are to move southward in the direction of the Gulf of Aqaba.

When next the locale becomes important in the background of the narrative, many years have passed and the Children of Israel are again encamped at Kadesh-barnea, to the south of Canaan.

The name *Kadesh* may have been used not only for a specific site but also in reference to a much larger area encompassing both the Wilderness of Zin, which lay southeast of Canaan, and the Wilderness of Paran, farther to the southwest. These were the territories in which the Children of Israel wandered during a large part of those silent thirty-eight years, probably moving from oasis to oasis according to prevailing conditions of rainfall. Tradition says that they remained at the home site of Kadesh for nineteen years, with the other nineteen spent in the surrounding areas (Ginzberg 1909–1938, 3:307). The settlement of Kadesh itself, still distinguished by a tower built in the tenth century B.C., has been identified by Albright (1957) as the present Ain-el-Qudeirat (p. 256).

The wanderings thus took them on a kind of circular tour through the central and eastern areas of the Peninsula of Sinai. The exact location of Kadesh as a specific locality is puzzling in terms of the biblical references to this site. It is mentioned at one point as being in the Wilderness of Paran (Num. 13:26). More frequently, Kadesh is described as being in the Wilderness of Zin, southeast of Canaan (Num. 20:1; 33:36). Nor is there always a clear distinction between the terms *Kadesh* and *Kadesh-barnea*. The former is thought to be the specific site of the encampment and the latter a larger area surrounding it. That the Children of Israel remained in this general locality for a long time, is expressed by Moses himself when he says in the introductory chapter of Deuteronomy, "So ye abode in Kadesh many days, according to the days that ye abode there" (1:46).

The Children of Israel probably led a seminomadic existence during this period, engaging in agricultural activities as well as caring for their flocks. Travelers have noted that the localities involved contained numerous springs that would have made such life-sustaining pursuits possible.

Martin Buber (1936) attributes particular significance to the favorable situation of these surroundings which, in spite of the usual hardships of wilderness life, enabled the Children of Israel to have the experience of a productive relationship with the land, a basic factor that prepared them for an agricultural existence in Canaan. He points out that Moses also was better able during those years to envision in more specific ways the needs and problems of a people attached to the land and to formulate with greater insight the precepts and commandments to guide them (pp. 175ff.).

It was probably during this long period of comparative stability that the leader had time for the important task of writing down much of the material that he wished to preserve for his people, both in the legislative area and in the narratives that make up the discourses of Deuteronomy. For it seems inconceivable that one who put so much emphasis on the need to transmit the remarkable story of a people's experience with its God would not himself have written it down if such a skill was available to him. And it is increasingly evident that writing was an accomplishment widespread throughout the lands of the ancient Near East centuries before the time of Moses. This process of recording is mentioned numerous times by the leader himself. The matters about which he spoke with such eloquence in the discourses must certainly not only have been written down with the usual writing materials of his time but were also relived in the mind and heart of the leader. How often he must have pondered on the meaning of those events during the quiet starlit nights or in the early hours of dawn in the strangely mystical atmosphere of the desert wilderness.

The Fortieth Year

The all-important fortieth year is introduced into the narrative so unobtrusively that the reader is scarcely aware of the lapse of time that has taken place since the last event was recorded. That occasion was associated with the episode of the twelve spies, when God said, "turn ye, and and get you into the wilderness by the way to the Red Sea" (Num. 14:25).

It is five chapters later (Num. 20) that we are told, "And the children of Israel, even the whole congregation, came into the wilderness of Zin, *in the first month*; and the people abode in Kadesh; and Miriam died there, and was buried there" (Num. 20:1) (italics added). One would have expected that after so much time had passed and two important events were being recorded in the very first verse, the move of the camp to Kadesh and the death of Miriam, the *year* would also have been mentioned, not just the *month*. But although it was the memorable fortieth year, that fact is omitted. One must wonder why. Moreover, not only Miriam's death but also Aaron's takes place in this same period, but the time of their passing is not noted. Only considerably later, after a great deal of intervening material, is the year of Aaron's death finally mentioned as part of a brief review detailing the stages of the journeys from Egypt to the Plains of Moab. "And Aaron the priest went up into mount Hor at the commandment of the Lord, and died there, *in the fortieth year* after the children of Israel were come out of the land of Egypt, in the fifth month, on the first day of the month. And Aaron was a hundred and twenty and three years old when he died in mount Hor" (Num. 33:38–39) (italics added). The exact time of Miriam's death can only be inferred from the general content as having taken place in that same year, probably in the first month (Num. 20:1).

The implication that can be drawn from the belated mentioning of that fortieth year is a psychological one pertaining to the leader himself. *Moses also was destined to die during that very year*, just before the Children of Israel would enter the Promised Land. Aaron passed away on the first day of the fifth month. There could not be much time left for the remaining member of that family. It was a fate to which Moses was not easily reconciled. The thought of this coming event evidently had to be pushed below the level of awareness. Omitting the dreaded words, "the fortieth year," helped to deny the reality.

The thought of his own imminent demise, however, could not have been too far beneath the surface of his consciousness. At the same time a lingering hope may have remained that he might yet persuade the Deity to hear his plea, as had happened on other occasions for other purposes.

The first appeal of this nature occurs in the book of Numbers. The context is in relation to the division of the Promised Land among the tribes, for which purpose a new census had been taken. A question is brought before Moses regarding the laws of inheritance in the event there were no sons in the family, as in the case of the daughters of Zelophehad (Num. 27:1–11). The right to inherit was decided in their favor, at the command of God. A feeling may have been triggered within Moses that everyone would have a share in the Land of Promise except himself. For now, suddenly, without seeming connection, a command comes from the Deity. "And the Lord said unto Moses: 'Get thee up into this mountain of Abarim and behold the land which I have given unto the children of Israel. And when thou hast seen it, thou shalt be gathered unto thy people, as Aaron thy brother was gathered; because ye rebelled against My commandment in the wilderness of Zin, in the strife of the congregation, to sanctify Me at the waters before their eyes.' These are the waters of Meribath-kadesh in the wilderness of Zin" (Num. 27: 12–14).

The response of Moses on this occasion seems to be one of complete submission, an acceptance of what was to come. He requests only that a worthy successor be appointed to take his place. "And Moses spoke unto the Lord, saying: 'Let the Lord, the God of the spirits of all flesh, set a man over the congregation, who may go out before them, and who may come in before them, and who may lead them out, and may bring them in; that the congregation of the Lord be not as sheep which have no shepherd.' And the Lord said unto Moses: 'Take thee Joshua, the son of Nun, a man in whom is spirit, and lay thy hand upon him; and set him before Eleazar the priest, and before all the congregation; and give him a charge in their sight. And thou shalt put of thy honour upon him, that all the congregation of the children of Israel may hearken.' And Moses did as the Lord commanded him" (Num. 27:15–23).

The inference to be gathered from the request of Moses to "set a man over the congregation" is that he himself does not know who his successor will be, although of course he knows quite well. We can only conjecture the motive for this request. Certainly it would be appropriate that God Himself should name the successor. But it had long been taken for granted that Joshua would become the leader after the death of Moses. He had been trained for many years to assume this role. Was the overt act of naming him difficult for the one who was to be displaced? Or was there another reason as well? Did Moses wish to spare himself the onus of disinheriting his own sons, preferring to let the responsibility for naming the one who would succeed him come from the Deity? In a sense his situation was similar to that of Zelophehad. The latter had no sons to inherit from him. Moses could not pass on the inheritance of his leadership to the sons he had.

Among scholars of Higher Biblical Criticism the theory about the mention of Moses' death at this time is that this was the logical place in the narrative for the actual event to have taken place. Two important preliminaries had now been satisfied, it seemed. Ostensibly, Moses had viewed the Promised Land and the transfer of leadership from him to Joshua had been confirmed by the Deity. Thus, the basic narrative had been completed in Numbers according to the reasoning of some critics. Deuteronomy, therefore, they suggest, must have been written at another time and come from another source (Sandmel 1963, 400ff.).

However, that kind of logic is not necessarily applicable to the biblical writing. Sequence was not always determined by chronology but could be influenced by the association of ideas. As suggested above, the command that Moses should view the land could have been stimulated by the Zelophehad affair, which may have aroused the feeling that all *he* would have of the Promised Land was a distant view. Significantly, the narrative does not say that Moses *actually carried out the command at this time, only that God told him to do so. The experience may have taken place in fantasy only, anticipatory in nature, an effort to prepare himself for what was to come.*

The impact of the impending death of Moses could have been a factor in the tone and quality of Deuteronomy and the sense of urgency that pervaded it. His concerns, his feelings and wishes for the good and welfare of his people along the lines for which he had tried to prepare them, thus find heightened expression in its eloquent passages.

From a literary viewpoint, this fifth book of Moses attains new heights in the beauty of its language, its clarity, and the vividness and variety of its metaphors. In terms of its religious and moral values it is as meaningful today as it was remarkable several thousand years ago.

The Concept of Covenant

Whereas the Ten Commandments form the basic law of Israel, the foundation of the covenant between the people and their God, the entire book of Deuteronomy has been described as "a covenant on a grand scale" (Hillers 1969, 54).

The concept of covenant goes back to the earliest period of Hebrew biblical life, the Age of the Patriarchs, when Abraham made his covenant with God (Gen. 17). This conception has played a unique and highly significant role in biblical history, reaching its most dramatic climax in the experience at Mount Sinai. Deuteronomy is the expression of its renewal and reaffirmation. In the words of Albright (1957), noted biblical scholar, "the concept of covenant dominates the entire religious life of Israel" (p. 16).

In the section "The Background of Deuteronomy" (chapter 18), the idea of *covenant*, as viewed against the general background of the ancient Near East, is more fully explored. Archeological findings have shown that agreements between two parties, as a form of treaty, was common practice between states or individuals and tended to follow a certain pattern of structure.

That Moses may have used this concept of treaty and rebuilt it into a grand plan for his own purposes, transforming it into a covenant between the Deity and the Children of Israel, should not be surprising. That his genius included a capacity for organization has been manifested many times throughout his leadership.

The Introductory Verses of Deuteronomy

The opening verses of Deuteronomy, which precede the first discourse, are difficult to understand. Since most of the content of this book is comparatively free from obscurity, a legitimate question arises about why these particular verses should have an enigmatic quality. They begin as follows: "These are the words which Moses spoke unto all Israel beyond the Jordan: In the wilderness, in the Arabah, over against Suph, between Paran and Tophel, and Hazeroth, and Di-zahab. It is eleven days' journey from Horeb unto Kadesh-barnea by way of mount Seir" (1:2).* Some of these geographic sites have not been identified by mod-

---

*All biblical references in this chapter, unless otherwise noted, are to the book of Deuteronomy.

ern scholars. Their use in this verse is unclear. It has been suggested by some of the ancient and medieval scholars that Moses intended to convey a veiled reproach here, indirectly related to the statement that it takes *eleven days* to make the journey from Mount Sinai (Horeb) to Kadesh-barnea by way of Mount Seir (by the Mount Seir road, the easternmost track from the Sinai encampment to Kadesh). Yet it took the Children of Israel forty years to accomplish that journey. (Hertz 1936, 736). This interpretation is further elaborated by Onkeles, a first-century translator of the Pentateuch into Aramaic, who treated the geographic names symbolically. He explains: "Moses reproved them because they had sinned *in the Wilderness*, had provoked God to anger *in the Plain* (Arabah) of Moab; *over against the Red Sea* (Suph), they murmured against God; *in Paran* they had spoken contemptuously (Tophel) concerning *the manna* (laban); and *in Hazeroth*, they angered him on account of the flesh and because they made *the Golden Calf* (di-zahad)" (Hertz 1936, 736).

Moses was trying to convey a certain thought, Onkeles suggests but was hesitant to do so openly. That may indeed be so. The leader may have wished to remind the people of their past transgressions as a background for his present discourse, perhaps to put them in a suitably repentant mood. At the same time he may also have wanted to establish a relationship of rapport with his listeners and therefore wished to modify any possible punitive image of himself stemming from memories of his severity in the past. The teachings he was preparing to impart to his people throughout the discourses had to be impressed on them through the strengthening of positive ties. Love as well as fear had to play a role. Thus, Moses may have used an indirect approach to remind the people that their wrongdoing in the past had brought unhappiness, but at the same time he did not wish to arouse undue resentment toward him at this crucial time.

After these ambiguous reminders of the past, Moses brings his listeners back to the immediacy of the moment by noting the time and place where he was now addressing them. About these facts there was no fuzziness. It was the fortieth year, on the first day of the eleventh month.

The leader concludes these introductory remarks by referring to the more positive experiences—the victories over the kings of Sihon and Og—that finally brought the Children of Israel to their present locality, the Plains of Moab. They were now directly opposite the point at which they were to cross the Jordan, where the conquest of the city of Jericho would be their first objective.

The First Discourse

The first discourse (1:6–4:40) begins with a historical review of events from the time of departure from Mount Sinai (here called Horeb) to the encampment at Kadesh-barnea. As related above, it was from that locality that spies had first been sent so long ago to survey the land of Canaan.

The disastrous consequences of that event are recalled, together with the judgment that followed because the Children of Israel lacked the faith and courage to enter upon the conquest of Canaan. They were to wander forty years in the wilderness.

At this point Moses unexpectedly introduces a personal note. The leader acknowledges that he was to share the same punishment as those others of his generation who had already died in the wilderness. He too would not be allowed to enter the Promised Land. Moses prefaces that painful fact with a defensive explanation: "Also the Lord was angry with me for your sakes [on your account], saying: 'thou also shalt not go in thither; Joshua, the son of Nun, who standeth before thee, he shall go in thither; encourage thou him, for he shall cause Israel to inherit it'" (1: 37–38).

The impression given here is that Moses too had been included in the judgment pronounced by God after the debacle following the report of the spies. But actually Moses himself had not shown a lack of faith on that occasion. Indeed, when God threatened to destroy the Children of Israel, the Deity had also declared his intention to make Moses "a nation greater and mightier than they" (Num. 14:12). The punishment of Moses had been pronounced at a different time and under different circumstances than that of the group. It was a consequece of his striking the rock at Meribah instead of speaking to it as God had commanded (Num. 20:8–13).

Moses evidently believed it to be true that his own fate had been brought about by the rebelliousness of the people. This attitude is clearly expressed in the words he had uttered on that fateful occasion referred to above: "Hear now, ye rebels; are we to bring you forth water from this rock?" followed by his own act of disobedience. The water did come forth "abundantly," satisfying the needs of the people and their cattle. "And the Lord said unto Moses and Aaron: 'Because ye believed not in Me, to sanctify Me in the eyes of the children of Israel, therefore ye shall not bring this assembly into the land which I have given them'" (Num. 21:12). As interpreted in an earlier chapter, the sin of Moses was more related to competitiveness with God on that occasion than the actual disobedience itself.

Because the personal consequences of his act at Meribah were the same as those meted out to the people after their rebelliousness following the report of the spies, Moses associated the two situations, evidently not thinking it necessary to distinguish between them. Indeed, the nature of his sin was similar to theirs —a lack of faith in the power of God. One is not competitive with another whose greater power is unquestionably accepted. In having to share the fate of those others of his generation, Moses was no longer special in an important respect. His own mortality was now clearly established.

In this recall of the eventful episode of the report of the spies, the personal feelings of the leader can be detected in several significant details that differ from the earlier account. As presented in Numbers, the suggestion for sending men to spy out the land comes from God Himself, Who said to Moses: "Send thou men that they may spy out the Land of Canaan" (13:1–2). As Moses now tells it, the idea came from the people. "And ye came near unto me, every one of you, and said, 'Let us send men before us that they may search the land before us, and bring back word of the way by which we must go up, and the cities unto which we shall come.' And the thing pleased me well" (Deut. 1:22).

By attributing the fateful suggestion to the people instead of to God, the leader unconsciously strengthens his justification of the oft-repeated statement that God was angry with him because of them. In the words, "And ye came near me, *every one of you*" (italics added), the latter phrase seems unnecessarily inclusive, giving an added emphasis to their role. Then he retreats somewhat, admitting, "And the thing pleased me well," thus acknowledging a share of the responsibility for an act that led to such unhappy consequences. Perhaps his own sense of justice required those ameliorating words.

There are further differences in the nuances of the narrative in Deuteronomy. God's suggestion that the men should be sent to spy out the land conveys only the idea of a realistic procedure preliminary to the invasion. When the plan is presented by the people to Moses, the purpose is more comprehensive. They say, "Let us send men *before us*, that they may search the land *before us*, and *bring back word* of the way by which we must go up, and the cities unto which we shall come" (italics added). Clearly, the people here are concerned about the difficulties they may encounter, indicating an anticipatory attitude of fear that is not apparent in the simple motive that the men "spy out the land."

One can observe in this presentation of material how unconscious factors can influence the manner of the telling, especially when a conflictful element is involved. The desire of Moses to vindicate himself in the eyes of the people also led to a confusion of the two different situations. By emphasizing that the people themselves were largely to blame for what had happened in the episode of the spies, Moses shifted the attention from his own disobedience at Meribah to the earlier rebellious behavior of the group. Yet even as he sadly talks of his own fate, Moses hastens to assure the people that they would not be left leaderless. Joshua was to take over his role.

Moses explains how he tried to strengthen and encourage the man who would succeed him. "And I commanded Joshua at that time, saying: 'Thine eyes have seen all that the Lord *your* God hath done unto these two kings (Sihon and Og); so shall the Lord do unto all the kingdoms whither *thou* goest over. *Ye* shall not fear them; for the Lord *your* God, He it is that fighteth for *you*'" (3:21–22) (italics added).

This renunciation of self, as manifested in the use of the pronouns that excluded him, seems to have evoked further feelings of pain and longing at the frustration of his dearest wish. Again, Moses pleaded with God on his own behalf. Even more openly, he shares this experience with his people. "And I besought the Lord at that time saying, 'Let me go over, I pray Thee, and see the good land that is beyond the Jordan, the goodly hill-country and the Lebanon'" (3:25–28). During this appeal Moses referred to God's greatness and power as manifested in the recent victories east of the Jordan that the Deity had granted to the Children of Israel. The underlying need may have been to demonstrate that his entering the Promised Land could not be construed as a competitive act with God—unconsciously, a form of rivalry with the Father for the possession of the motherland. Moses emphasizes that the Deity was great and powerful, whereas he himself was a humble suppliant, referring to himself as "thy servant."

But it was not to be. And again, Moses attributes blame to the people. "But the Lord was wroth with me for your sakes, and hearkened not unto me; and the Lord said unto me: 'Let it suffice thee; speak no more unto Me of this matter. Get thee up into the top of Pisgah, and lift up thine eyes westward, and northward, and southward, and eastward, and behold with thine eyes; for thou shalt not go over this Jordan'"(3:26–27).

An unresolved sense of grievance seems to have remained with Moses because of God's severity with him in this matter. That he himself had ever erred so grievously as to have merited the displeasure of the Deity to such an extent was something he could not consciously understand or accept. Therefore God must be angry with him *because of the people*. As the leader, he was being held responsible for their sins. That explanation was more acceptable to him than the underlying one of disobedience and competitiveness with God, in the episode of striking the rock. Moreover, it allowed that lingering sense of hurt in regard to the Deity.

However, both realistically and psychologically, it was necessary that the leadership of Moses should come to an end at the borders of the Promised Land. His mission had to do with the escape from Egypt, the covenant at Mount Sinai, and the years of training and discipline that prepared his people for the conquest of Canaan. Deep within him, Moses must have known that the end had been inevitable from the beginning. His failure to accept the situation fully attests to his humanness. Not even Moses was expected to be perfect, as the bibical tradition repeatedly makes clear.

There is no overt indication that Moses resented Joshua, the man who was to take his place. The latter had been selected by Moses himself for the purpose of bringing to fulfillment the great task for which the leader had prepared his people. Moreover, God directly commanded Moses several times to strengthen and encourage the new leader-to-be. Yet even in this relationship there are suggestions of some elements of rivalry with the man who was soon to succeed him. Oedipal feelings on the part of the father in this area of human relationships had been largely discharged by Moses in the rejection of his own sons, whose existence he had practically ignored. One might ponder the question of whether the inevitable guilt thus engendered provided an added source of an unconscious need for punishment from the Father-God, Who was soon to displace him with Joshua. Yet even with this chosen son figure there are indications of ambivalent feelings inadvertently revealed in the text.

In the account of the spies, *the two good men* who advocated an immediate advance into Canaan were Caleb and Joshua (Num. 14:6). Yet several times it is only Caleb who is mentioned in connection with this act of faith and loyalty, where both names logically would have been appropriate. At one point the text says, "And Caleb stilled the people toward Moses and said: 'We should go up at once and possess it (Canaan); for we are well able to overcome it'" (Num. 13:30). It is only after the people have reacted with fear and consternation to the negative report brought by the other ten spies that the statement is made: "And Joshua the son of Nun and Caleb the son of Jephunneh, who were of them that spied out the land, rent their clothes" (Num. 14:6), a gesture expressive of some great calamity. It is hard to imagine that Joshua, the warrior leader, was silent throughout all this turmoil, leaving Caleb to bear alone the onus of an unpopular report, while he joined the latter only in *rending his clothes.*

Shortly thereafter, when the Deity pronounces punishment on the people for their lack of faith, He adds, "But my servant Caleb, because he had another spirit with him, and hath followed Me fully, him will I bring into the land whereinto he went; and his seed shall possess it" (Num. 14:24). Again the name of Joshua is omitted for some inexplicable reason. It may be that the survival of the latter was taken for granted, since he was the one destined for leadership. Nevertheless, the omission of his name in the two instances where both men were so closely associated is rather striking. The two are indeed brought together several verses later when the Deity declares that of all the "evil generation" only Caleb and Joshua would live to enter the Promised Land (Num. 14:27–39). Yet even here, Caleb is given priority in the mentioning of their names. The latter is not a conflictful son figure for Moses and therefore does not arouse feelings of ambivalence. Yet on the whole, Joshua is unquestionably the man on whom Moses depended to carry on the task, and there must have been strong ties of positive feelings between the two during their long relationship.

Joshua is mentioned in juxtaposition with Moses on several occasions when the latter is told that he would not enter the Promised Land but Joshua would (Num. 27:18–21; Deut. 1:37–38; 3:27–28). The death of Moses and his replacement, Joshua, are thus closely associated in the mind of Moses. It is understandable that some element of ambivalent feelings should flow from the one thought to the other.

At yet another time, the third in Deuteronomy (1:37, 3:27, (4:21–22) Moses again gives expression to his sadness at the denial of his deepest wish. On this occasion the feeling is stimulated by his reminder to the Children of Israel of the special treatment they had received from God. Among all the peoples of the earth, they had been selected to enter into a relationship with Him. "But you hath the Lord taken and brought forth out of the iron furnace of Egypt, to be unto Him a people of inheritance, as ye are this day" (4:20). "As ye are this day" points to their situation more fortunate than Moses himself. He alone of that large assembly would not receive this inheritance of the Promised Land. And so the feelings again rush to the surface with even greater poignancy than before. And again they are prefaced by those brief words of blame, which serve not only to express his anger but also as a defensive measure to explain why he was being thus treated. "Now the Lord was angered with me for your sakes, and swore I should not go over the Jordan, into that good land, which the Lord thy God giveth thee for an inheritance, But I must die in this land, I must not go over the Jordan; but ye are to go over, and possess the good land. Take heed unto yourselves, lest ye forget the covenant of the Lord, your God, which He made with you, and make you a graven image, even the likeness of anything which the Lord thy God hath forbidden thee" (4:21–23). Since they were to be so privileged, let them beware of angering God because of idol worship. The leader's personal deprivation thus ends on a constructive note, being utilized to strengthen the sense of responsibility in his people to carry on the task. In exhorting them to be obedient to God's precepts, Moses may also be trying to deal with his own rebelliousness. His demands on them reflect the severity of his superego toward himself.

It is not the intent of this presentation to recapitulate the content of the discourse but rather to suggest that those precepts were emphasized that Moses may have felt would be of special relevance for his listeners at that time. His approach utilizes the events of their common past with an appeal to their sense of pride as a people elected by God for a special mission. He stresses their responsibility in the life situation that confronts them and its possibilities for good and evil.

The concept of justice is brought out early in the presentation. Moses recalls the problem of judging the increasing number of his people and the decision to select outstanding men of the tribes to assist him. It was Jethro, his father-in-law, who had first offered advice along those lines in the early months of the wilderness wanderings (Exod. 18). But this detail is not recalled now. On another occasion Moses had complained to the Deity that the burden of managing the people was too much for him, and God suggested that seventy elders be chosen to assist him in the task of governing (Num. 11:14). As Moses tells it now, the appeal to the Deity is omitted, but the advice is carried out. The leader reminds the people that he directed them to select from each tribe "wise men and understanding, and full of knowledge" (1:13–15). Perhaps it was closer to his purpose to stress the image of his own strength at this time rather than to dwell on earlier moments of weakness and feelings of inadequacy. Certainly it must have been easier for him to do so rather than to recall that the advice had again come from another source.

Moses uses the present opportunity to elaborate on the manner in which justice should be carried out. "And I charged you at that time, saying: 'Hear the causes between your brethren, and judge righteously between a man and his brother and the stranger that is with him. Ye shall not respect persons in judgment; ye shall hear the small and the great alike; ye shall not be afraid of the face of any man; for the judgment is God's; and the cause that is too hard for you ye shall bring unto me, and I will hear it'" (1:16–17). The principles and concepts set forth here are those we are still striving to attain in our own times. Even the right of appeal in difficult cases was provided for.

One might wonder whether questions of justice had a particular significance for Moses himself at this time. The theme occurs in the historical review at the point when the Children of Israel were about to set forth from Mount Sinai toward the land of Canaan. Moses recalls how God said: "Behold, I have set the land before you; go in and possess the land which the Lord swore unto your fathers, to Abraham, to Isaac, and to Jacob, to give unto them and to their seed after them" (1:8). Moses, however, would not be among those who would "go in and possess" it. The problem of justice in that situation may have continued to perplex him, but he could not question that "the judgment is God's."

Even in the long trek through the wilderness the Children of Israel were guided by laws of justice. The rights of other peoples with whom they came in contact were clearly defined. The journey toward Canaan was not one of indiscriminate warfare. Wherever peaceful means of traversing through the territory of other nations were possible, especially of those peoples related to them by kinship, open struggles were avoided (2:5–10; Num. 20:16).

An interlude in the discourse occurs when Moses interrupts the historical review to make a digression that reveals his scholarly interests. Occupied though he was with the immediate concerns of his own people and their future, Moses nevertheless pauses in the narrative to share with them a few of the details of history that had no immediate bearing from a practical viewpoint. He mentions the earlier inhabitants of Moab, "a people great, and many, and tall, as the Anakim but the Moabites called them Emim [the dreaded ones]. And in Seir dwelt the Horites aforetime but the children of Esau succeeded them; and they destroyed them from before them, and dwelt in their stead" (2:10–12). The Horites have been identified by some scholars as the Hurrians, an ancient race that left a strong cultural imprint on the Hittites, whose civilization had a considerable influence on the Hebrews as early as the time of Abraham (Hertz 1936, 744).

It is often by such seemingly unimportant details that aspects of personality are brought to light. The scholarly trait in Moses is not usually associated with his active role of leadership. Yet he could scarcely have been the great innovator in the area of ethical monotheism and the great lawgiver without a profound knowledge of history and the culture of his time. The surprising richness of that ancient cultural world is being brought to light increasingly in our own time.

In his final act of leadership, the delivery of the discourses as set forth in Deuteronomy, Moses reveals remarkable insight concerning the various ways of appealing to his people in order to impress his teachings on them. The time and place were especially appropriate for this purpose. The situation was not one of crisis or special exigency, when directives and commands had to be issued in order to overcome some impending disaster or to meet an immediate need on the part of the people. It was, rather, an occasion for relating to them on a person to person basis, as it were, for strengthening the bonds between them. Only on this level could his words have a more lasting effect.

Although the text emphasizes the repeated rebelliousness of the people toward their leader, it would be unrealistic to deny that there were also positive ties that bound them to him. There could be no question of his concern for their welfare or their acceptance of his moral leadership. At this point, when the loss of that leadership was imminent, they would be especially receptive to his words and moved by the openness with which he shared his personal feelings.

With an awareness of this increased bond of empathy between him and his listeners, Moses proceeded to give those words a special authority. He instructs his people, saying: "Ye shall not add unto the words which I commanded you, neither shall you diminish from it, that ye may keep the commandments of the Lord, your God, which I command you" (4:2).

This injunction served early as a *fence around the law*, to protect its integrity. The rabbis have pointed out that this precept did not alter the possibility of change or adaptation but that the latter should not be treated as further revelation from God (Hertz 1936, 750).

This instruction from Moses reveals his understanding of human nature. His approach is geared to the future, and he tries to anticipate the temptations and pitfalls to which his people may be subjected and to prepare them for it. This anticipatory process, the capacity to understand intuitively what the Children of Israel will have to face in their new environment, is indicative of a keen and imaginative mind. The task is as challenging in its way as the earlier responsibilities of leadership in the wilderness. Moses now has to reorganize and solidify what they had learned so they could adapt his teachings to a new situation. He utilizes various methods of reaching both their minds and their hearts. Frequently he appeals to their sense of pride as an inducement to keep the commandments. "Behold, I have taught you statutes and ordinances, even as the Lord my God commanded me, that ye should do so in the midst of the land whither ye go in to possess it. Observe therefore and do them; for this is your wisdom and your understanding in the sight of the peoples, that, when they hear all these statutes, shall say, 'Surely this great nation is a wise and understanding people.' For what great nation is there, that hath God so nigh unto them, as the Lord our God is whensoever we call upon him? And what great nation is there, that hath statutes and ordinances so righteous as all this law, which I set before you this day?" (4:5–8).

The contrast between their own concept of God and the idol-worshipping nations around is drawn with particular emphasis. Significantly Moses does not blame the pagan world for their worship of images and celestial bodies. He reminds his people that Israel has been blessed by *being chosen* for special enlightenment (4:20). He stresses the most memorable of their experiences, the receiving of the Law at Mount Sinai. "Did ever a people hear the voice of God speaking out of the midst of the fire, as thou hast heard, and live? Or hath God assayed to go and take Him a nation from the midst of another nation, by trials, by signs, and by wonders, and by wars, and by a mighty hand, and by an outstretched arm, and by great terrors, according to all that the Lord your God did for you in Egypt before thine eyes? Unto thee it was shown that thou mightest know that the Lord, He is God; there is none else beside Him" (4:33–35).

Out of that unforgettable event the basic theme is drawn and developed with an impassioned eloquence. "Take ye therefore good heed unto yourselves—for ye saw no manner of form on that day that the Lord spoke unto you in Horeb out of the midst of the fire lest ye deal corruptly and make a graven image, even the form of any figure, the likeness of male or female, the likeness of any beast that is on the earth." This theme is continued at greater length (4:15–19).

The incorporeality of God was thus emphasized as the foundation of the Hebrew religion. It was the distinguishing mark of that religion that set the Children of Israel apart from the surrounding peoples. The spirituality of God could not be embodied in any form. The significance of this concept is far-reaching and profound from a psychological as well as theological viewpoint. An invisible God cannot be experienced through the physical senses. The relationship with such a Deity can take place only on a psychic basis. As Freud (1939) says regarding this concept, "it signified subordinating sense perception to an abstract idea; it was a triumph of spirituality over the senses." Freud explains that this progress in spirituality is accompanied by an increase in self-confidence because it represents a successful effort in instinctual renunciation—the capacity to give up a pleasure of the senses for an intellectual achievement (pp.178–79). Such a step forward in individual development requires the aid of approval from a loved and respected authority. In childhood it is the parental figures who perform this function. Later, their internalized images, together with those of other significant adults, lead to the formation of the superego, which helps the ego make such renunciations. The reward is a sense of inner approval and of pride in the accomplishment.

In the cultural development of a group a similar process takes place under the guidance and inspiration of great leaders. Moses performed this significant role for the Children of Israel. He served the function of a group superego figure through whom was reflected and mediated the greater superego, the Deity Himself (Freud 1922, 110ff.; 1930).

It was now the task of Moses to make unnecessary the intermediary role of his presence, which had served as a bridge to bring the people closer to God. He had to help them strengthen their own capacity to experience a transcendental Being Who nevertheless was close to them. Intuitively, he tries to prepare them for the inevitable trauma of the loss of his leadership. No longer would they be able to plead as they had done at Mount Sinai, "Speak thou with us, and we will hear; but let not God speak with us, lest we die" (Exod. 20:16).

Through the laws and precepts that he gave them, Moses tried to provide security through structure. But structure alone would be like a body without a spirit. At one time, the spirit of Moses was imparted to the seventy elders who were to assist him in governing the people (Num. 11:25). Now, he strives to impart his spirit in more lasting ways to all the Children of Israel.

The leader does not hesitate, also, to instill fear of consequences into his listeners. The threat of punishment for those who disobey God's commandments is vividly portrayed. "Take heed unto yourselves, lest ye forget the covenant of the Lord your God, which He made with you, and make you a graven image, even the likeness of anything which the Lord thy God hath forbidden thee. For the Lord thy God is a devouring fire, a jealous God. When thou shalt beget children, and children's children, and ye shall have been long in the land, and shall deal corruptly, and make a graven image, even the form of any thing, and shall do that which is evil in the sight of the Lord thy God, to provoke Him; I call heaven and earth to witness against you this day, that ye shall soon utterly perish from off the land whereunto ye go over the Jordan to possess it. And the Lord shall scatter you among the peoples, and ye shall be left few in number among the nations, whither the Lord shall lead you away. And there ye shall serve other gods, the work of man's hands, wood and stone, which neither see, nor hear, nor eat, nor smell" (4:23–28).

But the frightening vision is followed with words of reassurance and comfort. If they seek out the Lord, he will show mercy (4:29). "And because He loved thy fathers," he told them, "and chose their seed after them and brought thee out with His presence, with His great power out of Egypt, to drive out nations from before thee greater and mightier than thou, to bring thee in, to give thee their land for an inheritance as it is this day" (4:37–38). The clear implication was that for all these reasons, the Children of Israel were obliged to keep God's commandments that it might go well with them and with their children.

As Moses delivers his discourses, one can visualize a towering figure of strength and courage, who must also have shown some signs of frailty, exhorting, pleading, threatening, trying to put his last imprint on them before leaving his people to the dangers of a new world that awaited them. Although the Bible maintains that his vigor was undiminishied to the end, Moses himself admitted, "I can no more go out and come" (31:2).

It seems that his intense wish to cross the Jordan with them was not only for a sense of personal fulfillment but also to continue his protective guidance of the people amid the new temptations and perils that lay before them. They were in a significant sense *his* creation, of which he felt himself to be a living part. The anxiety about separating from them seems to have been of a twofold nature: It was not only that he had to go on his own way without them but also that they had to go on without him. He was not to be part of the great adventure that lay before them.

The Three Cities of Refuge

After the exhortation that ends the first discourse, a puzzling change in style and content occurs. Instead of the direct address, the sentence structure reverts to the third person (4:41–43). "Then Moses separated three cities beyond the Jordan toward the sunrising: that the manslayer might flee thither, that slayeth his neighbor unawares, and hated him not in time past; and that fleeing unto one of these cities he might live; Bezer in the wilderness, in the tableland, for the Reubenites; and Ramoth in Gilead, for the Gadites; and Golan in Bashan, for the Manassites."

Altogether, there were to be six cities of refuge, three on each side of the Jordan. The other three are described in a later chapter (19:1–3). One can only speculate why the ones east of the Jordan were inserted in the text at this time. A logical assumption is that Moses included this material when he originally wrote down or edited the discourses. Perhaps the sequence from a geographic viewpoint took precedence over the harmony in terms of style. From their later perspective in the land of Canaan, the Children of Israel were not to forget that for those living *beyond the Jordan*, there were also cities of refuge.

The Second Discourse

The Second Discourse (4:44 through chapter 26) makes up the largest part of Deuteronomy. It embodies the laws by which Israel is to live, the religious foundation of the Covenant that sets forth the relationship between God and Israel, its spiritual nature and the moral demands that such a relationship makes on the Children of Israel. It contains a repetition of the Ten Commandments given at Mount Sinai, stating anew the Oneness of God and the duty incumbent on every individual of the house of Israel to love God with "all his heart, and with all his soul, and with all his might."

A large part of the Second Discourse (chaps. 12–26) is made up of what is known as the Code of Laws, to which fuller reference will be made further on.

As Moses recalls for the people the circumstances at Mount Sinai under which the Ten Commandments were delivered, he reminds them that the Covenant established at that time was not only for those present then but for all generations to come. The leader now repeats the Ten Commandments before the entire assembly of Israel.

The minor differences in the restatement, to which some scholars of Higher Biblical Criticism have attributed much importance in the controversy regarding sources and dates of composition, can be understood on the basis of the differences in the life situation of the people on the two occasions. The mystique of the Mount Sinai experience could only be reproduced verbally close to forty years later. But the memory was being recalled by the same magnetic personality who had initiated the first scene, Moses himself. He did not attempt to repeat himself perfectly. He was a vibrant human being and allowed himself a few deviations from the original wording. The purpose of the leader was not only to repeat but to impress the content on the minds of his listeners.

This solemn recall of the earlier event must have been deeply impressive in its own way, as the aged leader, on the Plains of Moab, faced a different generation from those at the foot of Mount Sinai.

Some of the more memorabale changes from the Exodus version occur in the text of the fourth commandment. The earlier statement begins with the words, "*Remember* the sabbath day to keep it holy" (Exod. 20:8) (italics added). In Deuteronomy the commandment begins, "*Observe* the Sabbath day, to keep it holy, as the Lord, thy God, commanded thee" (5:12) (italics added).

May Moses have wished to make a change in emphasis here? *Remembering* is a mental function, whereas *observing* has to do with action. When wandering in the wilderness, where the routines of life were very much the same day after day, it was important to *remember* the Sabbath in order to observe it. For the new life facing the people in the land of Canaan, where the daily activities would be more varied and the days of the week more clearly set apart from each other, the emphasis was more logically placed on *observance*, especially when the Children of Israel would be living among peoples who did not observe the Sabbath. Thus, *remembering* was not enough; the *observance* was all-important, the former being included in the latter. As a further distinction in the two versions, the rationale given in Exodus for remembering the Sabbath Day was because God rested on that day, after His work of creating the world in the first six days. Again, the emphasis there is on a mental or spiritual concept—God was the model for what man himself should do. In Deuteronomy, the reason for sanctifying the seventh day was oriented once more directly to human events. It was to serve as a reminder that the Children of Israel were once slaves in the land of Egypt and God had brought them out from there with a mighty hand. Therefore, the commandment to rest on the seventh day was to include all within the household, the servants and even the domestic animals. "And thou shalt remember that thou wast a servant in the land of Egypt" (5:15).

Moving from the fourth to the tenth commandment, one can detect there a subtle but not insignificant change in the wording.

On the assumption that Moses is unconsciously expressing aspects of himself in the choice of words, the following differences in the two versions are of interest. Exodus states: "Thou shalt not covet . . . thy neighbor's house; thou shalt not covet . . . thy neighbor's wife" (20:14). Deuteronomy puts it this way: "Neither shalt thou covet thy neighbor's wife; neither shalt thou *desire* thy neighbor's house" (5:18) (italics added). Here, in terms of sequence, *the wife* is placed before *the house*, suggesting a higher degree of value. But strangely, the word *desire*, with its stronger emotional connotation, is used in connection with the neighbor's *house*. It would have seemed more likely to desire the neighbor's wife and to covet his house. Psychoanalytically viewed, a defensive measure may have been at work here. The priority in sequence is counteracted with a form of denial about even the possibility of desiring the neighbor's wife.

Even more definitively, other differences in the Deuteronomic version can be understood as significant of changes in the thinking and feeling of Moses himself. Thus, in Exodus, the text is somewhat ambiguous about whether God Himself had written the Ten Words on the second Tables of the Testimony as the Deity had done on the first tables, those that Moses had destroyed in his anger because of the golden calf apostasy, (Exod. 34:27–28). Now, however, Moses clearly states that God had indeed inscribed the second set of commandments as well. On a further point, Exodus states that *they* (presumably Bezalel, the gifted craftsman) had made the Ark in which the Tables of the Law were placed (25:10). In Deuteronomy we are told that Moses himself had made the Ark (10:3). Did the aged leader remember those details *as he wished to recall them* and as he wanted the people to remember them? Such faulty recall is common indeed and indicates further the deeply human qualities of this great personality.

After the restatement of the Decalogue, Moses exhorts the people, in the name of the Deity, to obey all the commandments. "Ye shall walk in all the ways which the Lord your God commanded you, that ye may live, and that it may be well with you, and that ye may prolong your days in the land which ye shall possess" (5:30).

In this context the words that have become most familiar in

Jewish liturgy are pronounced. "Hear, O Israel, the Lord our God, the Lord is One. And thou shalt love the Lord thy God with all thy heart, and with all thy soul, and with all thy might. And these words which I command thee this day, shall be upon thy heart; and thou shalt teach them diligently unto thy children, and shalt talk of them when thou sittest down in thy house, and when thou liest down and when thou risest up" (6:4–7).

The *Shema*, as the first part of this commandment is known, is part of the daily morning and evening prayer in the synagogue. It is recited by the entire congregation on the many occasions, such as the Sabbath and the festivals, when the Torah is taken out of the Ark for the Portion of the Law to be read. It constitutes a confession of the faith that every pious Jew utters as his last words and which those martyred for their faith throughout the history of Judaism pronounce with their final breath. As Hertz (1936) puts it, "The *Shema* became the soul-stirring, collective expression of Israel's spiritual being" (p. 942).

Psychoanalytically, the first word of this declaration of faith, *Hear*, is related to the development of the superego in early childhood. It is through the *ear* that the child first learns of what he may or may not do, the beginnings of a sense of what he perceives as right and wrong (Fenichel 1945, 107; Freud 1923). The image of God, viewed developmentally as the projected figure of the father, is associated with the admonition *to hear* (Reik 1959, 168–69) (24). What Israel is to hear is that *God is One*. The oneness of God in contrast to the many gods of the idol-worshipping nations, symbolizes the mature, integrated oneness of the worshipper himself, the state of his psychic integration that results from the maturation of his personality, as instincts, ego, and superego develop into a unified self.

The growth of monotheism signifies a similar process in the cultural development of the group, as Freud points out in his *Civilization and Its Discontents*. On a group level, this shared sense of the oneness of God is accompanied by strengthened feelings of relatedness among the people. They are one because their God is one, and because the representative of God among them, Moses, their leader, is the earthly father figure, under whose guidance they are united (Freud 1922, 110ff.). At the same time, each individual remains as a separate and responsible member of the group. For only within the mind and heart of the person himself can thought and feelings take place.

The intermingled use of the singular and plural forms of the pronouns, which is so prevalent throughout the discourses, expresses both aspects of how Moses related to his people. In a fashion that seems almost indiscriminate, he seems to address both the individual and the group at the same time, a phenomenon to be more fully explored later in chapter 18.

As mentioned earlier, the commandment to love God was a unique feature in the development of religion. It seems strange that one should be *commanded* to love God and to regard this feeling as a duty. Can feelings of this kind be subject to command?

This concept of love is related to the love one so much desires from the superego, the inner sense of approval that what one is doing is right and good. It is the opposite of guilt, the punishment that the superego inflicts for disobedience to its commands. Developmentally, the fear of loss of love from the parental figure becomes a source of anxiety for the child. Unconsciously, it can mean abandonment and death. Such feelings can remain repressed in the adult and influence his yearning for the security of love from authority figures, from God, here the projected superego, and from his own inner voice, the superego that is part of his own psyche.

Biblical religion teaches that fear of the Lord and love of Him are not antithetical. Indeed, they belong together. As the Book of Proverbs declares: "The fear of the Lord is the beginning of knowledge" (1:7). Such knowledge (or wisdom) signifies an awareness between good and evil, an all-important step in the development of the superego. The commandment to love God is the commandment to love *good*, therefore, to *do* good, thus gaining the approval of the superego. Love as the act of doing can be understood as a commandment and a duty.

Following our usual approach, it is suggested here that there is a meaningful relationship between the frequent exhortations in Deuteronomy to love God and the role that love played within Moses himself. The duty to love God did not come easily to the leader even though it grew in intensity and passion throughout his life. His love for God involved a continuing struggle for an increasing degree of spirituality. This process of sublimation meant a transcendence over instinctual needs and wishes. In Deuteronomy Moses stresses more than ever the duty of loving God and the blessings that derive from it.

What implications from his own life situation might be drawn from this emphasis? Did Moses himself feel a need for the strengthening of this feeling at a time when his wish to enter the Promised Land was denied? By pleading with his people to love God, was Moses also pleading with himself not to give way to personal feelings of disappointment, with their negative connotations in relation to the Deity? Moreover, was Moses in need at this time of the special love of his people to sustain him in this disappointment and perhaps to counteract his anger against them? Was he fearful of losing their love at this final stage of his life because of his demands on them for controls on their own instinctual wishes and for progress in their spiritual growth? Did Moses increasingly see that love was indeed the most constructive and motivating force for good and that love alone would make possible the obedience to the laws that humanity requires to keep its instinctual forces in control and to foster the process of civilization? It was through his personal struggles that Moses saw the role of love in religion. Like other great biblical leaders, he was a true culture hero, carving out new paths for the group to follow.

The Code of Laws

Although precepts and commandments are found throughout Deuteronomy, a formalized arrangement of these statutes is concentrated in the so-called Code of Laws (chapters 12–26). This content is regarded by many as the nucleus of Deuteronomy, the center for which the colorful periphery was formed (Hertz 1936, 800). Many scholars consider the Code of Laws as the most ancient part of Deuteronomy and even some of the more radical concede to it a Mosaic origin.

The tendency of Higher Biblical Criticism was to equate this body of law with the statutes set forth in the so-called Book of the Covenant (Exod. 20–23). But in recent decades further exploration in this area has pointed in other directions. It has been suggested that if the Code in Deuteronomy was only an expansion of the Covenant in Exodus, why should more than three-fourths of the latter not have been included? (Archer 1964, 245). Evidently, repetition was not the basic motive of Deuteronomy. This fifth book of the Torah, as suggested earlier, emphasizes those aspects of the law that would be especially relevant for the future life of the Children of Israel in Canaan (Hertz 1936, 809).

The first commandment in the Code deals with the order to destroy the pagan sites of worship, the high places, in the land they are to conquer and occupy (12:2–4). Then comes the statute concerning the establishment of a central place of worship. To this one shrine the people must come from all parts of the land to celebrate the festivals, to bring their sacrifices, and to pay their tithes. Altars at local high places were thus forbidden, a protection against the temptation of using pagan sites of worship. A further motive must have been to strengthen the sense of national unity among the tribes. This commandment became a focal point among scholars of Higher Biblical Criticism for dating Deuteronomy in the time of Josiah (621 B.C.).

The site of this central sanctuary was to be chosen by God. At this point, Jerusalem was not specifically named (12:5–7), although ultimately that is the place that was chosen.

It is not within the scope of this study to enter into a description of the many precepts and commandments contained in the lengthy Code of Laws under discussion here. Many of them are touched on throughout the chapter and elsewhere in this volume as they relate to specific situations in regard to Moses himself within the fabric of his life situation. It could be noted that the Code of Laws is comprehensive in nature, dealing with every important aspect of both communal and individual living. In addition to the detailed statutes regarding religious practices and observances, there is considerable emphasis on relationships within the family, between neighbors, and with national and local government and on the rights of the workman and the slave, with specific laws involving the administration of justice and the practice of kindness and mercy.

Many of the laws that had previously been enunciated in terse legal form are here expanded into wider humanitarian applications, voiced with greater warmth and emotional commitment. This approach suggests the mellowing aspects of Moses' own personality at this stage in his life.

Although written so long ago, these laws are remarkable for the psychological insights and understanding they reveal, not only against the background of their times and in terms of the immediate needs and problems of the Children of Israel but also in lasting and universal terms.

The Third Discourse (Chaps. 27–30)

Moses was deeply concerned with a coming event that he personally was not to experience—the crossing of the Jordan River and the entrance into the Promised Land by his people. The right of the Children of Israel to the land of Canaan was based on a covenant with God. They were entitled to occupy it only on the basis of their obedience to the commandments of the Deity. Coming into the Promised Land would mark a historic change in their life situation. It had to be accompanied by appropriate ceremonials that would be expressive of its significance and would make this occasion an unforgettable one in their history.

In regard to Moses himself, it can be said that an important aspect of his personality was the capacity to integrate the realities of life with its essential mystery. It is not surprising, therefore, that an elaborate series of meaningful rituals should have been prepared by the leader for this occasion.

The crossing of the Jordan and the entrance into the Promised Land can be understood symbolically as a group rite of passage from adolescence to adulthood, similar to that which occurs in the developmental life of the individual (Reik 1959, 54) (25). It represented a transition, the emergence into a new state of growth and maturation for which the years in the wilderness had been a period of learning and preparation, a time of growing up as a people. The symbolism of God as the Father and the Promised Land as mother is representative of the family constellation. As in the earthly family, the man is both husband and father, so in the metaphor of the biblical narrative, God also relates to the Children of Israel in the two roles.

The entrance of the Children of Israel into Canaan symbolized a kind of marriage ceremony that climaxed their rite of passage into maturity. The very tones of the biblical phrases convey an intimation of such a relationship. "And Moses and the priests and the Levites spoke unto all Israel, saying: '. . . Keep silence, and hear, O Israel; this day thou art become a people unto the Lord thy God. Thou shalt therefore hearken to the voice of the Lord thy God, and do His commandments and His statutes, which I command thee this day'" (27:9–10).

Another aspect of this metaphor identifies the people of Israel with the land itself in terms of its relationship to the Deity. It was a *holy* land, inseparable from its people, who were often referred to as the *betrothed of God*. As one scholar put it, "The exclusive sanctity of the land of Israel is as fundamental a part of the priestly laws as the election of the people" (Kaufmann 1960, 129). At the covenant of Mount Sinai, the Deity had declared, "Now therefore, if ye will hearken unto My voice indeed, and keep My covenant, then ye shall be Mine own treasure from among all the peoples; for all the earth is Mine; and ye shall be unto Me a kingdom of priests and a holy nation" (Exod. 19:5–6).

The metaphor of Israel's relationship to the Deity and to the land, does at times assume a somewhat puzzling complexity. God is metaphorically both Husband and Father. In the latter role, He allows the sons to possess the land in a setting of holy matrimony. In the metaphor, as in the unconscious of man, the images of mother and wife sometimes become confused. It is in the process of achieving a greater degree of separation between these relationships that emotional maturity is more fully attained. Through the concept of an incorporeal God and a motherland, a pathway for projecting the oedipal conflict onto a more symbolic plane is provided. Because of the degree of sublimation and abstract thinking involved in this process, the cultural life of the group was aided in reaching a higher level of functioning. There was no confusion in terms of the laws that regulated marital life and the purity of family relationships. Through their acceptance of the commandments of the Father, the sons give up their rivalry with Him and enjoy His blessing in the possession of the land.

The dual roles of God as Husband and Father may reflect,

in part, the state of mind within Moses himself. Where did *he* belong in the scheme of things as pictured above? In his relationship to the Deity, Moses was a special and beloved son. But in the eyes of the people, as the prophet of God, as the leader and lawgiver, Moses was a father figure, not too remote at times from the image of God Himself. The latter association was one that Moses could not always escape in the recesses of his fantasies. Caught between the roles of son and father, he could not enter the motherland. Even in this symbolic and sublimated form, the wish to do so had to be denied because of its underlying oedipal significance. Such was the stern edict of his own superego, projected to God. Its reward was an increase in spirituality, a greater closeness to God.

Preparations for the Entrance into Canaan

The ceremonials prescribed for crossing the Jordan River and setting foot on the Promised Land are expressive of the significance of the event. "And Moses and the elders commanded the people saying: 'Keep all the commandments which I command you this day. And it shall be on the day when ye pass over the Jordan, unto the land which the Lord thy God giveth thee, that thou shalt set up great stones, and plaster them with plaster. And thou shalt write upon them all the words of this law, when thou art passed over; that thou mayest go in unto the land which the Lord thy God giveth thee, a land flowing with milk and honey, as the Lord, the God of thy fathers hath promised thee'" (27:1–3). The Children of Israel were thus bound to their God and to the land under the precepts of law, as in a marriage.

The stones, with the laws inscribed on the plaster, a procedure of recording not uncommon in those times, were to be erected on Mount Ebal. There too an altar was to be built. And the people were to eat of the sacrificial offerings and rejoice before God. Establishing peace with the Deity, which meant submission and obedience to His laws, had to precede their task of conquest. Such obedience, however, was not an abject act but an occasion for rejoicing.

The next ceremonial was one of the most solemn and impressive. It was to take place between the two mountain peaks, Ebal and Gerizim, each rising on opposite sides of the town of Shechem. Half of the tribes of Israel were to stand on the slope of Mount Gerizim, symbolic of the mount of blessing, and the other half on Mount Ebal, the mount of curses. Though not actually stated, the Levites evidently stood in the valley between them. The text says, "And the Levites shall speak, and say unto all the men of Israel with a loud voice: 'Cursed be the man that maketh a graven or molten image, an abomination unto the Lord, the work of the hands of the craftsman, and setteth it up in secret.' And all the people shall answer and say: 'Amen'" (27:14–15). In this manner the priests would call out each separate wrongdoing and its accompanying punishment while the people responded with *Amen*.

The first pronouncement, as quoted above, had to do with idolatry. Everything depended on the acceptance of the oneness of God and the manifold implications of that concept. The main content of the ceremonial injunctions dealt with matters of human relationships, the purity of family life, the humane treatment of the blind, and justice to the stranger, the fatherless, and the widow. Prominent among the forbidden deeds that were considered accursed, were violations of family taboos in regard to sexuality, especially those of incest. This type of crime must have seemed especially horrendous to Moses himself, second only to idolatry (27:11–26).

Chapter 28, which follows, is known in Hebrew as *The Warning*. Here the blessings for those who obey the commandments of God are given first. They are fewer in number than the curses that follow, the latter occupying a major part of the lengthy pronouncements.

The rhythmic quality of the language and the antiphonal responses from the people on the opposite mountain slope, the vividness and variety of the metaphors, with their use of contrast, and the impassioned quality of the content give these verses and the scene they conjure up an impact that is unforgettable.

The prediction of exile in this chapter as one of the punishments for disobedience to the laws has been used by some scholars of Higher Biblical Criticism as an indication of its postexilic origin. But exile was the common lot of conquered peoples and a fate readily predictable as a possible evil consequence. The curses are frequently the reverse of the blessings—the other side of the coin, as it were. The covenantal character of the relationship between the Children of Israel and God is clearly stated at the end of the chapter (28:69): "These are the words of the covenant which the Lord commanded Moses to make with the Children of Israel in the land of Moab, beside the covenant which he made with them in Horeb."

It is hard to realize that the portrayal of this lively pageantry describes what is to take place in the future and is not the actual event itself. A vivid imagination capable of projecting itself into another time and place, must have been at work here, as in so much of these discourses. The happening itself is enacted at a later date and recorded in a rather prosaic fashion, the chief purpose of which seems to be a dutiful statement that Joshua had fulfilled the commandments of Moses (Josh. 8:30–35).

The Clothes that Did Not Grow Old

Moses is now near the conclusion of his final discourse. All Israel is in solemn assembly before him. The purpose is to reestablish, or renew, the Covenant under which the people are bound in obedience to the Law. It was to be a Covenant for all time, not only for those present but for those who were to come.

This occasion must have been one of special significance for Moses, not only as the leader but on a personal level as well. He would not be present for the elaborate rituals that had been prepared for the Children of Israel on their crossing of the Jordan and when they stood on the shores of the Promised Land. Moses must have felt it incumbent personally to conduct the people through a reaffirmation of their allegiance to the Covenant established at Mount Sinai and to portray the consequences of disobedience to its laws.

It is understandable that the departing leader should experience anew certain underlying feelings about his own situation and that these should find expression inadvertently in his address to the people, leading to some ambiguities in the text.

The address begins: "And Moses called unto all Israel, and

said unto them: 'Ye have seen all that the Lord did before your eyes in the land of Egypt unto Pharaoh, and unto all his servants, and unto all his land; the great trials which thine eyes saw, the signs and those great wonders; but the Lord hath not given you a heart to know, and eyes to see, and ears to hear, unto this day'" (29:1–3). Then several verses follow that stand out because of a certain unrelatedness to the context both in the manner of presentation and obscurity of meaning. "And I have led you forty years in the wilderness: your clothes are not waxen old upon you, and thy shoe is not waxen old upon thy foot. Ye have not eaten bread, neither have ye drunk strong drink; that ye might know that I am the Lord your God" (29:4–5).

First to be noted is a grammatical change from the third person to the first, "And *I* have led you forty years in the wilderness" (italics added), leading to ambiguity about who is now doing the speaking, the Deity or Moses. Furthermore, in contrast to the generalizations voiced in the preceding material, the subsequent statements are highly specific in content.

The reference to the clothes and shoes that did not grow old in forty years suggests that God had performed another wonder for the people. However, no such happening had been mentioned before, in the light of which the present reference could be understood retrospectively. Nor was there any reality reason for such a miracle. The Children of Israel had flocks and herds as sources of material for their clothes and shoes. And certainly they did not lack the skill to produce these objects. God did not usually perform unnecessary acts to supply the wanderers with their needs nor tend to do so in a manner completely contrary to the laws of nature.

A detail that provides one of the clues for the interpretation to be presented here, is the use of the singular form in the expressions *thy shoe* and *thy foot*. Although the metaphoric use of the individual for the group is common throughout the discourses, the effect in the present instance conveys a certain sense of the inappropriate.

Psychoanalytically, *clothes may be a symbol for the person* (Fenichel 1945, 36). It is suggested here that the clothes and shoes that did not grow old may refer to the people themselves. The use of the singular pronoun in *thy shoe* and *thy foot* may indicate an unconscious identification on the part of Moses with the people, the wish that he might be in their shoes, as it were, that he, too, had not "waxen old" during the forty years in the wilderness. A sense of grievance may also have been involved. Moses may here be contrasting the comparatively youthful appearance of his followers with his own old age. To the elderly, those younger often appear unduly young even for their years. It must have seemed to the leader that the assembly before him looked remarkably youthful. And indeed, within the framework of the biblical narrative, they were a full generation younger than he, since his own contemporaries, except for Joshua and Caleb, had died in the wilderness. Was Moses here not only expressing a concealed wish but also giving indications of the familiar human emotions of disappointment and envy? If God had the power to have time stand still for the clothes and shoes of his followers (symbolically, the people themselves), couldn't the Deity have done the same for Moses? The leader would then have retained his youthful vigor and been able to cross the Jordan with his people. Such a fantasy was especially forbidden because it was contrary to God's plan for him.

The following verse (29:5) is even more puzzling. There is no reference to a specific occasion in the past when the people had refrained from eating bread or partaking of strong drink so that, in the words of the text, they might know "I am the Lord thy God."

It was Moses himself who, according to the narrative, did not partake of food and water for forty days while on Mount Sinai. On that memorable occasion, also at a time of the renewal of the Covenant, Moses had been granted a special closeness with the Deity and had come down from the mount with beams of light radiating from his face (Exod. 34:28–29). It was *Moses* to whom God had given "a heart to understand, and eyes to see, and ears to hear," not the people, whose lack of these capacities the leader deplored. Yet the miracle of remaining young, which had been conferred on them, had been denied to him. Implied in this situation is an underlying sense of grievance against God. In displacing to the people his own role in abstaining from food and drink, Moses may have been avoiding any direct expression of his own worthiness, which had gone unrewarded.

Another aspect may be involved in this highly elliptical verse. If the people had been given the capacity to understand, they would have known that "I (Moses) am like the Lord your God, who wrought the miracle of keeping your clothes and shoes (your persons) from getting old." Such a thought—competitiveness with the Deity, even momentarily displacing Him—could only find expression in highly distorted form .

If thoughts and feelings of a forbidden nature were striving for expression within Moses, the need to disguise such content would manifest itself in various forms of defensive measures unconsciously instituted by the ego and resulting in obscurities of the text. If the projections and displacements were removed and appropriate connections established, the thoughts and fantasies of Moses in the verses under consideration might have read as follows: "It was *I* who abstained from food and drink for forty days, *not you*, and it was to *me* that God gave the gift of understanding and closeness to Him, *not you*. Yet you are the ones for whom He caused time to stand still. Moreover, if God had granted you the necessary understanding, you would have known that *to you, I am as the Lord your God*, who kept you young in the wilderness for forty years."

The underlying wish may have been not actually to displace the Deity in their eyes but to present himself as having acted *in God's stead* regarding the miracle of the clothes and shoes. It was a role the Deity Himself had conferred on him before, in relation first to his brother Aaron (Exod. 4:16) and again, to the Pharaoh (Exod. 7:1). What Moses may actually have been seeking from the people was appreciation for himself and all he had done for them. He alone of all that vast assembly would not be crossing the Jordan to the Promised Land. The lowered sense of self-esteem that the occasion engendered may have sought relief through compensatory attempts at identification with the omnipotence of the Deity.

An acceptance of reality and a sense of his own identity is indicated by what follows. Moses reminds the people of their recent victories over the two kings east of the Jordan, Sihon and Og, "who came out against us unto battle, and we smote them" (29:6). By the use of the pronouns *us* and *we*, Moses is again allied with his people as their leader in the human sense. The confused meaning of the verses (29:1–5) are another indication of the depth and extent to which Moses experienced the deprivation of being denied the privilege of entering the Promised Land.

The Final Ceremonials

In the concluding chapters of Deuteronomy there is an increasing sense of the imminent death of Moses. A feeling of urgency is conveyed by the leader as though he were seeking to complete his tasks before the inevitable hour overtook him. At the same time he seemed to be pushing off that dreaded event by a series of leave-taking preparations on behalf of his people. All of those acts are clearly for the purpose of furthering the strength and stability of the Children of Israel after his departure. Yet as each preparatory ceremonial is prescribed and the action moves to a seemingly climactic end, it is succeeded by still another observance to be carried through, equally impressive and climactic. The impression is similar to that of a maestro conducting an orchestra, who is about to make his departure but keeps coming back to play one more piece, as though loath to leave.

In these final activities, as delineated in the text, the undercurrent of feelings within the leader can be detected in small ways. The greatness of a man, the largeness of his vision, does not necessarily free him from the frailties that are part of being human. It will be of interest to observe what conflictful personal issues disturbed Moses at this time, issues that, being unacceptable to his conscious mind, tended to show signs of their existence by minor disharmonies in the text or in the sequence of its contents.

Although conflicts may diminish for various reasons, they tend to leave traces behind. So it is understandable that even during those last days, though Moses had ostensibly come to terms with his fate, the old sensitivity about being displaced by another (this time Joshua), should give indications of its existence. In relation to the Deity also, there are some subtle implications that suggest competitiveness, as when the distinction between Moses and God are, on occasion, fleetingly lost sight of, as we shall see. Together with the prescribed impressive ceremonials of leave-taking, the importance of which are realistically valid, significant details also point to unconscious fantasies and feelings of Moses himself.

Chapter 31 opens with a dramatic statement that presents the situation succinctly: "And Moses went and spoke these words unto all Israel. And he said unto them: 'I am a hundred and twenty years old this day; I can no more go out and come in; and the Lord hath said unto me: Thou shalt not go over this Jordan. The Lord thy God, He will go over before thee; He will destroy these nations from before thee, and thou shalt dispossess them; and Joshua, he shall go over before thee, as the Lord hath spoken'" (31:1–3).

The impression is given that *the Deity would take the place of Moses* after the latter's death. Moses tells the people, "The Lord hath said unto me: '*Thou* shalt not go over this Jordan,'" adding immediately after, "*The Lord thy God, He will go over before thee*" (italics added). Here, it is God Who would take the place of Moses. One would have expected that Joshua would have been mentioned at this point as taking the place of Moses in the crossing of the Jordan. But it is only subsequent to this statement and after the added assurance that "He [God] will destroy these nations from before thee, and thou shalt dispossess them" that Joshua is brought in: "and Joshua, he shall go over before thee, as the Lord has spoken."

Joshua would also be there, but his presence would be incidental to that of God. Unconsciously perhaps, at this moment, Moses felt that only God would be acceptable to take his place.

The anxiety about how the loss of his leadership would affect the morale of the people in their coming struggle with the Canaanites continues to be a great concern of Moses. He exhorts them repeatedly: "Be strong and of good courage, fear not, nor be affrighted . . . for the Lord thy God, He it is that doth go with thee; He will not fail thee nor forsake thee." He now calls on Joshua to come before him "in the sight of all Israel" and repeats similar words of encouragement to him (32:7–8).

However, the chief structure that Moses leaves his people to guide and maintain them throughout the years is the *Law*. The giving of the Law to the Children of Israel, both at Mount Sinai and on the Plains of Moab, and indeed, teaching its beliefs and practices throughout their sojourn in the wilderness, was his outstanding contribution. It was as the great lawgiver that Moses was to be remembered. It was through his law that the Children of Israel were to preserve their identity in the role for which he had tried to prepare them, a people dedicated to the religion of One God, Whose commandments they had vowed to obey in a sacred covenant.

It is not surprising, therefore, that the ceremonials before his final departure should include important statements regarding the handing down of the Law to its proper custodians and to the people of Israel as a whole. The text says, "And Moses wrote this law, and delivered it unto the priests and sons of Levi, that bore the ark of the covenant to the Lord, and unto all the elders of Israel. And Moses commanded them, saying: 'At the end of every seven years, in the set time of the year of release, in the feast of tabernacles, when all Israel is come to appear before the Lord thy God in the place which he shall choose, thou shalt read this law before all Israel in their hearing. Assemble the people, the men and the women and the little ones, and the stranger that is within thy gates, that they may hear and that they may learn, and fear the Lord your God and observe to do all the words of this law'" (31:9–13).

Although the text says, "And *Moses wrote this law,*" certainly the intent was not to imply that he wrote it at this particular time, just before his death. The past tense is often used as the imperfect tense, indicating continuing activity. The significance of the ceremonial turning over of the Law and the commandment relating to its care and use is the understanding that the laws of Israel were not to be the sole possession of the priests and those in power. They were to be the possession of the people as a whole. Education, starting with the young, was thus a prime responsibility of the elders. The emphasis on educating the children is referred to frequently throughout Scripture. This tradition is well known and has been valued throughout Jewish history.

The Command to Write a Song

The next event in these impressive happenings that preceded the death of Moses takes place in a different setting. It is best described in the words of the text: "And the Lord said unto Moses: 'Behold, thy days approach that thou must die; call Joshua, and present yourselves in the tent of meeting, that I may give him a charge.' And Moses and Joshua went, and presented themselves in the tent of meeting. And the Lord appeared in the Tent in a pillar of cloud; and the pillar of cloud stood over the door of the Tent. And the Lord said unto Moses: 'Behold, thou art about to sleep with thy fathers; and this people will rise up, and go astray after the foreign gods of the land, whither they go to be among them, and will forsake Me, and break My covenant which I have made with them. Then my anger shall be kindled against them in that day, and I will forsake them, and I will hide My face from them, and they shall be devoured, and many evils and troubles shall come upon them; so that they will say in that day: 'Are not these evils come upon us because our God is not among us?' And I will surely hide My face in that day for all the evil which they shall have wrought, in that they turned unto other gods'" (31:14–18).

Although both men are in the tent, God addresses Moses only, reminding him that he is about to die. It seems that the Deity shared the same anxiety as Moses concerning the demoralization of the people when they would be left without their leader. The solution that God proposes is an unusual one. He says "Now therefore write ye this song for you, and teach thou it to the children of Israel; and put it in their mouths, that this song may be a witness for me against the children of Israel. For when I shall have brought them into the land which I swore unto their fathers, flowing with milk and honey; and they shall have eaten their fill, and waxen fat; and turned unto other gods, and served them, and despised Me, and broken my covenant; then it shall come to pass, when many evils are come upon them, then this song shall testify before them as a witness; for it shall not be forgotten out of the mouths of their seed; for I know their imagination how they do even now, before I have brought them into the land which I swore'" (31:19–21).

This undertaking evidently includes Joshua, for God says, "now therefore, write *ye* this song for you." But immediately following, there is a return to the singular pronoun as the Deity continues, "and teach *thou* it the children of Israel" (31:19) (italics added).

Initially, the only purpose mentioned for the theophany was that God might give Joshua a charge, the necessary authority and encouragement for his coming role (31:14). Yet in the actual enactment of the scene, the subject matter deals mainly with the directive about the song.

Another curious detail in the words spoken by the Deity is the phrase, "write ye this song *for you*" (italics added). Was not the song to be in behalf of the Deity Himself so that it might serve as a witness *for Him* against the Children of Israel? Why then the words *for you*? From the perspective of Moses himself, was this expression an unconscious acknowledgment that the wish for writing the song did indeed come *from him* and was to serve some need of his own?

This whole situation has a quality of strangeness. Associating the Deity with the command to write a song, no matter how worthy the purpose, seems quite out of character even for a relationship as unusual and intimate as that between Moses and God. This sudden desire for a poetic form of expression must have been unacceptable to Moses on some level, and thus the command had to be attributed to the Deity.

The charge to Joshua comes later, after the song has been completed. "So Moses wrote this song the same day and taught it to the children of Israel. And *he* gave Joshua the son of Nun a charge, and said: 'Be strong and of good courage; for thou shalt bring the children of Israel into the land which I swore unto them; and I will be with thee' " (31:23) (italics added).

Ostensibly it is God Who thus exhorts the future leader of Israel, but viewed grammatically, the antecedent of *he* is Moses, suggesting that he himself is the speaker (31:22–23). Moreover, an interval must have elapsed since the time of the theophany in the tent, the song having already been written and taught to the Children of Israel. Clearly, some displacement of time and place had occurred here. Commentators point out that the charge to Joshua logically should have followed the command for the two men to appear in the tent (3:14), but no explanation is given for the displacement.

It is suggested here that the confusing details in the text may again inadvertently reveal a reluctance on the part of Moses to yield his place of leadership to Joshua, especially in the hallowed area of the tent and through the words of the Deity Himself. Instead, the content of the theophany is diverted from Joshua to Moses and the song he is to write. Moreover, although the commandment seemingly included both men, Joshua evidently does not participate in this creative activity, for the text says, "So *Moses* wrote this song" (31:22) (italics added). Joshua is thus almost lost sight of in the scene, being only barely acknowledged by the occasional use of the pronoun *ye*. And when the charge is finally given, both the speaker and the locale are ambiguous.

Moses may not only have unconsciously been pushing Joshua aside but also fending off the approaching hour of death by this additional task that God Himself was now imposing on him. It may be as a defense against these impulses, unacceptable to his superego, that the unrealistic statement is made: "So Moses wrote this song the same day, and taught it the children of Israel" (31:22). For if the whole matter took only one day, then Moses wasn't actually being guilty of seeking ways to postpone the time of his death.

The inconsistencies involved in the above verses may also point to conflictful feelings in Moses about writing the song. Clearly, he wished to do so but seems to have had some superego pressures against undertaking this project. It may be that the creative process involved in such an endeavor was unconsciously perceived by Moses as a forbidden activity, an act of creation that was the sole prerogative of God Himself, the creator of all things. The recording of his people's history and the inscribing of the laws were necessary activities performed by Moses in his role of leader. But could he allow himself that more personal and creative form of expression, the writing of a song? Seemingly, only when commanded by God and in the service of God could such an activity be undertaken.

From earliest years, Moses had tended to think of himself as being inarticulate. At the theophany of the burning bush, his initiation into the service of God, Moses had pleaded "slowness of tongue" in an effort to avoid being sent on the mission for which the Deity was calling him (Exod. 4:10). As suggested in my study of this event, Moses in his childhood had to deal with forbidden competitive feelings in relation to his older brother Aaron, of whom God says, "I know that he can speak well" (Exod. 4:14). In that first theophany such feelings were dealt with and compensated for along positive lines by making Aaron into a supportive figure. He was to stand at the side of Moses and ostensibly speak for him in a time of need. Actually, Aaron generally served more as the silent partner, for in reality situations Moses rarely seemed to suffer from the "slowness of tongue" that he subjectively feared. It may be that the very presence of Aaron served as a form of reassurance for the younger brother that his ambivalent feelings had not harmed his sibling.

On other occasions too, as noted earlier in these studies, there were situations when Moses unconsciously associated the power of speech with forbidden feelings of omnipotence, dangerously related to competitive attitudes to the Deity Himself and thus to be avoided.

Now, at the close of his life, the suppressed desire within Moses for a creative experience in the free use of verbal expression overcomes its inhibition and finds fulfillment in the writing of the song. In the words of the aged Goethe, which Reik tellingly quotes in terms of himself, "Late resounds what early sounded" (Reik 1959, 50).

For the aged Moses, the time for the realization of this wish was now more favorable. Since the command to write the song had come from God Himself, there could be no question of competitiveness with the Deity. But even now, Moses had to face similar feelings in relation to Joshua, the son figure who was to displace him. The latter is drawn briefly into the scene during the theophany but soon becomes a silent partner, as did Aaron before him, and it is Moses who writes the song and teaches it to the people.

This activity may have met several needs of Moses at this time. It delayed the hour of his death. It also provided the leader with another opportunity to impress on the people the importance of keeping the covenant with the Deity through obedience to His laws, a motive close indeed to the heart of Moses.

As noted in "The Background to Deuteronomy" (chapter 18), Higher Biblical Criticism, for the most part, regards the Song of Moses as coming from another time and place, although its source is uncertain. Its appearance at this point in the biblical narrative is attributed to the work of an editor or redactor and is regarded as interfering with the continuity of the text. And indeed, if an unconscious motive of Moses was to delay the onward movement of events, such as his approaching death, it could have such an effect. One must wonder, however, why it is more reasonable to assume that another person, at a different time and place, would be more likely to write such a song, rather than Moses himself, who was in the midst of the situation that motivated it.

Following the episode of the song, there is a puzzling, seemingly repetitive reference to the writing down of the Law and turning its care over to the Levites. A somewhat ambiguous instruction is added this time. "Moses commanded the Levites, that bore the ark of the covenant of the Lord, saying: 'Take this book of the Law, and *put it by the side of the ark of the covenant* of the Lord your God, that it may be there *for a witness against thee*'" (31:25). (italics added). It had already been stated that the Law had been handed over to the "sons of Levi, that bore the ark of the covenant of the Lord" (31:9) Ostensibly, they had placed this valued object *inside* the ark at that time. Why then the instruction in the later reference to put the Law by *the side* of the ark?

It seems reasonable to assume that this second time, the word *Law* must have referred specifically to the Song of Moses, since it was the song that was to be used as a witness. Does this strangely worded directive, puzzling to scholars, reflect again the hesitancy of Moses to give his own personal creation the same honored position *within* the ark which was accorded to the rest of the Law? At the same time, does he *wish* to do so and thus settles the conflict by a compromise, putting the song at the side of the ark?

A further detail regarding the handing down of the Law, this time involving Joshua, also may reveal unconscious factors within Moses, indicating how emotionally significant these final ceremonials were to him. Both occasions that refer to the writing down of the Law and turning it over to the sons of Levi follow a scene in which Joshua is charged "in the eyes of all Israel" to take over the leadership and is assured that God would be with him (31:7–9, 31:23–26). Both of these times the attention moves from Joshua, the newly appointed leader, to another subject of importance, the Law, which was representative of Moses himself. Joshua is thus overshadowed by the spiritual heritage of the departing leader, which is entrusted to the tutelage and guardianship of the Levites, who are the true son figures of Moses.

To the strictly logical minds of those readers for whom the manifest aspects of reality are all-convincing, this kind of analysis may seem implausible. But to those who are attuned to the undertones and overtones of the biblical text, with its tendency to ambiguities and the significance of its sequences, this method of interpretation will not seem surprising. As mentioned earlier in these studies, much of human thinking is accompanied by a continuous current of unconscious fantasy, which may be involved with feelings we are not ready to acknowledge consciously but which seek discharge in their own way. When such influences manifest themselves in repetitive patterns, their significance cannot be ignored if the meaning of the communication is to be understood.

Content of the Song of Moses

Chapter 32 of Deuteronomy consists almost entirely of the Song of Moses, as this ode is familiarly known. Regardless of what other factors may have been involved in the production of the song, its tone, mood, and spirit express admirably the purpose for which it was written—a warning and exhortation to the people, dramatically depicting future disasters in the event of their sinful behavior during their life in Canaan.

The song is introduced to the Children of Israel in the last verses of the preceding chapter: "'Assemble unto me all the elders of your tribe, and your officers, that I may speak these words in their ears, and call heaven and earth to witness against them.' And Moses spoke in the ears of all the assembly of Israel the words of this song, until they were finished" (31:28–30).

The future is depicted in the song as though it were a reality that had already come to pass. Some critics thus assume that these verses must have been written at a much later date, perhaps after the Babylonian exile, hundreds of years after the Mosaic Era. However, this style of presentation could indeed have been used purposely to heighten the dramatic effect of the message. As the scholar Kaufmann points out, threats of disaster, especially the punishment of exile, which was a common consequence of defeat in war, were so prevalent in this type of literature that the events dealt with cannot be interpreted as reflecting historical reality (Kaufmann 1960, 204–205).

The opening words testify to the expansion of spirit within Moses as he now gives expression in the fullness of his feelings: "Give ear, ye heavens, and I will speak;/ And let the earth hear the words of my mouth./ My doctrine shall drop as the rain,/ My speech shall distil as the dew;/ For I will proclaim the name of the Lord;/ Ascribe ye greatness unto our God/" (32:1–3).

The song consists of forty-three verses. The content, though voiced in soaring eloquence, is along familiar lines. It is concerned with the goodness of God and, by contrast, the ingratitude of Israel. It anticipates the Children of Israel's future misconduct, a situation that Moses fervently wishes to help them avoid by confronting them with the evils that will be the consequences of their behavior, especially the sin of straying after false gods. The song describes movingly how God had selected Israel from among the nations as His inheritance, a people who belonged to Him in a special sense. It refers to the days in the wilderness, speaking of Israel as *Jacob* and relating how God "found him in the desert,/ And in the waste, a howling wilderness;/ . . . He made him ride in the high places of the earth./ And he did eat the fruitage of the fields;/ . . . But Jeshurun waxed fat, and kicked—/ . . . They roused Him to jealousy with strange gods,/ With abominations did they provoke Him . . ./ Of the Rock that begot thee,/ thou was unmindful,/ And didst forget God that bore thee (32:10–18).

But when Israel would be at its lowest ebb of despair, having suffered at the hands of its enemies, God would again come to its rescue. Then the people would understand that the gods in whom they had trusted were *no-gods*. The Deity declares, "See now that I, even I, am He,/ and there is no god with Me; . . . And there is none that can deliver out of My hand" (32:39). The song ends triumphantly with the verse beginning, "Sing aloud, O ye nations, of His people;/ For He doth avenge the blood of his servants" (32:43). Even the idol-worshipping peoples are called on to rejoice in the deliverance of Israel, for it was clear, even to them, the song implies, that the God of Israel is powerful in His deeds, unlike the *no-gods* they worship. The theme of the song conveys again the fear of Moses that the people would go astray without his leadership and only the mercy of God would eventually save them.

Was there also indirect rebuke to the Deity for exposing Israel to this danger by removing Moses as a leader at this inopportune time? And did this unconscious reproach have to be atoned for by an even greater emphasis on the power and righteousness of God, Who would eventually come to the rescue? The underlying protest at his coming death is drowned out near the beginning of the song as Moses assures himself that what God had decreed was right and just. The poem declares, "The Rock, His work is perfect;/ For all his ways are justice;/ A God of faithfulness and without iniquity,/ Just and right is He" (32:4).

Antiphonal in tone to the righteousness of God, there is also a strong undercurrent of anger in the song, which finds expression in the anticipated wickedness of the Children of Israel. The Deity had also given emphasis to this aspect at the time the commandment was given to write the song: "for I know their imagination how they do even now, before I have brought them into the land which I swore" (31:21). The future is predicted on the basis of the past.

Viewing this attitude on the part of God as a projection of Moses himself, one must assume that the leader was reluctant to accept the feelings of anger as part of himself. This intrapsychic struggle between anger and love can be understood as the consequence of a demanding superego within himself. His anger at the Children of Israel because of their lapses in the moral standards he set up for them may also have reflected a similar emotion against himself because he had not been able to hold them more firmly to his teachings.

The punishment Moses foretells about the future fate of the Children of Israel is portrayed with fiery eloquence, as though his followers had already been guilty of those heinous sins, rather than viewing these in anticipation of the future. One notes here a certain flexibility in the sense of time. A feeling of the continuity of history, the past as a living present, may have created within Moses a foreboding about the future as flowing irresistibly in a given direction on the basis of the past. Only by a conscious effort on the part of the people, and with the help of God, could that predicted future be changed. Then only would come God's forgiveness and the restoration of Israel to its position as the beloved of God, while the perverse nations, who had been the instrument of Israel's punishment, would be brought low.

If Moses felt verbally inhibited, he must have experienced a profound release from those bonds in the writing and delivery of the song. The pent-up emotions associated with his anxiety and fears for the future of the Children of Israel, his anger at their anticipated wrongdoings, and finally, his love and concern for them, find expression in the striking metaphors of the verses, the fiery zeal evoked by the power of words as well as the message. The rationale for presenting the material in this form, that it would be better remembered in its poetic cadence, does indeed have psychological validity. God says, "teach thou it the children of Israel; put it in their mouths, that this song may be a witness for Me against the children of Israel" (31:19).

It is of interest that at the conclusion of teaching the song Joshua is again briefly brought into the scene. But this time he is referred to as *Hoshea*, the name by which he was known as a youth. The text says, "And Moses came and spoke all the words of this song in the ears of the people, he and Hoshea, the son of Nun" (32:44). Is Joshua belatedly being mentioned here because of a twinge of conscience on the part of Moses? Did God not also include him in the command to write the song?

But why is the future leader of Israel here being called by the name of Hoshea? Did Moses, at this point, prefer to think of his successor in the image of the beloved youth who had faithfully ministered to him many years ago, rather than the stalwart military leader of the present, who was about to displace him? An insight into his human weaknesses lends credibility to Moses as a real person and makes even more astonishing the greatness of his achievments and the validity of his moral strivings.

The Blessing of the Tribes

The final duty that remained for Moses before ascending Mount Nebo to his death was the blessing of the tribes. This ceremonial followed the traditional patriarchal custom of a father toward his children as they gathered around his deathbed. The Children of Israel represented the family of Moses.

The blessing of the leader is modeled after that of Jacob for his twelve sons, the eponymous fathers of the tribes (Gen. 49). It is poetic in form like the latter and similarly prophetic in content, picturing the people of Israel as settled in their future home, the Promised Land.

Higher Biblical Criticism for the most part disclaims the Mosaic origin of the poem, since it describes conditions after the death of Moses. Scholars say that the language is difficult to categorize because of its antiquity, its many corruptions, and its epigrammatic style. On orthographic grounds, the poem has been placed by some scholars in the eleventh century B.C. (*EJ* 1972, 14:1580). Samdmel (1963) sums up the situation in a brief footnote: "The blessings are in context ascribed to Moses, but they are of unknown authorship and date, though presumably from a very early time" (pp. 400ff.). It is conceded however that the actual words of blessing by Moses over the tribes, contained within the larger structure of the poem, constitute the oldest part.

Within the frame of reference of this study, the emphasis will be on the psychological significance of the blessings in empathy with the perspective of Moses himself and his relationship with the various tribes as he might have perceived them at this point in his life. And, remarkably, it will be seen that from this viewpoint, one naturally assumed by the great commentators of old, from Talmudic times through the Middle Ages, the blessings have convincing psychological validity as the expression of the great leader himself. Moses, the human being as we have come to know him, reveals familiar ways of thinking and feeling in these final words to his followers. The hitherto nondescript mass of people known as the Children of Israel take on more specific features in their tribal identity as Moses recalls their past and predicts their future. While the content is, for the most part, presented in brief and often cryptic metaphoric language, largely associated with the personal histories of the eponymous fathers, it does nevertheless add color and distinctiveness to the specific tribes.

The mystery of the prophetic tone in which the blessings are presented is one for which there is no ready answer. Blessing and prophecy are generally linked in the biblical pattern. The projected image of the geographic location of the tribes as it is to take place in Canaan belongs to that prophetic category. However, it is not implausible that Moses might have had a hand in the preparatory phase of these plans. The land and its features must have been familiar to him (Num. 34), and it is not unlikely that he and Joshua, probably together with some of the elders of the tribes, had taken counsel on this matter. The actual distribution of the land west of the Jordan is described in the book of Joshua (14:1–2).

Chapter 33 of Deuteronomy consists entirely of the Blessing of Moses. It begins, "And this is the blessing wherewith Moses the man of God blessed the children of Israel before his death." There are introductory words about how God had repeatedly revealed Himself to His people and His love for them. It was because of this love that He gave them commandments through Moses. The blessings over the individual tribes then begin.

The sequence in which the tribes are named starts in accordance with the order of birth of their eponymous fathers, as did the earlier blessings of the Patriarch Jacob. However, deviations from this order soon appear, as will be evident. The events associated with the lives of the progenitors overflow broadly into the description of the tribes as though there was little distinction between the two entities.

In a large measure the blessings of Moses bear striking similarities to those of Jacob for his sons. It should be of special interest therefore to note any marked deviations from those earlier pronouncements and to consider the question of whether such changes may have involved the personal feelings and attitudes of the leader either toward the founder or the group called by his name. There is considerable difference in the length and emotional tone of the blessings devoted to the individual tribes, a number consisting of only a few lines while others are of much longer content.

The tribe of Reuben, stemming from the oldest son of Jacob, was the first to be considered but is quickly disposed of. The blessing consists of only two lines: "Let Reuben live, and not die/

The Moses of Deuteronomy 379

In that his men become few" (33:6). The Reubenites were already diminished in number and their future location east of the Jordan would be a hostile environment for them. And as it happened, during the time of David much of the Reubenite territory was taken over by the Moabites.

Moses could not have felt any special warmth toward the memory of Reuben, the first-born son of Jacob. Although endowed with all the advantages and dignity of that status, he became the wayward and unstable one, guilty of "defiling the couch of his father" by sleeping with the latter's concubine, Bilhah. He had acted out the oedipal conflict instead of mastering it. That such an example was not conducive to the future good of the progeny is the implication of his story. Survival was the basic need of the Reubenites and for that eventuality Moses prayed.

The blessing for the tribe of Judah follows immediately upon that of Reuben, although Judah was the fourth son of Jacob and was blessed in that order by the Patriarch. The question then arises of why the more usual procedure was not followed by Moses. It can be assumed that some other influence affected the situation. Perhaps Judah, the eponymous father of the tribe, had something in common with Reuben, his older brother, and this association of ideas was a determining factor in the sequence. It is not uncommon for this principle of mental functioning to take precedence over chronology in the biblical narrative. What this connecting link between Judah and Reuben may have been will be suggested as the study proceeds.

It should be of interest to note the striking contrast in the blessing of the Patriarch for his son Judah and that of Moses for the tribe that bore his name. Jacob refers to Judah as having the strength of a lion, as one who would be feared by his enemies. "Judah, thee shall thy brethren praise," Jacob declared. "Thy hand shall be on the neck of thine enemies;/ Thy father's sons shall bow before thee./ Judah is a lion's whelp;/ . . . The sceptre shall not depart from Judah./ Nor the ruler's staff from beneath his feet" (Gen. 49:8–10).

On the other hand, the blessing of Moses for this tribe is singularly lacking both in length and enthusiasm. There are a mere four lines of verse: "And this for Judah, and he said: 'Hear,

Lord, the voice of Judah,/ And bring him in unto his people;/ His hands shall contend for him,/ And Thou shalt be a help against his adversaries" (33:7).

These words are enigmatic and difficult to interpret. The prayer that Judah should be "brought in unto his people" sounds as though the tribe had been estranged from the rest of the Children of Israel. And why should this group be presented as though it were in a state of weakness and thus in need of special help from the Deity? The tribe of Judah was the largest in size among the twelve tribes of Israel. It occupied a position of strength and prestige in the tribal organization. When the Children of Israel were on the move, the tribe of Judah, flanked by Issachar and Zebulun, marched at the head of the host. During an encampment, they had an honored position along the eastern border of the Tabernacle (Num. 2:3–9).

Nor can the words of Moses be understood as prophetic of the future. The tribe of Judah was destined to take a leading role in the life of the nation. From its progeny were to come the most memorable kings of Israel, David and Solomon. One must wonder then what motivated this blessing? It was hardly a glowing tribute to the prestige and power of the largest tribe of Israel.

The blessing may be more meaningful when applied to Judah himself. An interplay of associations between thoughts of the individual and the group, so characteristic of biblical thinking, is especially applicable to the blessing of the twelve tribes, each so closely related to the lives of their eponymous fathers. Within that frame of reference, the implication is that it was *Judah, the individual*, who was separated from his people, and the plea is that *he* should be "brought in unto them again." The ambiguity of the wording may unconsciously serve to disguise some personal emotional involvement on the part of Moses. The brevity of the blessing may be indicative of a disapproving attitude regarding events in the life of Judah, which are here transferred to the group as a whole.

The question therefore arises: What was there about the story of Judah that could have set off reverberations within Moses, activating associations of a painful kind?

This fourth son of Jacob seems to have been a person of great vitality and a sense of adventure. He hobnobbed with friendly Canaanites from the villages of Adullam and Timnah, taking part in the sheepshearing festivities with his friend Hirah, the Adullamite. It was in the latter's village that he met and married the daughter of a woman named Shua. In due time she bore him three sons. After the death of his wife, Judah unwittingly had a liaison with his widowed daughter-in-law, Tamar, who had disguised herself as a harlot. It was a preconceived plan on her part for the purpose of reminding Judah that he had neglected to perform his duty to arrange a levirate marriage for her with his third son, Shelah, whose two older brothers, her previous husbands, had died.

The story of Judah and Tamar was a dramatic one of sexual misadventure. It was also significant, however, for revealing the strength of Judah's integrity in a difficult situation. He acknowledged his wrongdoing when confronted with the evidence and made the necessary reparation (Gen. 38).

Moses may have regarded Judah as having strayed from the fold, as it were, because of his alliances with non-Israelitish women. Since members of a kinship group were regarded as having certain qualities or characteristics in common (Pedersen 1926, 48), the tribe of Judah as a whole may have been associated in the mind of Moses with alien influences. And indeed tradition has it that early in its history this tribe had occupied a rather lowly status because it contained a larger non-Israelitish element among its descendants than any other tribe (*EJ* 1972, 14:1550). Realistically, however, in those far-off Patriarchal times, the sons of Jacob had few other sources from which to choose wives. Moreover, the tribe of Judah had long ago proved its strength and loyalty, a fact not noted in the tone and wording of the blessing pronounced by Moses. His response may have stemmed largely from unconscious sources, the evocation of associated feelings and fantasies rising from repression, as will be indicated.

Moses, too, had been separated from his people, had lived among strangers, and married one of them, a daughter of the Midianites. Judah, with his easy-going sexuality, may have represented a repressed aspect of Moses himself and his own long-rejected sexual impulses. If so, his view of the tribe as a whole could have been colored by feelings of ambivalence. He, who largely ignored his own sons, who were also from a non-Israelitish mother, may have found it difficult to accept descendants of sons of Judah from similar alliances, even though the passage of time and the force of logic made such feelings inappropriate.

The common tie between Judah and Reuben in the mind of Moses could have been that of sexual misdemeanor, the most serious aspect of which was Reuben's incestuous behavior with his father's concubine, Bilhah, and Judah's affair with his widowed daughter-in-law, Tamar. As noted earlier, the taint of incest on any level must have been especially abhorrent to Moses. He who longed for the motherland and was denied access to it, must have been involved in this human dilemma of forbidden but repressed desires and struggled with it through projection and displacement.

A more realistic reason may have also played a role in the unenthusiastic tone of Moses' blessing for the tribe of Judah. The very fact that it was indeed the largest and strongest of the tribes may have caused him some concern. For it was the tribe of Levi that had been entrusted with the leadership of a different kind, the spiritual guidance of the nation. The Levites were representatives of the Deity, the group that was to keep Israel as a distinctive people, set aside from the other nations for a specific purpose. Did Moses fear that the tribe of Judah might become a stronger influence in the development of the nation than the Levites, significant of a struggle between the material aspects of life and the spiritual goals of the people, goals to which Moses had dedicated his life? If so, the future of Judah had to be presented as precarious, threatened by adversaries, "contending with his hands," an emphasis on the physical rather than the spiritual side of the struggle. Only with the help of God, the blessing of Moses suggested, could Judah be brought "in unto his people," restored spiritually to the fold of the Children of Israel.

In terms of their actual future destiny, it was the tribe of Judah that gave its name to the descendants of Israel. Its people indeed had to learn to "contend with their hands" against their adversaries. They were often isolated in the midst of hostile forces. Their source of strength had to be twofold—within their own hands and through their faith in the Deity.

It is evident then that the figure of Judah had different

meanings for those two great father figures, Jacob and Moses, each in his own historic epoch, especially in their attitudes towards sons. To Jacob, whose own sexuality found ample expression, the birth of sons meant the fulfillment of his birthright as progenitor of a nation. Thus, for Judah, destined head of the dominant tribe of Israel, Jacob had only high praise, glorying in the strength of this son and predicting great things for him. To Moses, whose task was the molding of a people in the spirit of the Mount Sinai covenant, Judah represented those conflictful aspects of life with which the leader himself had to contend in his own struggles for sublimation.

In regard to the tribe of Simeon, a puzzling situation exists in relation to the blessing of Moses. This group is completely omitted in the ceremonial. Moses blesses only eleven of the twelve tribes of Israel, not even mentioning the Simeonites.

The reason for this surprising omission is not explained in the text, thus augmenting its mystifying effect. Since the members of this tribe were ostensibly a part of the assembly being addressed by Moses, it is difficult to understand that he would so blatantly *forget* them in his blessing, not even referring to the name of the tribe.

Let us go back to the history of the eponymous father. Simeon was the second son of Jacob. In the Patriarchal blessing, he and his brother Levi, the next in age, are mentioned together by their father and castigated for the violence of their behavior in the affair of Shechem, the Canaanite town where Jacob had settled and hoped to live in peace with his neighbors. But an unfortunate event changed this plan. The daughter of the family, Dinah, alone among so many brothers, innocently went forth to meet the "daughters of the land." "And Shechem the son of Hamor the Hivite, the prince of the land, saw her; and he took her, and lay with her, and humbled her" (Gen. 34:2). He then asked for her hand in marriage, but instead, in a clever strategy Simeon and Levi, to avenge this dishonor of their sister, subjected the entire town to severe punishment. In reply to their father's angry reproach, they said only, "Should one deal with our sister as with a harlot?" (Gen. 34:31).

It was this violence that Jacob remembered in his final words to these two sons, again severely reproaching them: "Simeon and

Levi are brethren;/ Weapons of violence their kinship./ Let my soul not come into their council;/ Unto their assembly let my glory not be united;/ For in their anger they slew men,/ And in their self-will they houghed oxen./ Cursed be their anger, for it was fierce,/ And in their wrath, for it was cruel;/ I will divide them in Jacob,/ And scatter them in Israel" (Gen. 49:5–7).

Whereas both sons are subjected to this strongly expressed displeasure, the destinies of the two tribes called by their names are quite different, as we shall see.

Although the Simeonites did not have an outstanding position in the tribal organization of Israel, they were nevertheless a recognized and distinctive unit, one of the twelve tribes. There is no indication that this group was discredited because of excessive violence, as their progenitor had been. Therefore, it must have been some other reason, something very disturbing to Moses, that could cause him to omit this tribe in his farewell blessing. And indeed the Simeonites were involved in a situation that might have brought about such an eventuality. The men of this tribe played a particularly conspicuous role in the Baal-peor affair, a happening that caused the leader much anguish of spirit and which brought severe punishment to the Children of Israel (Num. 25:1ff) (Cohen 1947, 1147).

As will be recalled, a number of the men of Israel were seduced by Moabitish (and Midianitish?) women during the time when the Children of Israel were encamped at Shittim, probably the very site on the Plains of Moab where Moses was now addressing them. The men were not only enticed into forbidden sexual practices but took part in orgies associated with the worship of the pagan god, the Baal-peor (Num. 25:1–9).

A plague was visited on the Children of Israel as punishment for this shameful episode. In the census taken shortly thereafter, it was noted that the Simeonites were now the smallest in number among the tribes. The implication is that many of them were stricken by the plague because of their involvement in the Baal-peor affair. Commentators suggest that since their location in the encampment was on the south side, they were the closest to the Moabite border and thus most exposed to the seduction by the women of that area (Hertz 1936, 682).

For Moses, the Baal-peor apostasy must have been a shocking

experience. It involved two acts of the most heinous kind—sexual misbehavior and idolatrous practices. The event had taken place so recently that its painful effects must still have been fresh in the mind of the leader. To give full vent to his feelings might have been too devastating for the remaining members of that decimated tribe. Or perhaps Moses was too fearful of the intensity of his own anger to allow it open expression. So he handled the difficult situation by an act of omission. This method was not a new one for him, as we have seen. Even his own sons had no place in his farewell blessings, either publicly or privately. As for the Simeonites themselves, perhaps it was easier for them to be forgotten than openly castigated for the sins of the group as a whole. Talmudic rabbis tended to agree that Moses omitted the blessing of the Simeonites because of the sin they had committed at Shittim (Ginzberg 1909–1938, 3:457, 6:155 n. 924).

In an effort to ameliorate the situation, the rabbis expressed an opinion that the blessing for the Simeonites was included in the one for Judah. This explanation seemed a logical conclusion, since the two groups were to share a common territory within Canaan. The tribe of Simeon had no separate geographic locality. They were given thirteen unconnected cities, each with surrounding villages and open lands, located in the southwestern portion of Judea. Like the tribe of Levi, they had no contiguous boundaries that defined the limits of their territory. And indeed Jacob had said in regard to Simeon and Levi, "I will divide them in Jacob,/ And scatter them in Israel" (Gen. 49:7).

However, the tribe of Simeon was not forgotten in the history of Israel. Although crowded into a corner of the territory of Judah, the Simeonites managed to preserve their tribal unity. Genealogies of Simeonite families are found in the Bible up to the end of the Kingdom of Judah (1 Chron. 4:24–43). During the period of the monarchy, however, their history was indivisibly tied to Judah (Ginzberg 1909–1938, 3:457, 6:155 n. 924; *EJ* 1972, 14:1549, 10:330).

The blessing for the tribe of Levi followed that of Judah. In spite of the displeasure expressed toward Levi as well as Simeon, in Jacob's farewell to his sons, the Levites had a quite different fate.

This tribe was chosen for special service to the Deity. They provided the priests and teachers, the workers in the Temple, all those who were responsible for maintaining the religious life of the community as commanded by the Law. The Levites thus had an opportunity to sublimate their aggressive impulses into service for God and when necessary, to fight in His name, as happened in the internal strife that followed the episode of the golden calf (Exod. 32:27).

Moses, who was also a Levite, had special ties with this group, whose functions were so close to his heart. In his blessing for the tribe, the leader refers to the Thummin and Urim, mysterious objects concealed within the breastplate of the high priest and used to cast lots for the purpose of determining the will of God in specific situations. The role of prophecy was thus fittingly associated with the Levites and the prophetic tone of Moses himself in his blessings.

The leader vividly portrays the wholehearted devotion to God demanded of the Levites. He speaks of the tribe in the familiar metaphor of an individual, as one who denies the very existence of parental ties, proof of total devotion to God. The Levite was one "who said of his father, and of his mother: 'I have not seen him;/ Neither did he acknowledge his brethren,/ Nor knew he his own children;/ For they have observed Thy word,/ And keep thy covenant./ They shall teach Jacob Thine inheritance,/ And Israel Thy law" (33:8–10).

These attitudes were characteristic of Moses himself. He also denied his parental figures by ignoring them and in his youthful fantasy of being adopted by the daughter of Pharaoh (see chapter 1).

There is a marked difference in the order of blessing between Jacob and Moses where the two youngest sons of the Patriarch, Joseph and Benjamin, are concerned. Jacob blesses them in the order of their birth, even though they are the progeny of his beloved Rachel and treasured above the others, Joseph especially being well known as the favorite. Moses, however, disregards this order of precedence and blesses the tribes of Joseph and Benjamin fourth and fifth, immediately after Reuben, Judah, and Levi. Benjamin even precedes the twin tribes of Joseph, Ephraim and Manasseh. Was the leader perhaps emulating the practice of favoring a younger son, the position occupied by Moses himself?

"And of Benjamin he said: "The beloved of the Lord shall dwell in safety by Him;/ He covereth him all the day,/ And He dwelleth between His shoulders" (33:12). The metaphor of Benjamin dwelling between the shoulders of the Deity may refer to the fact that the Temple in Jerusalem was destined to be situated in the territory of the tribe of Benjamin, against the *shoulder* of a rocky hill, with the courts of the Temple extending into the land of Judah. The blessing suggests that as Benjamin was beloved by his father, so too would the tribe be beloved by God, Whose presence was especially felt in the area of the Temple.

In the Patriarchal blessing for his youngest son, the words of Jacob are not so protective. He foresees the future tribe as being well able to take care of itself. Jacob declares, "Benjamin is a wolf that raveneth;/ In the morning he devoureth the prey,/ And at even he divideth the spoil" (Gen. 49:27).

These cryptic words may refer, in prophetic terms, to certain dramatic adventures in which the tribe of Benjamin became involved during the settlement in Canaan at the time of the Judges. A situation of conflict arose between the Benjamites and the other tribes of Israel. Although they fought valiantly, the men of Benjamin were overcome through a military strategy on the part of their opponents and lost a goodly number of their fighting force. How the decimated tribe was allowed to renew its population is graphically described in the biblical narrative (Judg. 19–21).

In regard to Joseph, the most beloved son of Jacob, the Patriarch's blessing overflowed with wishes and predictions regarding the good things of heaven and earth his descendants would enjoy. "Joseph is a fruitful vine,/ A fruitful vine by a fountain; its branches run over the wall./ The archers have dealt bitterly with him,/ And shot at him, and hated him;/ But his bow abode firm,/ And the arms of his hands were made supple,/ By the hands of the Mighty One of Jacob." Jacob also asks for him the "blessings of the breasts and of the womb, suggestive of fruitful progeny. The reference to "the archers who dealt bitterly with him" is, of course, to the brothers who hated him and whose enmity led to his being transported to Egypt.

With equal enthusiasm Moses also evokes the blessing of God on the descendants of Joseph, and the land they would inherit.

They were to be blessed with "the precious things of heaven,/ And for the precious things of the earth and the fulness thereof." The blessing is a long and glowing one, the word *precious* being used repeatedly, reflecting how precious this son of Rachel had been to his father, even some of the same expressions being used.

Moses then introduces a theme that has deeply personal associations. He asks for the tribes of Joseph "the good will of Him that dwelt in the bush;/ Let the blessing come upon the head of Joseph,/ And upon the crown of the head of him that is prince among his brethren" (33:23–26).

The expression "Him that dwelt in the bush" referred to the experience of Moses himself at the theophany of the burning bush. It indicated a close identification with Joseph, both being chosen by God for special missions. Both had been driven from the land of their birth and had suffered the trauma of totally new environments. Both shared the experience of a common background in Egypt. Joseph was a prince not only among his brethren but also in the court of Egypt, even as Moses had also once been, in terms of the biblical story. Joseph served as the connecting link between his ancestral patriarchal life in Canaan and the events that brought the Children of Israel to Egypt, leading eventually to the exodus, Mount Sinai, and the imminent return to the Promised Land.

The historic memory of Joseph must have been especially precious to Moses. In all the excitement and turmoil of the exodus an important duty was not forgotten. The text says, "And Moses took the bones of Joseph with him," for Joseph had so made his brethren promise: . . . "'and ye shall carry up my bones hence with you'" (Exod. 13:19).

The twin tribes of Ephraim and Manasseh, though the objects of those manifold blessings, practically lose their separate identities in the glowing words of Moses for their common ancestor. They are named only in the last two lines of the blessing, which explains to whom those praiseworthy words referred. "And they are the ten thousands of Ephraim,/ And they are the thousands of Manasseh" (33:17).

The blessings over the remaining tribes are brief and for the most part followed largely the tenor of thought and prophecy in the blessing of Jacob. Zebulun and Issachar are mentioned together, in contrast, but as supplementing each other. "And of Zebulun he said: Rejoice, Zebulun, in thy going out,/ And Issachar in thy tents" (33:18). Jacob's blessing was along similar lines, describing Zebulun's "going out" in terms of the tribe's future maritime activities. "Zebulun shall dwell at the shore of the sea, and he shall be a shore for ships,/ And his flank shall be upon Zidon" (Gen. 49:13).

The tribe of Issachar was portrayed as a stay-at-home people, scholarly in its pursuits. Tradition, in response to these words, pictures Zebulun metaphorically as the man of action, the merchant, helping to support Issachar, the man of learning, occupied in studying the Torah.

Regarding Gad, Moses recalls that this tribe had asked for and received land in Gilead, east of the Jordan. Their territory was larger than any occupied by the tribes west of the river. But while the people of Gad cultivated the fertile soil and pastured their flocks, they had to be ready to fend off attacks from marauding neighbors on the east, as the Ammonites and other nomadic tribes would sweep in from the desert.

The leader praises the men of Gad for crossing the Jordan with their brethren and helping in the conquest of Canaan. He depicts this tribe as possessing strength and prowess in war as well as righteousness. "And of Gad," he said, "Blessed is He that enlargeth Gad;/ He dwelleth as a lioness,/ . . . He executed the righteousness of the Lord,/ And his ordinances with Israel" (33:20–21).

In contrast, the blessing of Jacob for his son Gad is largely a play on words. He says, "Gad, a troop shall troop upon him;/ But he shall troop upon their heels" (Gen. 49:19). The words are descriptive of the neighboring tribes who raid his borders and the prediction that the Gadites would successfully repel them.

Regarding Dan, the words of Moses are again few. "And of Dan, he said: Dan is a lion's whelp,/ That leapeth forth from Bashan" (33:22). Like of cattle of Bashan, the Danites were strong and agile. The tribe had to strugggle for survival in the territory alloted to them in southern Judea. They were squeezed between the borders of Judah, Ephraim, and Benjamin. Their possessions were contested by the Canaanites, who tried to force them back from the coastal plain, which made up part of their territory, up into the foothills of the Judean hills (Judg. 1:34). The tribe of Dan was finally compelled to seek new territory and moved to the north, where they formed the most northern outpost of Israel, the boundaries of which are often described as reaching from Dan to Beersheba.

Jacob also speaks prophetically of the tribe of Dan and its struggles with oppressive foes impinging upon them. He says, "Dan shall be a serpent in the way,/ A horned snake in the path./ That biteth the horse's heels,/ So that his rider falleth backward" (Gen. 49:17–18). In their warfare with the Philistines, who used iron chariots and horses, the Danites had to resort to skill and cunning but without avail. It was in the days of servitude to their conquerors that the heroic stories of Samson, the Danite, took place (Judg. 13–16). It may be in reference to this folk hero of the future that Jacob begins his blessing with the more positive statement, "Dan shall judge his people,/ As one of the tribes of Israel" (Gen. 49:16).

The blessing of Moses for Naphtali, while also brief, was warm and positive in tone. "And of Naphtali he said: 'O Naphtali, satisfied with favour,/ And full with the blessing of the Lord;/ Possess thou the sea and the south'" (33:23). The territory of Naphtali, while starting south of the Sea of Galilee, lay chiefly to the north and west of it, making up a large part of eastern Galilee, reaching to the Jordan Valley.

During the period of the Judges, the men of Naphtali led the Children of Israel in the battles against the Canaanites, helping to secure the freedom of that important area under the leadership of Barak and the prophetess Deborah.

The blessing of Jacob for Naphtali may be understood prophetically regarding that historic event. The Patriarch says, "Naphtali is a hind let loose:/ He giveth goodly words" (Gen. 49:21). A hind is noted for its nimbleness and agility, as were the men of the tribe in battle. The *goodly words* may pertain to the triumphant Song of Deborah that followed the victory in the battle (Judg. 5).

Asher is the last of the tribes to be blessed. Jacob said of him, "As for Asher, his bread shall be fat;/ And he shall yield royal dainties" (Gen. 49:20). The territory assigned to the tribe was along the seacoast, offering opportunities for profitable maritime trade, which could provide delicacies fit for royalty.

From Moses, Asher also receives a goodly and even more lengthy blessing. "And of Asher, he said: Blessed be Asher above sons;/ Let him be the favored of his brethren,/ And let him dip his foot in oil,/ Iron and brass shall be thy bars/ And as thy days, so shall thy strength be" (33:24–25).

The reference to oil probably has to do with the abundance of olive trees in the area. The puzzling expression about iron and brass bars may suggest that the territory required such protection from enemies (Hertz 1936, 655). Asher's land was in the north and thus exposed to invading forces from that direction. Its long coastline could also make it vulnerable to attack from the sea. In actuality, the tribe led a comparatively tranquil existence and was able to develop its agricultural and maritime trade potentialities.

In considering the rather puzzling question of what factors determined the order for the sequence in the blessings both of Jacob and Moses, two conflicting influences seem to have been at work. First, there was the traditional one of primogeniture, which endows the oldest son with the role of leadership as well as a double portion of material possessions. Second, the tendency to favor a younger son is also evident, a pattern frequently found in the biblical narratives. The latter choice is generally motivated by the personal feelings of the father figure or leader. The spiritual value of the blessing was accounted of far greater significance than the material goods (Patai 1959, 221–28).

Moses on Mount Nebo

The Last Theophany

 CHAPTER SEVENTEEN

IN SPITE OF the long-expected summons, the ascent of Moses to Mount Nebo comes with a startling suddenness. This time there is no voice from God telling him the moment is at hand. Seemingly, Moses is guided by his own inner voice.

The blessing of the tribes has been completed. Moses now takes his departure in silence. There are no personal words of farewell to his people or to those especially close to him. There is nothing in the text of how the assembly must have felt as they saw the familiar figure of their leader turn away from them and begin his ascent of the mountain slope. Yet Moses must have done so in the sight of all Israel. Otherwise they would not have known what had become of him.

The death of Moses is recorded in the last chapter of Deuteronomy. The text says, "And Moses went up from the plains of Moab unto mount Nebo to the top of Pisgah that is over against Jericho. And the Lord showed him all the land, even Gilead as far as Dan; and all Nephtali, and the land of Ephraim and Manasseh, and all the land of Judah as far as the hinder sea;

and the South and the Plain, even the valley of Jericho the city of palm-trees, as far as Zoar. And the Lord said unto him: 'This is the land which I swore unto Abraham, unto Isaac, and unto Jacob, saying: I will give it unto thy seed; I have caused thee to see it with thine eyes, but thou shalt not go over thither.' So Moses the servant of the Lord died there in the land of Moab, according to the word of the Lord [literally, *mouth of the Lord*]. And he was buried in the valley of the land of Moab over against Beth-peor; and no man knoweth of his sepulchre unto this day. And Moses was a hundred and twenty years old when he died; his eye was not dim, nor his natural force abated. And the children of Israel wept for Moses in the plains of Moab thirty days; so the days of weeping in the mourning for Moses were ended" (34:1-8).* Immediately thereafter, the active life of the people is resumed. Joshua takes over the leadership.

In this scene before his death Moses says not a word. The time for protest is over. It is God Who speaks, pointing out that He has kept His promise to the Patriarchal ancestors. But why, one must wonder, was it necessary for the Deity to repeat on this occasion, those painful, well remembered words "but thou shalt not go over thither"? There was hardly any likelihood at this point that Moses was still beseeching God to let him "go over thither."

It is suggested here that these may be words of regret and resignation going through the mind of Moses himself, but experienced as coming from the Deity. The superego of Moses may have become indistinguishable from the voice of God. After viewing the Promised Land spread before him in the clear mountain air, spectacular in its beauty, Moses is again reminded of the sad fact, "but thou shalt not go over thither."

One level of gratification is now granted to Moses before his death. He is finally allowed to see the motherland from the mountaintop in Moab, where he was standing. On several previous occasions, this promise is not only referred to but is given as a command. (Num. 27:12–13, Deut. 3:27). And now, at this final moment, we are told that "the Lord showed him all the land" (34:1). It seems that only at God's command and under the tutelage of the Deity Himself, could Moses allow himself the fulfillment of even this wish, a substitute for the deeper longing to en-

---

*All biblical references in this chapter, unless otherwise noted, are to the book of Deuteronomy.

ter this territory toward which his goals had so long been directed.

The wish *to see* is related to the wish *to know,* both in its sexual and sublimated forms. This instinctual urge, starting in infancy, has far-reaching effects through the process of sublimation, on the development of civilization itself (Abraham 1927, 208; Freud 1910, 109; 1905, 56–57, 72). The unbounded curiosity of childhood, rooted in biological urges, can lead from such primary sources to the heights of abstract thought in its most profound forms of philosophy and religion. Moses seems to have been endowed with special capacities for visualizing in symbolic forms, concepts that were of absorbing significance to him, especially at crucial points in his own psychosexual development. For Moses, whose need to see and fear of doing so seems to have been especially strong, the concept of an invisible God may have involved feelings of renunciation to an unusual degree, leading to increased spirituality (Freud 1939, 212). Phyllis Greenacre has pointed out that gifted people frequently project their inner conflicts onto cosmic forces. Especially relevant here is her statement about the need that is involved in "gaining permission from an all-powerful Father . . . for penetrations into the mysteries of the cosmic Mother" (Greenacre 1963, 18–19).

The first theophany of Moses is one in which a mystical visual occurrence takes place. It occurs when he is shepherding his flock at the foot of Mount Sinai. Moses *sees* the strange sight of the burning bush that is not consumed. His first impulse is to turn away from it, as if in fear. It is only when God calls out to him that he dares to look (Exod. 3:1–4). At a later time, when his relationship with the Deity is on a more developed basis, Moses expresses a desire *to see* the glory of God, a wish in which abstract ideas are unconsciously intermingled with more physical intimations. This wish is also granted but on an equally mystical level. He gets a fleeting glimpse of the *back* of the Deity while he himself remains protected in a cleft within the mountain slope. Here in a sense it is Mother Earth who shields him from the total, terrifying vision of the Father, but with the Deity's consent (Exod. 33:17–23).

From the height of Mount Pisgah, a name whose meaning suggests a cleft, or opening, Moses is permitted to incorporate the symbolic mother with his eyes. Talmudic legend says that Moses yielded up his spirit by receiving a kiss on the mouth from God. (Ginzberg 1909–1938, 3:473). The "uncircumsized lips" are now made holy (Exod. 6:30). Thus, briefly, Moses unites within himself both parental images, the Mother and the Father. Was this mystical experience perhaps an act of reparation for the oedipal guilt, common to childhood, of wishing to separate the parents and having each of them for himself? He could now accept both without hostility or guilt.

In his youth, Moses had longed for more exalted parents than those of his own humble Hebrew origin. His fantasy provided him with an Egyptian princess as a mother and the Pharaoh as a frightening but all-powerful father. Now at this finale of his life Moses embraces the motherland with his eyes and then closes those eyes in a symbolic embrace by the Father. His last parental images were indeed of cosmic significance. As noted above by Greenacre, this capacity for abstraction and symbolization marks the creative personality.

It is of interest that the Promised Land, as pointed out to Moses by the Deity, is not described in terms of its scenic appeal but only along factual lines, dealing largely with the extent of its territory and borders. Again, only the Deity speaks. There is no mention of how Moses felt at this long-awaited sight—the beauty of the Promised Land, with its clearly delineated bodies of blue waters, the green-forested slopes of central Canaan, the reddish-tinted low-lying hills of the southland, the long, winding line of the Jordan River descending from the foot of Mount Hermon to the depths of the Salt Sea, and the broad stretch of coastline washed by the vast waters of the "hinder sea." There is not a word in the text of all this glorious view, so vividly described by travelers who have seen it from this same vantage point. Yet it was a sight that must have moved Moses profoundly.

But to take note of the symbolic mother from the aspect of her beauty may have been forbidden to Moses. Yet the reason for seeing this view from the mountaintop was not only to enlighten and inform but to provide gratification for the leader of *the wish to see* the land in all its varied splendor. The oedipal aspect of this wish had to remain hidden.

A brief digression may be relevant here. The figure of Moses on a mountaintop overlooking the Promised Land has been compared in psychoanalytic literature to that of Freud on the height of the Acropolis, overlooking the city of Athens. On that occasion, Freud (1936) had gone through a disturbing experience, the nature of which he had not understood for a long time. Many years later, in a charming essay written as an open letter to his admired friend Romain Rolland on the occasion of the latter's seventieth birthday, Freud revealed the inner meaning of this puzzling incident (5:303–312).

In this self-analysis Freud explores what he called a state of *derealization*, a sense of unreality, while standing amid the still-majestic remains of the Parthenon, with the view of the magical city below him.

Although this experience had taken place more than three decades earlier, Freud had often been troubled by the memory, the significance of which had puzzled him for so long. Now, at the age of eighty, the man who had ushered a new vision of truth into the world, finally undertook the task of reaching some insight into that bewildering episode.

The world of antiquity, especially the cities of Rome and Athens, had long held a special fascination for Freud. They were part of his youthful dreams of travel, the hope that he might someday be able to view them with his own eyes.

Freud's self-analysis revealed that the brief period of confusion he experienced, had stemmed from unconscious feelings of guilt in relation to his father. The son had dared to achieve a degree of fulfillment that the father had never attained, a situation epitomized by the opportunity of standing where he then stood, on the famed Acropolis, viewing the city of his youthful dreams. Even though it was Freud himself who had explained the symbolism of landscapes and cities in dreams as frequently representing the female figure (1900, 356, 366), he did not grasp fully the meaning of his own experience at this point in his self-analysis. Continuing interest in this essay by other psychoanalysts (Kanzer, Schur, Abbott, Stamm, Niederland, 1969) made it possible, with the use of other biographical material, to fathom more deeply the unconscious factors that caused the temporary disturbance within Freud. It was not only a moment of unconscious oedipal triumph in relation to his father and the subsequent guilt that had created the psychological unease, the memory of which had stayed with him for so long. Preoedipal feelings relating to the mother also played a significant role.

It was Dr. Harry Slochower, in one of his several studies on the subject, who pointed out that the view of the beloved city from the sacred precincts of the Acropolis may unconsciously have reactivated in Freud an infantile experience of a forbidden voyeuristic gratification involving the mother. Slochower (1970) observes, "Like Moses, Freud had seen the Promised Land and was forbidden to enter it" (see also, Slochower, 1971). In another of his essays on this theme (1975), the same author states, "the quest for the mother, in philosophic terms, for ontology, is a quest for the Absolute, for the unconditional pleasure principle which is denied to man."

Returning to the theme of Moses on Mount Nebo, his vision of the Promised Land must also have been symbolic of the mother. However, this experience by the leader of Israel took place under quite different circumstances from that of Freud. Moses surveyed the beautiful landscape, not only with the permission of the Father but at His command, thus apparently without guilt. The maternal image could now be admired and loved. But even this moment of gratification could take place only from a distant mountaintop in a neighboring land, at a time that marked the final moments of his existence. The superego thus asserts its control over instinctual impulses, a motif significant of the whole of the biblical story.

The burial of Moses is depicted with the brevity and austerity characteristic of this literature, especially in some of its most dramatic moments. The text says, "So Moses the servant of the Lord died there in the land of Moab, according to the word of the Lord. And he was buried in the valley of the land of Moab over against Beth-peor; and no man knoweth of his sepulchre unto this day" (34:5–6).

We are not told who performed the act of burial. For the Bible to have said that God Himself did so would have been too blatantly anthropomorphic. The Hagadda, which has no such compunctions, says that God Himself did indeed bury Moses and that it was done in a grave prepared for him at the time of creation (Hertz 1936, 916). A version of this fantasy is expressed in the wording of a poet, "the angels of God upturned the sod/ And laid the dead man there" (Alexander 1818–1875, 523).

The text says that Moses was buried "in a valley." Thus a space between two heights received the body of Moses. Symbolic here of all humanity, his return is to the womb of Mother Earth, a place indeed created for him, as for all, when the earth was formed.

But why "over against Beth-peor," the site where the men of Israel had sinned with the women of Moab and committed acts of apostasy? It was also from Beth-peor that Balaam, the false prophet, had blessed the people of Israel and later conspired against them, according to Moses (Num. 23:28; 25:5, 31:16). Why did the leader choose this locality for his last theophany and final resting place? Was it perhaps to demonstrate that, as the true prophet and servant of God, Moses, the superego figure for the Children of Israel, represented the overcoming of such sins among his people, the triumph of the God of Israel over the *no-god*, Baal-peor?

There is no attempt in the enigmatic biblical text to explain who wrote the words of this final scene on the desolate mountaintop, where the two participants were the man who died there and the incorporeal God Who showed him the land and reminded him of a promise to the Patriarchal ancestors that had been kept. The most widespread tradition is that Joshua wrote this account of the death of Moses, an opinion attributed in the Talmud to Rabbi Judah (Hertz 1936, 916).

It is not unlikely, however, that Moses himself, in anticipation of the event, may have written this brief and unassuming obituary. He must have imagined himself in this situation many times, looking down from the mountain peak at the wondrous beauty of the landscape before him and again being reminded that he would never set foot on that territory himself.

Rabbi Meir, of Talmudic fame, came close to the supposition presented here, that Moses himself wrote the account of his own death. He adds that the aged leader did so amid tears, at the dictation of the Deity (Hertz 1936, 916).

One wonders why the leader of a multitude planned such a lonely death for himself. Why did he visualize his departure from this world without the comfort of a friendly human presence or the assurance that human hands would bury him with appropriate dignity? One can only conjecture.

Throughout his life Moses had experienced the reality of God as a Living Presence. He may therefore have felt that he would not actually be alone. Nor could he have wished to share those final moments with the Deity in the presence of another human being. Death for him was the last theophany. He had been alone on a mountaintop with God for long periods of time on other occasions (Exod. 24:19, 34:28). And indeed, in terms of the biblical text, Moses experienced God during those last moments as being very much with him.

There is no indication in the narrative that Moses feared death itself. His reluctance to die seemed to express more his strong ties to life, motivated by the wish to remain with his people and to enter the Promised Land with them.

It is of interest that the lively imagination of the Talmudic rabbis centered more on legends and fantasies dealing with the supplications of Moses to ward off his death than on the circumstances of the event itself. Even the angels in heaven, it was said, had joined in pleading with the Deity to avert the dreaded decree, until finally God ordered them to bring Him no more appeals from Moses because his doom had already been sealed (Ginzberg 1909–1938, 3:418–419).

It is noteworthy that in all the ceremonials of leave-taking, there was no attempt on the part of Moses to suggest any form of ritual to commemorate his own life. There were to be no birthdays or death days to hallow his memory. Even the location of his grave was to remain unknown so that, according to rabbinic explanation, his burial place would not become a shrine for worship. Although these self-effacing tendencies in Moses may indeed reflect the true humility of the leader, there may have been a deeper, more unconscious basis for this failure to memorialize himself. Moses may still have hoped, on some level of his being, irrational though it was, that he was indeed a special person and would not be subject to mortality, the common fate of man.

Perhaps the tendency to identify himself with the Deity, against which he had to struggle, carried with it the hope for immortality, a God-like attribute. If so, associated with such a fantasy, there would be unconscious competitive feelings.

It is within the context of the oedipal situation that ambivalent feelings toward the father come to the fore. It was when Moses was competitive with God in striking the rock for water at Meribah-Kadesh that the punishment of the leader was pronounced—he was not to enter the Promised Land. Moses had been guilty of putting himself in God's place by unconsciously identifying himself with the Deity in the eyes of the people while ostensibly sanctifying God (Num. 20:7–13). It is at this point that the leader is promptly reminded of his own human condition—he too would die as his contemporaries had done.

The text says that Moses died in the full strength of his manhood. Although he was one hundred twenty years old, "his eye was not dim, nor his natural force abated" (34:7). This situation is in contrast to the manner in which the Patriarchs of Israel died. Abraham, Isaac, and Jacob, were all depicted as being "old and full of days," with the clear implication that they had exhausted their life force (Gen. 25:8, 35:39, 49:33).

What significance then can be attributed to the description of Moses and his youthful vitality at the time of his death? And why do we get a seemingly contradictory image of the leader here? In preparing the people for his demise Moses tells them of his frailty, that he can no more "go out and come in" among them (31:2). At the same time we are given an image of the leader as still being in the full vigor of his manhood, experiencing sadness and frustration because he cannot cross the Jordan with his people and bring them into the Promised Land. Both aspects can have validity. The magic of symbolism joins different levels of meaning (Jones 1912, 87ff.). The death of Moses was not only a physical reality event but can also be understood symbolically in terms of his relationship to the group.

Moses is wholly understandable psychologically as a human being although an extraordinarily exceptional one. Yet in the metaphor so commonly found in the biblical literature, he is also symbolic of the group. What takes place within the psyche of Moses reflects, as in microcosm, the psychodynamics of the people as a whole. The apparent contradiction concerning the vitality of Moses at the time of his death can be attributed to the two roles he plays, as a man and as a symbol, a point that will be amplified as the study proceeds.

The death of Moses has a subtle, underlying metaphoric quality, its meaning hidden yet pervasive. The hypothesis presented here is that the death of Moses represents both his human situation as a man, for whom death is inevitable, and the mythic role he played as representative of the group as a whole. In the latter aspect, the death of Moses can be understood symbolically as a form of rebirth, a transition from one level of maturation to a higher one. This kind of transition requires a *giving up* of the old for the sake of the new. Moses died in the flesh so that his spirit (superego) might live on in his people. His death both presages and symbolizes the developmental path to be taken by the group, the submission of *instinctual strivings* associated with the oedipal conflict, such as incestuous and aggressive impulses, to the influence of the superego.

In this frame of reference, the prolonged struggle of Moses against the edict of his death can be seen as expressing the persistence of such feelings, the reluctance with which instincts give up their aims, until finally they are relinquished in favor of substitute satisfactions of a higher order. As Freud (1923) succinctly expresses this basic premise of his thinking: "The superego is the heir of the oedipus complex" (pp. 47–48). In the sense, therefore, that the death of Moses symbolizes a transitional stage, a form of rebirth, he dies with his *natural force not abated.*

Through the surrender of his oedipal wishes Moses serves as the emergent superego of the group, reborn in them through the incorporation of his image into the collective superego (Reik 1959, 165–70) (26). The unconscious wish to displace the Father is sublimated into identification with His commandments.

This acquiescence to the will of God makes it possible for the people to cross the Jordan River and enter upon their inheritance, the Promised Land of their adulthood (Roheim 1955, 4:173) (27). There they would have to function without the physical presence of the familiar father figure, their leader. The authority of the visible father would now give way to the memory of his awesome presence and the duty of obedience to his laws (Freud 1930, 136; Reik 1959, 168–69).

To Moses, being forbidden to cross the Jordan becomes equivalent to the final conquest of oedipal impulses. His physical remains, the earthly strivings, are buried in Moab, but his image and his teachings become a part of the spiritual life of his followers. His demise represents a form of sublimation leading to a higher degree of spirituality for the group as a whole.

In terms of the concept of sacrifice and redemption, Moses was following in the footsteps of the Patriarchs, the progenitors of Israel. Abraham, Isaac, and Jacob, each in his own way, and in his own historic epoch, had to go through a struggle of overcoming feelings of competitiveness and hostility. Through some form of self-sacrifice, they came to terms with themselves and with a new vision of God, a Deity Who made moral demands on them. Abraham's growth in spirituality reached its high point in the experience of the near-sacrifice of Isaac. The latter, by acquiescing to this ordeal, testified to his own faith in the father by this act of submission, a faith that proved its justification in the father's triumph of love over ambivalence. As for the stronger-spirited Jacob, his capacity to struggle and endure was epitomized in his wrestling with the angel, an experience in which he sacrificed a portion of his flesh in return for a blessing of the spirit (Zeligs 1974). It is known psychologically that progress in spirituality is achieved by instinctual renunciation (Freud 1939, 180–81).

In this developmental group process, it was Moses who performed the most arduous accomplishment, bringing the Children of Israel a long way on the journey of their historic mission and psychic growth. In his resistance to death, Moses struggles with God as Jacob had once done with the angel. After his encounter, Jacob was free to cross a river (the Jabbok) and continue on his way to the land of his inheritance. His role was to produce sons who would provide the foundation for the physical structure of the twelve tribes, the eponymous fathers. The fate of Moses was different because his function was different. He yielded, not just a part of his body, but his entire earthly form, to the Deity and vanished physically from the earth. The superego, as a psychic process, has no physical substance.

As a culture hero who, through his own struggles presages and prepares the path for the group, Moses typifies in his personal life the various phases of development through which the group as a whole has to pass on its way to a higher level of cultural growth. As Freud (1930) has observed, "When . . . we compare the cultural process in humanity with the process of development or upbringing in an individual human being, we shall conclude without much hesitation that the two are very similiar in nature, if not in fact the same process applied to a different kind of object" (p. 133).

It is in the light of his symbolic significance for the group that added meaning can be attributed to some of the leave-taking ceremonials carried out by Moses before his departure. The transfer of the Book of the Law to the people signified that the *words of the father* must now replace the actual presence of the earthly parent figure. It is the father whose words in the form of verbal commands and instructions to the child mark the beginning of superego development (Freud 1923, 76; Reik 1959, 168–69).

The blessing of the tribes as part of the farewell ceremonies can be understood as a renunciation by the father figure of oedipal hostility toward the sons. The ascent of Moses to Mount Nebo and his burial there suggests the final attainment of spirituality. The earthly body has fully surrendered its claims. However, man being imperfect by the very fact of his humanity, Moses does not willingly surrender those oedipal wishes. Authentically human, he accepts yet protests his fate to the end. Only through love of the father and in identification with the superego wishes represented by the Deity, does Moses finally yield.

Talmudic scholars intuitively appreciated the concept of the great Lawgiver as a superego figure. They explain that Moses could not have led the Children of Israel into the Promised Land because he had become increasingly spiritual as he grew older. Moses was thus not qualified to serve as a military leader, a role that would have required an aggressive attack upon the land. The unconscious concept was that he could not enter upon the conquest of the symbolic oedipal mother. The man with the light of divinity shining on his face (Exod. 34:29–34) could function only as a moral and spiritual force in the lives of the people.

In its evaluation of Moses, the Talmudic view attributes greatness to him of a kind not achieved by any other prophet or leader of Israel. At the same time, there is a frank portrayal of his faults and weaknesses, often in the exaggerated form that is characteristic of rabbinic fantasy. The need to keep Moses human, to prevent him from assuming the guise of divinity in the minds of men, was basic to the biblical purpose. His greatness, while fully acknowledged, must never be construed as exceeding his human potential.

Perhaps the most outstanding quality in the character of Moses is the fact that throughout his leadership, a role made possible by his mystical relationship with God, he was able, in spite of conflictful feelings, to retain his own sense of identity as a human being. At the same time, the uniqueness of this relationship with the Deity is stressed again and again in the biblical literature. In the closing verses of Deuteronomy, the statement is made, "And there hath not arisen a prophet since in Israel, like unto Moses, whom the Lord knew face to face" (34:10).

Additional Notes on Deuteronomy

 CHAPTER EIGHTEEN

AN UNUSUAL feature in the discourses of Moses is the extent to which the leader makes use of both plural and singular forms of the pronouns as he addresses the people. Often within the compass of a single verse, Moses moves readily from the plural *ye* to the more intimate *thee* and *thou*.

This pattern has been puzzling to scholars, several of whom have made efforts in recent years to divide the material into two sources according to the use of these two pronoun forms. However, the attempt proved unsuccessful because the changes occurred so frequently and often without accompanying differences in other aspects of style (Oesterly & Robinson 1958, 46n.; *EJ* 1972, 5:1575; Driver 1903, 21).

It is suggested here that the alternating use of these pronouns may reflect underlying attitudes on the part of Moses himself. Clearly the Children of Israel had a special quality of *oneness* for the leader. The mission on which he had been sent was to rescue *a people* from slavery. He had led them to Mount Sinai as *a people*. Under his leadership they had made a covenant with

God as *a people*. But that this assembly was made up of separate persons must also have been a reality for Moses, who had lived with them as individuals through so many common experiences.

The Individual and the Group

The perception of the people as being one yet many, in a somewhat mystical sense that carries this concept beyond the ordinary, may have stemmed from the psychological situation within Moses himself. As a mediator between them and the Deity, the leader represented the group in its totality. He was *the people* before God and must have incorporated this image of himself within his own psyche. At the same time, Moses must indeed have experienced himself as a unique and separate person, one who had a special relationship with God.

The Deity also is portrayed as viewing the Children of Israel in the metaphor of *a person*. Very early in the mission of Moses, God instructs His newly appointed prophet to say to Pharaoh, "Israel is My son . . . My first-born" (Exod. 4:22). The attitudes of Moses and God in this respect thus mirror each other.

In his discourses Moses seemed to move intuitively from one form of address to the other precisely at those points when the change was most effective, thereby relating to the people both as leader of the group and also on a more intimate person to person basis. Thus, in anticipating the punishment of exile that would befall them for their disobedience to God's laws, he says, "But from there [the land of exile] *ye* will seek the Lord *thy* God; and *thou* shalt find Him, if *thou* search after Him with all *thy* heart and with all *thy* soul" (4:29)* (italics added). Here the people as a group suffer exile, but the return to God in the spirit of repentance could only take place in the heart of an individual, hence the use of the singular pronoun.

The unifying effect on the Children of Israel is strengthened by the implication of oneness. Thus, when Moses assures them of their specialness, he says, "For *thou* art a holy people unto the Lord *thy* God; the Lord *thy* God has chosen *thee* to be His own treasure, out of all the peoples that are upon the face of the

---

*All biblical references in this chapter, unless otherwise noted, are to the book of Deuteronomy.

earth" (7:6–8) (italics added). Their specialness as a people also makes each one of them special.

In trying to prepare them for their coming battles with the Canaanites, the departing leader uses the singular pronoun to involve the people subtly on two levels, both as individuals and as a group. "If *thou* shalt say in *thy* heart; 'These nations are more than *I;* How can I dispossess them?' *thou* shall not be afraid of them; *thou* shalt well remember what the Lord *thy* God did unto Pharoah and unto all Egypt'" (7:1–18) (italics added). The injunctions "thou shall not be afraid" and "thou shalt well remember" are appeals to each individual heart but delivered to the group as a whole. It also might be noted that these words are expressed not as advice but in the form of commands, again showing the remarkable psychological insight of the leader in his use of the power of suggestion.

The distinctive relationship between the individual and the group, characterized by both separateness and unity, also finds frequent expression in a similiar usage of singular and plural forms of address throughout the Prophets and in other parts of the biblical writings. There too the Children of Israel are often referred to in the metaphor of an individual. Just as Jacob became Israel, symbolic of the group, so Israel is also Jacob, the individual.

Even after the above interpretation, however, an element of puzzling ambiguity of meaning still remains. There is an impression of a lack of distinctiveness between the identity of the individual and the group that goes beyond the psychological considerations presented and raises further questions of possible significance. These aspects are largely beyond the scope of this study and are indeed quite speculative. But whatever impinges on a further understanding of the biblical literature merits some attention.

Pedersen (1926), the Danish scholar, whose work in the early decades of the twentieth century was devoted largely to the study of thought processes of the biblical Hebrews and their neighbors, stated his belief that the mentality of the individual in relation to his group had the characteristics of what he called a *corporate personality*.

According to this concept, the sense of self-identity was largely in terms of belonging to and being an integral part of a specific ethnic group. Moreover, Pedersen explains, a person was viewed by his environment as a prototype of the group, containing all its psychological qualities. As he puts it, "The individual is only a form of the predominant type" (Pedersen 1926, 1–2:110).

In regard to the Hebrews, Pedersen asks, "When are the Patriarchs tribes, and when are they individuals?" His response is, "this question is not in the spirit of the old legends, which do not acknowledge the sharp distinction between the history of the individual and that of the tribe. Therefore," he continues, "Patriarchs are neither merely individuals nor personifications of the tribes; they are *the fathers* who take part in the life of the tribe" (p. 14). He remarks at another point, "Jacob as a man and Jacob as a people are so intimately connected that no one can keep the two apart" (1–2:278).

Pedersen's concept of the corporate personality, which is both mechanistic and mystical at the same time, may denote a period in the cultural development of society when the mentality of man was closely bound to the specific group whose psychological processes he shared and reflected. There are critics, however, who feel that Pedersen's description of Hebrew life and thought contains a primitive element that does not do justice to the developmental aspect of social and religious life as depicted in the Scriptures (Hahn 1954, 71–73). His view was based on a theory, then widely held, that the Hebrews did not emerge from the civilized centers of Mesopotamia and surrounding cultures but from the more primitive nomadic tribes of the Arabian Desert (p. 13).

Some of the early theories in Higher Biblical Criticism about the personalities of the Patriarchal Period were of a much more bizarre nature. The characters in Genesis were not even portrayed by some commentators as human beings but as impersonations of pagan gods, as symbols of astral bodies, or as representing signs of the zodiac, among other things (Goldman 1948, 60ff).

The findings made possible by archeology and by an increased understanding of the newly found ancient texts led to a fuller knowledge of the widespread cultural life of the ancient Near East and the degree to which the Hebrews participated in it. A more realistic approach to the Patriarchal Period was then possible, and its leaders took on more understandable human qualities. Thus, even from its beginnings it can be said that a distinctive feature of Hebrew biblical life was that its leaders and heroes were psychologically understandable human beings (Zeligs 1974, intro.).

A Princeton psychologist, Julian Jaynes (1976), studied the development of human consciousness as revealed in the behavior of epic heroes in the literature of the ancient Near East and early Greek writings. He came to the conclusion that these heroic figures were lacking in the quality of consciousness and the power of self-direction characteristic of fully developed human beings from an emotional and psychological viewpoint. They behaved more like automatons, driven by forces outside themselves, either as projections of their own elemental instincts or in the shape of gods, mystically internalized as *inner* voices from what Jaynes calls the bicameral mind (Jaynes, Chap 3). He suggests that the true state of being conscious was a gradual development in the cultural history of mankind.

The point most relevant to the present study is that, according to the conclusions reached by Jaynes, it was not until the Mosaic Age that leaders and heroes, as manifested in the outstanding literature of that time, began to assume more genuinely human qualities (Jaynes, Chap. 6).

A psycholinguistic approach to the study of the biblical literature, especially the discourses of Moses, may provide a further avenue of understanding to the complexity of the relationship between the individual and the group.

From the time of the primal horde as visualized by Freud in his *Totem and Taboo* (1913), the *scientific myth* of how the first primitive religion and organized society came into being, together with its moral standards, man has been involved in finding a harmonizing relationship between the need for self-assertion and his equally basic need to be a part of society.

The covenantal concept in Hebraic biblical life made man a partner in the relationship with a Deity Who stood for morality, the power of the superego. This partnership not only offered *choice* in entering the agreement but the reward of *love* for obedience as well as the preexisting fear of consequences.

The internalization of this moral force in man and the sense of responsibility that came with the power to choose may have caused an increase in self-awareness and changed the relationship of the individual to the group. A wider path was thus opened for his emergent growth as a unique personality in the never-ending human experiment for harmonizing the basic needs of man in society.

Moses, the biblical culture hero, stands as a monumental figure in lifting man from the slavery of his own instincts as well as from the chains imposed by his fellowmen, to a new vision of the Promised Land where his fate depended on his own courage and initiative together with the strength to live in harmony with the Law given by Moses.

The biblical literature, with its somewhat mystifying intermingling of singular and plural pronouns, may represent a period of transition in cultural development that marked an increasing emergence of the individual from the anonymity of the group, ushering in a new period of freedom for the human psyche and its potential for creativity. In this frame of reference Moses can be seen in a further role as a culture hero who functioned in the transitional phase of psycholinguistic development attributed to this period.

The Background of Deuteronomy

The Mosaic origin of Deuteronomy remained unquestioned for many centuries. It was the one book that the Pentateuch itself ascribed to Moses (Deut. 31:9).

During the era of modern biblical criticism, however, the book of Deuteronomy became one of the most controversial subjects in this area of scholarship as far as questions of sources and dates of composition were concerned. Views regarding its origins ranged from the long-held traditional conviction that it was indeed written by the hand of Moses, to the other end of the spectrum of critical analysis, which held that Deuteronomy was largely a product of many centuries later, some even placing it in the postexilic period.

The dominant theory for close to one hundred fifty years, and one still retained by many scholars, was initiated by De Wette in 1805 (Kaufmann 1960; 173, 175). It was based on a biblical episode as recorded in 2 Kings, chapters 22–23, which relates that a scroll, described as a "book of the Law," was found amid the debris in the Temple of Jerusalem when that house of worship was being renovated in the year 621 B.C., during the reign of King Josiah.

The Bible describes this momentous event as follows: "And Hilkiah the high priest said unto Shaphan the scribe: 'I have found the book of the Law in the house of the Lord.' And Hilkiah delivered the book to Shaphan, and he read it. . . . And Shaphan the scribe told the king, saying: 'Hilkiah the priest hath delivered me a book.' And Shaphan read it before the king. And it came to pass, when the king had heard the words of the book of the Law, that he rent his clothes. And the king commanded Hilkiah the priest and Ahikam the son of Shaphan the scribe, and Asaiah the king's servant, saying: 'Go ye, inquire of the Lord for me, and for the people, and for all Judah, concerning the words of this book that is found; for great is the wrath of the Lord that is kindled against us, because our fathers have not hearkened unto the words of this book, to do according unto all which is written concerning us'" (2 Kings: 22).

Inquiry is then made of Huldah, the prophetess, who predicts that great evil would befall the place and the people because they had forsaken God and offered sacrifices to other gods. The religious reformation carried out under Josiah led to the abolishment of local shrines, where idolatry had been practiced. The Temple in Jerusalem was declared to be the only legitimate center for observing the festivals and for the offering of sacrifices.

The De Wette theory proposed that the internal historical data in Deuteronomy, especially the commandment establishing a central place of worship, identified the "book of the Law" found in the Temple with Deuteronomy, thus making it a product of the seventh century, B.C. (Hahn 1954, 4). It was conceded, however, that portions of the scroll probably went back to a much earlier time (Hahn 1954, 31–32).

The authorship of the scroll, according to this theory, was spuriously assigned to Moses in order to give it greater authority. The purpose of the deception, it was argued, was to motivate the king to carry out the long-needed religious reformation, as indeed happened.

Other scholars, however, pointed out that there is nothing in the biblical account which suggests that the "book of the Law," a term traditionally used to refer to Deuteronomy, was not, in fact, the real thing, the discovery of a long-lost book of Scripture. It was an old custom to place a sacred scroll, especially one containing laws and commandments, in a crevice or cornerstone of the walls when a public building was erected. As Rudolf Kittel, himself a noted scholar of Higher Biblical Criticism, observed in 1925, "There is no real evidence to prove that a pious or impious deceit was practiced on Josiah. The assumption of forgery was to be one of those hypotheses which once set up, is so often repeated that finally everyone believes it has been proven" (Hertz 1936, 939).

The De Wette theory, with its 621 B.C. date for the origin of Deuteronomy or a significant portion of it, was clung to with special tenacity by many scholars because it provided a kind of measuring point from which the dating of other parts of the Pentateuch could be established. Especially significant for this purpose was the commandment establishing a central place of worship and the obliteration of all local shrines. The process of cultic development in biblical history, it was reasoned, could now be more readily assessed on the basis of whether a central place of worship was involved. This concept became important in the evolutionary theory of Wellhausen, the most influential scholar of Higher Biblical Criticism in the nineteenth century. He saw Hebrew life as developing from a primitive nomadic state to progressively higher stages of civilization and sought to interpret the biblical literature along these lines. The seventh-century date for Deuteronomy thus became an important building block in the Documentary Theory and its further elaborations, a process that largely occupied biblical scholars for the second half of the nineteenth century and into the early decades of the twentieth, continuing on a much diminished level of activity since then.

More recently, especially since the 1950s, there has been a

renewal of interest in the origins of Deuteronomy, with a considerable swing back, on the part of some noted investigators, to the traditional view of its Mosaic origin, in whole or in part. It has been clearly shown, for example, that the Mosaic Age was not a primitive period. These views were based, not only on the conventional tools of literary analysis and internal historical data, but on more recent archeological findings of cultural life in the whole ancient Near East.

In terms of the historical references found within the contents of Deuteronomy itself, these scholars have maintained that specific instances clearly prove that the conditions described there are fully understandable for the epoch involved but do not fit into the times of the seventh century B.C. As Hertz (1936,) sums it up, "The internal evidence *against* the late composition of the book and *for* its Mosaic authorship is overwhelming. From whatever side the question is examined, we find the book and the history of Josiah's time do not fit each other" (p. 939). In regard to the argument that seventh-century Hebrew was distinguishable from that of the Mosaic period, another scholar states, "there are no expressions in the text of Deuteronomy which are not perfectly reconcilable with Mosaic authorship" (Archer 1964, 244).

An argument of special relevance is that the centralization of worship did not originate in the age of Josiah or even during the rule of his pious grandfather, Hezekiah, who had also initiated a period of religious reform. All through Israel's earlier history, a central place of worship was a feature of religious life. Even in the time of Moses there was the Tabernacle, the portable Tent of Meeting, erected at Mount Sinai and carried by the Children of Israel through the wilderness. Its historicity has received considerable scholarly validation in recent times (Albright 1957, 266). There was the sanctuary at Shiloh and, of course, the splendid Temple of Solomon, built in the tenth century B.C. (Hertz 1936, 140). But these chief sanctuaries did not forbid offerings at other altars that were designated by God under special circumstances. Furthermore, scholars affirm that the centralization of worship was not the main emphasis in Deuteronomy but rather the obliteration of local shrines, which were associated with pagan rites (Kaufmann 1960, 173).

It was in the 1950s, during the resurgence of interest in the sources of Deuteronomy, that George Mendenhall (1954), on the basis of archeological discoveries, found a connection between the style and content of Deuteronomy and early Hittite treaties of a kind that had been used extensively in the ancient Near East, going back to 1500 B.C. (pp. 26–46).

Even more recently (1976) Dr. Peter Craigie set forth cogent arguments for his theory that Deuteronomy was a product of the Mosaic Age, basing his reasoning on the above-stated fact that the treaty pattern underlying the book is consonant with that early period of time. Craigie elaborates his thesis on the early origins of Deuteronomy in a convincing fashion, pointing out that it bears striking similarities to the form of treaties commonly used throughout the Near East as long ago as the third millenia before the Common Era (p. 54–55). The form of the covenant usually consisted first of a historical approach describing the events leading to the need for such a treaty, then the content of the agreement itself, and finally a series of blessings and curses that were intended to serve as a way of enforcing compliance with the terms set forth.

Going back to the Patriarchal background, Craigie says, "The truly germinal period in the Israelite religious tradition is to be found in the religion of the patriarchs. The pattern was already set within which subsequent religious thought was to develop. The tradition of covenant and the commitment to one God were to play a determinative role in the later development of Israelite religious thought. It was within this framework, which had so limited a sphere of reference in the time of the patriarchs, that the creative movements in Israelite religion were to find full expression at the time of the exodus. In Deuteronomy similar recollections of ancient patriarchal traditions appear; they form, in effect, one of the sub-themes throughout the book" (p. 63; see also, Hillers, 1967, chap. 3).

In this connection the noted scholar, Albright (1957), observes, "One point I emphasized briefly in 1940–46 was the pre-Mosaic origin of the covenant between God and His people . . . [but] I failed to recognize that the concept of 'covenant' dominates the entire religious life of Israel" (p. 16).

A happening of special interest to biblical scholars was the excavation at Ebla (Tel Mardikh) near Aleppo in northern Syria, of 15,000 clay tablets at the Royal Archives of the king. They cover a period of 150 years, from 2400 to 2250 B.C. (BA, March, June, 1984). The discovery was an especially exciting one for biblical philologists because the tablets were inscribed in a form of cuneiform script previously unknown but associated with a Western Semitic language, the family to which Phoenician and Hebrew belong. It was considered akin to the biblical Hebrew spoken more than a thousand years later. The oldest previously known Western Semitic inscriptions had dates only from about 1400 B.C. Certainly the Ebla finding was further evidence that writing was a longknown skill in the time of Moses. A further interesting detail about the newly discovered tablets was the finding of familiar biblical names such as Abram, Ishmael, Esau, and even David, scattered through the writings.

Archeological excavation at Ebla and the arduous scholarship it continues to evoke and inspire has pushed back the boundaries of time and space. It has strengthened and enriched the knowledge already familiar to scholars—that Egypt and Mesopotamia were not the only great centers of culture and civilization in the ancient Near East. The lands that connected them, the so-called Fertile Crescent, were also significant cultural centers in their own right. Biblical scholars drew the further conclusion that the Patriarchal Period, so vividly depicted in the pages of the Bible, could have originated far earlier than previously believed. The validity of that epoch, in terms of its social and economic background had already long been validated (Baron 1952, 1:32–35).

The significance of the Ebla findings for the present study is to emphasize what has already been well known: that Moses, living more than a thousand years later than 2400 B.C., in the literate civilization of Egypt and in contact with surrounding cultures even during the period of the wilderness, would find nothing unusual in utilizing the written form to record what were to him experiences of great importance in the religious life of Israel under his leadership.

Still further diminished was the credibility of those scholars who placed the actual writing down of Deuteronomy in the postexilic period. One commentator, in his defense of the Mosaic origin of Deuteronomy, writes, "even the underprivileged Semitic miners at the turquoise mines in the Sinai Peninsula, were scrawling their alphabetic inscriptions as early as 1500 B.C., if not earlier. Even up at the northernmost tip of the Canaanite area, at Ugarit, the contemporaries of Moses were recording their pagan scriptures in alphabetic characters. It requires an excessive credulity to believe that the Hebrews alone were so backward that they did not know how to reduce to writing their most important legal and religious institutions until after 600 B.C. The Pentateuchal record itself abounds in references to writing, and portrays Moses as a man of letters" (Archer 1964, 87).

The tendency in recent decades is toward a more holistic view regarding the unity of Deuteronomy. The scholar M. Weiss says in this respect, "The biblical text must be studied as it is, with a perception of its wholeness and an emphasis on its intrinsic properties, which alone can explain the text" (Craigie 1976, 63). On this note Hertz (1936) observes, "No book of the Bible bears on its face a stronger impress of unity—the unity of thought, language, style, and spirit—than Deuteronomy. And there is no reason to doubt that the various Discourses proceed from one hand, and that the same hand was responsible for the Code of Laws." The scholar Paul Volz expresses the conviction that "Moses must have been a genius of the first order, a supreme Lawgiver, who shaped an inchoate human mass into a great spiritual nation. Can we deny such a genius the ability to deliver his Farewell Discourses?" (as quoted by Hertz 1936, 941).

A Psychoanalytic Note on the Function of the Bible

 CHAPTER NINETEEN

ONE OF THE concepts that emerged from my biblical studies has to do with the nature and function of the Bible as a whole. I see this body of literature (Old Testament) as an expression of the Hebraic approach to what is regarded from a Freudian viewpoint as the nuclear psychological conflict of each human being—the oedipal struggle.

These writings might be considered as performing the same function for the Hebrews as the *Oedipus Rex* dramas did for the ancient Greeks. However, instead of their heroes acting out the primordial crime as Oedipus did, the Hebrews, over a long period of time, evolved a form of sublimation, a *working through* of the conflict, which led to new paths in the fields of morality and religion.

The text of the Bible contains the story of this evolution. It is a remarkable expression of the development of the superego, outgrowth of the oedipal conflict, portrayed as a group drama, with its leaders as the representative actors.

The particular aspects of the conflict, its massive repression both of incestuous wishes toward the mother and the ambivalence between father and son, the efforts to overcome this hostility along constructive lines, the instinctual renunciations that led to identification with a monotheistic Father-God and increased feelings of kinship in the group—all of these forces can be observed in the lives of many of the biblical heroes.

The theme that runs like a unifying thread through the various books of the Bible is the story of man's struggle between his instinctual impulses and his wish and need for socialization. This is indeed the kernel of the oedipal conflict.

In the life of Moses, as in the studies of biblical figures that preceded him, there were many instances in the text of the *return of the repressed,* the longing for the mother, which came out in disguised and symbolic ways, indicating a resistance to the process of identification with the commandments of the Father.

The Bible repeats the oedipal theme through various media, in the realistic personal conflicts of its leaders and heroes, through legend and symbolism, in poetic and prophetic expression, and through song and proverb. At the same time, since aspects of this struggle were on the level of unconscious conflict, the mechanisms of defense employed by the ego sought to deny and to disguise the forbidden impulses.

Thus, the Bible is a story of human conflict and endeavor rather than the portrayal of heroes as perfect examples to be emulated. As the civilization of Israel progressed from early times through the centuries, this struggle took on a more purified form until it reached a high degree of sublimated expression in the writings of the prophets. But its basic nature was the same—man's efforts to find a *modus vivendi* between his instinctual wishes and his conscience.

Different stages of civilization create areas of special psychic significance common to a people as a whole. "Men who share an ethnic area, a historical era, or an economic pursuit, are guided by common images of good and evil," said Erik Erikson (1959, 18). The Bible can be seen as a unique product of the Hebraic group at a certain period of its development. The leaders through whose experiences the stories are told reflect not only their individual struggles and aspirations but also those of the group. It is because their conflicts are typical and yet new solutions are attempted that these people are leaders.

In the mass oedipal involvement that the Bible expresses, the feelings for the mother were sublimated in a love for the *land,* which became the good mother, "flowing with milk and honey," and in an acceptance of the Torah, or religious law, *the words of the father* (Brenner 1952; Rosenzweig 1940).

It is significant that after the first loss of the land suffered by the Hebrews through the Babylonian conquest in 586 B.C. and the burning of the Temple, the subsequent happy return to Canaan fifty years later was marked by two events, the rebuilding of the Temple and a renewed emphasis on the study and observance of the Torah. The relationship is clear: Only by worshipping God and obeying His commandments would they feel any security in possessing the land.

In the later destruction of the Kingdom of Judah by the Romans (70 A.D.) and the more widespread exile of Jews to other lands, a further substitution of the law for the land was achieved, and the Jews became the People of the Book. Thus, even the symbolic mother had to be renounced and in its place came a more spiritualized, internalized identification with the commandments of the Father. He granted His followers a way of life in which adult sexuality was sanctioned and a benign superego exerted a controlling but permissive influence over the whole of existence.

This concept of the purpose and function of the Bible offers some explanation of the unique role it has played in the Judeo-Christian culture of the Western world. The powerful affects associated with the oedipal conflict and the formation of the superego are related to this body of literature. Perhaps that is the reason, also, why even psychoanalytic investigation of the text has been so surprisingly limited in this field. To look at *the father* critically can become a forbidden form of voyeurism. But only by daring to do so can we fully appreciate how the very human struggles of these group fathers led to the growth and development of the social and moral concepts which are the foundation of our own present-day Judeo-Christian culture.

Some Brief Remarks on Biblical Exegesis

 CHAPTER TWENTY

As ONE REVIEWS the history of man's efforts to probe into the origins of the Bible, one fact stands out impressively: how little we know with certainty about the true birth pangs of this priceless literature. Yet it seems safe to say that the Bible has evoked more scholarly interest and research than any other comparable number of written words.

The following brief discussion of the complex area of biblical criticism is intended to provide some background for the lay readers. For them also several introductions to this field and some other volumes of related interest are suggested (see p. 428).

The Bible is a body of literature made up of a number of books that deal with a variety of material in a diversity of literary forms. Yet all are tied together by a common theme—the religious life and history of a people.

Just the process of gathering this content together and the tasks of compiling, editing, and putting it into the form familiar to us today went on for about a thousand years, approximately from the tenth century B.C. to the first century of the present era. Some of the material it contains goes back even further, perhaps to the middle of the second millenium B.C. It is now amply clear that written sources for the ancient Near East go back to a much earlier date than had previously been supposed (*BA*, 1984).

Not only does obscurity veil the beginnings of the Bible, but even the time of its final canonization is indefinite. This latter procedure is one that declares the writings to be holy, thereby no longer subject to change (Rowley 1961, 169).

It has been claimed that the Pentateuch attained the status of canon sometime in the days of Ezra and Nehemiah, around 400 B.C. This assumption stemmed from the biblical reference to the ceremony then observed of reading the Torah in public assembly, a practice initiated by Ezra in Jerusalem (Neh. 8–10). More recent scholarship, however, points with some degree of assurance to the preceding period of the Babylonian exile as the time when the work of *final collecting, fixing, and preserving of the Torah took place* (*EJ* 1972, 4:823). It is noted, though, that there is no record of any special ceremonial that marked the ritual of canonization.

The Five Books of Moses (the Torah) came down to us as a unit. If they were ever known as separate scrolls, we have no record of such a time. A possible exception, however, is the widely held belief that the book of Deuteronomy does have such a distinction and is synonymous with the book of laws discovered by King Josiah in the Temple in 621 B.C. (Rowley 1961, 29).

What we know with certainty about that part of the Bible known as the Prophets, which makes up the second of its three main divisions, is that it was obviously made up of independent scrolls. There is a tradition that the canonization of the prophetic writings took place during the Persian period of control over Judea, that is, about 323 B.C. (*EJ* 1972, 4:824).

The third of the tripartite division of the Bible, the Writings, is surrounded by the same inconclusiveness regarding its final achievement of canonization. It is considered highly probably that the individual books were canonized quite early. Their collection as a unit may not have been fixed until well into the second century A.D. (*EJ* 1972, 4:824).

The final compilation of the Bible as a whole is ascribed by tradition to a synod of Jewish scholars at some time around the end of the first century of the present era. Their motivation evidently was to preserve this literature during the period of turmoil following the destruction of Jerusalem at the hands of the Romans in the year 70 A.D. Some scholars, however, tend to the opinion that this latter event may have been only a reaffirmation of the status of canon, whose actual date could have been much earlier. As is evident from the above statements, there is little known with certainty about the whole matter of canonization either in regard to parts of the biblical literature or its totality.

However, it should be noted that concerning the Pentateuch itself, there is widespread opinion that a standard copy of it was deposited in the Temple long before the common era and was used as a guide by scribes to correct their own scrolls (Goldman 1948, 37). Thus, in spite of the human tendency to error, much effort went into the preservation of the text from earliest times. Suffice it to say, we have known the Bible basically in its present form for about two thousand years.

For many centuries the Bible was regarded as divine revelation and therefore not subject to imperfections. Problems involving obscurities of the text were attributed to man's limited capacity to understand. Nevertheless, critical approaches to the study of the biblical text were not wanting, even among the rabbis of Talmudic days. They were cognizant of its many inconsistencies and puzzling features that centuries later became the subject of so much intensive study among the scholars of modern biblical criticism. Nor was this kind of awareness lacking during the Middle Ages, when the atmosphere of the church was even more forbidding. Scholarly and inquiring minds covertly expressed and sought answers to the mysteries of the holy text.

The critical study of the Bible in modern times is generally regarded as having its beginnings in the middle of the eighteenth century, reaching its peak among the German theologians of the mid-nineteenth century and continuing into the twentieth. There was a new aura of excitement in the freedom with which scholars now felt able to penetrate boldly into this hitherto sanctified field and face the challenging problems of the Bible's origins and structure.

Under the impetus of the scientific method and the Darwinian theory of evolution, an increasing number of scholarly investigators became involved in biblical research, producing a large body of material dealing with theories about the authorship of the Bible and the history of its development.

Certain criteria were formulated on the basis of which the biblical content, particularly of the Pentateuch and Joshua, was separated into what was thought to be the original sources, or documents, from which the Bible as we know it now was compiled and edited. These criteria, growing out of the internal evidence of the Bible itself, were based on intensive study of its literary characteristics and an analysis of the historical data it contained. Thus evolved the Documentary Theory. Its proponents came from the school of Higher Biblical Criticism, so called because its areas of interest transcended Lower Biblical Criticism, the study of textual problems as such. The theory that the Pentateuch was a composite work was then used to explain most of the puzzling features of the text.

One of the major conclusions of the Documentary Theory was that these first six books of the Bible, now called the *Hexateuch,* were mainly the work of four writers, each of whom had produced his material at different times, these accounts being later combined into one narrative by various redactors or editors. This theory of composite authorship reached further proportions in which the four chief sources were either subdivided or added to again and again, indicating a much larger number of original authors. Many times, even a single verse of the Bible was divided into parts and attributed to different sources. This process became known as the Fragmentation Theory and led others to challenge this whole area of scholarship and to wonder how such a patchwork could have resulted in so effective a body of literature (Goldman 1948, 48).

Some of the more basic assumptions of the Documentary Theory, such as its division into four major sources, were widely accepted during the better part of the past two hundred years and still provide a basic foundation for Higher Biblical Criticism, although much more subject to prevailing winds of change. It might be stated, however, that at no time was there unanimous agreement on any of the theories even in regard to its major premises; concerning details, there was always wide room for differences of opinion.

The zeal for this so-called scientific approach to the understanding of the biblical text led to other departures. There was a reformulation of early Hebrew history, one of the chief proponents of which was Wellhausen, a German scholar of the late nineteenth century. He saw the ancient Hebrews as a group that had a long evolutionary history, beginning as an illiterate, nomadic tribe with a polytheistic religion. He questioned the historical value of the Pentateuch, declaring that the early history of the Hebrews it described was legendary, made up at a later date and projected backward in time to provide a suitable background for the later, more authenticated historical epochs. This viewpoint found widespread acceptance until disproved by later scholarship.

While the work of literary and historical analysis of the biblical sources still continues, it has diminished in importance. Its task seems to have been largely accomplished. The one outstanding conclusion to which most modern scholars would subscribe is that the Pentateuch is a composite work. The Documentary Theory with its four basic sources, together with some variations, is still more widely accepted than any other single theory in spite of the setbacks to which it has been subjected in the last half century.

In regard to this whole field of Higher Biblical Criticism, the esteemed scholar, H. H. Rowley (1961), comments, "To treat modern theories as the older traditions were so long treated, as dogmas to be defended at all costs, whose difficulties are to be resolved by special pleading, in so far as they are openly recognized at all, is to deny the modern method whereby they were reached. It is wise to recognize that, like all scientific theories, they only hold the field until more satisfactory theories are forthcoming, and that from the ferment of recent challenge something more satisfactory may yet emerge, though in few cases does it seem yet to have done so" (p. 10).

Another important school of thought was that which emphasized the role of oral traditions, a process believed to have preceded the written form. These traditions, it was believed, arose in different localities, perhaps at similar times, a mode of group communication reaching back to the very beginnings of Hebraic life. The scholar's task, as this school saw it, was to penetrate the facade of the written material and find the original nucleus of the oral tradition that had gone into its making. It was felt that the tendency of the redactors had been to preserve as much of the original form and content as possible and thus had kept intact the literary characteristics of its popular origin. The documentary sources were now seen by these scholars, not so much as the work of individual authors, but rather reflecting *schools of writers* in various areas, who gathered the folk traditions and compiled them. In these terms, the biblical material would represent more genuinely the collective expression of a people (Hahn 1954, 135ff.; Nielson 1954).

Regarding both the antiquity of the Torah and the authenticity of its language, Solomon Goldman refers to the opinion of the noted Israeli scholar, Y. Kaufmann, as follows, "although he readily admits that the Pentateuchal Canon might not date back earlier than the age of Ezra (about 400 B.C.), he is convinced that the documents it comprises stem not alone in part or general content but in actuality of composition, in style, and in their very letters from remotest antiquity (Goldman 1948, 62).

The most far-reaching and dramatic influence on biblical scholarship in recent times has come through the revelations stemming from archeological research. Hundreds of sites through the entire Near East have been excavated. A whole new world that had been buried for centuries beneath the sand was brought into the light of day. Thousands of clay tablets and other forms of written records, the most exciting example of the latter being the Dead Sea Scrolls, made available an increasing body of knowledge about the previously shadowy backgrounds of early biblical life. Discoveries in this field not only brought to vivid reality the world of those days but also made possible comparative studies of the literature and history of Israel and her neighbors at a period contemporaneous with the very beginnings of Hebrew existence.

It became evident that the whole ancient Near East, though made up of various peoples and political entities, was united by many bonds of cultural and economic ties and characterized by an advanced state of civilization. Clearly, the Hebrews had emerged as a distinctive people, not from a primitive state as Wellhausen had thought but against the background of a complex culture in which they had shared. Thus, the earlier reconstruction of Hebrew history based on an evolutionary concept was seen as invalid.

One of the consequences of archeological research was to restore the Patriarchal Period as described in the Bible to its traditional place as the true beginnings of Hebrew life. Although no evidence was unearthed to prove the existence of the specific personalities immortalized in its narratives, the whole social and economic background so colorfully described in the Bible was indeed an authentic picture of those days. Albright (1949), an outstanding authority on biblical archeology, says in this connection, "Abraham, Isaac, and Jacob no longer seem isolated figures, much less reflections of later Israelite history; they now appear as true children of their age, bearing the same names, moving about the same territory, visiting the same towns (especially Haran and Nahor), practicing the same customs as their contemporaries. In other words, the patriarchal narratives have a historical nucleus throughout (pp. 236–37).

Salo Baron (1952), the noted historian of the Jews, also comments on this theme, referring to "the now prevalent assumption of a solid kernel of authentic historic tradition in the biblical narrative." He goes on to say, "The lifelike description of the human strengths and weaknesses of Abraham, Jacob, and Joseph, in the book of Genesis is also more likely to reflect actual historical personalities than mere personifications of later Hebrew tribes. Few biblical historians would still profess to be shocked by even the extreme statement that 'it is no longer a matter of argument that behind the biblical Abraham an eminent historical personality is manifest'" (1:34).

E. A. Speiser (1964), an esteemed authority on the biblical Near East, commented on the reality of the functions which these leaders carried out in the early formation of a people. He writes, "Although there is no proof so far of Abraham's historicity, many biblical historians would probably agree that if some such figure had not been recorded by the ancients, it would have to be conjectured by the moderns" (p. xlv). He continues, "While it is true that Israel as a nation would be inconceivable without Moses, the work of Moses would be equally inconceivable without the prior labors of the Patriarchs. The covenant of Mount Sinai is a natural sequel to God's covenant with Abraham . . . the internal evidence of the Bible itself goes hand in hand with the results of modern biblical study based in large measure on the testimony of outside sources. Both sets of data point to the Age of Abraham; each in its own way enhances the probability of Abraham as a historical figure" (p. 1).

In the first comparative studies made possible by archeological discoveries, the tendency of certain scholars was to point out the similarities between the culture and literature of ancient Israel and that of her polytheistic neighbors, with the implication that the contribution of Israel was therefore not as great as originally thought. But the work of other able scholars, through their translation of the ancient texts, demonstrated that it was the *differences* that were important and that gave to the Hebrew religion and to the biblical writings their unique and distinctive aspects (Sarna 1966).

The field of biblical exegesis is so comprehensive in scope and content that the numerous other approaches cannot even be touched on in these few pages. The purpose here is to indicate to the layman the existence of this vast school of thought that the Bible has stimulated, as it continues to exert its profound influence, not only on the hearts but also on the minds of men.

A predominant characteristic of the present era in this field is the tendency to find greater unity in the biblical literature in contrast to earlier tendencies to fragment it. The quest is to deepen the understanding of what held this diverse body of writings together and gave it so important a place in the world of religion. It was recognized that the underlying motive animating those who wrote down and preserved this literature was primarily religious. As one scholar put it, "This recognition of the unifying religious motivation of Hebrew historiography was the most important development in *Old Testament* criticism of the last two decades" (Hahn 1954, 260). It can be said that the same holds true for the several decades that have followed since that statement. And as religious feeling is part of the psychological nature of man, it seems fitting that psychoanalysis should also have a voice in this quest for understanding.

Suggested Bibliography

Burrows, Millar. 1941. *What Mean These Stones?* New Haven, CT: American Schools of Oriental Research.
Driver, S. R. 1913. *An Introduction to the Literature of the Old Testament.* New York: Charles Scribner's Sons.
Gordon, C. H. 1958. *The World of the Old Testament.* New York: Doubleday.
Hahn, Herbert. 1954. *Old Testament in Modern Research.* Philadelphia: Muhlenberg Press.
Oesterly, W., & Robinson, T. 1934. *An Introduction to the Books of the Old Testament.* New York: Meridian Books.
Orlinsky, Harry. 1956. *Ancient Israel.* Ithaca, NY: Cornell University Press.
Prichard, James B. 1958. *The Ancient Near East: An Anthology of Texts and Pictures.* Princeton: Princeton University Press.
Robinson, H. W. 1937. *The Old Testament: Its Making and Meaning.* London: University of London Press.
Rowley, H. H. 1952. *The Old Testament and Modern Study.* Oxford: Oxford University Press.
―――. 1959. *The Changing Pattern of Old Testament Studies.* London: Epworth.
Sandmel, Samuel. 1963. *The Hebrew Scriptures.* New York: Alfred A. Knopf.
―――. 1972. *The Enjoyment of Scripture.* New York: Oxford University Press.

Notes

1. The specific version of the Bible on which this analysis was made is an English translation, *The Holy Scriptures,* "According to the Masoretic Text," published by the Jewish Publication Society of America, 1917. It is highly regarded from a scholarly point of view. Compared to the King James Bible, I found this translation to be somewhat more literal, at times sacrificing the smoothness of phraseology for the exactness of meaning. The Hebrew text, which was freely consulted for this study, is from *The Pentateuch and the Haftorahs,* edited by the scholar Dr. J. H. Hertz (2d ed., Soncino Press, 1973), which also makes use of the above-mentioned English translation.

2. Much of Freud's *Moses and Monotheism* has a quality of subjectivity that sets it apart from Freud's other works. His original title for parts one and two of the work was "The Man Moses, an Historical Novel." He was reluctant to publish it, commenting in a letter to Jones, "The necessary historical evidence for my theory is lacking, and since my results, which contain a refutation of the Jewish national mythology, seem to me to be very important, I am not inclined to submit it to the easy criticism of opponents" (Jones 1957, 3:207).

3. Reik calls the burning bush "a late descendant of a primeval plant-totem" (p. 113).

4. Some believe that the bush may have been illuminated by a sudden shaft of sunlight and thus created a temporary hallucinatory effect.

5. The phrase to lay one's hand in one's bosom is an idiom in Hebrew, as in German, for inactivity (cf. Psalm 74:11).

6. Circumcision, a widespread rite, is usually performed at the time of puberty among primitive tribes; among Arabic peoples and the Egyptians in connection with the marriage ceremony; on the eighth day after birth among the biblical Hebrews and the Jewish people since that time (Gen. 17:9–12). See Reik 1931b for the psychoanalytic significance of circumcision.

7. Fenichel points out that inhibitions of speech and thinking are closely connected and may manifest themselves only in certain situations.

8. Jones (3:363; 374), explains that Freud derived this hypothesis from an interpretation by the biblical critic Sellin, who based it on a passage in Hosea but adds that it was said Sellin later withdrew this interpretation as being inconclusive.

9. Buber compares this vision of the form of God to the experience of Isaiah at the time of his appointment as a prophet. Isaiah beholds an image of God seated on a throne in the Holy of Holies within the Temple at Jerusalem. The future prophet exclaims: "mine eyes have seen the King,/ the Lord of hosts" (Isa. 6:5). But as Buber explains, "He senses his seeing in the radiance as being a seeing of the Radiant."

10. Dr. Richard Robertiello suggested in a personal communication that the figure of the calf could have served as a *transitional object* in terms of Winnicott's theory; that is, as a link between the absent figure, usually the mother, and the child, who thus seeks comfort for the lost parent.

11. In "The Shofar" (1919) Reik offers an interpretation of the golden calf episode from the viewpoint of psychoanalytic anthropology.

12. Freud was clearly influenced by Higher Biblical Criticism, which tends to emphasize the fragmented nature of the text in terms of the so-called documentary sources.

13. For another interpretation of the *moment in time* that this statue projects see Rudy Bremer, "Freud and Michangelo's Moses," *American Imago* 1976; 33:60–75.

14. There are two biblical representations of the Tent of Meeting in the wilderness. One, as described in Exodus 33, is pitched "afar off from the camp." The traditional view is that this tent is an entirely different one from the large Tabernacle, which was always set up in the center of the encampment and guarded by a group of Levites who ministered there.

15. The expression "God's glory" has been variously interpreted by scholars: Hertz (1936) "His eternal qualities," p. 363; Driver (1911) "His full majesty," p. 362; Heschel (1956) similar to the "goodness of God," p. 82; Abraham ben Ezra, "God Himself" (Cohen 1947, 359); Rashi, "the reflection of the glory of God" (Cohen 1947, 359).

16. From these familiar verses the Talmud derived the so-called Attributes of God, which have become an integral part of Hebraic prayer and liturgy.

17. This author states: "In an autonomous superego, male and female features are combined and not in conflict with each other."

18. The actual numbers mentioned are not accepted literally by most scholars. They point out that the word *thousands* may refer to a unit, such as a troop, rather than having an exact numerical value.

19. Legendary giants. See Gen. 6:4.

20. In a personal communication Dr. Patai gave me his own translation of the Hebrew verse Deut. 32:18: "Thou didst forget the Rock that bore thee/ and didst not remember God Who brought thee forth." His comment:

"Both Hebrew verbs used clearly mean *to bear,* the female function." *The Hebrew Goddess* (Patai 1967) provides general background on the anthropological and psychological aspects of the role of the mother figure in the development of religion.

21. The brazen (bronze) snake of Moses was kept for a long time as a sacred relic. It was destroyed many years later by King Hezekiah in the eighth century B.C. because he feared that it might become an object of worship (2 Kings 18:4).

22. Maimonides also considered this episode as having occurred in a dream or vision of the night (see Hertz 1936, 671).

23. Recent evidence suggests that Moab may have been under a Midianite protectorate of some kind in the period under consideration (*E J* 1972, 121).

24. "The auditory sphere may claim an exceptional position in the development of the superego. God need not be seen. It is only necessary to harken to his inward words" (Reik 1959, 168–69).

25. "The puberty rites of all people have certain features in common in spite of great differences of civilization" (Reik 1959, 54).

26. Dr. Reik sees the Exodus-Sinai events and the later crossing of the Jordan and entrance into the Promised Land as having striking analogies to the puberty rites of primitive peoples. He shows how the patterns of earlier rituals based on this important rite of passage from youth to manhood reemerge in sublimated form (1959, 165–70).

27. "I have conjectured that the Exodus was originally not from Egypt to freedom, but from youth to manhood." Roheim (1955) admits his limited expertise in the area of Semitic ethnography (p.169n.).

Abbreviations:
EJ: Encyclopaedia Judaica
IB: Interpreter's Bible
IDB: Interpreter's Dictionary of the Bible
Peake's: Peake's Commentary on the Bible
ELB: Encyclopedia of the Living Bible (Illustrated)
BA: Biblical Archaeologist

References

Abbott, John B. 1969. Freud's repressed feelings about Athena on the Acropolis. *American Imago* 26:355–363.

Abraham, Karl. 1927. Transformations of scoptophilia. In *Selected Papers on Psychoanalysis*. London: Hogarth Press, 1949.

Albright, William. 1942. *Archaeology and the Religion of Israel*. Baltimore: Johns Hopkins.

———. 1954. *The Archaeology of Palestine*. London: Penguin Books.

———. 1957. *From the Stone Age to Christianity: Monotheism and the Historical Process*. New York: Doubleday Anchor Books.

Alexander, Cecil F. (1818–1875). "Burial of Moses." In *Standard Book of British and American Verse*. New York: Garden City.

Archer, Gleason L., Jr. 1964. *A Survey of Old Testament Introduction*. Chicago: The Moody Press.

Arlow, Jacob. 1951. The consecration of the prophet. *Psychoanalytic Quarterly* 20:374–97.

———. 1955. Notes on oral symbolism. *Psychoanalytic Quarterly* 24:63–74.

———. 1961. Ego psychology and the study of mythology. *Journal of the American Psychoanalytic Association* 9:383ff.

Barag, G. G. 1946. The mother in the religious concepts of Judaism. *American Imago* 4:32–53.

Baron, Salo. 1952. *A Social and Religious History of the Jews*, vol. 1. Philadelphia: Jewish Publication Society of America.

Benno, Jacob. 1942. The childhood and youth of Moses. In *Essays in Honor of the Very Rev. Dr. J. J. Hertz*. London: Edward Goldston.

Bleich, David. 1976. New considerations on the infantile acquisition of language and symbolic thought. *Psychoanalytic Review* 63:55–56.

Brenner, Arthur B. 1952. The covenant with Abraham. *Psychoanalytic Review* 39:38.

Buber, Martin. 1936. *Moses, the Revelation and the Covenant*. New York: Harper Torchbooks, 1956.
———. 1968. Job. In *On the Bible: Eighteen Studies*. Ed. Nahum M. Glatzer. New York: Schocken Books.
Cohen, Abraham, ed. 1947. *The Soncino Chumash*. London: The Soncino Press.
Craigie, Peter C. 1976. *The Book of Deuteronomy*. Grand Rapids, MI: Wm. B. Eerdmans.
Cross, Frank M. 1947. The tabernacle. *Biblical Archaeologist* 10:45–68.
Driver, S. R. 1903. *The International Critical Commentary*, vol. 5. New York: Charles Scribner's Sons.
———. 1911. *Cambridge Bible. Exodus*. Revised version, with introduction and notes. London: Cambridge Univ. Press, 1953.
Encyclopaedia Judaica. 1972. Jerusalem: Keter Publishing House.
Erikson, Erik H. 1959. Ego development and historical change. In *Psychological Issues*, vol. 1, Monograph 1. New York: International Universities Press.
Evans, William N. 1972. The mother: Image and reality. *Psychoanalytic Review* 59:193–96.
Feldman, A. Bronson. 1955. Mother-country and fatherland. *Psychoanalysis: Journal of Psychoanalytic Psychology* 3:27–45.
Fenichel, Otto. 1945. *The Psychoanalytic Theory of Neurosis*. New York: W. W. Norton.
Fodor, A. 1951. Was Moses an Egyptian? In *Psychoanalysis and the Social Sciences*. Ed. Geza Roheim. New York: International Universities Press.
Frankfort, Henri. 1948. *Ancient Egyptian Religion: An Interpretation*. New York: Harper & Row.
Freud, Anna. 1946. *The Ego and the Mechanisms of Defense*. New York: International Universities Press.
Freud, Sigmund. 1893. A case of successful treatment by hypnosis. In *Collected Papers*, vol. 5. London: Hogarth Press, 1950.
———. 1893. *Studies on Hysteria*. New York: Basic Books, 1957.
———. 1900. *The Interpretation of Dreams*. New York: Basic Books, 1955.
———. 1905. *Three Essays on the Theory of Sexuality*. London: Imago Publishing Co.
———. 1908. The relation of the poet to day-dreaming. In *Collected Papers*, vol. 4. London, Hogarth Press, 1950.
———. 1909. Family romances. In *Collected Papers*, vol. 5. London, Hogarth Press, 1950.
———. 1910. The antithetical sense of primal words. In *Collected Papers*, vol. 4. London: Hogarth Press, 1950.
———. 1910. *Leonardo Da Vinci*. Trans. by A. A. Brill. New York: Random House, 1947.

———. 1910. Psychogenic visual disturbances according to psychoanalytical conceptions. In *Collected Papers,* vol. 2. London: Hogarth Press, 1950.
———. 1913. *Fausse reconnaissance* in psychoanalytic treatment. In *Collected Papers,* vol. 2. London: Hogarth Press, 1950.
———. 1913. *Totem and Taboo.* New York: W. W. Norton, 1952.
———. 1914. The Moses of Michelangelo. In *Collected Papers,* vol. 4. London: Hogarth Press, 1950.
———. 1915. Thoughts for the times on war and death. In *Collected Papers,* vol. 4. London: Hogarth Press, 1956.
———. 1922. *Group Psychology and the Analysis of the Ego.* New York: Liveright, 1949.
———. 1923. *The Ego and the Id.* London: Hogarth Press, 1950.
———. 1926. *The Problem of Anxiety.* Trans. by Henry Bunker. New York: The Psychoanalytic Quarterly Press & W. W. Norton, 1936.
———. 1928. *The Future of an Illusion.* New York: Liveright, 1953.
———. 1930. *Civilization and Its Discontents.* London: Hogarth Press, 1951.
———. 1933. *New Introductory Lectures on Psychoanalysis.* New York: W. W. Norton.
———. 1936. A disturbance of memory on the Acropolis. In *Collected Papers,* vol. 5. London: Hogarth Press, 1950.
———. 1939. *Moses and Monotheism.* New York: Alfred A. Knopf, 1949.
Funk, Robert. 1976. The watershed of the American biblical tradition: The Chicago school, first phase, 1892–1920. *Journal of Biblical Literature* 95:6.
Ginsberg, Asher (Ahad Ha'am). 1904. *Moses: Selected Essays.* Philadelphia: Jewish Publication Society of America, 1912.
Ginzberg, Louis. 1909–1938. *The Legends of the Jews,* vols. 1–7. Philadelphia: Jewish Publication Society of America.
Glueck, Nelson. 1946. *The River Jordan.* Philadelphia: Jewish Publication Society of America.
Goldman, Solomon. 1948. *The Book of Books: An Introduction.* Philadelphia: Jewish Publication Society of America.
———. 1949. *In the Beginning.* Philadelphia: Jewish Publication Society of America.
———. 1956. *The Ten Commandments.* Ed. and with an introduction by Maurice Samuel. Chicago: Univ. of Chicago Press.
Greenacre, Phyllis. 1956. Experiences of awe in childhood. In *The Psychoanalytic Study of the Child,* vol. 2. New York: International Universities Press.
———. 1957. The childhood of the artist. In *The Psychoanalytic Study of the Child,* vol. 12. New York: International Universities Press.
———. 1958. The family romance of the artist. In *The Psychoanalytic Study of the Child,* vol. 13. New York: International Universities Press.

———. 1963. *The Quest for the Father*. New York: International Universities Press.

Hahn, Herbert P. 1954. *Old Testament in Modern Research*. Philadelphia: Muhlenberg Press.

Hertz, Joseph H. 1973. *The Pentateuch and the Haftorahs*. Hebrew text, English translation and commentary. 2d ed. London: Soncino Press.

Heschel, Abraham J. 1955. *God in Search of Man*. New York: Straus & Cudahy.

Hillers, Delbert R. 1969. *Covenant: The History of a Biblical Idea*. Baltimore: Johns Hopkins Univ. Press.

Hirsch, Samson R. 1960. *The Pentateuch: Exodus*, vol. 2. Trans. by Isaac Levy. 2d ed. London: Isaac Levy.

The Interpreter's Bible. 1957. Vols. 1–2. New York, Nashville: Abingdon.

The Interpreter's Dictionary of the Bible. 1976. Nashville, Abingdon.

James, Fleming. 1950. *Personalities of the Old Testament*. New York: Charles Scribner's Sons.

Jaynes, Julian. 1976. *The Origin of Consciousness in the Breakdown of the Bicameral Mind*. Boston: Houghton Mifflin.

Jones, Ernest. 1912a. The nature of auto-suggestion. In *Papers on Psychoanalysis*. Baltimore: Williams & Wilkins, 1950.

———. 1912b. The theory of symbolism. In *Papers on Psychoanalysis*. Baltimore: Williams & Wilkins, 1950.

———. 1953, 1955, 1957. *The Life and Work of Sigmund Freud*, vols. 1–3. New York: Basic Books.

Kanzer, Mark. 1969. Sigmund and Alexander Freud on the Acropolis. *American Imago* 26:324–54.

Kaufmann, Yehezkel. 1960. *The Religion of Israel*. Trans. by Moshe Greenberg. Chicago: Univ. of Chicago Press.

Keller, Werner. 1964. *The Bible as History*. New York: William Morrow & Co., 1969.

Kohut, Heinz. 1971. *The Analysis of the Self*. New York: International Universities Press.

Kris, Ernst. 1952. *Psychoanalytic Explorations in Art*. New York: Schocken Books, 1964.

Lewin, Bertram D. 1973. *Selected Writings of Bertram D. Lewin*. Ed. by Jacob A. Arlow. New York: Psychoanalytic Quarterly Press.

Mendenhall, George E. 1955. *Law and Covenant in Israel and the Ancient Near East*. Pittsburgh: The Biblical Colloquium.

Niederland, W. G. 1969. Freud's "déjà vu" on the Acropolis. *American Imago* 26:373–378.

Nielson, Eduard. 1954. *Oral Traditions: A Modern Problem in Old Testament Introduction*. Chicago: Allenson.

Noth, Martin. 1968. *Numbers: A Commentary.* London: SCM Press.
Oesterley, W. O. E., and Theodore H. Robinson. 1958. *An Introduction to the Books of the Old Testament.* New York: Meridan Books, Inc.
Orlinsky, Harry. 1954. *Ancient Israel.* Ithaca: Cornell Univ. Press.
Otto, Rudolf. 1923. *The Idea of the Holy.* London: Oxford Univ. Press.
Patai, Raphael. 1959. *Sex and Family Life in the Bible and the Middle East.* Garden City, NY: Doubleday & Co.
———. 1967. *The Hebrew Goddess.* Rev. ed. New York: Avon Books, 1978.
Peake's Commentary on the Bible. 1953. New York: Abingdon-Cokesbury.
Pedersen, Johs. 1926. *Israel, Its Life and Culture.* vol. 1–2. London: Oxford Univ. Press.
Peto, Andrew. 1960. The development of ethical monotheism. In *The Psychoanalytic Study of Society*, vol. 1. Ed. by Warner Muensterberger & Sidney Axelrod. New York: International Universities Press.
Pfeiffer, Robert H. 1941. *Introduction to the Old Testament.* New York: Harper & Bros.
Rank, Otto. 1909. *The Myth of the Birth of the Hero.* New York: Robert Brunner, 1952.
Rank, Otto, and Hanns Sachs. 1913. The significance of psychoanalysis for the humanities. *American Imago* 1964; 21:43.
Reik, Theodor. 1919. The Shofar. In *Ritual: Psychoanalytic Studies.* New York: International Universities Press, 1958.
———. 1931a. Couvade and the psychogenesis of the fear of retaliation. In *Ritual: Psychoanalytic Studies.* New York: International Universities Press, 1958.
———. 1931b. The puberty rites of savages. In *Ritual: Psychoanalytic Studies.* New York: International Universities Press, 1958.
———. 1948. *Listening with the Third Ear.* New York: Garden City Books, 1951.
———. 1959. *Mystery on the Mountain.* New York: Harper & Row.
Ricoeur, Paul. 1970. *Freud and Philosophy: An Essay in Interpretation.* Trans. by Denis Savage. New Haven, CT: Yale Univ. Press.
Roheim, Geza. 1955. Some aspects of Semitic monotheism. In *Psychoanalysis and the Social Sciences*, vol. 4. New York: International Universities Press.
Rosenfeld, Eva. 1951. The Pan-headed Moses: A parallel. *International Journal of Psychoanalysis* 32:83–93.
Rosenzweig, E. M. 1940. Some notes, historical and psychoanalytical on the people of Israel, with special reference to Deuteronomy. *American Imago* 1:4.
Rowley, H. H. 1961. *The Growth of the Old Testament.* New York: Harper Torchbooks.

Rubenstein, Richard L. 1968. *The Religious Imagination: A Study in Psychoanalysis and Jewish Theology.* New York: Bobbs-Merrill Co.
Sandler, Joseph. 1960. On the concept of superego. In *The Psychoanalytic Study of the Child,* vol. 15. New York: International Universities Press.
Sandmel, Samuel. 1963. *The Hebrew Scriptures.* New York: Alfred A. Knopf.
Sarna, Nahum. 1966. *Understanding Genesis: The Heritage of Biblical Israel.* New York: Schocken Books, 1970.
Schafer, Roy. 1960. The loving and beloved superego in Freud's structural theory. In *The Psychoanalytic Study of the Child,* vol. 15. New York: International Universities Press.
Schlesinger, Kurt. 1972. *Origins of the Passover Seder in Ritual Sacrifice.* Paper read at the San Francisco Psychoanalytic Society.
Schur, Max. 1969. The background of Freud's "disturbance" on the Acropolis. *American Imago* 26:303–323.
Shengold, Leonard. 1966. The metaphor of the journey in *The Interpretation of Dreams. American Imago* 23:316–31.
Slochower, Harry. 1970. Freud's déjà vu on the Acropolis: A symbolic relic of *Mater Nuda. Psychoanalytic Quarterly* 39:100.
———. 1971. Freud's *Gradiva: Mater Nuda Rediviva:* A wish-fulfillment of the "memory" on the Acropolis. *Psychoanalytic Quarterly* 40:646–662.
———. 1975. Philosophical principles in Freudian psychoanalytic theory: Ontology and the quest for Matrem. *American Imago* 32:16.
Speiser, E. A. 1964. *The Anchor Bible: Genesis.* Trans. with introduction and notes. New York: Doubleday & Co.
Stamm, Julian L. The problems of depersonalization in Freud's "Disturbance of Memory on the Acropolis." *American Imago* 26:364–372.
Ticho, Ernst A. 1972. The development of superego autonomy. *Psychoanalytic Review* 2:219.
Von Rad, Gerhard. 1960. *Moses.* New York: Association Press.
Zeligs, Dorothy F. 1960. The role of the mother in the development of Hebraic monotheism: As exemplified in the life of Abraham. In *The Psychoanalytic Study of Society,* vol. 1. Eds. Munsterberger, Warner, Axelrad, Sidney. New York: International Universities Press.
———. 1974. *Psychoanalysis and the Bible: A Study in Depth of Seven Leaders.* New York: Bloch Publishing Co.

Glossary of Psychoanalytic Terms

Affect: A feeling-tone, pleasurable or unpleasurable.

Alter ego: Someone who represents an externalization of one's own ego or self; another "I."

Altruistic surrender: Withdrawal from a more advantageous position in favor of someone else, usually accompanied by an identification with the other and a vicarious enjoyment of the latter's gratification.

Ambivalence: The coexistence of opposite feelings, especially love and hate, without either feeling modifying the other; in neurotic conflict, one aspect of the feelings is unconscious.

Analysand: One who is being analyzed.

Castration anxiety: An unrealistic fear, usually unconscious, of genital injury or loss, related to the oedipal stage of psychosexual development; may be displaced in later life to other parts of the body; includes the childhood fantasy that female genitals result from loss of a penis.

Cathexis: The investment of psychic energy in a mental representation.

Compensatory (also over-compensatory): Descriptive of a process, generally unconscious, by which an individual tries to make up for real or fancied deficiencies.

Compulsion: An urge to perform an action which may seem incomprehensible to the subject or against his conscious wishes and standards, but the omission of which would cause anxiety; may represent the acting out of an unconscious fantasy or a defense against unacceptable wishes.

Condensation: A psychic process, often present in dreams, in which two or more concepts are fused so that a single symbol represents the multiple components.

Conflict, intrapsychic: The clash between opposing emotional forces within the self; a common characteristic of psychic life and a significant cause of psychologic disorders.

Glossary of Psychoanalytic Terms

Defense mechanisms: Specific intrapsychic processes, working unconsciously, which are used by the ego to protect itself from anxiety or guilt in relation to forbidden wishes or drives.

Defusion: The separation of emotions, especially love and aggression, so that the former fails to modify and restrain the full force of the latter.

Déjà vu; (*Already seen*): The feeling, somewhat uncanny, of having perceived or experienced something before of a similar nature; the feeling may stem from an association with something in the unconscious.

Denial: An unconscious mechanism of defense by which the ego seeks to protect itself from an intolerable idea or feeling by denying some aspect of reality.

Displacement: The transference of emotions from the original idea or person to which they were attached, to less significant substitutes; the motive is to spare the ego the pain of knowing the real source of the feelings while, at the same time, allowing discharge of these emotions.

Ego: That part of the psyche which develops through the influence of the external world upon the more primal structure of the id; serves as the regulatory part of the personality, guiding perception and muscular activity; acts as the mediator between the demands of the id and the world of reality.

Ego ideal: That part of the personality, related to the superego, which has to do with the self-image of how the person feels he should be; based on identifications with admired and significant figures in early life, especially the parents; partly unconscious; *narcissistic ego ideal*—a childish image of the perfect self as the individual would like to believe he is or ought to be.

Ego-syntonic: That which is in harmony with the standards of the ego (and ego ideal), therefore causes no anxiety.

Empathy: The capacity to think and feel oneself into the psyche of another person for the purpose of understanding him.

Free association: The psychic process in which one thought leads spontaneously to another, together with the accompanying emotions, because these ideas are unconsciously related or *associated* with each other in some manner; because of reality factors, this kind of thinking is customarily controlled and censored so that unacceptable ideas can be withheld; Freud discovered the technique of *free association* as a path to the unconscious and established it as a fundamental tool in psychoanalytic therapy.

Id: That part of the personality structure which comprises the instinctual strivings and repressed, unconscious content; aspects of the id can reach consciousness only through some form of representation in the ego or find discharge through derivatives expressed in dreams or symptoms.

Identification: A psychic, unconscious process by which an individual patterns himself after another; an important mechanism for the development of one's personality, in which the parents and other significant figures of early life play a major role.

Imago: An unconscious mental image, usually idealized, of an important person in the early life of an individual.

Incorporation: A primitive defense mechanism, functioning unconsciously, in which a person, or parts of him, are figuratively ingested, and thus felt to be within, or part of one's self.

Inhibition: Interference with, or restriction of, specific activities or functions; may result from an unconscious defense against forbidden instinctual drives.

Internalized object: The mental representation of someone, with accompanying emotions, with whom one formerly had a relationship in the external world.

Intrapsychic: Taking place within the psyche.

Introjection: The psychic act of taking into one's ego system the image of a person, as one perceives that person to be, together with the accompanying emotions that one had toward him in the external world; related to the more primitive method of incorporation.

Isolation: An unconscious mechanism of defense in which an unacceptable impulse, idea, or act, is separated from its original memory source, thereby removing the emotional charge.

Latent content: The hidden, unconscious meaning as opposed to the *manifest content*, or the surface meaning; especially related to dreams, fantasies, and works of art and literature.

Libido: Psychic drive, or energy, usually associated with or derived from the sexual instinct; in its broad sense used to include all warm relationships and pleasurable feelings.

Masochism: Sexualized pleasure in association with physical or psychological pain; often related to an unconscious sense of guilt and a consequent need for punishment to obtain relief.

Melancholia: A severe depression characterized by an intrapsychic conflict in which a severe superego berates the ego, leading to a loss of self-esteem.

Narcissism: Self-love as opposed to object love; an over-estimation of self; *narcissistic identification*—identifying with another person who unconsciously represents aspects of oneself; a love relationship on this basis is thus largely a form of externalized self-love; *narcissistic injury*—an injury to one's sense of self-esteem; a certain amount of narcissism, or self-love, is necessary for a healthy psyche.

Object love: Love for another person outside the self.

Oral stage: The earliest period of psychic development in the infant, when the mouth is the main erotogenic zone; it is the chief organ with which he experiences the world, taking in good objects, like mother's milk, and spitting out what he doesn't like.

Overdetermination: The multiple causality of a single symptom or emotional reaction.

Paranoid: Characterized by oversuspiciousness; paranoid trends can vary from mild tendencies within the range of normalcy, to severe pathology involving grandiose or persecutory delusions.

Passive-aggressive personality: Descriptive of aggressive behavior expressed in passive or covert ways in order to conceal the underlying hostility.

Phallic mother: Refers to the fantasy of the child that the mother, being a powerful person, must also have a penis, perhaps a hidden one; the fantasy is repressed but may remain active in the unconscious.

Pleasure principle: The concept that man instinctively seeks gratification and pleasure and strives to avoid pain and discomfort; related to early stages in personality development; soon comes in conflict with the frustrations imposed by reality and, normally, is modified as one matures, by an acceptance of the *reality* principle.

Preoedipal: Preceding the oedipal period; refers to the oral and anal stages of psychic development; *preoedipal mother*—the infant's image of the mother during this period.

Primal scene: The real or fantasied observation by the child of parental or other heterosexual intercourse.

Projection: A defense mechanism which unconsciously attributes to others that which is unacceptable to the self; these qualities, however, are real to the self and influence the person's behavior accordingly.

Rationalization: The process, frequently unconscious, of finding reasons for that which one wishes to believe or do, without regard for the real, underlying motives.

Reaction-formation: Development of a character trait that conceals and tries to keep under control another trait, which is usually of the exactly opposite type.

Regression: Reverting to an earlier pattern of mental functioning, usually in periods of stress.

Repression: The process of keeping unacceptable ideas from consciousness; these ideas may remain active in the unconscious and seek an outlet in disguised ways, such as dreams or symptoms.

Sadism: Sexualized pleasure derived from inflicting physical or psychological pain on others.

Sublimation: A diversion of psychic energy from instinctual drives which are unacceptable to the self to channels which are personally and socially approved, as in the fields of art, religion, or social service.

Superego: That part of the psyche out of which conscience develops; formed in early childhood by identification with the standards and wishes of the parents and other significant adults, as the child perceives these to be; the self-criticizing aspect of the personality which, under certain conditions, can become overly severe and even sadistic, causing guilt and anxiety. In his earlier writings Freud used this terms synonymously with "ego ideal." The latter is now usually viewed as part of the superego.

Index to Biblical References

GENESIS
1 . . . 273
6:4 . . . 430
11:26 . . . 33
17 . . . 335
17:9–12 . . . 429
18:20–23 . . . 167
25:8 . . . 400
34:2 . . . 383
34:31 . . . 383
35:39 . . . 400
38 . . . 381
49 . . . 377
49:5–7 . . . 383–384
49:7 . . . 385
49:8–10 . . . 379
49:13 . . . 389
49:17–18 . . . 390
49:19 . . . 389
49:20 . . . 390
49:21 . . . 390
49:27 . . . 387
49:33 . . . 400

EXODUS
1 . . . 41–42, 44
1:7 . . . 42
1:9–10 . . . 41–42
1:15–17 . . . 43
1:21 . . . 43
2 . . . 41
2:1 . . . 29
2:1–10 . . . 25
2:10 . . . 34
2:11 . . . 36, 47
2:11–12 . . . 35
2:12 . . . 61
2:13–15 . . . 37
2:14 . . . 258
2:14–5 . . . 48
2:16–17 . . . 50
2:20 . . . 51
2:21–22 . . . 51–52
3 . . . 71, 72
3:1–4 . . . 394
3:1–11 . . . 59
3:10–11 . . . 63
3:11–12 . . . 184, 327
3:12 . . . 64, 140
3:13–14 . . . 64, 96, 184
3:16–18 . . . 72
3:19 . . . 71, 94
3:19–22 . . . 71
3:20 . . . 71
3:21–22 . . . 66
4 . . . 71
4:1 . . . 71

4:2–5 . . . 73
4:6–7 . . . 73
4:9 . . . 74
4:10 . . . 75, 274, 370
4:11 . . . 75
4:12–16 . . . 99
4:14 . . . 370
4:14–16 . . . 99
4:14–17 . . . 76
4:16 . . . 274, 364
4:16–17 . . . 103
4:17 . . . 93
4:18 . . . 80
4:19 . . . 83
4:19–20 . . . 80
4:20 . . . 82, 103
4:21 . . . 83
4:21–26 . . . 83
4:22 . . . 176, 406
4:22–23 . . . 122
4:24 . . . 86, 110
4:24–26 . . . 79, 262
4:26 . . . 87, 88
4:26–27 . . . 231
4:27 . . . 88
4:28–31 . . . 92
5:1–2 . . . 93
5:22–23 . . . 94
6:1 . . . 94, 99
6:2 . . . 96
6:2–3 . . . 95, 99
6:3 . . . 95
6:12 . . . 98
6:13 . . . 95
6:14–27 . . . 99
6:18–21 . . . 249, 257
6:20 . . . 29
6:30 . . . 100, 274, 395
7:1 . . . 364
7:1–2 . . . 100, 274
7:8–10 . . . 104
7:17–18 . . . 104

7:19–20 . . . 105
7:20 . . . 120
7:28 . . . 106
8:1–2 . . . 105
8:8–9 . . . 106
8:12–13 . . . 107, 112
9:20 . . . 172
10:24 . . . 107
10:26 . . . 107
10:28–29 . . . 107
11:2–3 . . . 69
11:4–8 . . . 109
12:11 . . . 109
12:13 . . . 109
12:31 . . . 109
12:35 . . . 110
12:35–36 . . . 69
12:51 . . . 328
13:2 . . . 209
13:19 . . . 388
14:4 . . . 111
14:5–9 . . . 111
14:10–11 . . . 111
14:13–14 . . . 111
14:14 . . . 173
14:15–16 . . . 111–112, 273
14:17–18 . . . 111, 112–113
15 . . . 114
15:20 . . . 232
15:23–26 . . . 120
15:24 . . . 270
15:25 . . . 122
15:27 . . . 123
16:1 . . . 328
16:1–3 . . . 123, 212
16:4–5 . . . 123
16:6–8 . . . 124
16:9–12 . . . 125
16:10 . . . 125
16:13 . . . 222
16:14–15 . . . 126
16:15 . . . 126

Index to Biblical References

17:1–4 . . . 127
17:1–7 . . . 267
17:5–7 . . . 129
17:6 . . . 275
17:8 . . . 130
17:9–13 . . . 131
17:14 . . . 133
17:14–16 . . . 132, 133
17:15 . . . 132
18 . . . 343
18:1–6 . . . 229
18:1–7 . . . 228
18:2 . . . 228
18:2–5 . . . 89
18:5 . . . 230
18:7 . . . 229
18:8–12 . . . 230
19:1 . . . 230, 328
19:1–2 . . . 136
19:3 . . . 138, 139
19:3–5 . . . 142
19:3–8 . . . 137
19:5–6 . . . 358
19:6 . . . 212, 324
19:8 . . . 138, 139
19:8–9 . . . 176
19:9 . . . 140
19:10–13 . . . 141
19:14–15 . . . 142
19:16–17 . . . 150
19:16–25 . . . 144
19:18, 20 . . . 145
19:19 . . . 145, 150
19:20–23, 33 . . . 151
19:24 . . . 156
19:24–25 . . . 146
20–23 . . . 355
20:1–2 . . . 146
20:1–3 . . . 149
20:8 . . . 351
20:14 . . . 352
20:15–16 . . . 185

20:15–18 . . . 151
20:16 . . . 348
20:19–23:33 . . . 151, 187
24:1–2 . . . 153
24:3 . . . 152
24:4–8 . . . 152
24:9–11 . . . 154
24:12 . . . 156, 188
24:13–14 . . . 162
24:14 . . . 156
24:15 . . . 156
24:16 . . . 157
24:16–18 . . . 157
24:19 . . . 399
25–31 . . . 196
25:1–9 . . . 196
26:6 . . . 198
28:1 . . . 206
28:1–2 . . . 200
30:15 . . . 197
31:18 . . . 188
32:1–6 . . . 162
32:7–8 . . . 166
32:9–10 . . . 167
32:9–14 . . . 167
32:10 . . . 173
32:16 . . . 188
32:17 . . . 156
32:19–28 . . . 316
32:20 . . . 169
32:21–23 . . . 169
32:24 . . . 166
32:25–28 . . . 170
32:27 . . . 386
32:29 . . . 172
32:32 . . . 173
32:33–35 . . . 173
33 . . . 430
33:1–6 . . . 175
33:2 . . . 179
33:3–6 . . . 175
33:4 . . . 175

33:7–11 . . . 177, 203
33:10–12 . . . 182
33:11 . . . 178
33:12 . . . 66
33:12–13 . . . 179
33:13 . . . 180
33:14 . . . 179
33:15 . . . 180
33:15–17 . . . 179
33:16 . . . 184
33:17–23 . . . 394
33:18 . . . 180
33:19 . . . 181, 186
33:20–23 . . . 182
34:1 . . . 188
34:1–7 . . . 186
34:6–7 . . . 245
34:8 . . . 186
34:9 . . . 186
34:10–16 . . . 187
34:27–28 . . . 352
34:28 . . . 188, 189, 190, 399
34:28–29 . . . 363
34:29 . . . 191
34:29–34 . . . 403
34:29–35 . . . 190
35:21–22 . . . 193
35:31–34 . . . 202
37:1 . . . 189
39:42–43 . . . 193, 201
40:17 . . . 192

LEVITICUS

8:10 . . . 192, 204
9:22–24 . . . 204
10:1–2 . . . 205
10:1–3 . . . 259
10:2 . . . 206
10:7 . . . 207
24:7 . . . 199

NUMBERS

1:1–3 . . . 194
2:3–9 . . . 380
2:17–19 . . . 301
3:53 . . . 281
4:13 . . . 252
4:28–38 . . . 284
10:11 . . . 328
10:11–12 . . . 192, 194
10:29 . . . 53
10:29, 31 . . . 54
11 . . . 224, 226, 228, 234, 272
11:1–3 . . . 213, 214
11:4–6 . . . 214
11:6–9 . . . 214
11:10–11 . . . 215
11:10–15 . . . 216
11:14 . . . 343
11:16–17 . . . 218
11:18–20 . . . 219
11:21–22 . . . 219
11:23 . . . 219
11:24–25 . . . 220
11:25 . . . 348
11:25–28 . . . 220
11:31–34 . . . 221
12 . . . 225
12:1 . . . 228
12:1–16 . . . 226
12:3 . . . 235
12:4–9 . . . 234
12:8 . . . 248
12:14–15 . . . 236
13:1–2 . . . 338
13:26 . . . 330
13:28–29 . . . 240
13:30 . . . 341
13:32 . . . 240
13:33 . . . 240
14:1–4 . . . 242
14:1–25 . . . 329
14:5 . . . 242, 270

Index to Biblical References 447

14:6 ... 341
14:6–9 ... 242, 258
14:7–12 ... 243
14:10 ... 245
14:12 ... 337
14:13–19 ... 243
14:20–25 ... 244
14:24 ... 341
14:25 ... 331
14:26:34 ... 244
14:27–39 ... 342
14:40 ... 245
15:20 ... 252
16:1–4 ... 251
16:3 ... 260
16:4 ... 251
16:5–11 ... 251
16:12–14 ... 253
16:13 ... 222
16:15 ... 253
16:19–22 ... 254
16:23–25 ... 255
16:23–27 ... 257
16:32 ... 257
17:1–5 ... 259
17:6 ... 260
17:7–10 ... 261
17:11–15 ... 262
17:20 ... 264
17:23–24 ... 264
17:27–28 ... 264
20 ... 331
20:1 ... 330, 331, 332
20:1–2 ... 280
20:1–5 ... 270
20:6–13 ... 271
20:7–8 ... 273, 279
20:7–13 ... 400
20:8 ... 275
20:8–13 ... 337
20:10–11 ... 276
20:11–12 ... 276

20:12 ... 271
20:14–18 ... 287
20:16 ... 344
20:22–29 ... 280
20:23–26 ... 290
20:23–29 ... 288
20:24 ... 271
20:29 ... 280
21:2–3 ... 293, 294
21:4 ... 295
21:4–9 ... 296
21:5 ... 295
21:12 ... 338
21:16–18 ... 282, 299
21:24–26 ... 299
21:27–30 ... 299
22:2–3 ... 303
22:4 ... 315
22:5 ... 312
22:5–6 ... 303
22:8 ... 303
22:9–12 ... 304
22:16–17 ... 304
22:18–19 ... 304
22:20 ... 304
22:21–22 ... 305
22:22–35 ... 306
22:35 ... 307
22:37–38 ... 309
22:41 ... 309
23:3 ... 309
23:7–10 ... 310
23:11 ... 310
23:25–28 ... 310
23:28 ... 398
24–25 ... 312, 315
24:1 ... 312
24:1–9 ... 311
24:10–14 ... 311
24:17 ... 302
24:17–18 ... 316
25:1–3 ... 313

25:1–9 . . . 384
25:5 . . . 398
25:7–8 . . . 314
25:8–9 . . . 313
25:14–15 . . . 313
25:17–18 . . . 314
26:10 . . . 257
27:1–11 . . . 332
27:12–13 . . . 393
27:12–14 . . . 333
27:14 . . . 272
27:15–23 . . . 333
27:18–21 . . . 342
31:1–2 . . . 316, 320
31:8 . . . 312, 319–320
31:16 . . . 316, 321, 398
31:17 . . . 319
31:19–24 . . . 319
33:36 . . . 330
33:38–39 . . . 332
34 . . . 378

DEUTERONOMY
1:2 . . . 329, 335
1:6–4:40 . . . 337
1:8 . . . 344
1:13–15 . . . 343
1:16–17 . . . 344
1:22 . . . 338
1:37 . . . 271, 342
1:37–38 . . . 337, 342
1:46 . . . 330
2:1–18 . . . 297
2:4–6 . . . 297
2:5–10 . . . 344
2:9 . . . 297
2:17–19 . . . 301
3:11 . . . 300
3:14 . . . 369
3:21–22 . . . 339
3:23–27 . . . 290

3:25–28 . . . 340
3:26 . . . 271
3:26–27 . . . 340
3:27 . . . 342, 393
3:27–28 . . . 342
4:2 . . . 345
4:5–8 . . . 345
4:11 . . . 148
4:15–19 . . . 347
4:20 . . . 342, 346
4:21 . . . 271
4:21–22 . . . 342
4:21–23 . . . 343
4:23–28 . . . 348
4:29 . . . 348, 406
4:33–35 . . . 347
4:37–38 . . . 349
4:41–43 . . . 349
4:44–26 . . . 350
5:12 . . . 351
5:15 . . . 351
5:18 . . . 352
5:30 . . . 352
6:4–7 . . . 353
7:1–18 . . . 407
7:6–8 . . . 407
9:21 . . . 169
10:1–5 . . . 188
10:3 . . . 352
12–26 . . . 350
12:2–4 . . . 356
12:5–7 . . . 356
12:26 . . . 350, 355
15:13–18 . . . 71
19:1–3 . . . 349
27–30 . . . 357
27:1–3 . . . 359
27:9–10 . . . 358
27:11–26 . . . 360
27:14–15 . . . 360
28 . . . 360
28:69 . . . 361

29:1–3 . . . 362
29:1–5 . . . 365
29:4–5 . . . 362
29:5 . . . 363
29:6 . . . 364
31 . . . 366
31:1–3 . . . 366
31:2 . . . 349, 400
31:7–9 . . . 372
31:9 . . . 372, 410
31:9–13 . . . 367
31:14 . . . 369
31:14–18 . . . 368
31:19 . . . 368, 376
31:19–21 . . . 368
31:21 . . . 375
31:22–23 . . . 369
31:23 . . . 369
31:23–26 . . . 372
31:25 . . . 372
31:28–30 . . . 373
32 . . . 373
32:1–3 . . . 374
32:1–43 . . . 321
32:4 . . . 375
32:7–8 . . . 366
32:10–18 . . . 374
32:18 . . . 282, 430
32:39 . . . 374
32:43 . . . 374
32:44 . . . 376
33 . . . 378
33:2 . . . 295
33:6 . . . 378–379
33:7 . . . 379–380
33:8–10 . . . 386
33:12 . . . 387
33:17 . . . 388
33:20–21 . . . 389
33:22 . . . 389
33:23 . . . 390
33:23–26 . . . 388

33:24–25 . . . 391
34 . . . 133
34:1 . . . 393
34:1–8 . . . 392–393
34:5–6 . . . 397
34:7 . . . 400
34:10 . . . 404

JOSHUA
8:30–35 . . . 361
14:1–2 . . . 378

JUDGES
1:34 . . . 390
4:11 . . . 53
5 . . . 390
13–16 . . . 390
19–21 . . . 387

FIRST KINGS
3:12 . . . 235

SECOND KINGS
18:4 . . . 431
22, 23 . . . 411

ISAIAH
6:5 . . . 430

JEREMIAH
1:5 . . . 63
8:22 . . . 300

PSALMS
74:11 . . . 429

PROVERBS
1:7 . . . 354

NEHEMIAH
8:10 . . . 421

FIRST CHRONICLES
4:24–43 . . . 385
6:22 . . . 258
23:14–16 . . . 230

Index

Aaron (brother of Moses), 21, 30, 54–55, 85, 116, 230, 242, 269–270
  brings Moses to Children of Israel, 92
  and covenant at Mount Sinai, 144, 146, 153–154, 156
  death of, 271, 280, 287–293, 332
  and golden calf, 161–166, 169, 172, 173, 174
  guilt of, at Kadesh, 278–280
  as high priest, 192, 199–200, 264
    garments of, 200–201
  jealousy of, 227
  and Moses before Pharaoh, 100–107, 109, 269, 274
  passivity of, 163, 290, 292–293, 371
  punishment of, 270–271, 287–288
  and revolt of Korah, 250–254, 258–264
    stops plague, 262–263
  and rod of God, 73, 102–103, 104–107, 270, 273
  suffers loss of two sons, 204–209
  supportive role of, 76–77, 88–90, 99, 274
  as voice of Moses, 76–77, 99, 124, 292, 371
  in the Wilderness, 124–126, 128, 131
Abihu (son of Aaron), 153, 154, 200, 205–206, 208–209
Abiram, 39, 81, 249, 250, 253–258; *see also* Dathan
Abraham, 22, 23, 33, 53–54, 400, 402, 426
  contrasted with Balaam, 318
  as father figure, 33, 34
  his covenant with God, 167, 335
Albright, William F., 135, 165, 203, 330, 335; (quoted), 414, 426
Amalek, 130–133, 240
Amalekites, battle with, 130–132, 246
Amram (father of Moses), 21, 30, 31, 55, 63, 115, 232
Aqaba, Gulf of, 48, 295, 314, 319, 329
Ark of the Covenant, 198–199, 246, 352–353
Arlow, Jacob A. (quoted), 324
Arnon River, 298–299, 301
Asher (son of Jacob), tribe of, 390–391

Balaam, 302–322, 398
  conflict with superego, 307, 308–311

Balaam (*continued*)
  Oracles of, 310
  symbolism in story of, 318–321
Balak, 302, 303, 309–312, 319
Baron, Salo (quoted), 426
Bashan (region east of the Jordan), 299–300
Benjamin (son of Jacob), tribe of, 386–387
Bezazel, 189, 202, 352
Bible
  compilation of, 420–421
  concealed oedipal conflict in, 417–419
  critical study of, 421–427
  development of collective superego in, 22, 417
  exegesis, 95, 420–427
  psychoanalytic concepts in, 19–23, 417–419
  received text, psychological validity of, 16–23
  see also Higher Biblical Criticism
Blessing of the Tribes, 324, 376–391, 403
Buber, Martin, 32, 97, 165, 330–331, 430; (quoted), 33, 41, 98, 203–204, 266
  on circumcision, 80, 87
  on revolt of Korah, 250
  on theophany of the burning bush, 65
Burning bush, theophany of, 40, 57–62, 77–81, 85, 87, 90, 94–98, 101, 103, 121, 140, 142, 157, 184, 274, 394, 429

Caleb, 240, 242–243, 284, 329, 341–342
Canaan, 298, 301, 330, 395
  conquest of, 133, 324, 328, 337, 340, 389
  and report of the spies, 240, 246, 300, 329
  rituals for entrance into, 359–361, 365–367, 389
Canaanites
  defeat of Children of Israel by, 246, 329
  destruction of Hormah, 293–294
Castration anxiety, 248, 438; *see also* Circumcision as symbolic castration
Children of Israel, 15, 64, 66, 78, 113
  battle with the Amalekites, 130–132
  construction of Tabernacle, 192–193
  covenant at Mount Sinai, 137–160, 184–187, 190–192, 211, 222, 321
  fears of Promised Land as preoedipal mother, 240–241, 246–247, 256;
    see also Rubenstein, Richard I.
  and golden calf, 161–172, 174, 177, 193; *see also* Golden calf
  maturation of, 224, 327, 357–358
  oneness of, 405–408
  rebelliousness of, 126–131, 212–222, 241–246, 256, 258, 260, 294–295, 338, 345
  punishment following, 221–222, 241–246, 263, 295–296
  relationship with God
    the conditional promise, 120
    covenantal character of, 361
    as Father Who disciplines, 224
    gratitude expressed in building tabernacle, 193
    and metaphor of marriage, 358
  sexual misconduct among, 312–314, 382, 384–385
Circumcision as symbolic castration, 79–80, 86–88, 89, 98, 110, 429
Cities of refuge, 349–350

Clothes, symbolism of, 362–364
Code of Laws, 355–356
Covenant, concept of, 334–335, 361, 409–410, 414
  Book of Covenant, 151, 187, 355
  see also Ten Commandments
Craigie, Peter (quoted), 414

Dan (son of Jacob), tribe of, 389–390
Dathan, 38–40, 81, 249, 250, 253, 254, 255, 258; *see also* Abiram
David, 258, 380
Dead Sea (Salt Sea), 287, 295, 297, 301, 395
Death
  of Aaron, 271, 280, 287–293, 332
  of Miriam, 269, 280, 281, 331–332
  of Moses, 15, 266–267, 326, 392–400
    psychological significance of, 401–403
Deuteronomy book of, 323–327, 334, 356, 373, 405–407, 421
  authorship of, 323–324
  critical theories about, 410–412
  DeWette theory of, 411–412
  more holistic view of, 416
  psychological validity of Moses in, 324
  social concepts in, 327, 334–335, 343–344, 350, 353–355, 356–357, 367, 406–407
Driver, S. R. (quoted), 80, 104, 147, 204

Ebla, archeologic findings at, 414–416
Edom, 287, 294–295, 297
Ego
  collective, represented by hero, 45
  definition of, 439
  and ego ideal, 218, 245, 247, 248
  and id, 132
  regression in the service of, 21
  in relation to storyteller, 18, 27, 29
  and superego, 122, 132, 167, 247, 248
Eisenstein, Ira, 11
Eldad and Medad, 220
Eleazar (son of Aaron), 200, 207, 259, 286–293, 333
Eliezer (son of Moses), 21, 86, 208, 228, 229, 230
Elim, oasis of, 123, 212, 328
Empathy, in applied psychoanalysis, 19
Ephraim (son of Joseph), tribe of, 338
Erickson, Erik (quoted), 418
Esau, 33, 131, 297
Evans, William N. (quoted), 217–218
Exodus, book of, 29–30, 41, 44, 114, 159, 351–352

Family romance, 28–31, 34–36, 40, 45, 46, 115, 220
  condensation of and myth of the birth of a hero, 29–31
  see also Myth, of the birth of a hero
Fodor, A., 27
Freud, Sigmund (quoted), 24, 27, 401, 402–403
  and acquisition of knowledge, 183
  at Acropolis, compared to Moses on Mount Nebo, 396–397
  counter-will and antithetic ideas, 272
  on cultural development of group, 45, 353
  on hero as ego storyteller, 18
  interpretation of Michelangelo's Moses, 168–169
  on latency period and religious feelings, 40
  on mechanisms of defense, 77, 78

Freud Sigmund (continued)
  Moses and Monotheism, 28, 56, 429
    as viewed by Ricoeur, 17
    on myth of Moses' birth, 26–29
    on significance of incorporeality of God, 347
    on theorized murder of Moses in wilderness, 128
    on theory of composite image of Moses, 56–57
  Totem and Taboo, 128, 409
    on the totem meal, 155
    views on religion, 117
Funk, Robert (quoted), 16

Gad (son of Jacob), tribe of, 300, 301, 389
Gershom (son of Moses), 21, 52, 86, 208, 228, 229, 230
Gilead, balm of, 300
Ginzberg, Louis (quoted), 281
God, concepts of
  attributes of, 160, 181, 190
  as good therapist, 116
  incorporeality of, 160, 346–347, 358
  monotheistic nature of, 45, 160, 418
Golden calf
  people's anxiety related to, 162–163
  punishment for, 169–172, 174, 177, 185
  reparation for, 192–193, 196
  and role of Aaron, 161–166, 169, 172, 173, 174
  symbolism of, 165–166
Goldman, Solomon, 405; (quoted), 135
Goshen, 109
Greenacre, Phyllis, 35, 394

Haggada, 48, 397
Hahn, Herbert P. (quoted), 427

Hammurabi, Code of, 159
Hero
  cultural, 355, 402, 410
  function of, in group, 23, 45, 55
  and myth of the birth of, 18, 26, 28, 31, 40, 46
Hertz, Joseph H., 69, 253, 293; (quoted), 64, 148, 262, 268, 276, 413
Higher Biblical Criticism, 16, 19, 72, 124, 125, 136, 141, 412, 423–424
  on blessing of the tribes, 377
  on burning bush, 59, 95
  on death of Moses, 334
  on Discourses, 350, 355, 356
  and Documentary Theory, 423
  on golden calf, 165, 175
  methods of, 16
  and Patriarchal period, 408
  and Pentateuch, 19–20, 95, 158
  on revolt of Korah, 250
  on rod of God, 103
  on Song of Moses, 371
  on Tabernacle, 202, 203
  on Ten Commandments, 158, 159
Hobab, 53, 54; see also Jethro
Horeb, 89, 129–130, 267, 269, 337, 361
Hormah, 293–295
Hur, 131, 132, 156, 162

Ibn Ezra, 328
Idolatry, struggle against, 360; see also Golden calf
Incest, biblical taboos against, 360, 382
Individual, the, and the group, 354, 406–410
  as expressed in use of personal pronoun, 406–410
  in metaphor of Moses as *the people*, 406
  in oneness of Children of Israel, 405–408

in Petersen's concept of corporate
personality, 407–408
Isaac, 34, 400, 402, 426
Isaiah, 430
Issachar (son of Jacob), tribe of, 389
Ithamar (son of Aaron), 200, 207

Jacob
blessings of tribes, 378, 384,
386–387, 389–391
and Esau, 33, 131
house of, 139, 381
as patriarchal figure, 34
Jaynes, Julian, 409
Jebel Musa, 135
Jereboam, 165
Jeremiah, 63, 300
Jericho, 301, 324, 337
Jerusalem, Temple of, 411
Jethro, 21, 47, 52–57, 80, 82, 228, 268
and concept of justice, 343
daughters of, 50–57, 227, 317
as father figure, 41, 55, 89, 103, 317
names of, 53, 54
reunion with Moses, 89, 229-230
Jochebed (mother of Moses), 21, 25,
29, 30, 44, 115, 232
meaning of name, 97
Jones, Ernest (quoted), 268
Jordan River, 297–298, 300–301,
324, 359, 395
crossing of, 337, 349, 357, 366,
400, 401
Joseph (son of Jacob), 33, 386, 426
tribes of (Ephraim and Manasseh),
386–388
Joshua, 21, 128, 220–221, 284, 361,
371, 376
battle with Amalekites, 131–132
book of, 378, 423
and death of Moses, 342, 370, 398

leadership of Children of Israel,
133, 333–334, 365, 366,
368–370, 372–373, 393
at Mount Sinai, 155–156
as scout, 240, 242–243, 329, 341
Josiah, 411–412, 421
Judah (son of Jacob), tribe of,
379–383, 385

Kadesh (Ain-el-Qudeirat)
death of Miriam in, 280, 331
site of, 135, 330
spies sent out from, 329
striking the rock at, 267, 269, 272,
273, 275, 283–285
Kanzer, Mark, 10
Kaufmann, Yehezkel, 203, 373–374,
425
Kittel, Rudolf (quoted), 412
Korah, revolt of, 249–265

Laws, 187, 344–346, 366–367; *see also*
Code of Laws
Leadership, 23, 24, 249; *see also*
Moses, as leader
Lelyveld, Arthur J., 9
Levites
blessing of, 385–386
and golden calf, 170, 172
relationship of Moses to, 31–32,
76, 257, 386
and revolt of Korah, 251, 257, 260
role in entrance into Promised
Land, 360, 373
role in priesthood, 146, 209, 252,
260, 385–386
Leviticus, book of, 204
Love, significance of concept of,
354–355

Magic, role of, 73–75, 78, 121
Maimonides, 431

Manasseh (son of Joseph), tribe of, 301, 388
Manna, 123–124, 126, 214–215, 216
Marah, 120–122
Medad and Eldad, 220
Mendenhall, George, 44
Michelangelo, 168–169, 191
Midian
    Moses en route to, 48–49
    Moses' family in, 89, 227, 229
    Moses in, 37, 47–78, 80, 90–91
Midianites, war with, 312–320
Midrash, 38, 62
Midwives; see Puah, Shiprah
Miriam (sister of Moses), 21, 25, 30, 31, 44, 114, 225–238, 318
    death of, 269, 280, 281, 331–332
    jealousy of, 227–228, 231, 233
    mother figure, 232, 280
    punishment of, 226, 235–237
Miriam's well, 281, 282
Moab
    Balaam in, 302–319
    burial of Moses in, 397, 401
    Children of Israel on borders of, 282, 393
    last days of Moses in, 15, 133, 272, 324, 326, 392
    site of, 297–299, 301, 431
Monotheism
    as basis for morality, 360
    contribution of Moses to, 345–346
    Freud's concept of, 353
Moses
    and Aaron, 76, 85, 88–89, 90, 100–101, 104–105, 169, 172, 225–238, 287–293, 376; see also Aaron
    ambivalence of, 116, 139, 144, 153–154, 220, 257, 281, 291–292
    and Balaam, 317–318, 320–321
    birth of, 15, 25–26
    myths of, 26, 34
    burial of, 397–398, 401, 403
    burning bush, 40, 57–58, 90, 157, 274, 317, 394; see also Burning bush
    and Children of Israel, relationship with
        confusion of, in sense of identity, 97–98, 176
        as family, 355, 377
        maternal feelings toward, 217, 223
        superego figure for, 347, 398, 401
    compassion of, 117, 169, 216, 258
    covenant at Mount Sinai, 135, 137–160, 195–196; see also Mount Sinai
    as culture hero, 77, 355, 402, 410
    death of, 15, 267, 326, 392–403
    defenses against incestuous feelings, 21, 70, 91
    derivation of name, 33, 34
    flight from Egypt, 49–50, 77, 82, 108, 267
    and God, relationship with
        anxiety toward, 95, 99, 116, 117, 179, 218
        competitiveness with, 71, 219, 273, 364, 365, 371, 399–400
        conflictful feelings toward, 216, 218, 223–224, 235
        desire for omnipotence, 98, 101
        element of narcissism in, 100, 116
        idealized father figure, 101, 116–117, 245
        identification with, 94, 95, 99–100, 184–185, 223, 283
        love of, 117, 178, 354–355, 360
        significance of knowing by special names, 96–97, 99, 184

wish to know better, 180–184, 394
and golden calf, 166–172, 192
guilt feelings, 98, 171, 176–177, 181–182, 258, 263, 271, 279, 284–285, 341
as intermediary and intercessor, 138, 157, 167, 176, 185, 236, 247, 295
and Jethro, 21, 52–57, 80, 82, 89, 103, 229–230; *see also* Jethro
and Joshua
  conflicting feelings toward, 341–342, 365, 369–370, 376
  as son figure, 220, 341, 361, 371
  strength of relationship with, 155–156, 342
  as successor to, 221, 333, 339, 341, 365–366, 369, 376
and concept of justice, 343–344
latency period, significance of, 32, 35, 40
as lawgiver, 117, 158–159, 345, 366–367, 403, 416
as leader, 21, 24, 90, 112, 118, 124, 162, 171, 177, 345, 347, 403
marriage of, 51–52, 55, 57, 90, 317; *see also* Zipporah
meekness of, 225, 231, 235, 238
in Midian, 37, 47, 50–78, 80, 90–91
narcissism of
  in personality of prophet, 97, 106, 110, 113, 116, 172, 223
  struggle against, 90, 100, 278
oedipal feelings
  and entry into Promised Land, 358–359, 397, 403
  in relationship with God, 22, 91, 98, 223
  in striking the rock, 283, 400, 401
  toward Pharaoh, 39, 41, 84, 108, 110, 115

parents of, 21, 173; *see also* Amram, Jochebed
  ambivalence toward, 29, 395
and Pharaoh, 21, 31, 37, 40, 50, 66
  ambivalence toward, 72, 82, 99, 115
  competition with, 71, 98
  contest of wills with, 85, 93–94, 102, 108
psychological validity of, 15
the return to Egypt, 79–91, 92–117
and rod of God, 72–76, 80, 83, 104, 129, 130, 267–285
siblings, 21, 225–238, 281, 291; *see also* Aaron, Miriam
Song of, 268, 282, 295, 321, 324, 367–376
sons of, 21, 52, 89
  attitude toward, 173, 208, 229–230, 259, 291, 385
  circumcision, 79–80, 110, 228
strikes down the Egyptian taskmaster, 35–40, 48, 50
striking the rock, 129–130, 267–285, 337, 400
sublimation, capacity for, 316, 319
as superego figure, 347, 398, 401
Tabernacle, planning of, 195–196
"uncircumcised lips," 98–99, 395
unconscious fantasies of, 21, 45, 183, 366
  and Balaam, 320–321
  birth and rescue, 29, 31, 35–36
  and Egyptian taskmaster, 38–39
  in family relationships, 172–173
  and flight from Egypt, 81
  and golden calf, 176
  and Miriam, 232
  and return to Egypt, 82–85
  and revolt of Korah, 257–263
  and striking the rock, 268, 269, 274, 279, 285

Mother image
  fear of, 248, 256, 258
  preoedipal concept of, 215, 217–218, 241, 248, 256
  Promised Land as, 241–242, 248, 357, 395–397
Mount Hor, death of Aaron at, 287–293
Mount Nebo
  death of Moses at, 392–403
  Moses beholds Promised Land from, 301
  symbolic significance of, 395–397, 401–404
Mount Pisgah, 392, 394–395
Mount Sinai, 78, 114, 129, 182, 186, 212, 328
  construction of Tabernacle at, 192–193, 195
  covenant at, 134, 137–160, 184–192, 222, 245, 281, 295, 321, 358, 361
  departure of tribes from, 194, 213
  Moses descends from, emanating radiance, 190–192
  physical description of, 135, 147
Myth
  of the birth of a hero, 18, 26, 28, 31, 40, 46
  of rescue, 29–31, 34, 36, 45

Nachmanides, 278
Nadab (son of Aaron), 153, 154, 200, 205–206, 208–209
Names, significance of, 33, 34, 45, 53, 95–97, 181
Naphtali (son of Jacob), tribe of, 390
Narcissism; *see* Moses, narcissism of
Negev, 293
Nile River, 74, 120

Noth, Martin (quoted), 276
Numbers, book of, 224, 286, 328, 332, 338

Oedipal struggle
  in biblical heroes, 22, 23, 72, 97, 417–419
  repression of, 44–45
  significance of for Freud at Acropolis, 396–397
  sublimation of, 417
  symbolism of Promised Land, 248, 358–359, 397
  see also Moses, oedipal feelings
Og (king of Bashan), 300, 339, 364
Oholiab, 202
Otto, Rudolf, 142–143

Passover, 109–110, 114, 328
Patai, Raphael, 10–11, 430
Pedersen, Johs, 142, 155, 407–408; (quoted), 147
Pentateuch, 15, 62, 158, 159, 318, 325, 410
  Documentary Theory, 423–424
  and Higher Biblical Criticism, 16, 19, 95, 158, 423
Peto, Andrew, 80
Phallus, symbolic significance of
  body as, 183
  in circumcision, 86
  rod of God as, 73–74, 75–76, 103, 264
  serpent as, 296
  small boys as, 319
Pharaoh, 37, 39–40, 48–50, 58–59, 83–86, 93, 102
  as ambivalent father figure, 40, 49, 66, 82, 84, 89, 99, 108, 115–116

and Children of Israel, 41–43
   daughter of, 25, 29, 30–31, 32, 34, 115, 386
   and ten plagues, 101–110, 112
   see also Moses, and Pharaoh
Phenix, Philip H., 9
Phinehas (grandson of Aaron), 314
Postbiblical legends
   Balaam, 318
   death of Aaron, 290, 291–292
   death of Moses, 397–399
   Jethro, 53
   Miriam, 281
   Moses' flight from Egypt, 48–49
   Nadab and Abihu, 208–209
   striking the rock, 281–284
   Ten Commandments, 148
Promised Land
   division of, 332–333, 376–391
   oedipal significance of for Moses, 285, 395–397, 400
   relationship of Children of Israel to, 246, 300–307, 324, 326–327, 357–358, 359–361, 401
   and report of the spies, 239–248
   symbolism of, 248, 294, 321–322, 327, 357–358
   see also Canaan; Children of Israel, fears of Promised Land
Psychoanalysis, applied, techniques of in research, 17–18
Psycholinguistic approach to biblical research, 409
Puah, 42–45

Rachel, 33, 386
Rank, Otto, 18, 29; (quoted), 28
Rashi, 158
Reik, Theodor, 20, 29, 32, 79, 97, 430, 431; (quoted), 40, 429

Rephidim, 126, 129, 130–133, 136, 230, 267–269
   battle with the Amalekites, 130–133
Repression
   definition of, 441
   as expressed in text, 40, 50–51, 171, 231, 237
   in latency period, 40
   in relation to God's special name, 87
   in relation to mother image, 45
   "return of the repressed," 21, 22, 87, 418
Reuben (son of Jacob), 378–379, 382
   tribe of, 250, 300, 301, 379
Reuel, 53, 54; see also Jethro
Ricoeur, Paul (quoted), 17
Robertiello, Robert C., 11, 430
Rod of God
   used by Aaron, 73, 102–103, 104
   used by Moses, 72–73, 80, 83, 102, 129, 130, 267–285
Roheim, Geza, 79, 431; (quoted), 28
Rowley, H. H. (quoted), 424
Rubenstein, Richard I., 256, 317

Sabbath, 351
Sachs, Hanns (quoted), 28
Samuel, 33
Sandler, Joseph, 117
Sandmel, Samuel, 11; (quoted), 377
Sanua, Victor D., 11
Sea of Reeds, 114, 118, 128, 281
Serpent, brazen, 295–296, 431
Sexual symbolism
   in burning bush, 59–60, 142
   in rod of God, 102–103
Shafer, Roy, 117
Shekinah, 60
Shema, the, 353
Sherman, Murray H., 10
Shiprah, 42–45

Sibling rivalry, 39, 86, 233, 291
  displaced to Dathan and Abiram, 258
  in use of rod of God, 77, 104
Sihon (king of Amorites), 299, 337, 339, 364
Simeon (son of Jacob), tribe of, 383
Simeonites, omitted in blessing of Moses, 383–385
Sinai Peninsula, 48, 56, 114, 118, 135
Slavery, in Egypt, 70, 71
Slochower, Harry, 10; (quoted), 397
Solomon, 380, 413
Speiser, E. A. (quoted), 426
Suez, Gulf of, 114
Superego
  collective, 22, 133, 153, 160, 401
  definition of, 441–442
  development of, 90, 91, 347, 353–354, 403, 417, 431
  God as, 117, 181, 237, 254, 403, 410, 419
  and id, 131, 308
  projected onto God, 121, 167, 247, 254, 359, 393
  struggle of Moses with, 21, 88, 142, 221, 359, 370, 375
  sublimation of as sexual energy, 60, 67
  symbolism of in death of Moses, 402
  as voice of the father, 62–63, 77, 150

Tabernacle, 192–193, 195–210, 211, 413
  Ark of the Covenant in, 198–199, 264
  consecration of, 204–205
  garments of high priest, 200–201
  revolt of Korah, 252, 259–260, 261
Ten Commandments
  and Code of Hammurabi, 159
  covenant at Mount Sinai, 146, 148
  renewal of covenant, 187–192
  restatement in Second Discourse, 351–352
Tent of Meeting, 203, 220–221, 226, 261, 413, 430
  theophany of, 177, 178, 182–183, 238, 254

Volz, Paul, 416

Water
  importance of in wilderness, 119–122, 280
  Miriam's well, 280–282
  struggle at Kadesh, 129, 275–278
  struggle at Rephidim, 124, 126–127
Weiss, M., 416
Wilderness
  physical description of, 119
  struggle for water in, 119–122, 126–127, 129, 275–278
Wilderness of Paran, 194, 330
Wilderness of Zin, 123, 212, 269, 272, 330, 331

Zebulun (son of Jacob), tribe of, 389
Zelophehad, daughters of, 332–333, 334
Zimri, 313–314
Zipporah (wife of Moses), 21, 51–52, 55–56, 80
  meaning of name, 45
  object of jealousy, 227, 231–233
  performs rite of circumcision, 79–80, 83, 86–97, 110, 228
  reunion with Moses, 229–231
  separation from Moses, 89, 228, 317